Tableau Cookbook for Experienced Professionals

Over 60 advanced recipes for maximizing performance, interactivity, and platform potential

Pablo Sáenz de Tejada

Daria Kirilenko

Tableau Cookbook for Experienced Professionals

Portfolio Director: Sunith Shetty
Relationship Lead: Nilesh Kowadkar
Project Manager: Hemangi Lotlikar
Content Engineer: Ayushi Bulani
Technical Editor: Seemanjay Ameriya
Copy Editor: Safis Editing
Proofreader: Ayushi Bulani
Indexer: Tejal Soni
Production Designer: Nilesh Mohite
Growth Lead: Bhavesh Amin
DevRel Marketing Coordinator: Shruthi Shetty

First published: April 2025
Production reference: 2281125

Published by Packt Publishing Ltd.
Grosvenor House
11 St Paul's Square
Birmingham
B3 1RB, UK.

ISBN 978-1-83546-974-3
www.packtpub.com

To my mother, Pilar, and to the memory of my father, Nacho, for their constant support and for teaching me the value of hard work and dedication.

– Pablo Sáenz de Tejada

To the incredible Tableau community, whose passion for discovery and innovation continues to inspire. And to my students and colleagues – your curiosity and dedication make this journey worthwhile.

– Daria Kirilenko

Contributors

About the authors

Pablo Sáenz de Tejada is a Tableau specialist with over 10 years of experience helping people and organizations improve their data and Tableau skills and 20 years of experience as a consultant. He began his journey in data as a market research analyst specializing in survey data and analysis. Between 2015 and 2020, Pablo was part of The Information Lab (UK), helping people make sense of data as a data analyst, consultant, and certified Tableau trainer. In 2020, he became the managing director of The Information Lab (Spain). In 2022, Pablo joined Salesforce as a Tableau lead solution engineer, and then in 2024, he joined Snowflake as a senior partner sales engineer.

I would like to express my gratitude to my co-author, Daria, for her invaluable contributions and support during this journey.

A special thank you to the entire team at Packt for their professionalism and dedication in bringing this book to life.

Lastly, to my partner, Alexandra, thank you for your patience, encouragement, and love.

Daria Kirilenko is a Tableau consultant with over 8 years of experience in business intelligence and analytics. As the founder of DSCOVR Analytics, she leads a dynamic consulting firm dedicated to delivering data-driven solutions to Fortune 500 companies across North America. In 2022, she led a global Tableau training initiative for Salesforce employees, which was widely recognized for accelerating skill development and driving the adoption of Tableau tools in the organization. Daria also serves as a seasoned instructor at Stanford University, where she conducts regular training sessions and customized workshops. Her approach combines technical depth with real-world applications, enabling participants to transform how they work with data.

This book would not have been possible without the dedication, expertise, and support of many incredible people.

First and foremost, I want to thank my co-author, Pablo. Your expertise, dedication, and willingness to take on the heavy lifting made this collaboration both productive and truly enjoyable. I couldn't have asked for a better partner in this endeavor and I'm grateful for the opportunity to have worked alongside you.

A heartfelt thank you to our content editors, whose sharp insights and thoughtful feedback elevated this book to its best possible form. Your commitment to accuracy and quality is what makes this book a trusted resource for Tableau professionals.

I'm also deeply grateful to the technical editors who meticulously reviewed each recipe – testing code, verifying results, and making sure each technique was practical and well-explained. Your contributions have strengthened this book in countless ways.

A huge thank you to the product managers who made the authoring process as seamless as possible. Your guidance and support kept us on track and helped bring this project together smoothly.

Lastly, I want to thank my partner, Mitchel, for his unwavering support throughout this journey. From patiently listening to my endless Tableau talk to pretending to be fascinated by calculated fields at dinner, you deserve a medal – or at least a Tableau certificate of achievement.

To everyone who contributed to bringing this book to life, I am incredibly grateful. Your efforts have made this project something I am truly proud to share with the Tableau community.

About the reviewers

Amber Reed has a bachelor's in healthcare administration from the University of Northwestern Ohio and is currently pursuing a master's in data and analytics at Franklin University. Her career began in clinical roles within healthcare and pharmacy, transitioning over the past five years to data analytics. Currently, she is a data analyst at CoverMyMeds, a healthcare technology company. Amber's expertise in analytics focuses on data visualization and storytelling, particularly using Tableau, where she excels in transforming complex datasets into clear, impactful insights.

Eric Summers has been called the Swiss Army knife of data products—able to source data, uncover its value, and build the tools and data products that deliver clear answers. He brings what colleagues call an *unfair advantage*: a rare mix of technical range, common sense, and the ability to talk with both engineers and business leaders. As the creator of TableauAdmin.com, Eric helps teams simplify how they manage content, metadata, and monitoring in Tableau. Whether building dashboards, automations, or self-service tools, he focuses on delivering work that's not just useful—but valuable, trusted, and easy to act on.

Join our community on Discord

Join our community's Discord space for discussions with the authors and other readers:

```
https://packt.link/ds
```

Table of Contents

2

Managing Content and Security at Scale in Tableau   35

3

Leveraging Tableau Cloud's Data Management and Advanced Management   71

Part 2: Optimizing Performance and Mastering Complex Calculations

4

Maximizing Workbook Performance 101

5

Mastering Advanced Calculations to Answer Complex Business Questions

145

Part 3: Building Interactive Dashboards and Data Apps

6

Creating Interactive Dashboards

189

7

Interactivity and Zone Visibility: From Dashboards to Data Apps   219

Part 4: Exploring Geospatial Solutions, Developer Tools, and Design Best Practices

8

Advanced Geospatial and Mapping Use Cases — 241

9

Extending Tableau with Developer Tools and APIs — 269

10

Core Techniques for Impactful Data Design   303

Index   337

Other Books You May Enjoy   346

Preface

Data is the foundation of modern decision-making. Organizations that effectively harness data rely on it to drive strategy, measure performance, and uncover new opportunities. Tableau has played a transformative role in democratizing data, giving analysts, business leaders, and decision-makers a powerful, intuitive platform to visualize and explore insights. However, as Tableau deployments grow in scale and complexity, businesses often struggle with performance bottlenecks, governance issues, and the need for deeper analytical capabilities.

This book is designed for those who want to stay ahead of the curve. It goes beyond the fundamentals, offering a deep dive into the strategies, techniques, and innovations that will transform the way you build, optimize, and deploy Tableau solutions.

The *Tableau Cookbook for Experienced Professionals* begins by exploring scalable data architecture and security, ensuring your Tableau environment is not only efficient but also future-proofed for enterprise-level use.

From there, it delves into performance mastery, teaching you how to fine-tune calculations, optimize rendering speeds, and leverage Tableau's built-in diagnostic tools.

Then, it shifts the focus to interactive analytics, exploring advanced dashboard actions, dynamic zone visibility, and parameter-driven visualizations that create an intuitive, seamless user experience.

Finally, it takes a developer-focused approach, pushing the limits of Tableau through APIs, geospatial techniques, and advanced automation, turning dashboards into fully-fledged data applications.

Whether you're a consultant, analyst, or business leader, this book will equip you with the real-world, practical skills to drive measurable impact with Tableau, transforming dashboards into decision-making engines that shape business outcomes.

Welcome to the next step in your Tableau journey. Let's get started!

Who this book is for

This cookbook is tailored for Tableau professionals, BI administrators, developers, and data analysts eager to deepen their expertise and explore advanced techniques:

- **Tableau professionals**: Individuals with a good grasp of Tableau Desktop who are eager to expand their knowledge with more complex and sophisticated Tableau methods

- **BI administrators**: Experienced BI administrators who want to expand their knowledge of Tableau's advanced features and learn how to manage and optimize Tableau environments effectively

- **Developers**: Developers looking to refine their Tableau skills and implement advanced strategies for building scalable and efficient data applications

- **Data analysts**: Analysts looking to boost their proficiency with Tableau and apply advanced methods to address common business challenges

What this book covers

Chapter 1, Building Advanced and Efficient Tableau Data Models, provides an overview of how to create robust data models by leveraging logical and physical tables, optimizing relationships, and using multi-fact models. It also covers the differences between Tableau Desktop and Tableau Prep for various data preparation and modeling tasks.

Chapter 2, Managing Content and Security at Scale in Tableau, provides an overview of how to enable users to connect to data and share insights while maintaining security, scalability, and governance. It introduces various techniques for securing data and managing content to improve user trust and adoption on the Tableau platform.

Chapter 3, Leveraging Tableau Cloud's Data Management and Advanced Management, offers an overview of Tableau's Data Management and Advanced Management features, emphasizing their role in simplifying content management at scale and improving data governance. It then dives into the key features of the Content Migration Tool, Metadata API, and virtual connections, providing a thorough understanding of how these tools centralize data access and optimize data management processes.

Chapter 4, Maximizing Workbook Performance, provides a comprehensive framework for optimizing workbook performance in Tableau. It introduces best practices to address performance bottlenecks, improve data structures, and streamline calculations, to ensure high performance and greater user engagement.

Chapter 5, Mastering Advanced Calculations to Answer Complex Business Questions, provides an in-depth exploration of Tableau's calculation types, highlighting their critical role in creating customized metrics and refining data for more insightful analysis. It uses practical examples to solve complex data scenarios with table calculations, **Level of Detail** (**LOD**) expressions, and the order of operations framework.

Chapter 6, Creating Interactive Dashboards, focuses on exploring different types of actions in Tableau worksheets and dashboards, such as filter, highlight, parameter, and set actions. It provides practical examples and techniques for using these actions to build advanced, interactive tools that empower users to engage with data in new ways.

Chapter 7, Interactivity and Zone Visibility: From Dashboards to Data Apps, focuses on transforming traditional dashboards into more user-friendly data applications by using features such as **Dynamic Zone Visibility (DZV)** and interactivity. It demonstrates how to apply DZV and guided analytics to create flexible, dynamic data apps that improve user experience and communication of insights.

Chapter 8, Advanced Geospatial and Mapping Use Cases, demonstrates how to integrate spatial data with traditional analysis to create more insightful visualizations. It covers key spatial functionalities such as working with multiple map layers, performing spatial calculations, and handling Shapefiles to address location-based business questions with practical examples and challenging use cases.

Chapter 9, Extending Tableau with Developer Tools and APIs, offers an overview of how Tableau can be extended using developer tools and APIs to automate tasks, integrate with external systems, and manage resources more efficiently. It covers key features such as using Tableau's REST API for maintenance task automation, Python and R integration, Metadata API GraphQL, and VizQL Data Service for more powerful data management and unique visualization requirements.

Chapter 10, Core Techniques for Impactful Data Design, focuses on the core principles and best practices for designing impactful dashboards that deliver strategic insights and real value. It explores the basics of audience-centric design, color usage, and the importance of creating a style guide to maintain visual consistency. Additionally, the chapter covers how to create advanced tables, highlighting their role in adding sophistication and depth to your dashboards.

To get the most out of this book

Software/hardware covered in the book	OS requirements
Tableau Desktop 2025.1 or later	Microsoft Windows 8/8.1, Windows 10 (x64), or Windows 11 macOS Big Sur 11.4+, macOS Monterey 12.6+ (for Tableau 2022.3+), macOS Ventura (for Tableau 2022.3+), macOS Sonoma (for Tableau 2022.3+); Apple Silicon machines require the use of macOS Ventura (13+) or newer
Tableau Cloud	
Python version 3.9 to 3.12.	
R version 4.4.3	

If you are using the digital version of this book, we advise you to type the code yourself or access the code via the GitHub repository (link available in the next section). Doing so will help you avoid any potential errors related to the copying and pasting of code.

Download the example code files

You can download the example code files for this book from GitHub at `https://github.com/PacktPublishing/Tableau-Cookbook-for-Experienced-Professionals`. In case there's an update to the code, it will be updated on the existing GitHub repository.

We also have other code bundles from our rich catalog of books and videos available at `https://github.com/PacktPublishing/`. Check them out!

Conventions used

There are a number of text conventions used throughout this book.

`Code in text`: Indicates code words in text, database table names, folder names, filenames, file extensions, pathnames, dummy URLs, user input, and Twitter handles. Here is an example: "For this recipe, we will start from the `Chapter 6. Recipe 2. Global Dashboard sheet` in the `Chapter 6 – Starter workbook`."

A block of code is set as follows:

```
token_name = 'pat-name'
token_secret = 'paste-here-your-pat-secret'
my_tableau_url = 'https://10ax.online.tableau.com/'
api_v = '3.24'
site = 'pablosite'
```

When we wish to draw your attention to a particular part of a code block, the relevant lines or items are set in bold:

```
@echo off
"C:\Program Files\Tableau\Tableau Content Migration Tool\tabcmt-runner" --logfile="logfile_path" "migration_plan_tcmx_path"
```

Any command-line input or output is written as follows:

```
pip install --upgrade pip
pip install tableauserverclient
```

Bold: Indicates a new term, an important word, or words that you see onscreen. For example, words in menus or dialog boxes appear in the text like this. Here is an example: "Select the **Edit Data Source** button."

> **Tips or important notes**
> Appear like this.

Sections

In this book, you will find several headings that appear frequently (*Getting ready*, *How to do it...*, *How it works...*, *There's more...*, and *See also*).

To give clear instructions on how to complete a recipe, use these sections as follows.

Getting ready

This section tells you what to expect in the recipe and describes how to set up any software or any preliminary settings required for the recipe.

How to do it...

This section contains the steps required to follow the recipe.

How it works...

This section usually consists of a detailed explanation of what happened in the previous section.

There's more...

This section consists of additional information in order to make you more knowledgeable about the recipe.

See also

This section provides helpful links to other useful information for the recipe.

Get in touch

Feedback from our readers is always welcome.

General feedback: If you have questions about any aspect of this book, mention the book title in the subject of your message and email us at `customercare@packtpub.com`.

Errata: Although we have taken every care to ensure the accuracy of our content, mistakes do happen. If you have found a mistake in this book, we would be grateful if you would report this to us. Please visit `www.packtpub.com/support/errata`, select your book, click on the Errata Submission Form link, and enter the details.

Piracy: If you come across any illegal copies of our works in any form on the Internet, we would be grateful if you would provide us with the location address or website name. Please contact us at `copyright@packt.com` with a link to the material.

If you are interested in becoming an author: If there is a topic that you have expertise in and you are interested in either writing or contributing to a book, please visit `authors.packtpub.com`.

Reviews

Please leave a review. Once you have read and used this book, why not leave a review on the site that you purchased it from? Potential readers can then see and use your unbiased opinion to make purchase decisions, we at Packt can understand what you think about our products, and our authors can see your feedback on their book. Thank you!

For more information about Packt, please visit `packt.com`.

Share your thoughts

Once you've read *Tableau Cookbook for Experienced Professionals*, we'd love to hear your thoughts! Scan the QR code below to go straight to the Amazon review page for this book and share your feedback.

`https://packt.link/r/1835469744`

Your review is important to us and the tech community and will help us make sure we're delivering excellent quality content.

Free Benefits with Your Book

This book comes with free benefits to support your learning. Activate them now for instant access (see the "*How to Unlock*" section for instructions).

Here's a quick overview of what you can instantly unlock with your purchase:

PDF and ePub Copies

Next-Gen Web-Based Reader

Access a DRM-free PDF copy of this book to read anywhere, on any device.

Use a DRM-free ePub version with your favorite e-reader.

Multi-device progress sync: Pick up where you left off, on any device.

Highlighting and notetaking: Capture ideas and turn reading into lasting knowledge.

Bookmarking: Save and revisit key sections whenever you need them.

Dark mode: Reduce eye strain by switching to dark or sepia themes

How to Unlock

Scan the QR code (or go to `packtpub.com/unlock`). Search for this book by name, confirm the edition, and then follow the steps on the page.

Note: Keep your invoice handy. Purchases made directly from Packt don't require one

Part 1: Scaling Tableau Capabilities – Data, Security, and Cloud Excellence

In this part, you will learn how to build well-structured data models, manage content and security at scale, and strengthen governance with Tableau Cloud's specialized tools, such as the Content Migration Tool and the Metadata API. You will also explore how to secure and simplify data connectivity with virtual connections to ensure that users can access the information they need with confidence.

This part includes the following chapters:

- *Chapter 1, Building Advanced and Efficient Tableau Data Models*
- *Chapter 2, Managing Content and Security at Scale in Tableau*
- *Chapter 3, Leveraging Tableau Cloud's Data Management and Advanced Management*

1

Building Advanced and Efficient Tableau Data Models

It might sound obvious, but without data, there is not much we might be able to analyze and visualize in **Tableau**. To start using data in Tableau, first, we need to create a **data source**.

Each data source has a **data model**. A data model is a diagram needed before starting an analysis to allow Tableau to understand what data we want to use, any specific adjustments we might want to make to the fields, such as renaming or changing the data type of any of them, and, if we want to use more than one table at the same time, how the different tables are related in order to query the data correctly and get meaningful results.

It's common not to spend too much time on the data modeling and data source creation phase and jump to the analysis and visualization as quickly as possible. But creating a good data model is key, especially if we have different tables that we need to combine and use together.

Additionally, it can save us a lot of time if we find out afterward that something was not correct initially and a good data model can improve our dashboard and query performance in more complex scenarios.

In this chapter, we're going to cover the following recipes:

- Building a basic data model
- Combining logical and physical layers in our data model
- Building multi-connection schemas
- Optimizing data model relationships
- Building multi-fact models with Tableau 2025.1
- Crafting data models with Tableau Desktop versus Tableau Prep

> **Free Benefits with Your Book**
>
> Your purchase includes a free PDF copy of this book along with other exclusive benefits. Check the *Free Benefits with Your Book* section in the Preface to unlock them instantly and maximize your learning experience.

Technical requirements

For this chapter, we will use six different tables available on GitHub at `https://github.com/PacktPublishing/Tableau-Cookbook-for-Experienced-Professionals/tree/main/Chapter_01`.

For this chapter, all the images and examples will be provided using Tableau Desktop Public Edition, version 2024.3. Everything we will cover can also be done through the web interface of Tableau Cloud or Tableau Server, but we recommend using Tableau Public Edition or Tableau Desktop to follow along.

> **Note**
>
> The look and feel of the **Data Source** page are a bit different in Tableau's most recent version, 2025.1. Additionally, one of the topics covered in the chapter – multi-fact data models – has only been supported since version 2024.2. For this reason, we recommend updating your version of Tableau Desktop or installing Tableau Public Edition version 2024.2 or higher for this chapter. If you can't have the latest version, keep in mind that some images might look slightly different from what you see in your Tableau version.

Additionally, for the last recipe, *Crafting data models with Tableau Desktop versus Tableau Prep*, you will need to have a full Tableau Creator license to be able to use Tableau Prep Builder or Tableau Prep in the web browser.

Building a basic data model

Data models can be very simple (a single table) or more complex (dozens of tables). For this recipe, we will start with a simple data model relating two different tables together to better understand the data source page and how to create relationships and what they are.

There are two main ways to create a data model:

- Using **Tableau Desktop** or **Tableau Desktop Public Edition**
- Using the web interface from **Tableau Cloud** or **Tableau Server**

In this recipe, we will use the first option, but you can follow along using the web interface if you prefer. To create a workbook and connect to new data from the Tableau Cloud or Tableau Server web interface, check the first two steps in this guide if you don't know how to do it: `https://help.tableau.com/current/pro/desktop/en-us/getstarted_web_authoring.htm`.

Getting ready

You can download the tables we will be using for this recipe in the GitHub repository shared in the *Technical requirements* section at the beginning of this chapter.

More specifically, we will use these files:

- `ch1_visits.csv`: This table has a row for each visit in a hospital, with fields specifying the ID of the visit, the date the visit took place, the patient ID and doctor ID for the visit, and the duration of the visit in minutes

- `ch1_patients.csv`: This table has a row for each patient, with fields specifying the patient ID, gender, blood type, and **date of birth** (**DOB**) of each patient

Let's start by opening the `ch1_visits.csv` file in Tableau Desktop or Tableau Public Edition.

How to do it...

Building your first data model is easy. Let's explore the main areas of the Tableau user interface when we connect to data and create a data model.

1. To connect to the visits table, open Tableau and click on **Text file** in the **Connect** panel on the left side, as shown in *Figure 1.1*.

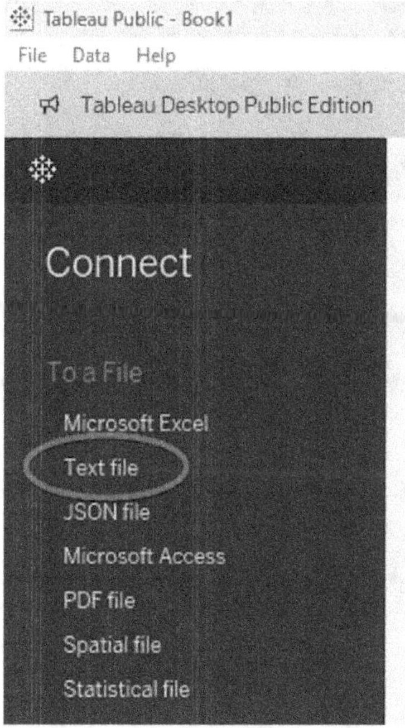

Figure 1.1 – Connecting to a CSV file

2. Then, select the `ch1_visits.csv` file that you downloaded from the GitHub repository and click **Open**.

If you have connected to the CSV file correctly, you should see the **Data Source** page.

The **Data Source** page has four main sections:

- The **left pane** shows the connection or connections we have set up in the workbook and the different files or tables available.

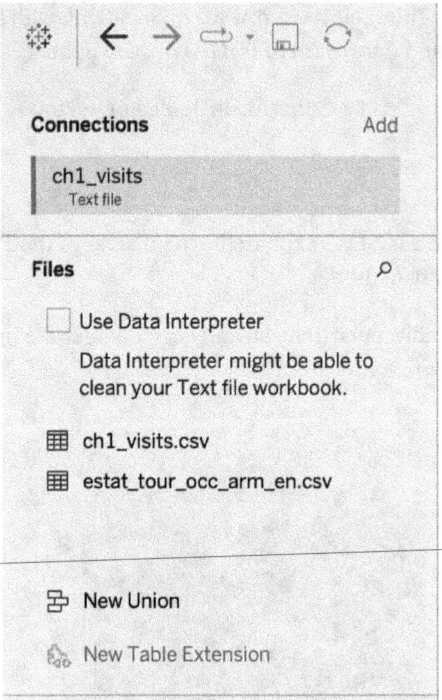

Figure 1.2 – The left pane of the Data Source page

- The **canvas** shows the logical layer of the data model, the tables added to it, and the relationships between them.

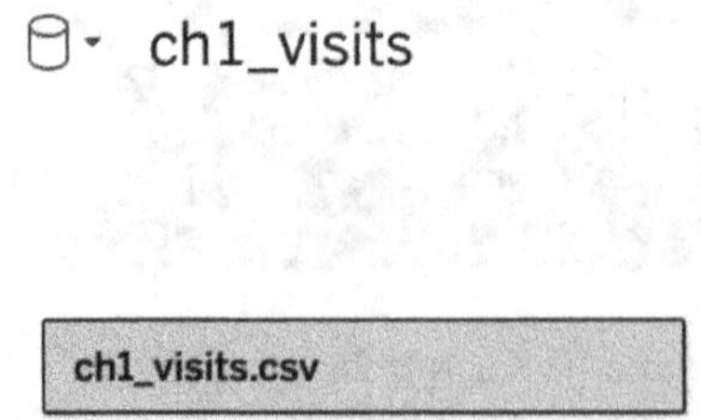

Figure 1.3 – The canvas of the Data Source page

- The **data grid** shows the first rows of the table selected in the canvas.

Abc ch1_visits.csv **Visit ID**	Abc ch1_visits.csv **Patient ID**	🗓 ch1_visits.csv **Visit Date**	Abc ch1_visits.csv **Doctor ID**	# ch1_visits.csv **Duration in Minutes**
VIS00001	PAT07841	13/6/2022	DOC081	17
VIS00002	PAT05395	9/9/2022	DOC029	12
VIS00003	PAT05789	15/11/2022	DOC100	15
VIS00004	PAT03069	17/2/2022	DOC055	8
VIS00005	PAT03095	18/2/2023	DOC077	15
VIS00006	PAT07083	14/1/2022	DOC080	11
VIS00007	PAT07093	1/9/2022	DOC038	13

Figure 1.4 – The data grid of the Data Source page

- The **metadata grid** shows a list of the fields in the table selected on the canvas and their main properties.

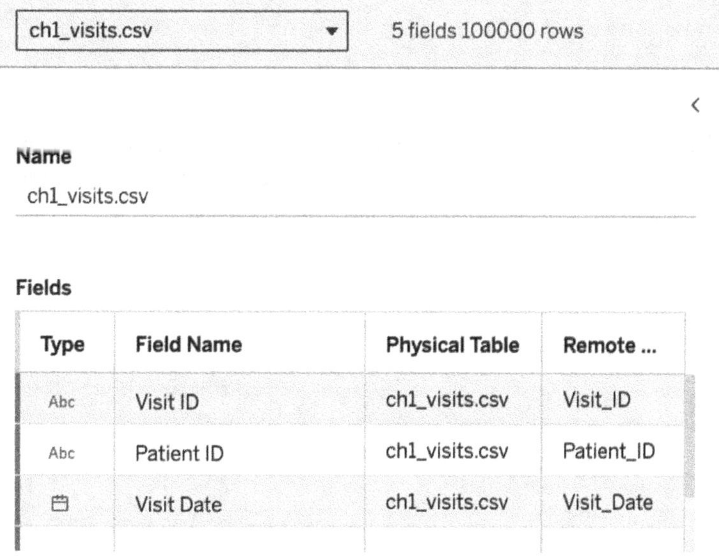

Figure 1.5 – The metadata grid of the Data Source page

Now that we better understand the **Data Source** page, let's create our first model combining the two tables mentioned before.

3. Drag the `ch1_patients.csv` file from the left pane to the canvas next to the `ch1_visits` table until you see a node connecting both tables. Drop the patients table there, as shown in *Figure 1.6*.

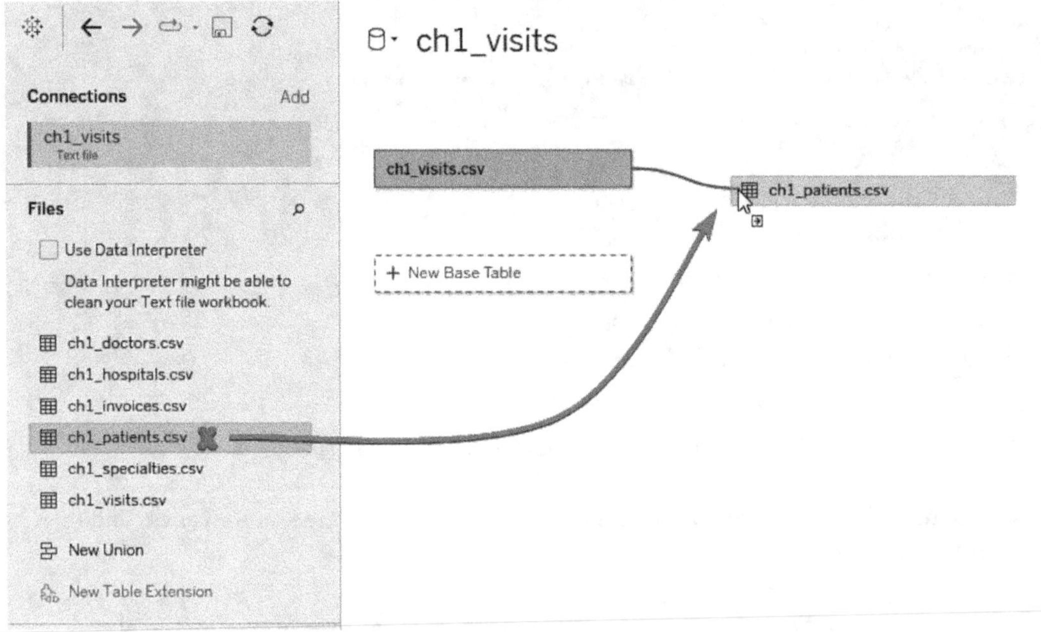

Figure 1.6 – Adding the second table to our data model

4. Click on the node or line connecting both tables. At the bottom, you can configure the relationship between both tables. In our case, the relationship between them is the `Patient ID` field from each table. Review that the relationship is correct.

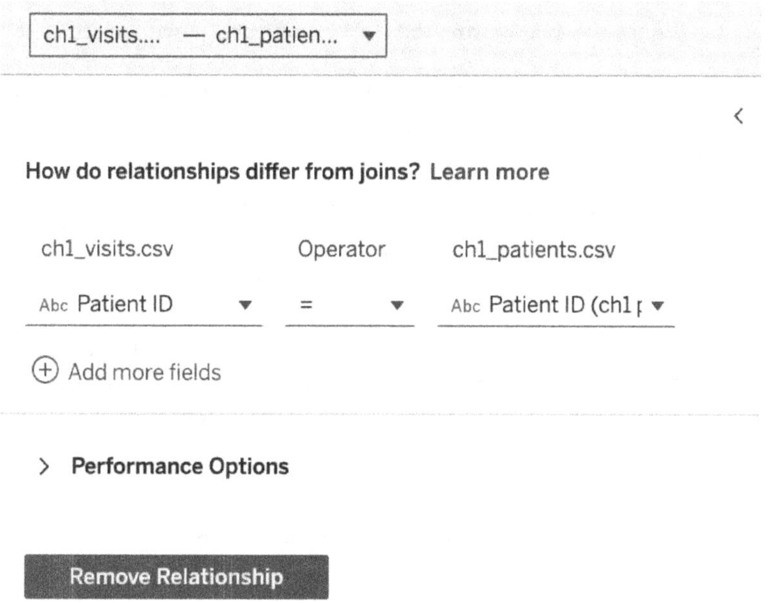

Figure 1.7 – Checking the relationship between the visits and patients tables

5. There are a few more things we can adjust in our data model. At the top of the canvas, you should see a *database* icon with the default name that Tableau assigns to our data source. In our case, it is **ch1_visits+**. Click on the name to rename it to something more meaningful such as Hospital visits and patients.

6. Additionally, right-click in each of the rectangles representing the tables in the canvas and click on *rename* to rename ch1_visits.csv to Visits and ch1_patients.csv to Patients. Your data model should look as shown in *Figure 1.8*.

⊟· Hospital visits and patients

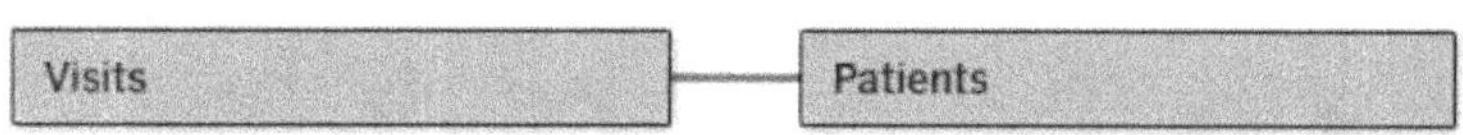

Figure 1.8 – Final stage of our data model after renaming the data source and tables

You have just created a data model with a relationship between two tables!

There are several more things you can do from the **Data Source** page, including the following:

- Add a data source filter from the top-right **Add Filters** button. Adding a data source filter means less data will be available in workbook. Think about data source filters as a WHERE clause in your SQL query if you are more familiar with SQL.

- Change the field names and types from the data or metadata grids.

- Include additional actions for specific columns, from hiding them to changing aliases, creating groups, and so on by right-clicking on each field in the data grid.

For now, we have done everything we need for our first model. You can now go to the **Sheet 1** tab at the bottom and start your analysis. Let's dig into the data model a bit further to understand the differences between the logical layer and the physical layer in the next recipe.

> **Note**
>
> Tableau has a data type for geographic information. Relationships can't be defined based on geographic fields so it's important to have this in mind when creating your data model. We will see different ways to handle geographic data in *Chapter 8*.

Combining logical and physical layers in our data model

In the previous recipe, we related two tables using what we called the **logical layer**, but Tableau's data model allows us to use two different layers:

- The **logical layer** is the default view in the **Data Source** page. When you add tables to your model, those are related through **relationships**, which have been the default way of combining tables in our data model since Tableau version 2020.2.

- The **physical layer** allows us to combine tables using traditional joins and unions. Before 2020.2, this was the only layer available. Each logical layer can contain one or more physical tables.

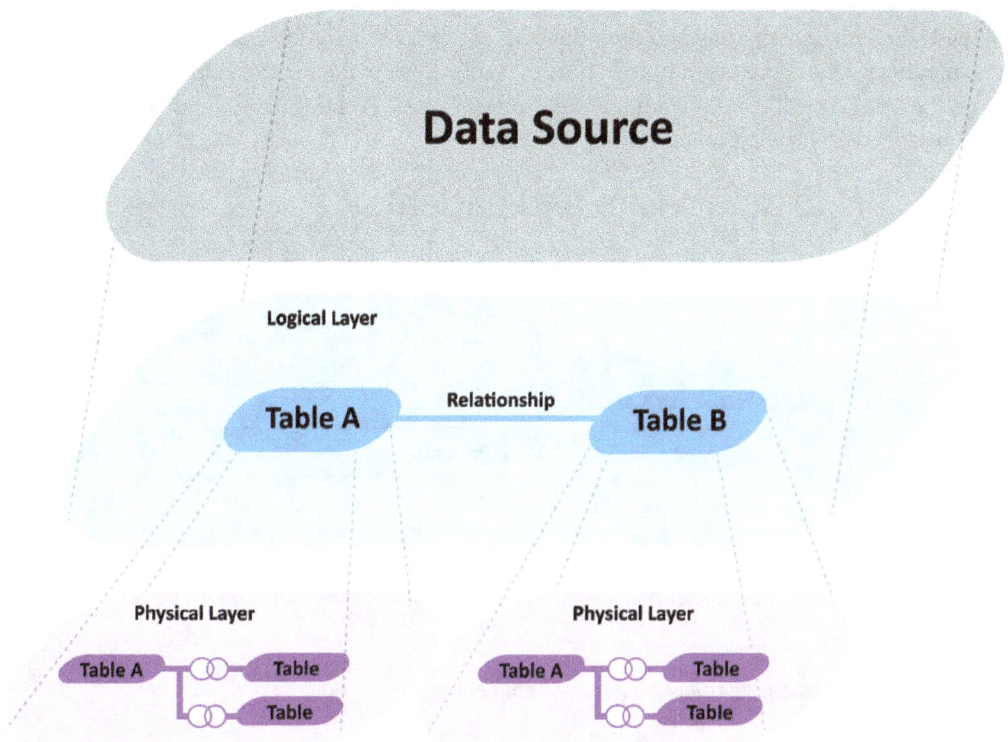

Figure 1.9 – Tableau's data model

The main benefit of having a logical and physical layer is the higher flexibility to build data models based on your needs.

In most scenarios, working with the logical layer should be enough, but if you need to perform traditional joins or unions, you'll need to do them in the physical layer. How can we then use the physical layer of each table?

Getting ready

We will add more data to the model built in the previous recipe. The `Visits` table also has a `Doctor ID` field that we would like to combine with the `ch1_doctors` table. And the `ch1_doctors` table is also related to the `ch1_hospitals` and `ch1_specialties` tables.

What we are going to do is add the `Doctors` table as another logical table related to the `Visits` table based on the `Doctor ID` field in the same way we add the `Patients` table in the previous recipe.

From the **Data Source** page, drag and drop the `ch1_doctors.csv` file from the left pane to the canvas, making sure it's connected to the `Visits` table. Review the relationship to make sure it's based on the `Doctor ID` field of both tables, as in *Figure 1.10*. Feel free to also update the name of the `ch1_doctors.csv` logical table to `Doctors`.

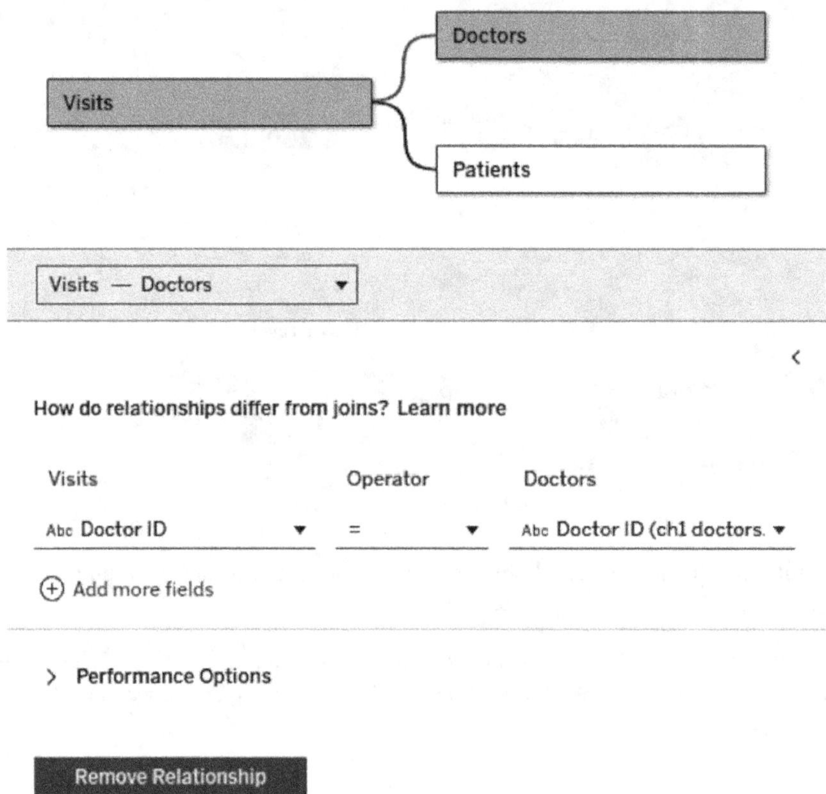

Figure 1.10 – Adding the Doctors table to the data model as a third logical table

How to do it...

Now, let's access the physical layer of the `Doctors` table to add the hospitals and specialties files as traditional joins:

1. Double-click the `Doctors` table in the canvas, or right-click on it and select **Open** to access the physical layer of the `Doctors` logical table. You should then see in the canvas the `Doctors` table's physical layer, as in *Figure 1.11*.

Figure 1.11 – The physical layer of the Doctors table

2. Drag the `ch1_hospitals.csv` file from the left pane and drop it next to the `ch1_doctors.csv` table. You'll see that this time, there's no relationship shown before dropping the table. By default, Tableau will create an inner join between both tables. Click on the Venn diagram to check the type of joins available and the field used in the join, as in *Figure 1.12*.

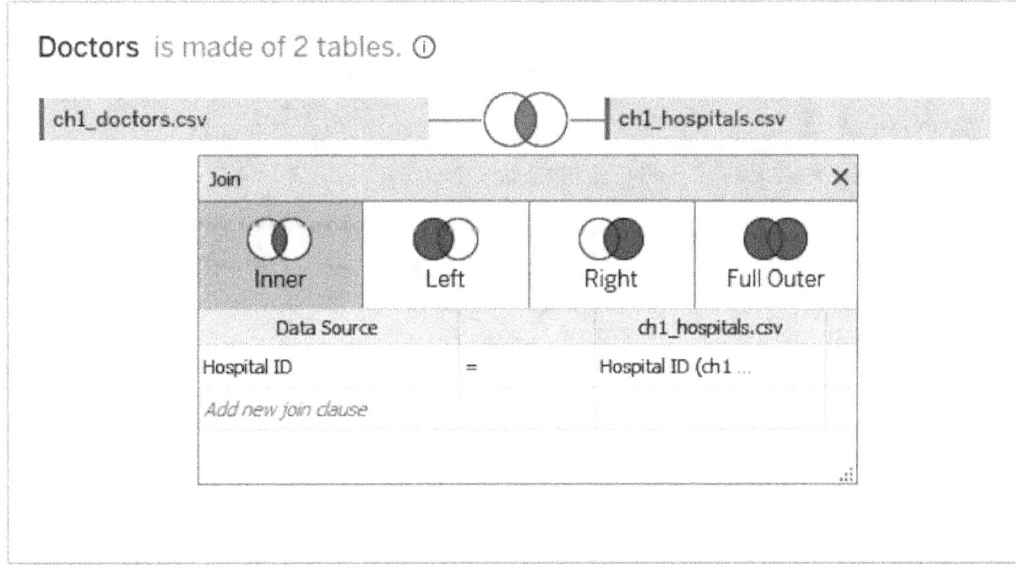

Figure 1.12 – Configuring the join in the physical layer

3. Make sure the relationship between both tables is based on the `Hospital ID` field and change the join to a left join. Close the join window with the Venn diagram.

4. Repeat *Steps 2* and *3* but with the `ch1_specialties.csv` table. The join between `ch1_doctors.csv` and `ch1_specialties.csv` should be based on the `Specialty ID` fields of each table. The physical layer of the `Doctors` table should now look like *Figure 1.13*.

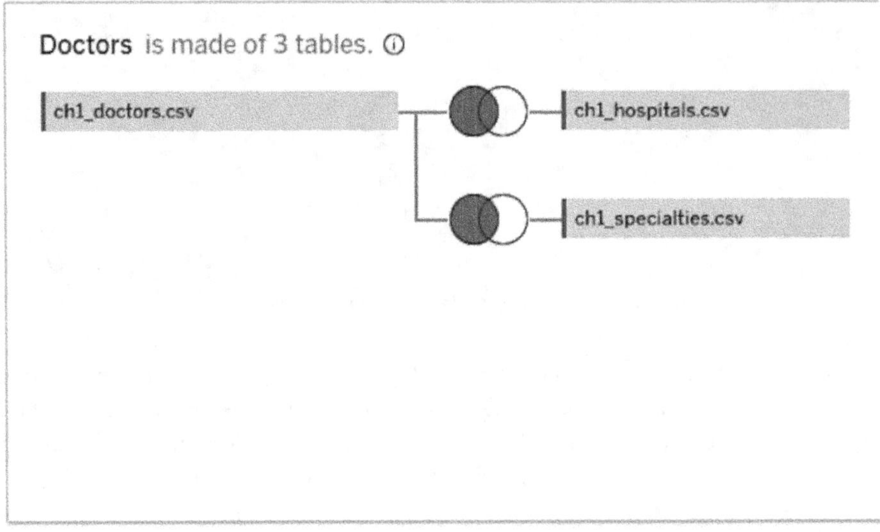

Figure 1.13 – Final state of the physical layer of the Doctors table

5. Close the physical layer of the `Doctors` table by clicking on the **X** in the top-right corner. Your updated data model should look like *Figure 1.14*.

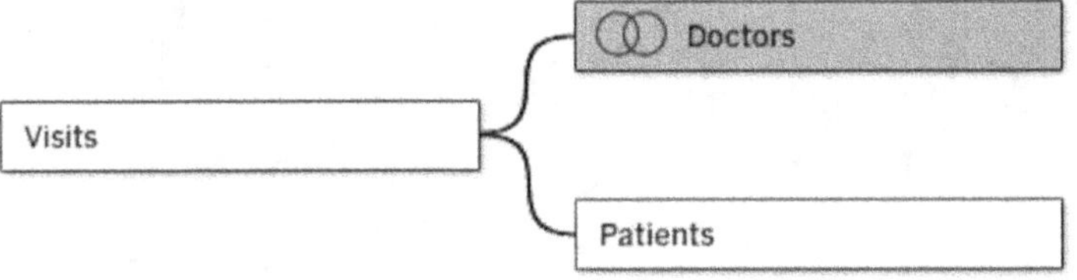

Figure 1.14 – The end state of our data model combining logical and physical layers

How it works...

With our data model ready, we could now start our analysis. The best thing about it is that for end users, there is no difference at all when analyzing data from different tables, no matter whether they are related in the logical layer or the physical layer.

The combination of the logical layer and the physical layer allows you to build different data model schemas, from a single table to star schemas and snowflake schemas.

Use the one that best fits your needs for your analysis, but it's always a good idea to think about the best way to organize your data model.

> **Note**
>
> When creating relationships or joins, it's important to remember that the data types of the fields used must match. One of the most common errors when creating data models is not paying attention to the data types of the fields being used. Make sure to keep an eye on the data types when configuring your relationships.

See also

- For more information about star and snowflake schemas in Tableau, check this page from Tableau's documentation: `https://help.tableau.com/current/pro/desktop/en-us/datasource_datamodel.htm#star-and-snowflake`

- For a detailed explanation of the differences between relationships and traditional joins, read this article: `https://help.tableau.com/current/pro/desktop/en-us/datasource_relationships_learnmorepage.htm`

Building multi-connection schemas

So far, we have seen how to build data models and data sources using one single data connection type. Our example has been with CSV files, but the same logic will apply when using data from Snowflake, Google BigQuery, Amazon Redshift, Azure SQL Database, or any other connection type.

In a lot of use cases, data might not be in the same database type or in the same file type. Very frequently, analysts need to combine data from a database with data from a CSV file; data from an Excel file with data from a CSV file; or even data from Snowflake with data from Amazon Redshift for instance.

How can we create a data model in Tableau that combines different connection types? Learning how we can build **multi-connection** or **cross-database schemas** is the main objective of this recipe.

Getting ready

For this exercise, I'll use some of the datasets we have used already during this chapter. If you don't have them, please go to the beginning of the chapter to find the link from which you can download the data. In my case, I'll also use a Snowflake database, but you could do the same with any database you might use or even save a copy of the `Doctors` and `Hospital` tables as Excel files instead of CSV.

In my case, I'll use the `Visits` table and combine it with `Doctors` and `Hospital` located in a Snowflake database.

If you don't have access to a database, you can make a copy of the `Doctors` and `Hospital` tables and save them as `.xslx` files to have different data types and build your own multi-connection data source.

How to do it...

The process is very simple, but a lot of Tableau users don't know how to do it because they might have missed where they can add several connection types to a data source:

1. First, let's start by connecting to our `visits.csv` file as the first table of our data model. Open Tableau Desktop or Tableau Public, go to **Connect | Text File**, and select the `visits.csv` file provided at the beginning of the chapter.

2. In the **Data Source** window, look at the top of the left panel where it says **Connections** and click on the **Add** button next to it, as shown in *Figure 1.15*.

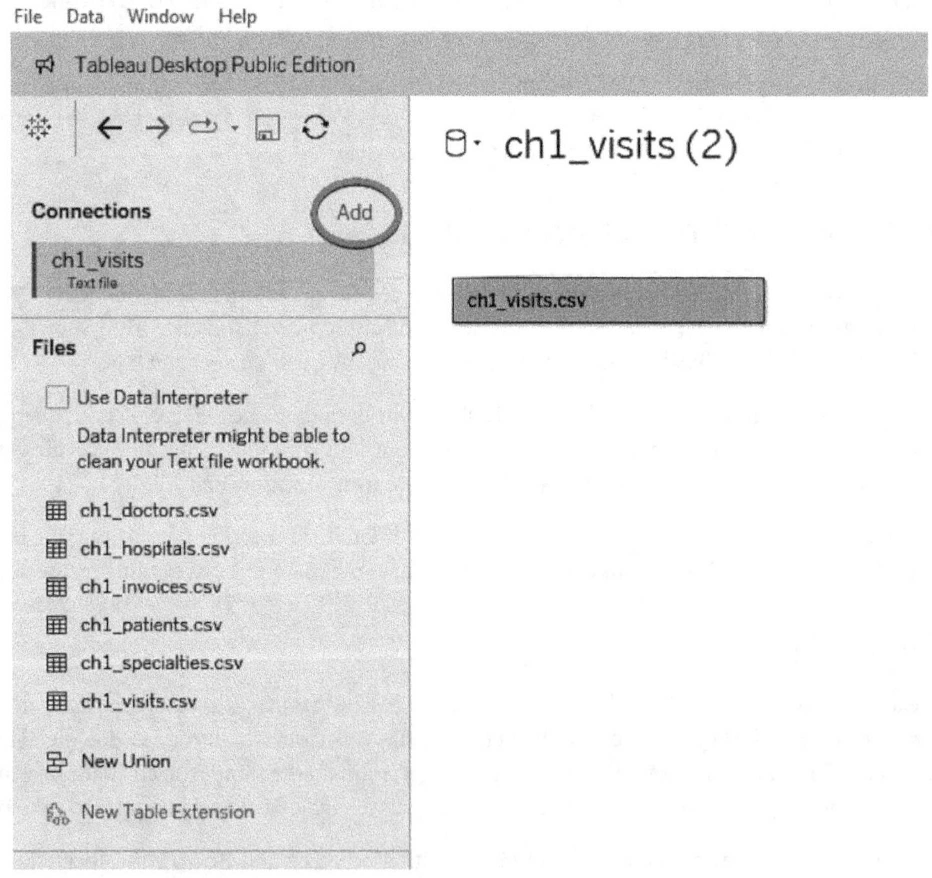

Figure 1.15 – Adding a second connection to our data model

3.   Select the new connection you want to add to your data model. As mentioned earlier, I'll use a Snowflake database, but you can use a copy of the `Doctors` table saved as an Excel file. In that case, select **Microsoft Excel** as your new connection. Then, find the `Doctors` file or the `Doctors` table in the database you want to use if you have access to one.

4.   Now, you should see two different connections in the left pane, one with a blue line and the second one with an orange line, as in *Figure 1.16*. Click on each to show the files or tables available in each connection.

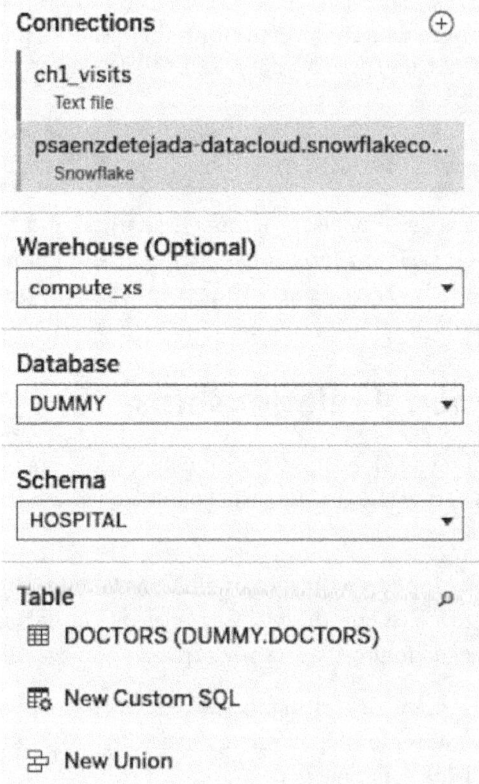

Figure 1.16 – Working with data from multiple connections on the left pane

5.   Drag and drop the `Doctors` table from the second connection from the left panel to the canvas and build the relationship as we have already learned in this chapter based on the `Doctor ID` fields.

Congratulations! You have just built a data model with a different connection type, also called a multi-connection or cross-database model. This can be very useful in scenarios where users need to combine their curated company data with some local Excel files to enrich the analysis or when data lives in different databases or is stored in different file types.

> **Note**
>
> When creating data models with cross-database joins, it's important to keep in mind that performance might be affected. For each connection in a cross-database join, Tableau sends queries independently for each data source and stores the results in a temporary table. This means that during your analysis, the speed of your results will depend on the slowest source used.

See also

Multi-connection or cross-database models have some limitations and considerations to keep in mind when combined with joins. Have a look at the documentation to improve performance for cross-database joins: `https://help.tableau.com/current/pro/desktop/en-us/joins_xbd_perf.htm`.

Optimizing data model relationships

In many scenarios, when creating relationships between tables, you'll not need to do anything other than specify the related fields between them. This will guarantee you get meaningful results and, in general, a good performance.

Sometimes, with complex data models with a lot of different tables or big datasets and complex relationships, you might want to adjust how the tables are related to let Tableau know specifically how to perform those relationships and improve query performance and overall speed.

Tableau allows us to do this by manually setting the **cardinality** and **referential integrity** of each table in a relationship. It is important to keep in mind that setting these options incorrectly can also translate into wrong results during your analysis.

A best practice is to only adjust the following settings when you have a deep understanding of your data, especially of the fields you are using to relate your tables.

Getting ready

Before learning how we can set the tables' cardinality and referential integrity, let's understand what those options mean and what they are used for.

Cardinality between tables refers to whether a row from one table could be related to more than one row from another table. You can set up the cardinality for each table you are using in a relationship by selecting one of the two options available: **Many** or **One**. Because cardinality can be set up for each table in a relationship, this will allow you to have four possible scenarios for a relationship between two tables: one-to-one, one-to-many, many-to-one, or many-to-many. Let's understand what each scenario means:

- A **one-to-one** cardinality means each value from the related field in one table is related to no more than one value of the shared field in the related table. For example, imagine you have the following tables:

  - *Table A*, with information about different hospitals in your city. Each row represents a hospital and there are no duplicate rows. The table has two columns: `Hospital ID` and `Hospital Name`.

  - *Table B*, with details of those hospitals. Again, each row represents a hospital and there are no duplicate rows. The table has the following columns: `Hospital ID`, `Address`, `Number of rooms`, and `Number of patients attended during the current year`.

  Because the `Hospital ID` value is unique in each table, we could specify *one* has the cardinality of each table in the data model, creating a one-to-one cardinality between the tables. Because we know both tables have unique values, a `Hospital ID` value in *Table A* can only appear once in *Table B*, and vice versa.

- The **one-to-many** and **many-to-one** scenarios are similar, and they just depend on where in the data model each table is. These configurations might improve performance in scenarios where one of the tables has unique values for the shared field, and the other table can have multiple rows for the same value in the related table. Let's see an example:

  - *Table A* is the same as in the previous scenario: hospitals in your city. Each row represents a hospital and there are no duplicate values. The fields in the table are `Hospital ID` and `Hospital Name`.

  - The second table, *Table C*, has information about doctors in those hospitals. Each row represents a doctor, and the fields available are `Doctor Name`, `Specialty`, `Main Hospital ID`, `Age`, and `Years Working at the Hospital`.

  Both tables are related by `Hospital ID`. However, because several doctors work in the same hospital, the same `Hospital ID` value will appear several times on the *Table C*, the Doctors table. This is a one-to-many cardinality between *Table A* and *Table C*, and setting up the cardinality accordingly might improve query processing and performance.

- Finally, we have the **many-to-many** scenario. This is also the default configuration Tableau defines for every relationship if we don't update the cardinality configuration. In this case, multiple values of the shared field of one table can be related to multiple values in the other table. Here is an example:

  - *Table D* has information about patient visits. Each row represents a visit from a patient to a doctor. The fields available are `Visit ID`, `Visit Date`, `Doctor ID`, and `Patient ID`.

  - *Table E* has prescription information. Each row represents a medical prescription made by a doctor to a patient during a visit. The fields available are `Visit ID`, `Product ID`, and `Product Name`.

  The relationship between both tables is the `Visit ID` value. But because, in a visit, a doctor can prescribe multiple products and a patient can see more than one doctor and specialist during the same visit, the cardinality between tables is many-to-many.

A related concept to cardinality in data models is **referential integrity**, which is used to specify whether every value in the shared field of one table has a matching value in the other table.

This configuration setting has only two options for each table in our data model: **Some records match** or **All records match**.

The naming is quite self-explanatory but let's see an example to better understand both options.

Imagine the last scenario we explained: *Table D* has information about patient visits, and *Table E* has prescription information. Every single prescription should have a `Visit ID` value (if there are no data quality issues) because each prescription in a hospital visit has to be done by a doctor during a medical appointment. On the contrary, not every patient who visits a doctor receives a medical prescription so some `Visit ID` values will appear in *Table D* but not in *Table E*.

In this scenario, in *Table D*, our visits table, referential integrity should be **Some records match** and in Table E, our prescription table, it should be **All records match**.

As mentioned before, this assumes there are no data quality issues or null values on each table. That's why it's so important to understand our data very well before setting up these settings.

How to do it...

Let's see how we can set up cardinality and referential integrity with the dummy hospital data we downloaded at the beginning of the chapter. Make sure you have unzipped the folder before starting the exercise:

1. Open Tableau Desktop or Tableau Public.

2. Click on **Connect** | **Text file** and select the `ch1_visits.csv` file in the folder you have downloaded and unzipped the files (see *Figure 1.1*). The **Data Source** page should appear, with the `Visits` table already on the canvas as part of your data model.

3. Drag the `ch1_doctors.csv` file from the **Files** panel on the left to the canvas next to the `Visits` table to create a relationship between both tables.

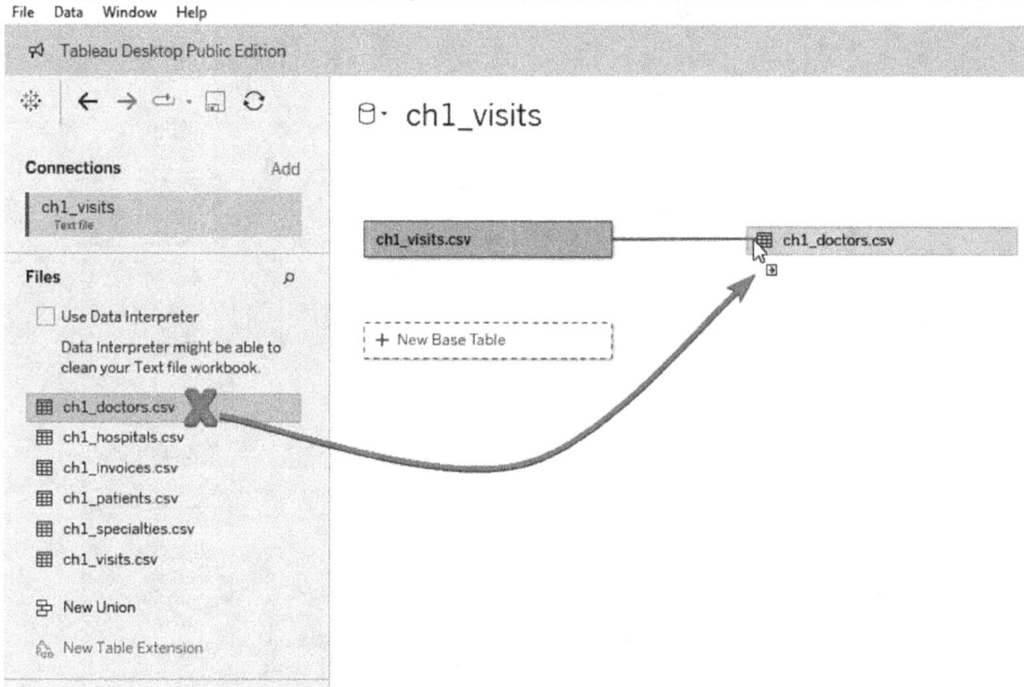

Figure 1.17 – Adding the doctors table to the data model

4. Click on the line that connects both tables and check the relationship between them at the bottom pane. The relationship must be the following:

```
Doctor ID = Doctor ID (ch1_doctors.csv)
```

5. Click on **Performance Options** to expand the cardinality and referential integrity settings.

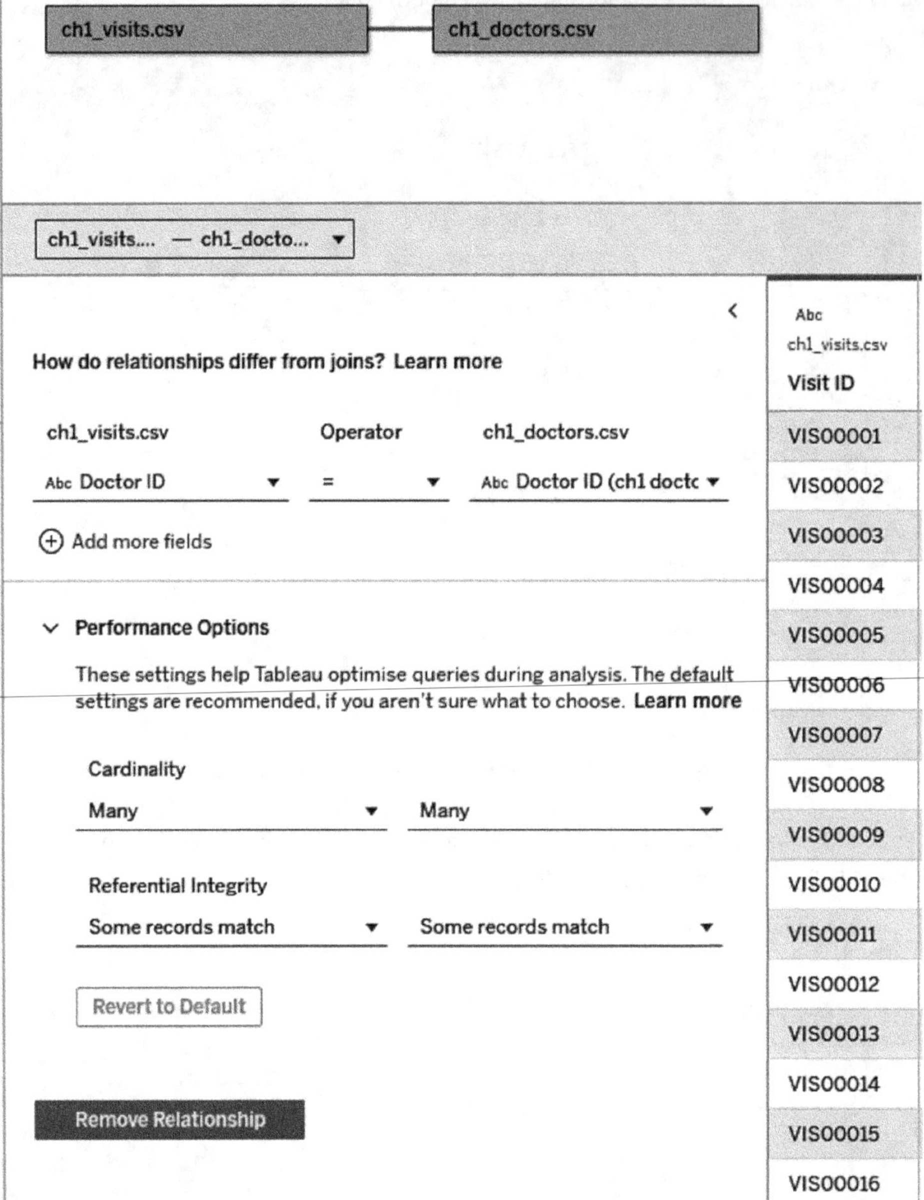

Figure 1.18 – Expanding Performance Options

6. In our example, a `Doctor ID` value will appear more than once in the `Visits` table as more than one patient can visit the same doctor. But our `Doctors` table has unique `Doctor ID` values so the Cardinality should be **Many** (visits) to **One** (doctor). All `Doctor ID` values in the `Visits` table match a `Doctor ID` value in the `Doctors` table, and vice versa, so the referential integrity is **All records match – All records match**.

It is as easy as that! You have specified the cardinality and referential integrity of both tables. Now, Tableau can optimize queries and improve performance when combining data from the two tables.

Just remember, these options can cause incorrect values during your analysis if they are set up incorrectly. That's why it's important to check the following steps:

1. Only change the default settings if you are 100% sure of the cardinality and referential integrity of your tables.

2. If you are not sure, leave the default options.

How it works...

Once we set up the cardinality and referential integrity of a relationship, the benefits are transparent to anyone using the data model. Keep in mind that if your dashboard's performance is already good, you might not be aware of any benefit. But let's understand better what Tableau does behind the scenes.

The cardinality defines when Tableau aggregates data when using both tables. If the cardinality is set to **Many**, Tableau will aggregate the data it needs before creating any required join for our analysis. When set to **One**, Tableau will first join the data and aggregate afterward. As mentioned before, this optimizes queries but can show duplicate aggregate values when set to **One** when, in reality, the field values aren't unique.

The referential integrity is related to the type of join used during the analysis. When set to **Some records match**, Tableau will use outer joins to get dimension values for a measure. This is safer during the analysis but might impact performance. If we know there is referential integrity and set it to **All records match**, Tableau will use inner joins when combining the data. The resulting query will be an optimized and more efficient one.

Building multi-fact models with Tableau 2025.1

Tableau allows us to build data models quickly and easily. However, it lacked a concrete type of data model that is common in some companies and scenarios: multi-fact data models.

You may have noticed that all the models we have seen so far have one base table. The base table is the first table we add to the data model, and every single table we add afterward must be connected to it directly or through another table.

This has been an obstacle for a long time to developing more complex data models with different base tables not connected between them, and it has been solved with Tableau version 2024.2.

Getting ready

For this recipe, we will use the same `Hospital` tables we used earlier in the chapter. Practice what you have learned in previous recipes to create a data model that combines `Visits`, `Patients`, `Doctors`, `Hospitals`, and `Specialties`, as shown in *Figure 1.19*.

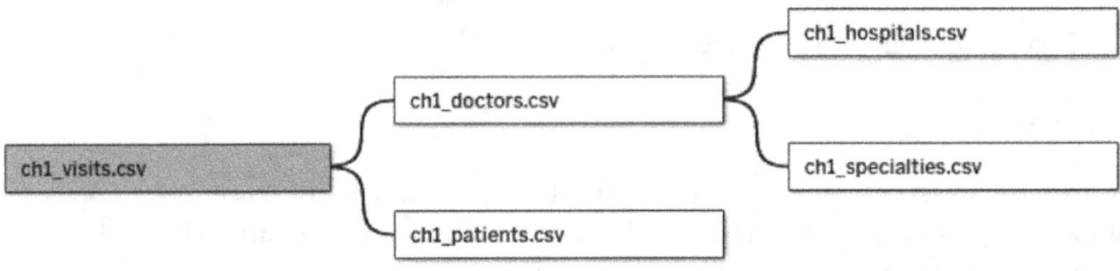

Figure 1.19 – The starting data model

With this model as a starting point, let's learn how to create a multi-fact data model.

How to do it...

Multi-fact data models allow us to use more than one base table in our model without requiring those base tables to be related together, but sharing common dimension tables.

> **Note**
>
> Remember that multi-fact analysis and data models are only available from Tableau version 2024.2 onward. If you have a previous version of Tableau Desktop, you won't be able to reproduce this recipe as you won't be able to add a second base table to the data model.

In our example, we might want to analyze not only the hospital visits but also the invoices without having a separate data source and connect the `Invoices` table to the `Patients` and `Doctors` tables, which are common dimension tables with `Visits`. To do so, follow the next steps:

1. Drag the `Invoices` table from the left panel. Once you start dragging it into the canvas, you will see a box that says **New Base Table**. Drop the `Invoices` table into the box, as in *Figure 1.20*.

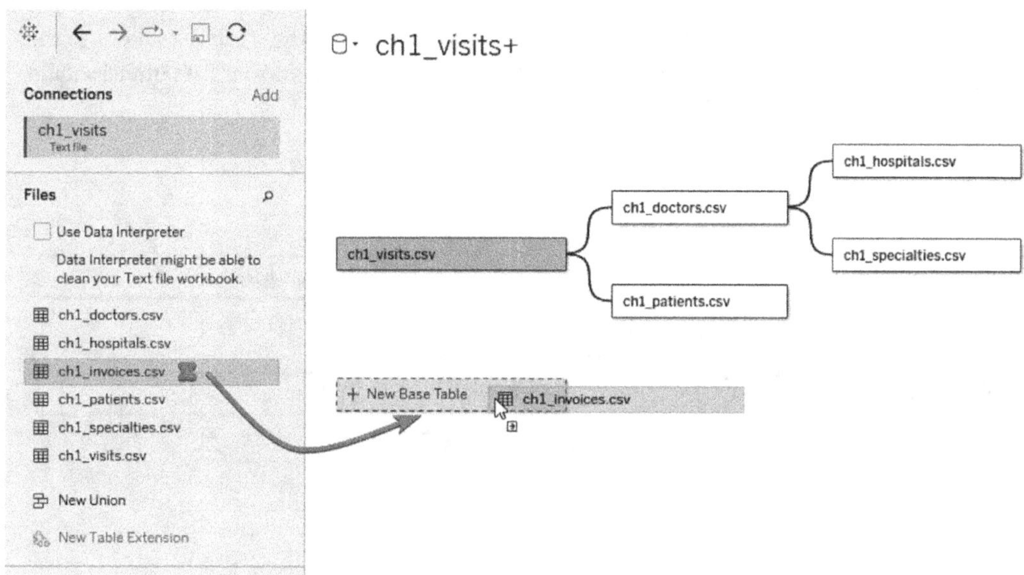

Figure 1.20 – Adding a second base table to the data model

2. We have our second base table, but we need to relate it with the common dimension tables it shares with the `Visits` table. To connect the new `Invoices` table to the `Doctors` table, hover over the `Invoices` table in the canvas until you see a + icon next to it. Click the + icon and drag it next to the `Doctors` table to connect the `Invoices` and `Doctors` shared dimension table, as in *Figure 1.21*. Make sure the relationship between both tables is based on the `Doctor  ID` fields.

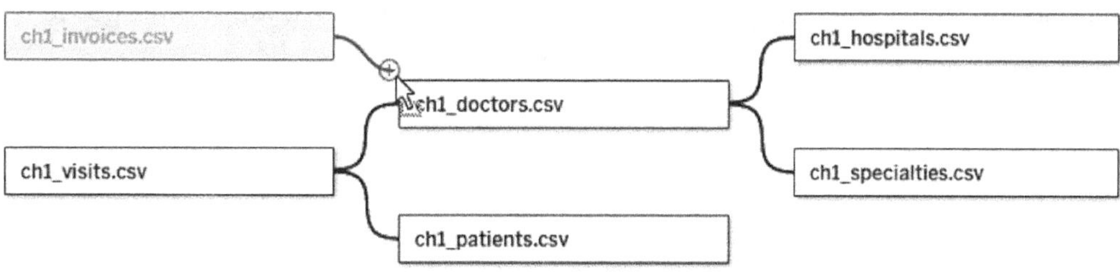

Figure 1.21 – Creating a relationship between the Invoices and Doctors tables

3. Repeat *Step 2* to connect the Invoices table with the Patients table. Make sure the relationship between both tables is based on the Patient ID fields. Your data model should look as shown in *Figure 1.22*.

⊖· Visits and Invoices

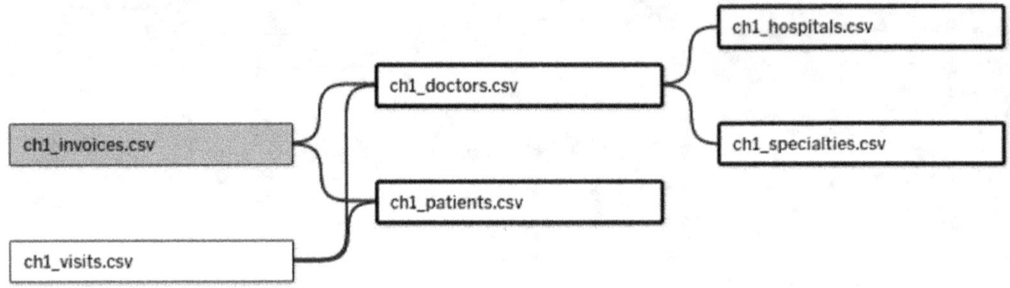

Figure 1.22 – Our final multi-fact data model

4. Feel free to change the data source name at the top to something more meaningful than the default name, such as Visits and Invoices.

We have our multi-fact data model. Now, let's see how this works when we are doing our analysis. Go to **Sheet 1** in your workbook to start analyzing the data.

How it works...

As you can probably notice, apparently nothing changes when we go to a sheet to start our analysis. We could then drag our Invoice Date field from the Invoices table to the **Columns** shelf and the Amount field from the same table into the **Rows** shelf to analyze the total amount of the invoices monthly.

You might have noticed something different on the data pane on the left. If you pay attention to all the fields in the Visits table, they are not grayed out, as shown in *Figure 1.23*.

✓ ⊞ **ch1_patients.csv**

   Abc Blood Type

   🗓 DOB

   Abc Gender

   Abc Patient ID (ch1 pati...

   # *ch1_patients.csv (C...*

✓ ⊞ **ch1_specialties.csv**

   Abc Medical Specialty

   Abc Specialty ID (ch1 sp...

   # *ch1_specialties.csv ...*

✓ ⊞ **ch1_visits.csv**

   Abc Doctor ID

   Abc Patient ID

   🗓 Visit Date

   Abc Visit ID

   # Duration in Minutes

   # *ch1_visits.csv (Cou...*

Figure 1.23 – Unrelated table fields are grayed out in a multi-fact analysis

If you hover over any of the grayed-out fields, you will see also an icon representing a data model crossed, and when hovering over the icon, you will see the following message:

Not related to any dimensions in the viz. If used, this field can show combinations of values in the viz that don't exist in the data.

Not related to any measures in the viz. If used, measure values will repeat for this field.

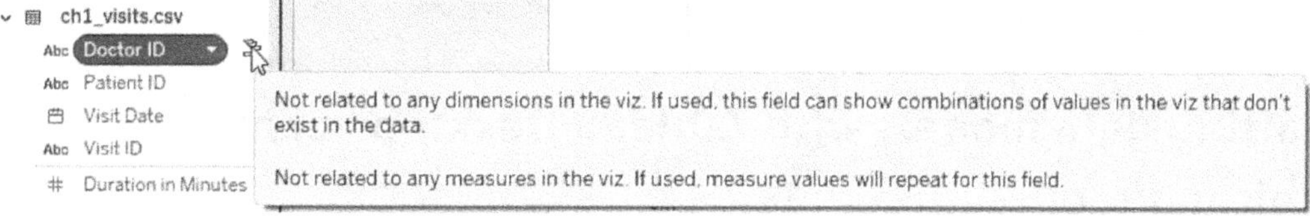

Figure 1.24 – Explanation of why fields from our Visits table are grayed out in our analysis

Tableau is warning us that, in the current sheet we are working on, if we use any fields from the `Visits` table, we might get inconsistent results. This is because the `Invoices` and `Visits` tables are not related together in our multi-fact model.

In fact, we still can just drag a field from the `Visits` table, such as the `Duration in Minutes` field, and try to add it to our view.

If you now drag and drop that field to the **Rows** shelf, Tableau will show another warning, as in *Figure 1.25*.

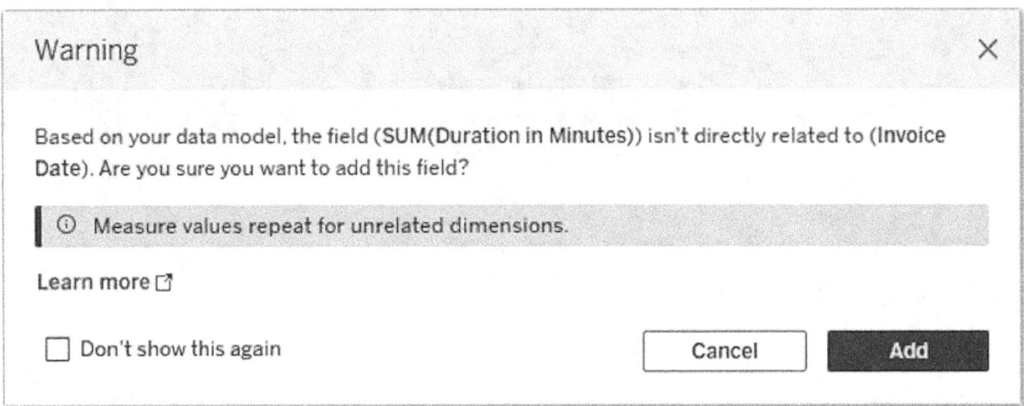

Figure 1.25 – Warning received when trying to add a non-related table field to the view

We can then decide to cancel the action or add the field to the view, but if we do, we will not get meaningful results. Instead, Tableau will just show the total value of duration in minutes for the entire table, repeated for each month.

See also

For a deeper explanation and considerations about multi-fact analysis in Tableau, we recommend checking the *About Multi-fact Relationship Data Models* article in the Tableau documentation: `https://help.tableau.com/current/pro/desktop/en-us/datasource_mfr_multiple_base_tables.htm`.

Crafting data models with Tableau Desktop versus Tableau Prep

One of the main benefits of Tableau is the efficiency of **Tableau extracts**. An extract is a snapshot of the data that Tableau gets from the original source and saves locally or on your own Tableau Server or Tableau Cloud environment.

Tableau extracts have some benefits, the two most important being improved performance and reduced workload from the original source when users run queries using the extract.

As you can imagine, Tableau extracts also have some downsides. They can take a long time to run if the original data is very big, and to date (Tableau version 2024.2), it's not possible to create data models combining Tableau extracts.

Fortunately, Tableau has another tool called Tableau Prep, or Tableau Prep Builder, that allows us to combine different Tableau extracts and also perform additional data preparation tasks before creating our Tableau extract, similar to what you can achieve with **Extract, Transform, Load** (ETL) tools.

> **Note**
>
> You need a full Tableau Creator license to use Tableau Prep Builder or Tableau Prep in the web browser. You can also request a Tableau Developer free sandbox through `https://www.tableau.com/developer` for developing and testing purposes that includes a Creator License, an Explorer License and a Viewer License.

How to do it...

We will use the `Doctors` and `Visits` tables available at the beginning of the chapter. Make sure you have both tables as extract files published on your Tableau Cloud or Tableau Server, or two Tableau extracts in your computer if you are using Tableau Prep Builder.

As you can see in *Figure 1.26*, I have two extracts published on my Tableau Cloud site.

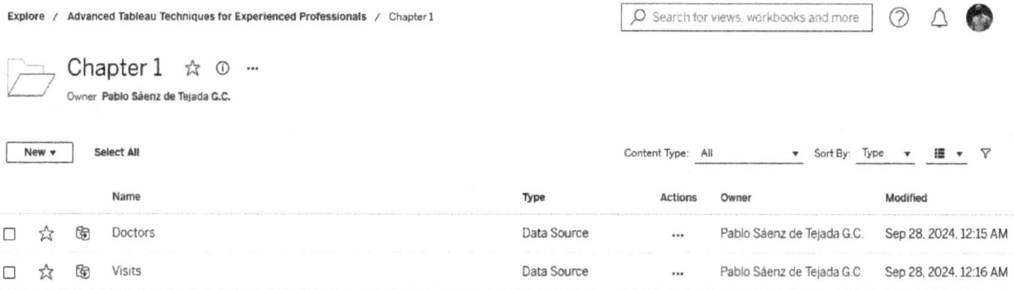

Figure 1.2 – Tableau extract data sources published in Tableau Cloud

As you might already know, if I want to combine those two data sources with Tableau Desktop, I won't be able to. Tableau Desktop doesn't allow us to create joins or relationships. I'd have to connect to each data source independently and use blending to combine both data sources. But as we learned earlier in this chapter, blending can impact performance if we are using big amounts of data, and it is not as easy to understand for end users.

Instead, we can use Tableau Prep to join both data sources together and publish a third data source that combines visits and doctors:

1.   Go to the **New** button in Tableau Cloud or Tableau Server and select **Flow**, as in *Figure 1.27*.

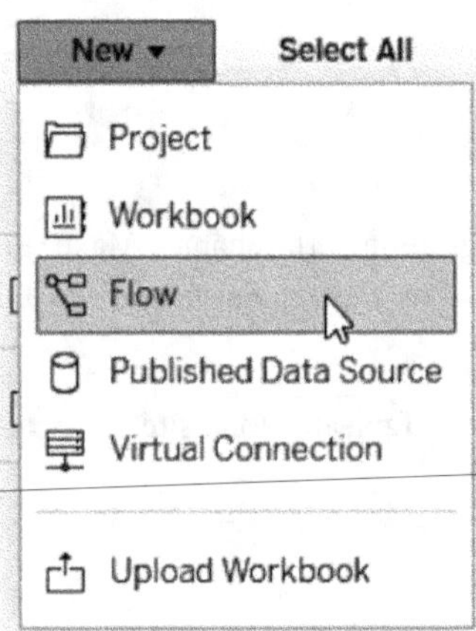

Figure 1.27 – Creating a new flow

2. On the new Tableau Prep flow that opens, click **Connect to Data** and select **Tableau Server** to connect to an extract saved in your Tableau Cloud or Tableau Server environment or **Tableau extract** to connect to a locally saved extract.

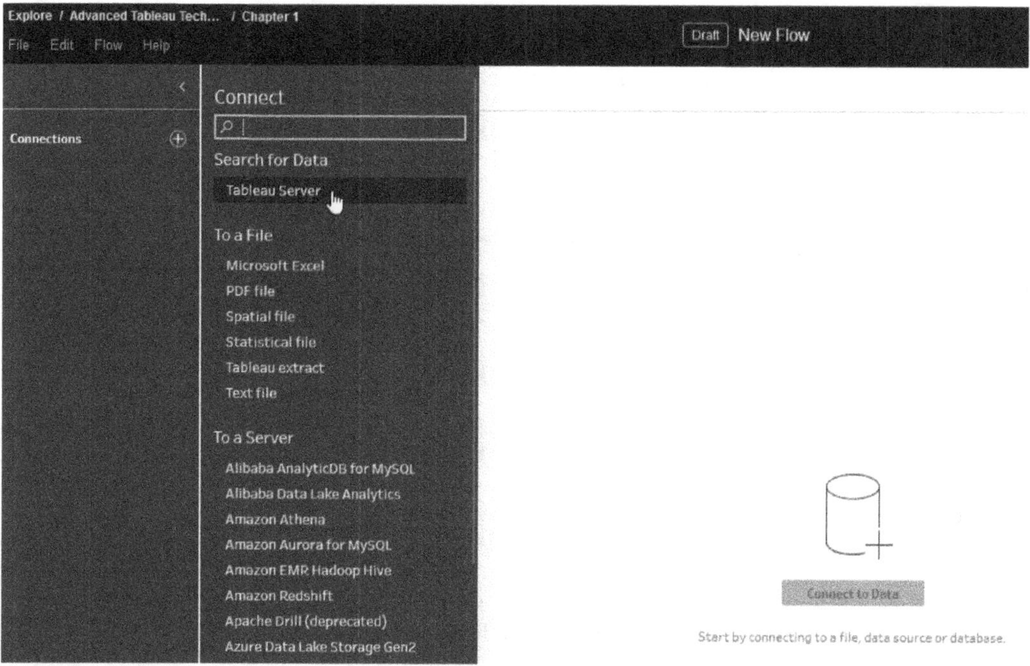

Figure 1.28 – Connecting to a data source saved in your Tableau Cloud or Tableau Server environment

3. Find the **Visits** data source extract and click **Connect**. Click on the + sign next to **Connections** on the left panel and repeat the process to connect to the **Doctors** data source. You should now have your Tableau Prep Flow with both data sources in the flow pane, as in *Figure 1.29*.

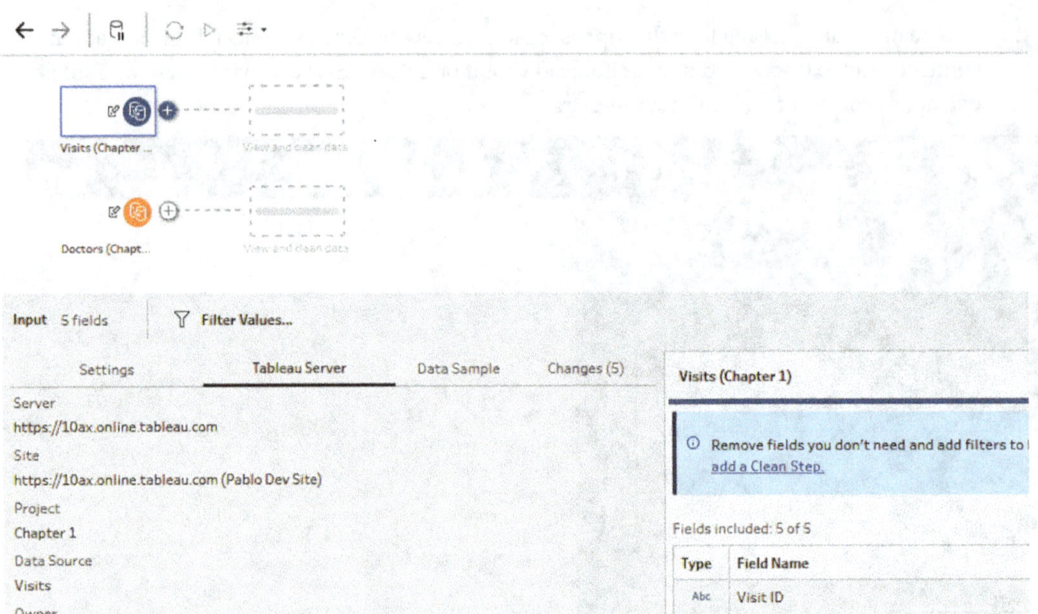

Figure 1.29 – Starting your Tableau Prep flow

This is not meant to be a proper Tableau Prep lesson, so we will just learn how to join two Tableau extracts or published data sources together.

4. Drag one of the data source icons, for example, **Doctors**, and move it close to the **Visits** icon. You'll see three icons appearing: **Replace**, **Union**, and **Join**. Drop the data source into the **Join** icon, as in *Figure 1.30*.

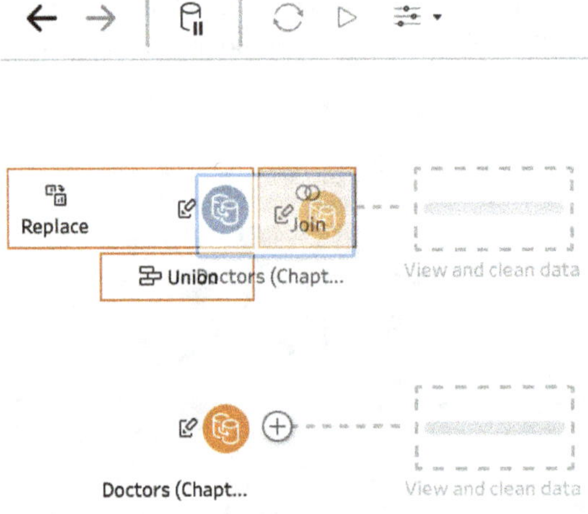

Figure 1.30 – Joining two extracts in Tableau Prep

5.   A Venn diagram representing the join between both sources should appear. At the bottom, we can define the type of join we want to use and the join clause, but in this case, the default one should be fine. We will use an inner join using the Doctor ID value from each table.

6.   Finally, you can click on the + icon next to the Venn diagram in the flow pane and add an **Output** step to save the combined data source locally or to your Tableau Cloud or Tableau Server environment.

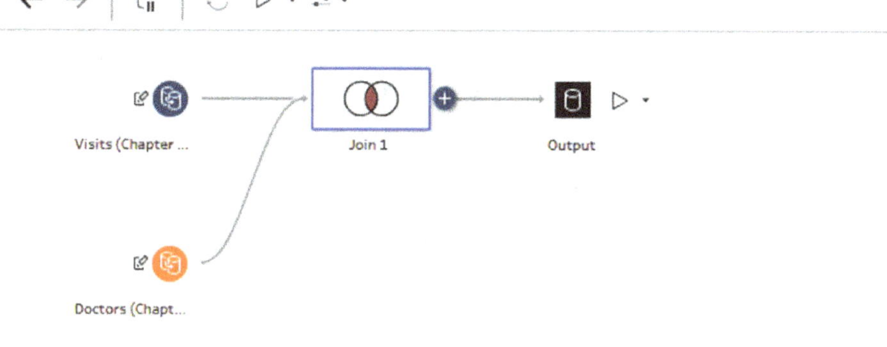

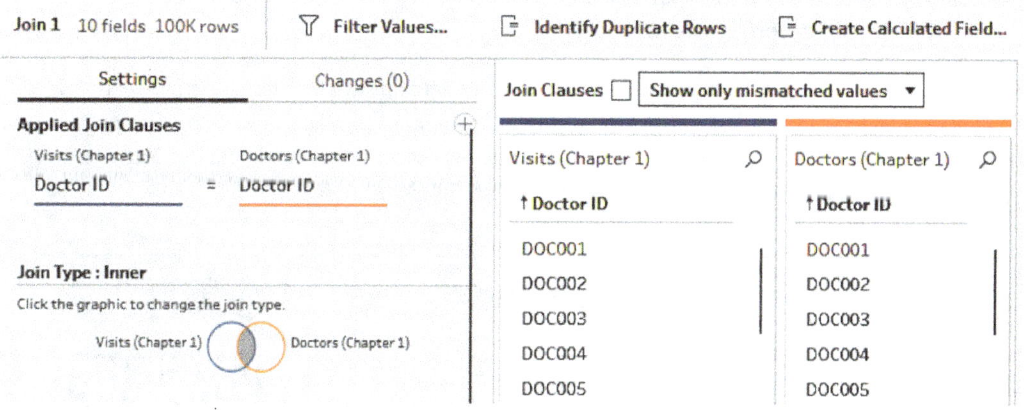

Figure 1.31 – Setting up the join and creating the output

One important difference between data sources and models created with Tableau Desktop versus Tableau Prep is that Desktop-created data models can be updated and edited more easily.

On the other hand, to change the final extract created by a Tableau Prep flow, we will need to edit the flow and rerun the extract again.

How it works...

As you might have noticed, there are some important differences between data sources created with Tableau Desktop and the ones created with Tableau Prep. Let's understand a bit better when to use each method.

You should create data sources in **Tableau Desktop** in these scenarios:

- You want to have full control of the data model and define the physical and logical layers

- You want to be able to edit the data model easily and add or remove tables

- Your data is quite clean from the original source, and you don't need complex data preparation tasks or data transformations

You should create data sources in **Tableau Prep** in these scenarios:

- You don't need control over the logical and physical layers and having traditional joins is enough for you

- You need to perform more advanced and complex data preparation and data transformation tasks before analyzing your data, such as aggregations, creating lots of calculations, and so on

- You need to combine several published data sources or extracts together, and you can't or don't want to rebuild the original data models

Because you can create relationships with Tableau Prep and just traditional joins, my suggestion is to use Tableau Desktop as your first option due to the advantages of the data model creation page. You should use Tableau Prep only when you can't create the data source you need with Tableau Desktop.

Get This Book's PDF Version and Exclusive Extras

2

Managing Content and Security at Scale in Tableau

Modern analytical platforms try to keep a balance between **self-service** and **control**. On one hand, you want to allow users to connect to data easily, run their analysis, and share their insights quickly. On the other hand, you need to make sure not everyone can do and access everything but also make security and control easy to maintain and audit.

In this chapter, we'll learn how to make it easier for IT and **data stewards** to manage data and other **assets** in a secure and scalable way in Tableau.

By the end of this chapter, you will know how to scale your Tableau platform to secure your data, manage your content, and improve users' trust and adoption.

More specifically, we're going to cover the following recipes:

- Understanding governance and permissions best practices
- Setting up row-level security (RLS) the traditional way
- Setting up centralized RLS with virtual connections
- Configuring column-level security
- Managing content description, metadata, and data labels with Tableau Data Management
- Using data lineage and Tableau Catalog to perform impact analysis

Technical requirements

Tableau has an additional module licensed separately called **Data Management**, which makes it easier to discover, understand, connect, and trust your data and assets. Although this module is licensed separately, it's also included in the free sandbox available for Developers. You can sign in and get your own Developer sandbox here `https://www.tableau.com/developer`. In *Chapter 3*, we will cover the Data Management module in even more detail. You can also review Tableau's official website to learn more about it: `https://www.tableau.com/products/data-management`.

In this chapter, we will cover several use cases of how to use this module to manage content and security and scale to make data stewards' lives easier. If you don't have Data Management, you will not be able to follow most of the recipes of this chapter but, hopefully, it's useful as an overview of what's possible and what benefits can offer you.

The benefit of the Data Management module in Tableau Cloud is that if you have it already, there's nothing you need to set up. In the left menu of Tableau Cloud's main page, if you see a section called **External Assets**, it means you have the module in your environment and access to it.

Apart from Data Management, everything covered in this chapter will be using Tableau Server or Tableau Cloud's web interface, so a **Tableau Server** or **Tableau Cloud** environment with an **administrator role** is required to follow along.

Understanding governance and permissions best practices

In any data platform, governance is critical to ensure data is managed as a valuable asset and supports the organization's goals. In Tableau, governance is critical not only to keep the platform secure but also to drive adoption and make sure the right data and content are available for the right users when they need it and that finding and understanding those assets is as easy as possible.

Getting ready

When we talk about governance, it is important to distinguish between data governance and content governance:

- **Data governance** is the process of guaranteeing the right data is available to the right user. This includes any metadata that might help users trust and understand the data.

- **Content governance** is the process of guaranteeing users can discover, consume, and create content with confidence. It includes content organization and permissions, content validation, and usage audit.

The following is an overview of the different governance topics in an analytical platform such as Tableau:

Data governance

Data source management	Data quality
Enrichment & preparation	Data security
Metadata management	Monitoring & management

Content governance

Content management	Authorization
Content validation	Content promotion
Content certification	Content utilization

Figure 2.1 – Governance in Tableau

In this recipe, we will focus on **content governance** as, based on my experience, it is one of the areas where people struggle most during the first steps of their Tableau journey.

Content management in Tableau refers to how we organize the different assets and define different permissions in Tableau to help enable users to discover and share data and insights while we meet our governance requirements.

To better understand content management in Tableau, there are several terms we need to feel comfortable with:

- **Content type**: Tableau has different types of content we can organize and set permissions on. These content types are projects, data sources, workbooks, and flows. If we have Tableau Data Management, there are also databases, tables, and virtual connections. Content types are also called **assets**.

- **Permission**: Permissions define the ability to perform different actions or capabilities on a piece of content.

- **Capability**: Capabilities are the type of action we want to allow or deny permissions for. Examples of capabilities are viewing a project, filtering a workbook, connecting to a data source, and so on.

- **Permission rule**: Permission rules are the setting for each capability for an individual user or group of users.

Defining permissions properly is key for correct, sustainable, and scalable content management in Tableau.

How to do it...

Let's learn the best practices for content management and permissions in Tableau:

1. The first important thing to learn about governance and permissions in Tableau is the role of the **Default project**.

    Of all the projects we might have in our Tableau environment, the Default project is also fundamental in making content management easier. In Tableau, when a new top-level project is created, it will use the permission rules of the Default project as a template.

    When a new project is created nested or inside another project, the parent project is the one used as a template for the permission rules of the new child project.

    Because of how the Default project behaves, it's key to define some best practices on it to make future projects more secure and manageable.

2. Remove all permissions in the Default project.

    As mentioned previously, when a new top-level project is created, it will use the permission rules of the Default project as a template, copying all the permission rules from it to the new top-level project.

    This makes the Default project the perfect place to start making effective permissions easier to manage and to understand as well as to avoid users accessing content they should not be able to.

    Tableau recommends deleting all the rules in the Default project for all content types and all capabilities. This way, when creating a new project, the default state will be to deny all capabilities to all content types.

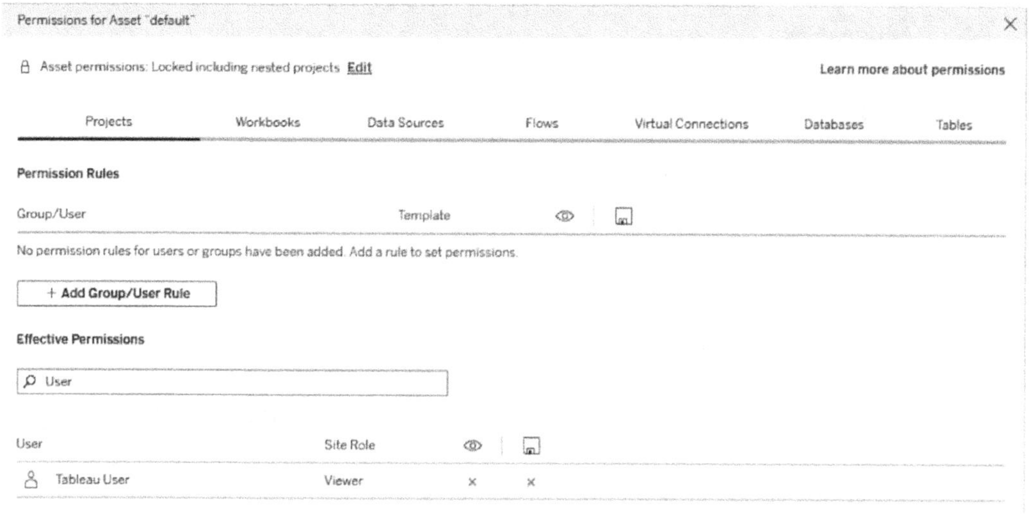

The screenshot below represents the permissions panel for the asset "default":

Permissions for Asset "default"   ×

Asset permissions: Locked including nested projects **Edit**   **Learn more about permissions**

| Projects | Workbooks | Data Sources | Flows | Virtual Connections | Databases | Tables |

Permission Rules

Group/User   Template

No permission rules for users or groups have been added. Add a rule to set permissions.

[+ **Add Group/User Rule**]

Effective Permissions

[🔍 User]

User   Site Role

👤 Tableau User   Viewer   ×   ×

Figure 2.2 – Removing all permissions in the Default project

The only exception will be administrator users who have full access to the Tableau environment.

3. Lock asset permissions.

    When a new permission rule is applied at the project level, this acts as a default for the content saved in the project. These rules can apply in two different ways: as enforced rules that only administrators or project owners can change (asset permissions are locked), or as preliminary rules, which can be modified for individual assets by administrators, project owners, or content owners (asset permissions are customizable).

    We recommend avoiding the customizable option in the asset permissions setup of a project. Letting administrators, project owners, or content owners define specific permission rules for individual assets is the perfect way to end up losing control of your content permissions.

    Because of this, it is best practice to lock asset permissions at the project level and nested projects. Applying this setup to the Default project will ensure any new top-level project follows this best practice too.

Asset Permissions

◉ 🔒 **Locked:** Assets inherit project permission rules. Asset-level permissions can't be modified. (Recommended)

☑ Apply to nested projects

◯ 🔓 **Customisable:** Assets start with project permission rules. Permissions can be modified by users authorised to do so.

Cancel   Save

Figure 2.3 – Locking asset permissions at the project level

4. Apply permission rules to groups instead of individual users.

    Another best practice is to only apply permission rules to groups of users and avoid setting up individual user permission rules at all costs. Applying permission rules for individual users can be tempting to add exceptions to our permissions and governance strategy but can also end up in a mess very quickly.

    As a best practice, avoid individual user permission rules in your projects. If individual user permission rules are needed, use them as a rare exception in your environment, trying to have those rules documented and identified.

5. Use sandbox and production projects.

    It's also a best practice to use sandbox and production projects. Sandbox projects should contain ad hoc, uncertified, or work-in-progress content, while production projects should only contain validated and certified content and assets.

    Using sandbox projects will allow users to freely run their analysis and publish content with ad hoc analysis. On the other hand, production projects are a very good approach to improving trust. It's also key to make sure users understand the difference between those two types of projects when making decisions based on the data and workbooks they have access to. Some best practices related to sandbox and production projects include the following:

    *   Management, main users, and viewers, in general, should have access mainly to production and certified content. Especially in big organizations, you want to avoid people having access to a lot of sandbox content. If they are less used to Tableau, it will create noise and make them less confident about the content they are accessing.

    *   Publishing to production projects should be limited to small groups of users. These users should be aware of the content management tasks required when publishing in production projects.

- Use descriptions, labels, warnings, certifications, and tags for your production content. The more information you provide about the quality and context of each asset, the more trust you will build in your organization.

- Permission management for production projects should be limited to data stewards and permissions should be blocked at the project level, as explained previously in this chapter.

Permissions can be applied to each content type inside the Tableau project – workbooks, data sources, flows, virtual connections, and so on. You can use the tabs at the top of the window to switch between the different content types and define the permissions for each content type in the project based on your security needs.

The following is an example of how permissions look for a group and for a specific user.

Projects	Workbooks	Data Sources	Flows

Permission Rules

Group/User		Template							
United Kingdom	•••	Custom	▾	✓	✓	✗	✗	✗	✗
Pablo Sáenz de Tejada G.C.	•••	Administer	▾	✓	✓	✓	✓	✓	✓

+ **Add Group/User Rule**

Figure 2.4 – Permission Rules for Workbooks

In this case, the members of the **United Kingdom** group should be able to see and filter any workbook in the project but will not be able to perform any additional action, whereas a specific user, **Pablo Saenz de Tejada G.C.**, can perform more actions in the workbooks.

Now, if you think of a company with hundreds or thousands of users, you can probably imagine why group permissions are best practices. Handling a few group rules is manageable, but handling individual permissions for hundreds of users is not sustainable from a maintenance point of view.

Setting up row-level security (RLS) the traditional way

Very often, organizations don't want to let users access all the rows of data available in a data source. A lot of times, especially in bigger companies, you will need to filter the data based on the user accessing it. Some examples and scenarios for this are the following:

- An HR manager needs to see salaries, personal data, and other sensitive information of the employees of the country they manage, but not from others.

- A salesperson needs to see their own individual sales figures, while the sales managers see all the data for salespeople reporting to them.

- Different marketing teams must see the performance and metrics of the campaigns related to the products they work with, while the marketing manager needs to see the overall picture of all campaigns.

When we need to filter the data for different users, we use the term RLS to refer to the different techniques to achieve this. In Tableau, there are different ways we can manage RLS.

Getting ready

There are four different ways you can perform RLS in Tableau:

- Let the database manage the RLS and not embed credentials for the data source in Tableau. This means each user who accesses the data will need to authenticate the database, query the data directly, and only receive back the rows they have access to. This method implies performing the RLS in the database, which is not always possible.

- Create a user filter in Tableau and map users to values manually at the workbook level.

- Use a dynamic user filter at the data source level.

- Centralize the RLS at the connection level using virtual connections with Tableau Data Management.

Let's focus on the third method, which is set up in the Tableau data source and doesn't require Tableau Data Management.

The key benefits of using a dynamic user filter at the data source level are as follows:

- It's set up at the data source level instead of at the workbook level

- The only way to remove the RLS is by editing the data source, normally limited to a reduced number of users

- Any workbook connected to the data source will inherit the security

Let's go through it in more detail. For this example, we will publish a new data source to our Tableau environment. You can find the data source we will use in our GitHub repository: `https://github.com/PacktPublishing/Tableau-Cookbook-for-Experienced-Professionals/tree/main/Chapter_02`.

How to do it...

In this exercise, we will use Tableau groups to make sure only members of certain groups can see the relevant data to the segment they belong to in our company:

1. First, let's create four groups in Tableau, named as follows:

    *   `Management`

    *   `Consumer`

    *   `Home Office`

    *   `Corporate`

    Feel free to add some users to each group to test the security later with those users.

> **Note**
>
> If you need help creating groups or adding users to groups, review Tableau's official documentation here: `https://help.tableau.com/current/online/en-us/to_add_users_groups.htm`.

2. Now that we have our groups ready, we can start publishing the data source.

    Go to the **Explore** section in Tableau Cloud or Server and click on **New | Published Data Source**.

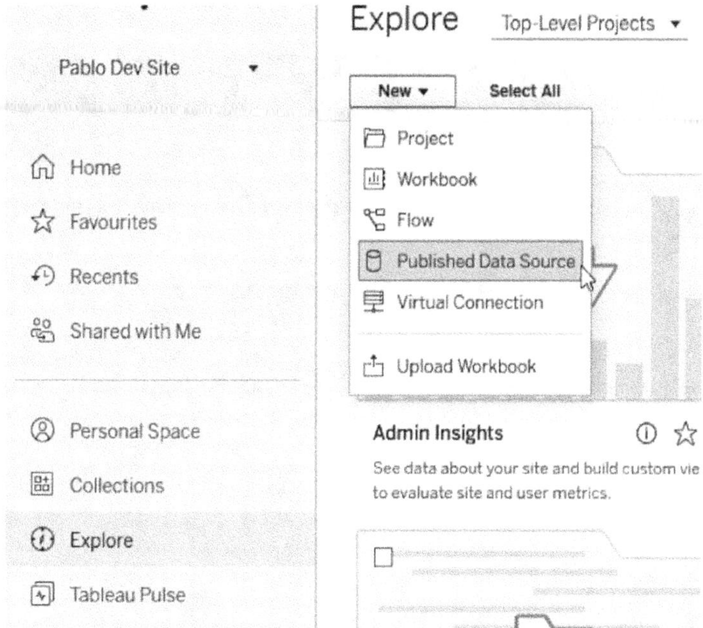

Figure 2.5 – Creating a new published data source

3. Go to the **Files** tab and drag and drop the `Sample - Superstore.xls` file to the **Connect to Data** window or click the **Upload from computer** button and search for the file in your computer.

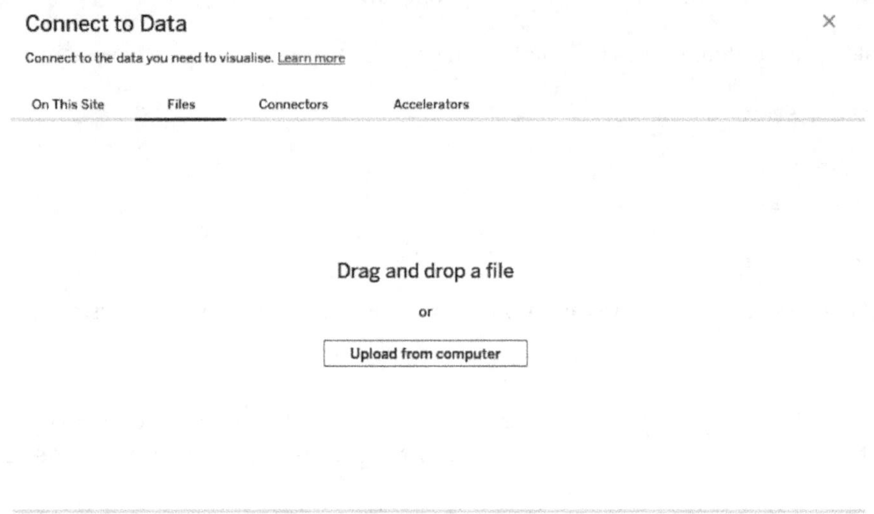

Figure 2.6 – Loading the CSV file from the Files tab

4. Double-click the `Orders` table or drag and drop the `Orders` table from the left-hand side to the data model window.

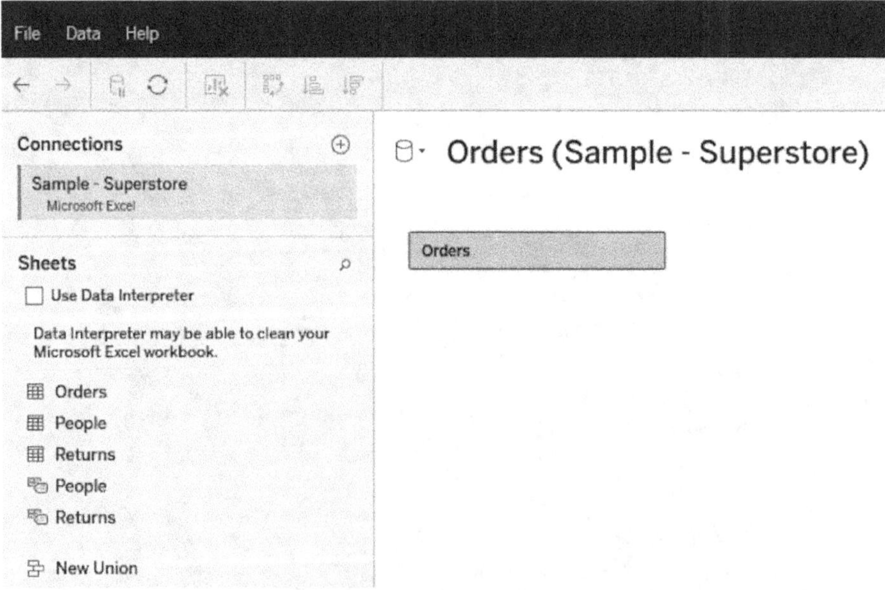

Figure 2.7 – Adding the table to the data model

5. We have our data ready; now we need to create a security field before publishing the data source.

6. Create a dynamic calculated field using a security field. For this example, let's imagine we want to have security at the row level, or RLS, with the following rules:

    *   Members of the **Management** group can see every row in the data.

    *   Members of the **Consumer** group can only see rows with the value of Consumer in the Segment field.

    *   Members of the **Home Office** group can only see rows with the value of Home Office in the Segment field.

    *   Members of the **Corporate** group can only see rows with the value of Corporate in the Segment field.

7. To achieve this, we need to create a calculated field following that logic and then add the calculated field as a filter in the data source before publishing it.

8. Right-click on the Segment field and go to **Create | Calculated Field…**.

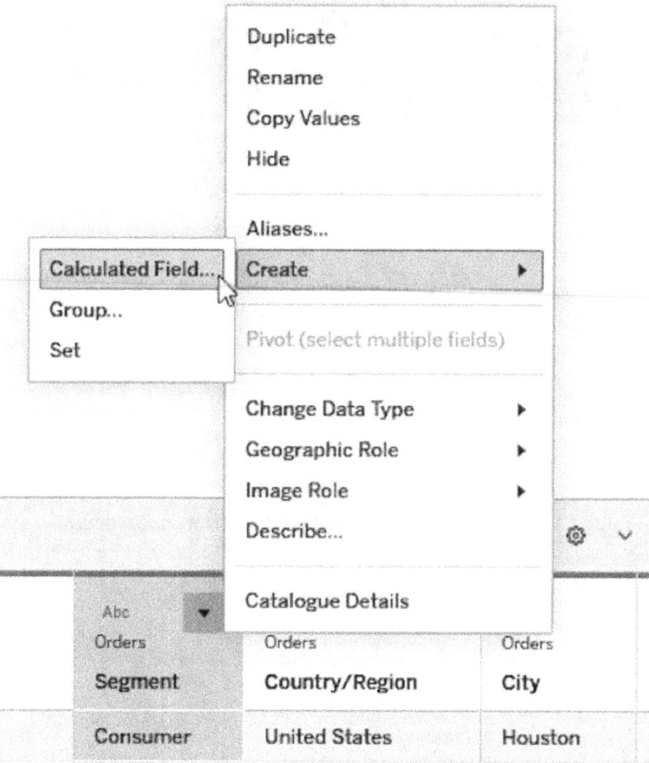

Figure 2.8 – Creating the calculated field

9. Give the field a meaningful name (such as RLS). Now, we can build the logic. What we need to get is a calculation that returns a TRUE value for the rows of data each user should be able to see and FALSE for any other row. To do this, we can leverage Tableau's ISMEMBEROF functions. The calculated field should be something like this (make sure to be careful with the parenthesis):

```
ISMEMBEROF("Management")
OR (ISMEMBEROF("Consumer")
    AND [Segment]="Consumer")
OR (ISMEMBEROF("Home Office")
    AND [Segment]="Home Office")
OR (ISMEMBEROF("Corporate")
    AND [Segment]="Corporate")
```

10. Click **OK** once the calculation is ready.

11. Add the field as a data source filter and publish the data source.

12. Now, we need to add the new calculated field created as a data source filter. Click on the **Add** button in the top-right section of the **Data Source** window.

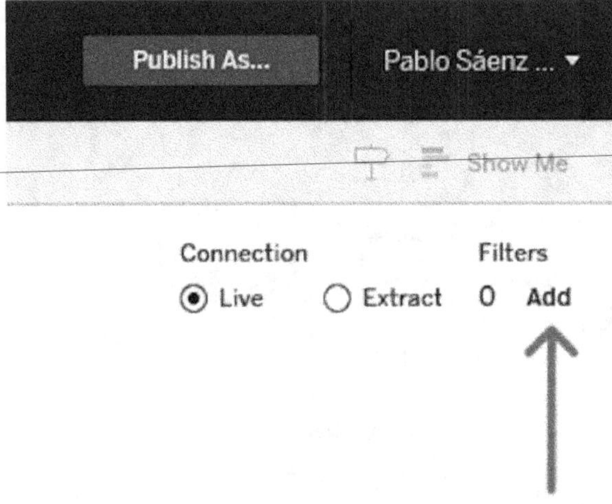

Figure 2.9 – Adding the calculated field as a data source filter

13. A new window should pop up. Click **Add Filter** and select the RLS calculated field we just created.

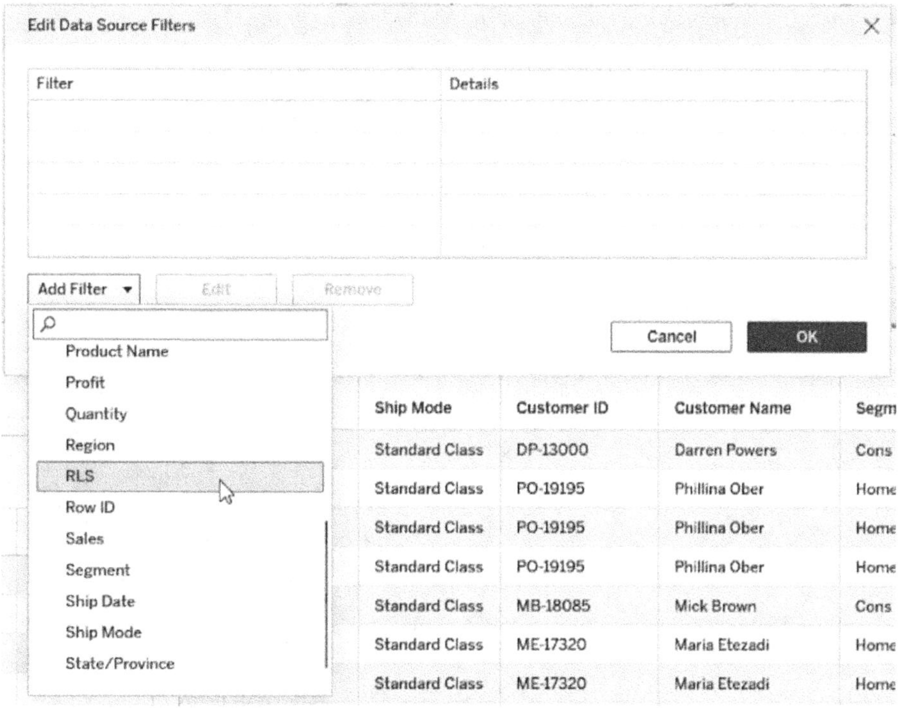

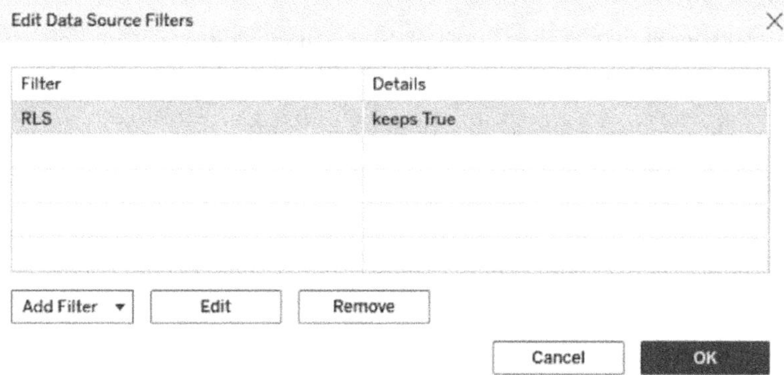

Figure 2.10 – Setting up the data source filter

14. Make sure to keep just True values from the **Select from list** menu or use the custom value list and type True to make sure we just keep records following the logic built in our calculation. Then, click **OK** and make sure the **Edit Data Source Filter** window looks something like *Figure 2.10* before clicking **OK** again to close the window.

Figure 2.11 – Checking the data source filter

Now, it's time to test it and make sure the RLS is working as expected.

15. Make sure that your user is a member of the **Management** group.

16. Go to the data source we just created and create a new workbook from it.

17. Create a view to make sure our user sees all the data, for instance, **Sales across Order Date by Segment**, as in *Figure 2.11*. Save the workbook.

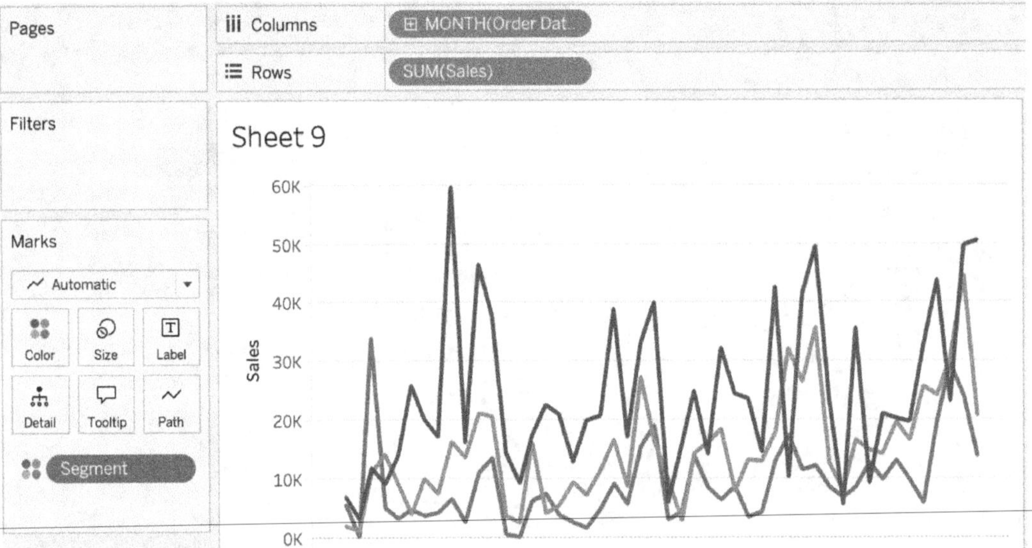

Figure 2.12 – Building a view to test RLS

18. If you open the view, you should see three lines, one for each segment. Now, let's change our user's group membership. Go to **Users**, find your user, and click on **Actions | Group Membership**. Make sure to change it so your user is not part of the **Management** group, and include it in the **Corporate** group.

19. Go to the workbook again and open the sheet. Now, you should see only one line, corresponding to the **Corporate** segment.

Well done! You have just set up a data source with RLS embedded.

How it works...

Remember that the benefits of this approach are as follows:

- The RLS is built at the data source level. End users might not be aware of the fact they are not seeing all the data. Letting them know adding meaningful description messages in the data source and workbooks will improve trust and make end users' lives easier.

- Only users with permission to edit the data source can update or remove the RLS.

- Any workbook connected to the data source will inherit the security without analysts needing to set up the security again.

Now, it is time to see an even more advanced, centralized, and robust way of setting up RLS.

Setting up centralized RLS with virtual connections

Virtual connections are an additional content type such as data sources, workbooks, or flows that allows data stewards and Tableau admins to simplify data connectivity, providing a central access point to your data sources, improving data governance, and allowing the creation of RLS via data policies at the connection level instead of the data source or workbook level. The main benefits of virtual connections are as follows:

- Centralizes access to your database, reducing maintenance times when credentials are updated

- Reduces data proliferation by consolidating extracts and reducing the load on your data warehouse

- Allows creators to build data models without requiring them to have database credentials

- Centralizes RLS

- Combines live and extract connections to different tables in the same data model

All within the Tableau platform!

Getting ready

Virtual connections are only available with Tableau Data Management, an additional module for Tableau that activates a set of premium data capabilities including data catalog, Tableau Prep Conductor, and other data governance and security controls. To set up Data Management, make sure that you check the *Technical requirements* section.

How to do it...

Let's start:

1. Create a virtual connection. Creating a virtual connection is very easy. From the **Home** or **Explore** page of Tableau Server or Tableau Cloud, click **New | Virtual Connection**.

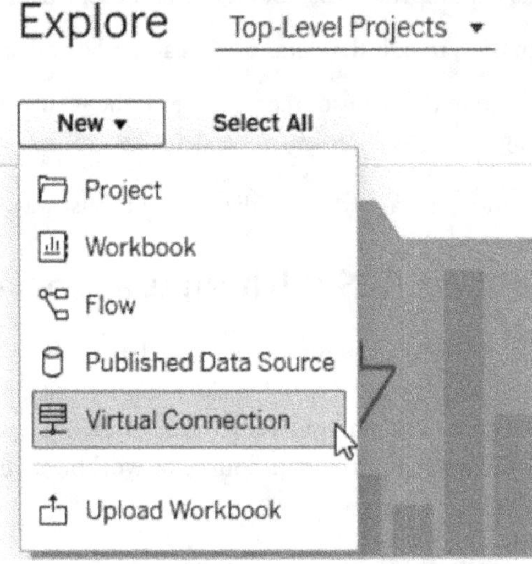

Figure 2.13 – Creating a new virtual connection

2. Select the connector from the list to sign in and connect to your data.

3. Enter the information required by the connector. The credentials you enter are saved in the virtual connection, so users aren't required to enter credentials to connect to the data once the virtual connection is set up.

4. Click **Sign In** and select, if needed, the database and schema you want to connect to. Drag and drop the tables you want to include in the virtual connection from the **Connections** pane on the left to the canvas where it says **Add tables**.

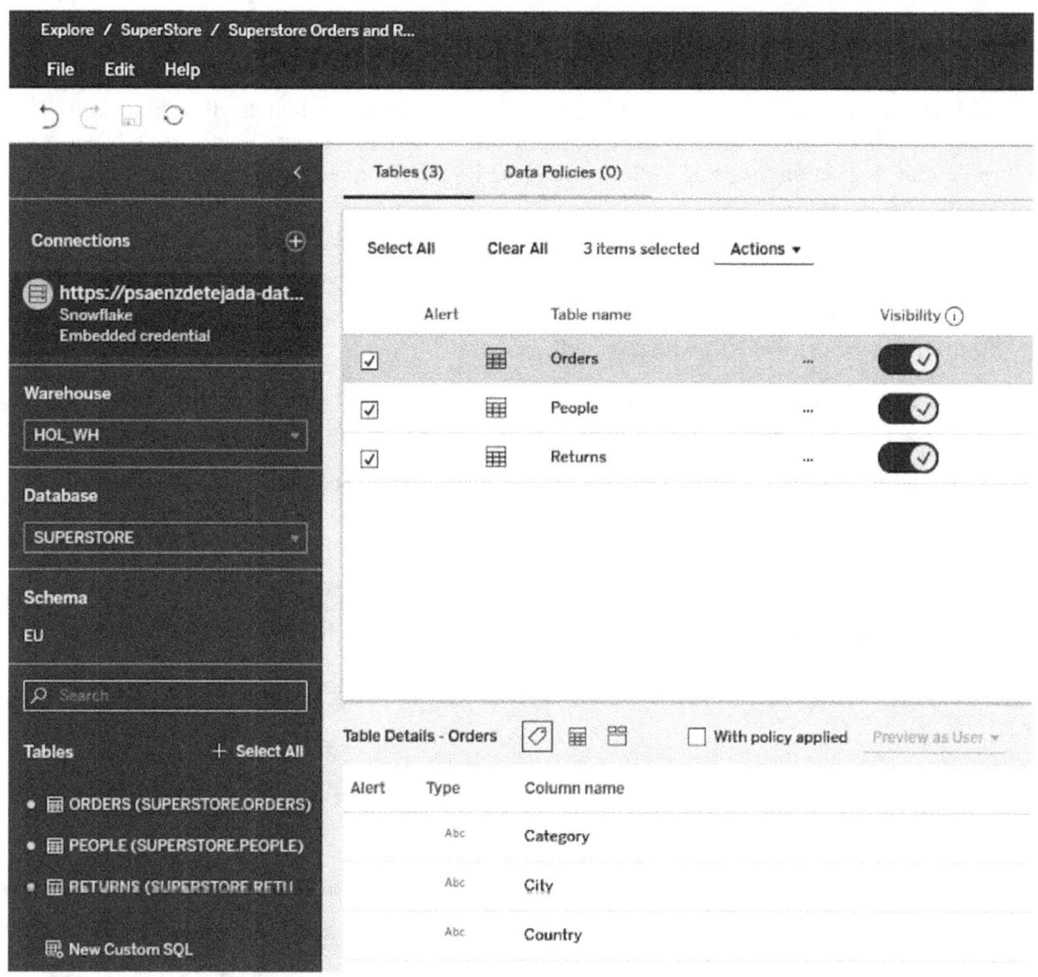

Figure 2.14 – Adding tables to the virtual connection

5. Perfect, you have just added the tables you want to give access to as part of the virtual connection. Here, you can see the details for each table by clicking on each one. Additionally, you can make simple edits such as the following:

- Change a table name.

- Hide or rename columns.

- Change data types.

- Select live or extract mode for individual tables or all of them.

- Turn on/off individual tables' visibility. When turned off, users can't see the data in the table. This might be useful while configuring and testing RLS and data policies.

> **Note**
>
> It is important to remember that creating a virtual connection is only available through the web browser in Tableau Server and Tableau Cloud. Unlike other content assets such as data sources, workbooks, or flows, which can be published using the Tableau Desktop or Tableau Prep Builder applications or using Tableau's REST API, virtual connections can only be created using the web interface.

If we just publish and save the virtual connection now, we will get the benefits of a centralized access point to our tables in the database, but we still haven't set up data policies and RLS. Let's learn how we can build RLS with data policies.

6. Create a data policy for RLS. To add RLS in a virtual connection, we need to add a **data policy**. A policy is a rule we apply to one or more tables in the virtual connection to filter data for users.

    When we navigate to the **Data Policies** tab we see three main sections:

    -   On the left, the list of tables in the virtual connection

    -   In the center, a list of the policies we have already created, if any

    -   At the bottom, the table details where we can see the different fields for each table and check the policies we create

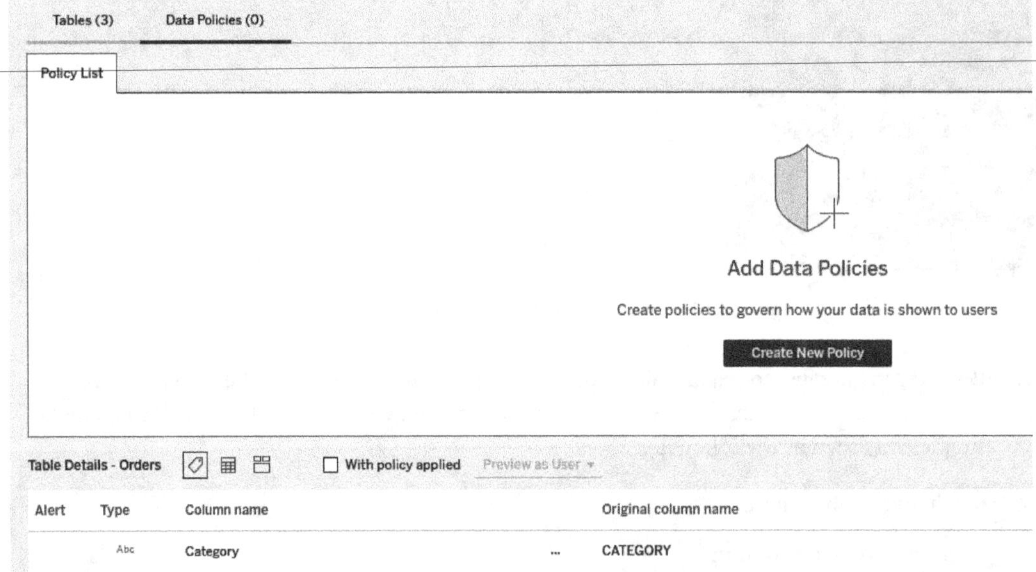

Figure 2.15 – The Data Policies window

7. We are going to create a data policy like the one created in the previous recipe of this chapter to show only rows of each `Segment` value to the members of each segment group. To create a data policy, complete the following steps:

I. Click on **Create New Policy**.

II. A new tab will appear with the name **Policy 1**. Double-click the policy name to change it. In our case, we are going to create a policy based on the segments so I'll call it `Segment Policy`.

III. Drag any tables you want to include in the policy from the left panel. This means any tables we want to apply RLS for, in our case, the `Orders` table. Once you drag the table to the center of the screen, a new option will appear to specify whether you want to add the table as a policy table or as an entitlement table. Policy tables are tables we want to apply security to. Entitlement tables are master tables we can use to map our security to specific users. For this use case, we want to manually build our policy condition so we will not use an entitlement table. Drag the `Orders` table to the **Add as Policy Table** section.

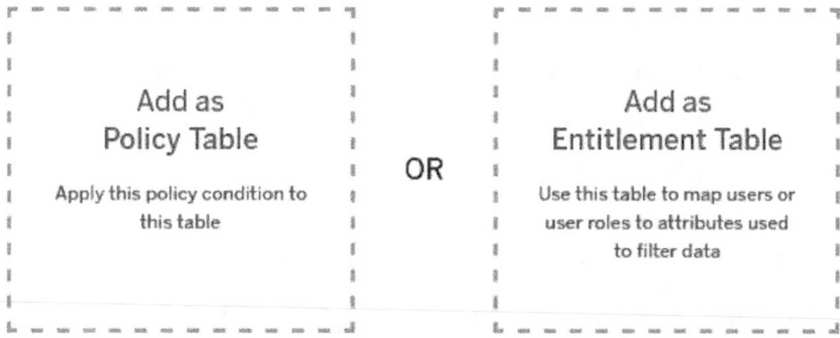

Figure 2.16 – Policy tables and entitlement tables

IV.   Now, we need to map our table to a column in order to create the policy. Click on the **Add Column to Map** button and select the **Segment** field.

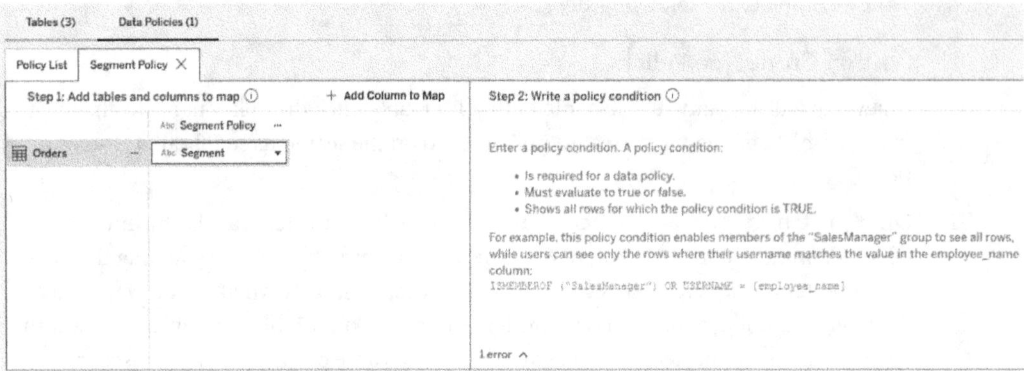

Figure 2.17 – Data policy configuration

V.   It's time to write the policy condition. We will use the same one as in the previous section, but in this case, you will need to use the name of the column in the **Step 1** mapping.

VI.   In the **Step 2: Write a policy condition** section, write the following:

```
ISMEMBEROF("Management")
OR (ISMEMBEROF("Consumer")
    AND [Segment Policy]="Consumer")
OR (ISMEMBEROF("Home Office")
    AND [Segment Policy]="Home Office")
OR (ISMEMBEROF("Corporate")
    AND [Segment Policy]="Corporate")
```

The data policy should be ready. Now, it's time to check that it works as expected.

8.   Another benefit of RLS with virtual connections is that we can check more easily whether the policy is working. On the table details at the bottom of the screen, change the view to **Show Table Data**, select the **With policy applied** checkbox, and click **Preview as User** to see the data a specific user will have access to.

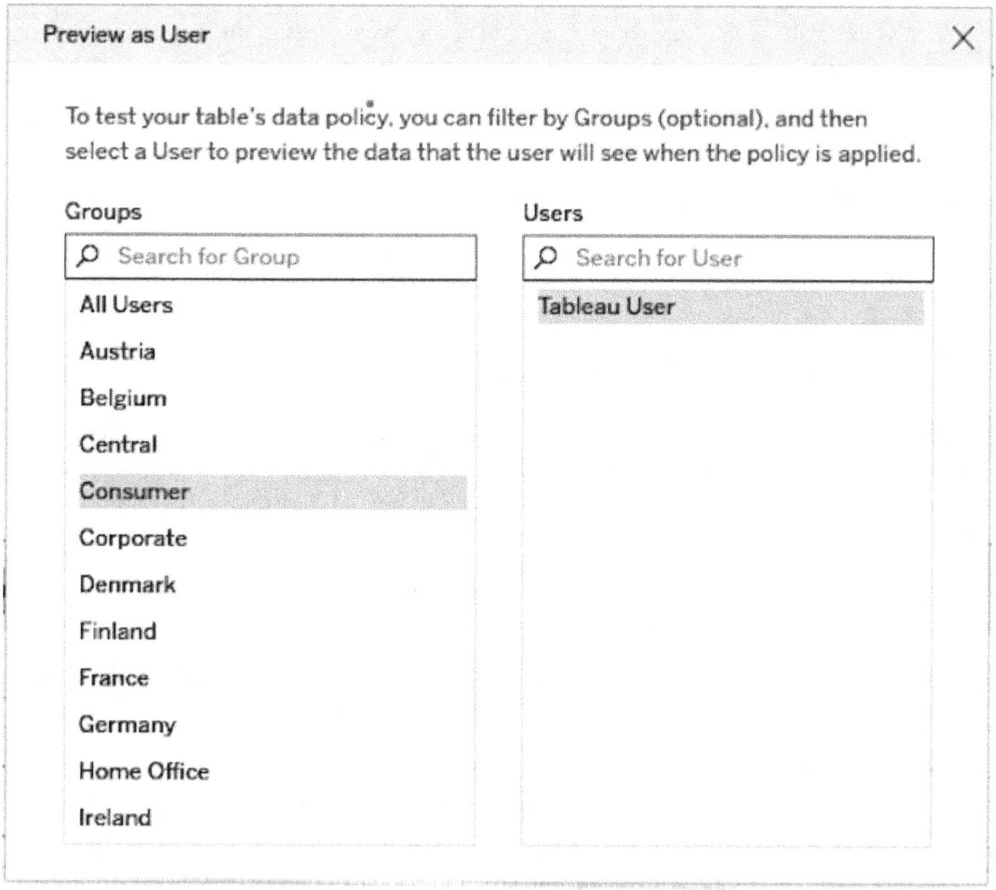

Preview as User   ✕

To test your table's data policy, you can filter by Groups (optional), and then
select a User to preview the data that the user will see when the policy is applied.

Groups   Users

🔍 Search for Group   🔍 Search for User

All Users   Tableau User

Austria

Belgium

Central

Consumer

Corporate

Denmark

Finland

France

Germany

Home Office

Ireland

Figure 2.18 – Previewing the data policy as user

Once you close the **Preview as User** window, you will be able to see the total rows the members
of the group will be able to see. In our case, members of the **Consumer** group will only see
around half the total number of rows.

Now, you can save the virtual connection. Creator users can now create and publish new data sources,
but instead of connecting to the original database, they will be able to use the virtual connection if
they have permission to connect to it.

There's more...

Some additional benefits of virtual connections include the following:

- Creators don't need to have database credentials as those are embedded in the virtual connection.
  Creators can still build new data models, but only a few analysts who are empowered to create
  virtual connections need to have database credentials.

- When your database changes, you just need to apply the changes in the virtual connection, instead of updating every single data source using that database as the origin.

- You can centralize your extract creation and data refresh at the virtual connection level, reducing possible database consumption and saving Tableau resources.

- You can combine live and extracts in the same data model.

- You can apply centralized RLS to any data source connected to the virtual connection, as the RLS will be applied to any workbook and data source that uses the virtual connection.

Configuring column-level security

We just saw two different ways of setting up RLS in Tableau. But what happens if we want to apply **column-level security**? Column-level security can be useful in different scenarios where we might not want to filter the rows of the data different users see, but instead, control whether specific users can see or not a specific column of our data.

Unfortunately, column-level security is not a native capability of Tableau as of version `2025.1`. However, there are workarounds to make this possible. Let's see an example.

Imagine you work in the HR department of an organization and need to develop some analysis about the company's headcount, time off left, average salary, and several other metrics.

Some of that information might be open to all employees (headcount) but other information is very sensitive and only organization leaders and management should be able to see it, such as salary data.

One option would be to create different data sources, but in order to avoid data proliferation, we are going to see how we can hide data for a specific profile of users in Tableau when creating the data source.

Getting ready

For this example, we are going to use employee compensation data from the City of Phoenix, available at *data.world* at the following link: `https://data.world/city-of-phoenix/2b41f4f8-fe6f-48d3-8097-ad44ee5bd616`.

Register and download one of the CSV files available for each calendar year. I have downloaded the file for 2021 for this recipe. Or download the file from the chapter's GitHub repository at `https://github.com/PacktPublishing/Tableau-Cookbook-for-Experienced-Professionals/tree/main/Chapter_02`

How to do it...

Let's start:

1. First, let's connect to the data and review the information available for context:

    I.   From the Tableau Cloud or Tableau Server interface, create a new data source from the **Explore** or **Home** pages.

    II. Connect to the CSV file from the link in the *Getting ready* section and drag the table to the data model.

    You should see three columns related to each employee's yearly compensation: `Regular Pay`, `Overtime Pay`, and `Other Pay`. Let's assume `Regular Pay` is the one we want to base our analysis on and the one we need to hide for any user unless they are part of the **Management** Tableau group.

2. Now, we must create a calculated field that will show the `Regular Pay` field only for members of the **Management** group and a null value for the rest:

    I.   Right-click on the `Regular Pay` field and select **Create | Calculated Field**.

    II. Now, we are going to use the `ISMEMBEROF` function. The `ISMEMBEROF` function returns a `True` value if the current user is a member of the group we specify in the calculation and returns `False` otherwise. We need to use the following calculation: `IIF(ISMEMBEROF("Management"),[Regular Pay],NULL)`

    III. Give the calculated field a name (`Pay`, for example) and click **OK** to confirm the calculated field.

3. The original `Regular Pay` field is still part of the data source. We need to hide the field so users cannot query the original field for their analysis and just the calculation created in *Step 2*.

    I.   Right-click on the `Regular Pay` field and select **Hide**.

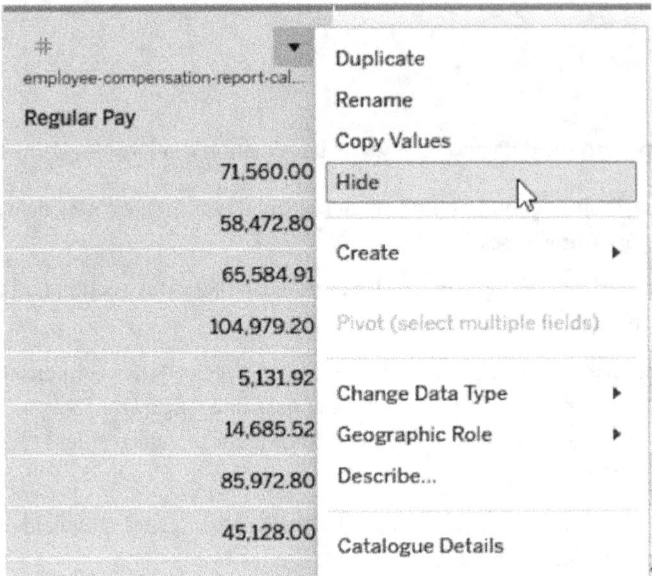

Figure 2.19 – Hiding the original field

    II.   Publish the data source to a project.

4.   The last step is just to make sure the column-level security is working correctly. To do this, you can do the following:

    I.   Create a workbook connected to the data source we just published and make sure the original field, `Regular Pay`, is not on the **Data** pane.

    II.   Do some analysis and visualizations using the `Pay` field we created and save the workbook.

    III.   Access the workbook using different users to test. If the user accessing the workbook is a member of the **Management** group, they should see the `Pay` data. If not, values should be null.

If something is not working as expected, edit the data source, check the calculated field, and make sure the group name is spelled in the same way as in the calculated field.

There's more...

Congratulations, you have used calculated fields to set up column-level security in your data source. There are some additional tips you might want to have in mind when using this approach:

- Let users know in the workbooks and dashboards that they might not see all the data due to security restrictions related to data privacy.

- If you have Tableau Data Management, add a **sensitivity label** to the table asset, the data source, and/or the column so users are aware of the particularity of the data. Data and sensitivity labels will be covered in the next recipe, *Managing content description, metadata, and data labels with Tableau Data Management*.

- Restrict (as much as possible!) the number of users that have edit permissions for data sources with column-level security using this method.

See also

- **Tableau Ideas** is a section of the Tableau Community that allows users to vote for product ideas they are interested in and add their own ideas as suggestions. It's a great way to be part of the Tableau Community and see what features other users around the world are willing to see in Tableau. You can see all the ideas submitted already at `https://community.tableau.com/s/ideas`.

- At the time of writing, there is an idea already published in Tableau Community Forums to have native column-level security in virtual connections. You can join Tableau Community Forums and vote for this idea here: `https://community.tableau.com/s/idea/0878b000000IDOnAAO/detail?t=1717339981645`.

Managing content description, metadata, and data labels with Tableau Data Management

The increasing volume of data and the pace at which data changes make it harder to track how data is being used, keep metadata updated, and keep end users informed of data quality issues.

In the *Setting up centralized RLS with virtual connections* recipe in this chapter, we covered the use and benefits of virtual connections, one of the key capabilities of Tableau Data Management, to centralize data access and RLS. However, Data Management offers many more benefits and allows you to do the following:

- Set data quality warnings.

- Perform lineage and impact analysis.

- Let users get data details while accessing workbooks.

- Add descriptions and labels to databases, tables, and columns.

- Certify databases and tables.

- Access additional REST API metadata methods to programmatically add, update, and remove external assets, and add additional metadata to Tableau's content.

Tableau Data Management allows data stewards to add labels to databases, tables and columns, data sources, flows, virtual connections, and virtual connection tables. Data labels, specifically, are metadata that you can attach to those asset types to help classify data and pass the information to end users. Some use cases are as follows:

- Add a data quality warning to a data source to let users know it's deprecated or not updated.

- Add a sensitive label to a column to inform users to take special care when using the data.

- Add column descriptions to include business definitions for fields to make sure all users are referring to the same concepts and improve trust and alignment.

How to do it...

In this recipe, we will cover some of these additional benefits to improve data trust and add metadata directly in Tableau.

Creating custom label categories and data labels

Except for the certification of published data sources, it's important to remember that a Tableau Data Management license is required for all operations related to data labels.

Additionally, from Tableau version 2023.3, Tableau administrators can create, edit, and manage label categories and labels through the REST API and the web interface in the new **Data Labels** section on the side panel of Tableau Cloud and Tableau Server.

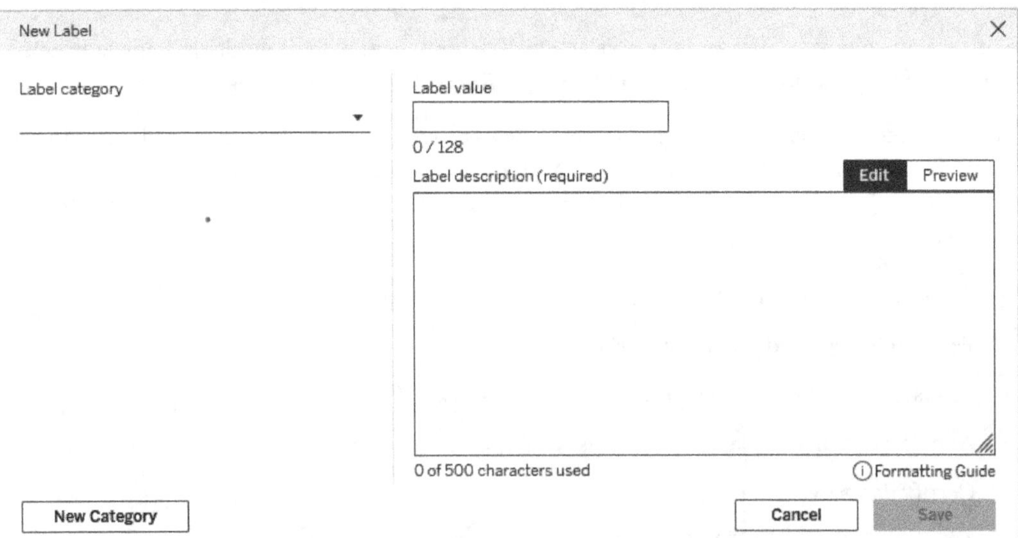

Figure 2.20 – Editing data labels and adding new categories

From the **Data Labels** section (bottom left sidebar), you can add new labels and label descriptions to the built-in categories such as **Quality Warning** and **Sensitivity** and even create new categories to identify assets according to your needs.

For new labels in the **Quality Warning** and **Sensitivity** categories, you can also specify the visibility level of the new labels: **Standard** or **High visibility**. High visibility labels show notifications in affected views and emails.

Adding sensitivity labels and descriptions to a column

Imagine we have some sensitive data in our HR department that includes each employee's full name and the annual salary they earn. Of course, we would probably like to limit who has access to this sensitive data, but we might also want users who have access to this data to be aware of it to take special care when analyzing and visualizing it.

Like data quality warnings, **sensitivity labels** appear on the assets they are applied to and in any downstream asset from the one they're added to. Sensitivity labels can be added to the following asset types:

- Databases
- Tables
- Virtual connections
- Virtual connection tables
- Data sources
- Columns

Adding a sensitivity label to an asset of a column is very simple:

1. First, navigate to the asset you want to add the sensitivity label to or the asset that contains the column you are interested in.
2. Click on the **Actions** menu (the three dots, ...) of the asset you want to add the label to.
3. Navigate to the **Data Labels** menu and select the type of label you want to add, in this case, **Sensitivity**.
4. A new window will appear where you need to specify the label you want to add and an optional message.

As an example, imagine we want to add a sensitivity label to a column that contains the full name of each of the employees of a company.

Navigate to the table that contains the column through the **External Assets** menu or search through Tableau's search bar. Click on the **Actions** menu of the Name column, as in *Figure 2.20*, and check the available label categories.

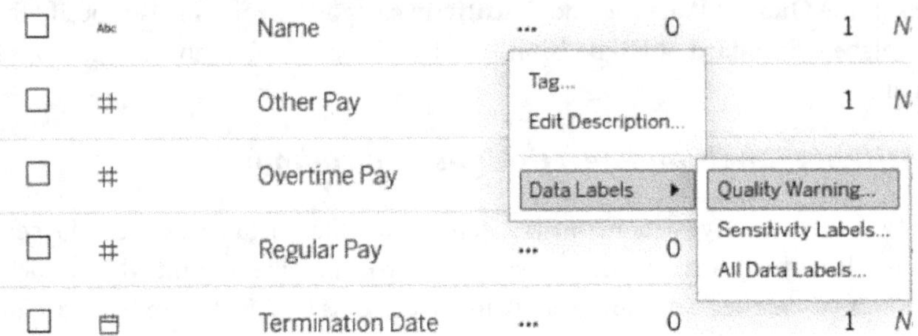

Figure 2.21 – Add a label to a table column

In the new window, select the **Sensitivity** label category, check the label or labels to add, enter a message (optional), and finally, click **Save**.

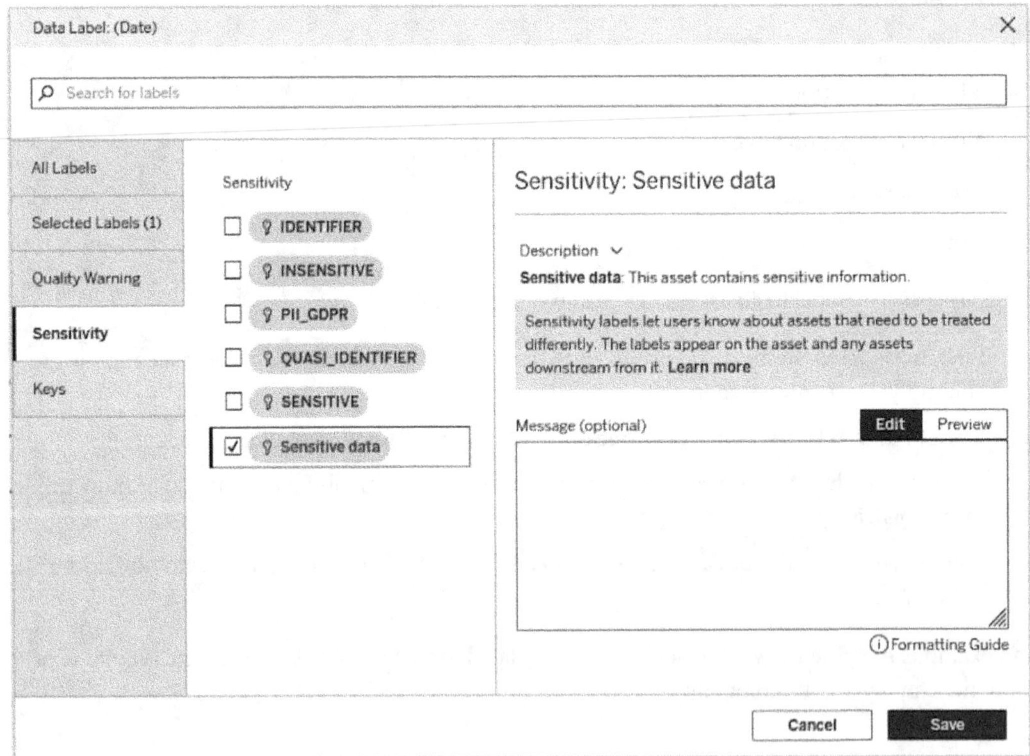

Figure 2.22 – Adding the sensitivity label type and message

The sensitivity label will appear now in the **Column** labels and the full message will appear when clicking on the label.

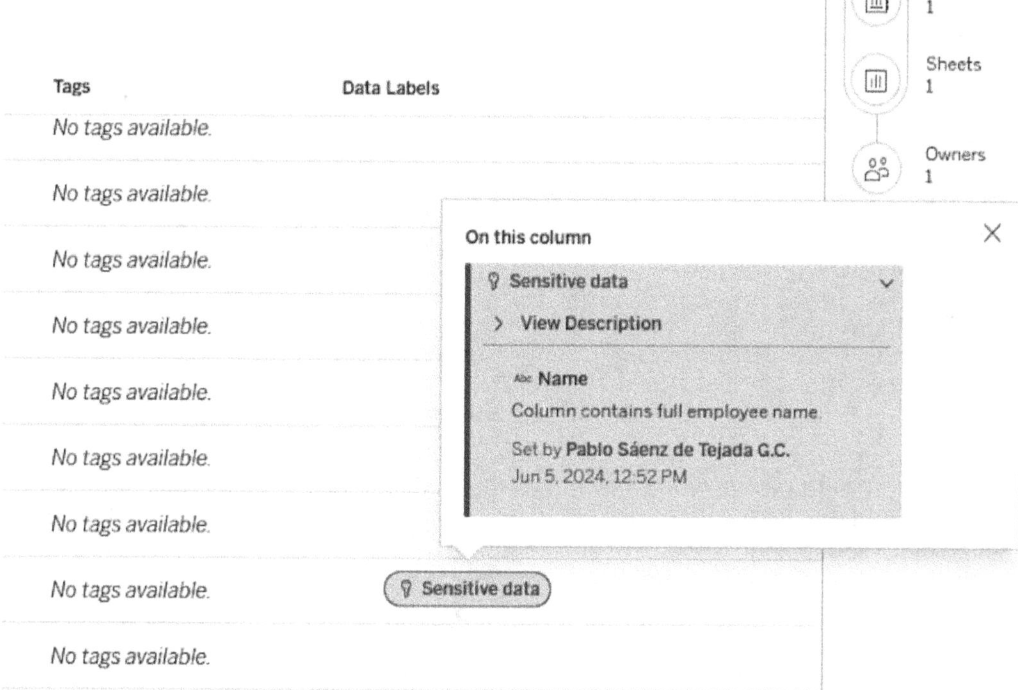

Figure 2.23 – The label and message in the data catalog

One of the advantages of managing labels in this way is that the label will be inherited by the downstream assets. Additionally, because this specific label is high visibility, when a user accesses a view connected to this data source, a notification will appear notifying the user that there's a sensitivity label affecting the view, and a link to see the full data and label details.

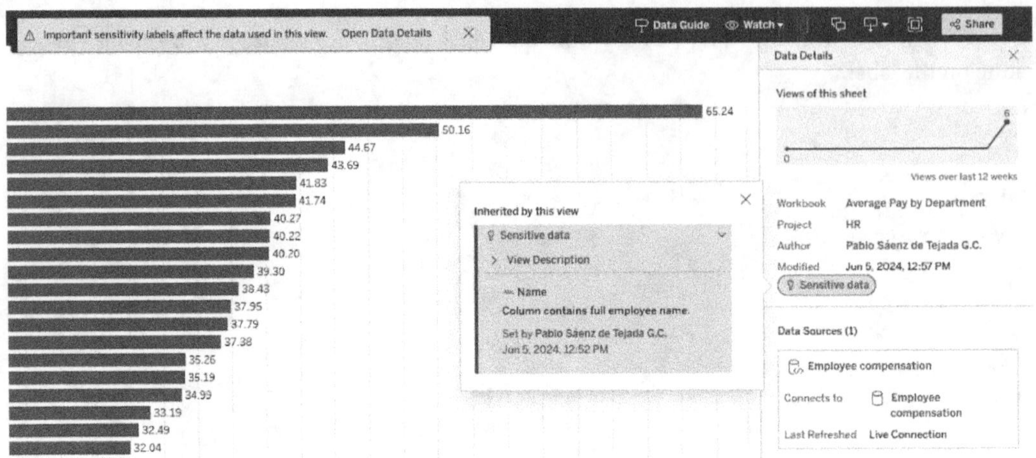

Figure 2.24 – The label and message in the data details as a viewer

Additionally, if we add a column description in the table, the description will also be inherited and shown in the data details for end users, allowing us to integrate corporate data catalogs and business definitions in the flow of work.

Additional use cases for data labels and metadata

Data labels and descriptions are a great way to help drive trust across the Tableau platform by including critical metadata such as sensitivity labels and definitions, as well as certifications, warnings, and any customized label requirements, all directly in the analytics experience.

Some of the most popular use cases of labels, certifications, and warnings are as follows:

- Notify users when a data source is deprecated, under maintenance, or other required warnings

- Certify content to make sure users know which databases, tables, and data sources can be trusted in large environments

- Add customized labels to categorize data in a different way from certification, warning, and sensitivity, such as to label the department the asset belongs to, for instance.

Spending time adding metadata, descriptions, and labels to your assets will not only make content easier to find for users but will also develop trust and develop a data culture across your company.

Now, let's see how we can also use Data Management's lineage to perform impact analysis.

Using data lineage and data catalog to perform impact analysis

To trust your data, you need to know where your data comes from and where it's being used. In Tableau, you can use Tableau Catalog and lineage, two of the main features of Data Management, to help you accomplish this.

You can see the lineage for any Tableau asset, including databases, tables, virtual connections, virtual connection tables, flows, data sources, workbooks, dashboards, and sheets.

Getting ready

To access the lineage, first, navigate to the asset you are interested in by doing one of the following:

- Search for the asset you are interested in using Tableau's search bar in the top right-hand corner of any page on your Tableau Server or Tableau Cloud site.

- Navigate to the asset from the **Explore** section on your Tableau Server or Tableau Cloud site.

How to do it...

Let's learn how we can use Tableau's data catalog and lineage to better understand the dependencies between your Tableau assets and perform an impact analysis:

1. Once you are in the asset you are interested in, click on the **Lineage** tab to see the assets upstream and downstream from your selected asset, or the **anchor**:

    - **Upstream** assets are the ones *above* the anchor and show elements your selected asset is dependent on

    - **Downstream** assets are the ones *below* the anchor and show elements that depend on your selected asset

    As you can see in the following figure, I have selected the virtual connection created during the *Setting up centralized RLS with virtual connections* recipe earlier in this chapter called **Superstore Orders and Returns** and navigated to the **Lineage** tab.

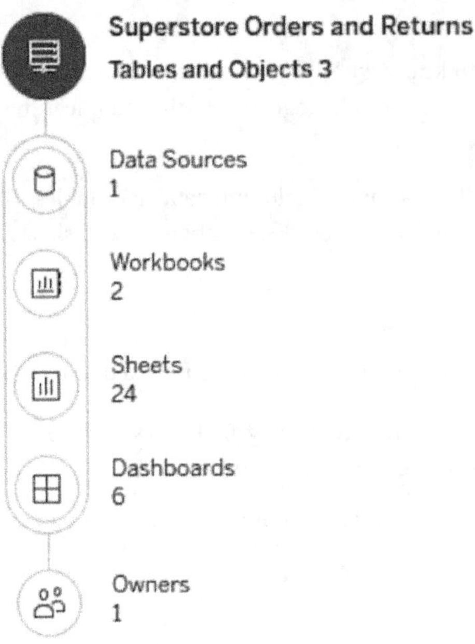

Figure 2.25 – The data lineage

2. The lineage shows the following information:

- The virtual connection contains three tables: `Orders`, `People`, and `Returns`.

- The `Orders` table is certified, and it's used in one data source and two workbooks.

- The `People` table is not used in any workbook or data source.

- The `Returns` table is used in one data source but no workbooks.

This is already very useful for cleaning up our virtual connection and reducing the extract workload in our Tableau environment. Potentially, I could remove the `People` table as it is not being used by any user in any data source or workbook.

3. From the **Lineage** diagram on the right-hand side, I can also navigate to any of the upstream/downstream assets from my anchor: the **Superstore Orders and Returns** virtual connection. Let's dig in a bit more:

- Click on the data source downstream from the lineage.

The main window will show all the downstream data sources dependent on the virtual connection.

- Click on the **Orders and Returns** data source.

Now, we are looking at the **Orders and Returns** data source, and navigating to the **Lineage** tab again, it has become our new anchor point.

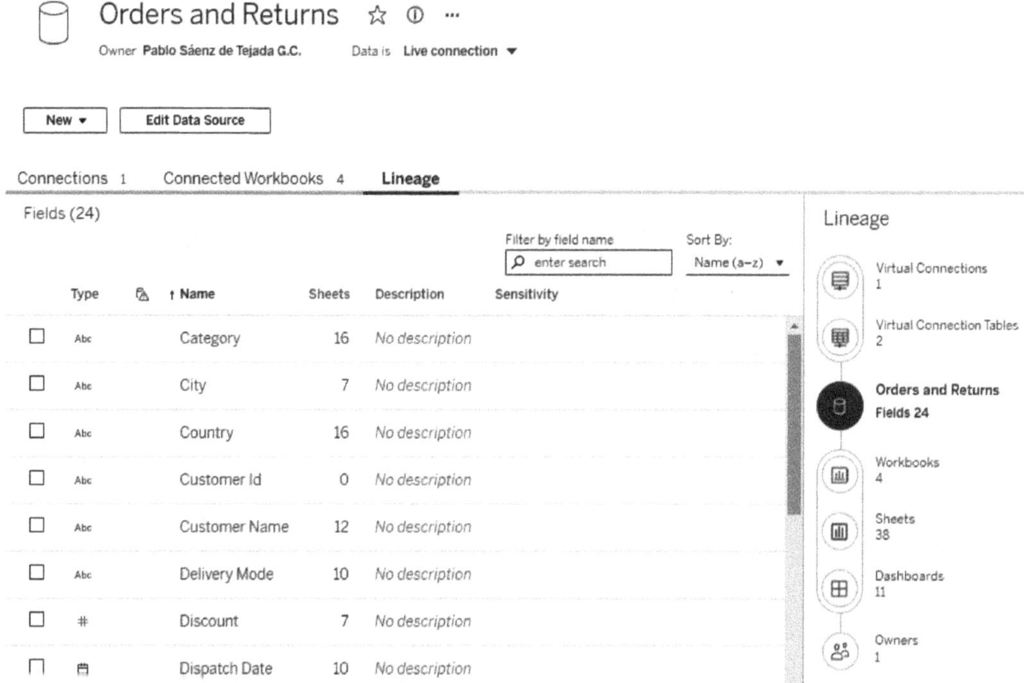

Figure 2.26 – Data source lineage and catalog with column metadata

4. Here, we can see all the fields that are part of the data source and information for each one:

- How many sheets in total are being used
- The description of each field
- Any data quality warnings each field might have
- Any sensitivity labels each field might have

5. One of the main advantages of **Lineage** is that it allows us to perform impact analysis and notify content owners directly from Tableau's interface. Following the previous example, let's keep digging a bit more into our data source and see how the `City` field is being used in our platform by selecting the `City` field in the field list:

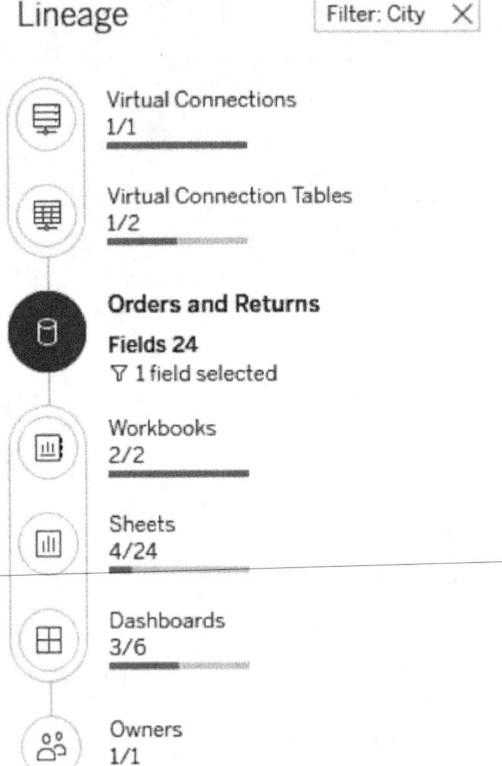

Figure 2.27 – Checking the lineage and impact of a specific column

I can see the `City` field is used in two workbooks, four different sheets, and three dashboards, and there's just one owner.

6. Clicking on the downstream sheets in the **Lineage** diagram, I'll get a list of the four sheets that are being used.

7. Additionally, at the bottom of **Lineage**, I have **Owners**. This refers to users assigned as owners or contacts for any content downstream of our anchor.

Imagine we want to apply some changes in the `City` field and we want to notify content owners of them to avoid any disruption to their workbooks and analysis. In this case, I could notify them directly from the Tableau interface using the lineage.

> **Note**
>
> The **Overwrite (Save)** capability on the **Lineage** anchor content is required to have permission to email owners directly from the data lineage.

To notify the owners, please follow these steps:

I.   Select **Owners** to see the list of people in the lineage.

II.   Select the owners you want to send a message to.

III.   Click **Send Email** to open the message box.

IV.   Enter the subject and message text and click **Send**.

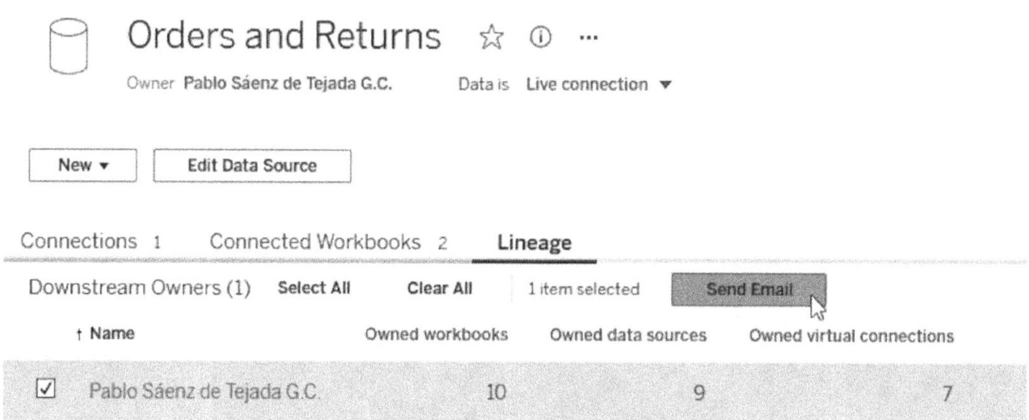

Figure 2.28 – Notifying content owners using the lineage

Using the lineage is a great way to understand how your content is being used and notify users directly of any changes in your data.

Join our community on Discord

Join our community's Discord space for discussions with the authors and other readers:

`https://packt.link/ds`

3

Leveraging Tableau Cloud's Data Management and Advanced Management

An enterprise-ready BI and analytic solution is not just about data visualization and analytical capabilities. It should also provide the capabilities to manage content at scale and provide ways to discover, understand, connect, and trust data in an easy and efficient way but also manage and secure the platform properly.

Tableau's Data Management and Advanced Management features were developed to make organizations' daily jobs easier for these types of tasks.

More concretely, **Advanced Management** makes it easier to understand your Tableau ecosystem regardless of whether you're using Tableau Cloud or Tableau Server. This includes the following:

- Managing content at scale with the **Content Migration Tool** (**CMT**) for robust content lifecycle management requirements

- Enhanced security allowing Tableau Cloud customers to manage their own encryption keys

- Additional storage and refreshing capabilities, with 5 TB of storage, a maximum file size of 25 GB, and up to 25 concurrent extract refreshes

On the other hand, **Data Management** activates a set of additional data functions for Tableau, such as the following:

- An analytics data catalog

- Tableau Prep Conductor to allow flow management and scheduling

- Data quality warnings, data labels, and certifications to enhance data governance directly in the analytics experience

Here, we aim to provide a better understanding of some of these capabilities and help you get the most out of your Tableau environment in more complex scenarios or demanding organizations.

In this chapter, we'll be covering the following recipes:

- Using the CMT to back up content at scale
- Scheduling a migration plan to execute it periodically
- Updating data source connection details at scale to change from development to production databases
- Keeping data curated and user's trust – data certification and quality warnings with Data Management
- Adding column description metadata from a data dictionary to Tableau Cloud with the Metadata API
- Centralizing data access with virtual connections

Technical requirements

This chapter might be the one with the highest requirements in this book in terms of Tableau licensing. Any of the following licensing options will allow you to complete all the recipes in the chapter:

- Tableau Cloud with Advanced Management and Data Management
- Tableau Server with Advanced Management and Data Management
- Tableau Enterprise
- Tableau+

Using the CMT to back up content at scale

For this recipe, we will need Tableau Server or Tableau Cloud with **Advanced Management**, which used to be bought separately from the regular Tableau licenses. It's now also included in the **Tableau Enterprise** and **Tableau+** packages.

One of the features included with Advanced Management is the CMT. The CMT simplifies copying or migrating content between Tableau sites, whether on a single installation or separate instances. The CMT guides users through creating a **migration plan**, which can be used once or as a template for multiple migrations.

Getting ready

If you have Advanced Management as part of your Tableau deployment, you can download the CMT for Windows and Linux from `https://www.tableau.com/support/releases/advanced-management`.

Use the preceding link to download and install the CMT before continuing with this recipe.

How to do it...

Once you have the CMT installed, open it and click on **Create a new plan**. Creating a plan forms the foundation of the migration process. This plan can be saved for future use, modified, or updated as required.

When you create a new plan, you should see the main migration plan menu, as in *Figure 3.1*.

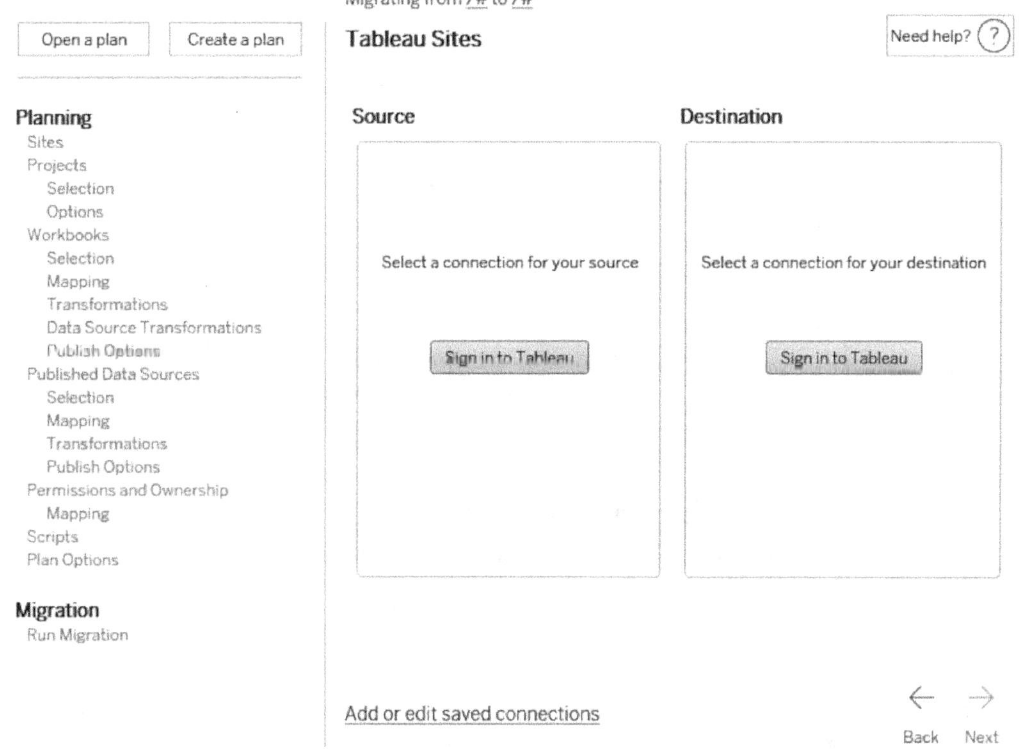

Figure 3.1 – An overview of the main migration plan menu

You can see the different steps of the migration plan available to configure. The CMT allows us to perform a wide range of tasks, so, normally, we will not need to configure each single section.

For this recipe, we will focus on the **Workbooks** section, but first, we need to specify our source and destination for our backups:

1. Click on **Sign in to Tableau** in the **Source** section to specify the Tableau Cloud or Tableau Server site that you want to connect to as your source site: the one you want to get workbooks from to back up.

2. We recommend to then click on **Add or edit saved connections** to store connection credentials and details in the CMT. Also, use **personal access tokens** (**PATs**) for a more secure connection to your Tableau environments, as in *Figure 3.2*. For additional guidance on how to create a PAT, see the *Authenticating in Tableau's REST API* recipe in *Chapter 9*.

Figure 3.2 – Saving credentials in the CMT

3. Repeat *Steps 1* and *2*, but this time, for the **Destination** section. If you are using PATs and the source and destination sites are the same, you will need different PATs for the source and destination.

4. Once ready, click **Next** on the bottom-right icon. We will then navigate to the **Projects | Selection** area. Here, you can specify the Tableau projects we want to work with. In our example, we want to back up all workbooks with the `certified` tag, so we will just select **All Projects** in the radial selector and click **Next** again.

5. As we don't want to perform any action with our projects, unselect any boxes marked in the **Projects | Options** tab and click **Next**.

6. Now, we're in the **Workbooks | Selection** tab, where we need to select which workbooks we want to back up. At the top, we have a radial button with three options:

    - **Specific Workbooks**: To manually select the workbooks we want to work with

    - **Rule Based**: To select workbooks based on certain conditions

    - **All Workbooks**: To perform actions in all workbooks

7. Select the **Rule Based** option as we want to select only workbooks with the `certified` tag. In our production-ready projects, we can use the options available to automatically select the workbooks that match our criteria. In my case, I'm selecting 12 different `certified` workbooks. This way, the workbook selection is based on those with that specific tag.

8. Click **Next** to navigate to the **Workbooks | Mapping** tab. Here, we can add some additional transformations to the workbooks such as renaming them or changing the destination project for those workbooks. Select the **Change Project** option from the **Add Mapping** drop-down menu to change the project into which the selected workbooks will be copied.

9. Select **All Projects** in the **Source** section and the **Backup** project you want to copy your workbooks to, as in *Figure 3.3*. You can also add a new project directly from the CMT.

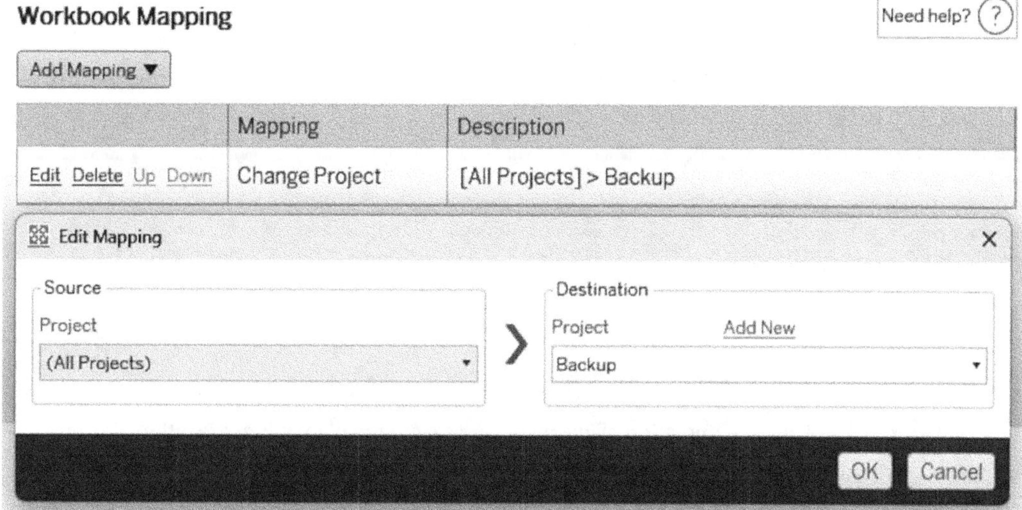

Figure 3.3 – Mapping workbooks to a new Destination project

10. Click **Next** until you reach the **Workbooks | Publish Options** tab and check the **Overwrite Newer Workbooks** tab to make sure newer versions of the workbooks are overwritten if we run the backup more than once.

11. Now, click **Next** several times until you reach the **Plan Options** tab. Give your plan a name, as shown in *Figure 3.4*, and save the plan using the **Save Plan** button to make any updates in the future if needed and to store the plan in a saved location of your convenience. We will also use the saved plan in the next recipe to schedule the backup.

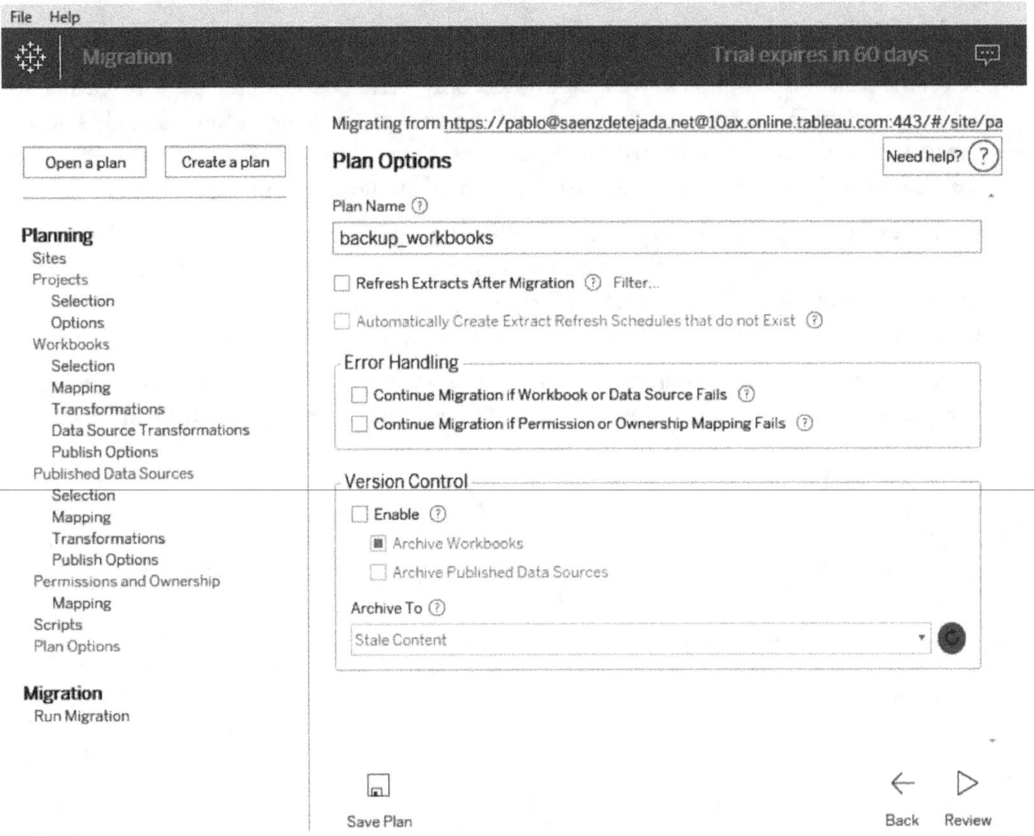

Figure 3.4 – Giving the migration plan a name and saving the plan before execution

12. Now, click on **Review** at the bottom right to check the migration plan and click on **Run** when you are ready to execute it.

How it works...

The CMT will start looking for the workbooks with the `certified` tag in the projects we have specified and copy those in our **Backup** project. The CMT will also show the full details of the migration plan, as in *Figure 3.5*. In my case, I have copied and backed up two workbooks to my **Backup** project.

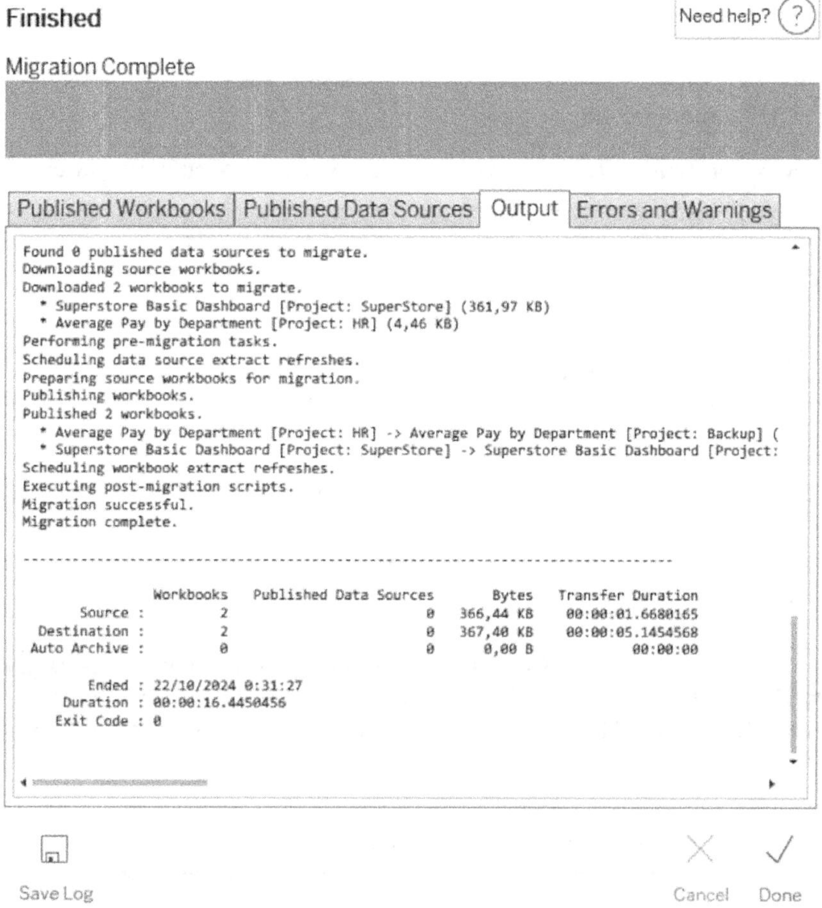

Figure 3.5 – Migration plan output

Well done! You have just learned how to use the CMT available with Tableau's Advanced Management to back up workbooks based on specific conditions, including tags and projects they belong to.

> **Note**
>
> Remember that the CMT can be used for much more than just backing up content. Its main purpose is to migrate and promote content from different Tableau sites or environments.

Scheduling a migration plan to execute it periodically

In the previous recipe, we learned how we can use the CMT available with Tableau's Advanced Management to back up specific workbooks based on a tag or tags they have and the projects they are located in. As Tableau Cloud doesn't have a built-in backup solution, this can be very helpful to make sure we have a copy of our most relevant workbooks and reports to make sure we don't lose them by accident.

However, what happens if we want to run this or any other migration plan on a schedule, avoiding the manual process of running the plan ourselves?

In this recipe, we will learn how we can use Windows Task Scheduler to automate the execution of a migration plan from the command line.

Getting ready

One very useful capability of the CMT is that it includes a command-line utility for running migrations, `tabcmt-runner.exe`, located in the installation folder. The default installation folder for the CMT is `%PROGRAMFILES%\Tableau\Tableau Content Migration Tool` but the location can be changed during the installation.

Keep in mind also that to schedule scripts and tasks with Windows Task Scheduler, you might need *Administrator* permissions on your computer.

How to do it...

Let's imagine we want to run the migration plan we developed in the previous recipe, which I named `backup_workbooks`, every day at 9 AM. We can use the CMT command line to build a very simple script, save it as a `.bat` file, and schedule it with the Windows Task Scheduler application.

Let's see how step by step:

1. First, we need to learn how we can use the CMT command line to execute the migration plan. To do this, open a new **Command Line** or **Terminal** window and type the following command:

    ```
    "C:\Program Files\Tableau\Tableau Content Migration Tool\tabcmt-
    runner" --logfile="logfile_path" "migration_plan_tcmx_path"
    ```

2. If you haven't used the default location for the CMT, replace `'C:\Program Files\Tableau\'` with the location where you have installed the CMT. Also, replace `'logfile_path'` with the location where you want the log file to be saved with the migration results, and replace `'migration_plan_tcmx_path'` with the location where you saved the `.tcmx` file when creating the migration plan, as shown during *Step 11* of the previous recipe.

3. You can execute the command to make sure it runs properly.

4. Now, we need to create a script to run the command. Open a Notepad application or any simple text editor or code application and paste the previous command from *Steps 1* and *2*, adding @ echo off at the beginning, like this:

```
@echo off
"C:\Program Files\Tableau\Tableau Content Migration Tool\tabcmt-
runner" --logfile="logfile_path" "migration_plan_tcmx_path"
```

5. Save this file with a .bat extension, for example, "backup_workbooks.bat", in a location you can easily access.

6. Press the *Windows* key + *R* to open the **Run** dialog, type taskschd.msc, and press *Enter* to open Task Scheduler.

7. Now, we need to create a new task. In Task Scheduler, click on **Create Task…** in the right-hand **Actions** pane, as shown in *Figure 3.6*. Give the task a name in the **General** tab and select **Run whether user is logged on or not**.

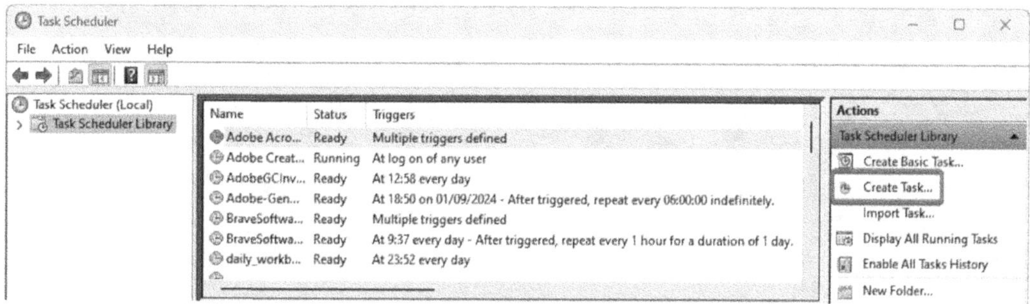

Figure 3.6 – Creating a new task with Task Scheduler

8. Go to the **Triggers** tab to specify when you want the task to run. Click **New** to create a new trigger.

9. On the **New Trigger** screen, from the **Begin the task** drop-down menu, select **On a schedule** and then the frequency you want to execute the task – in our case, as shown in *Figure 3.7*, **Daily** at **9:00** AM. Check the **Enabled** option at the bottom and click **OK** when you are ready.

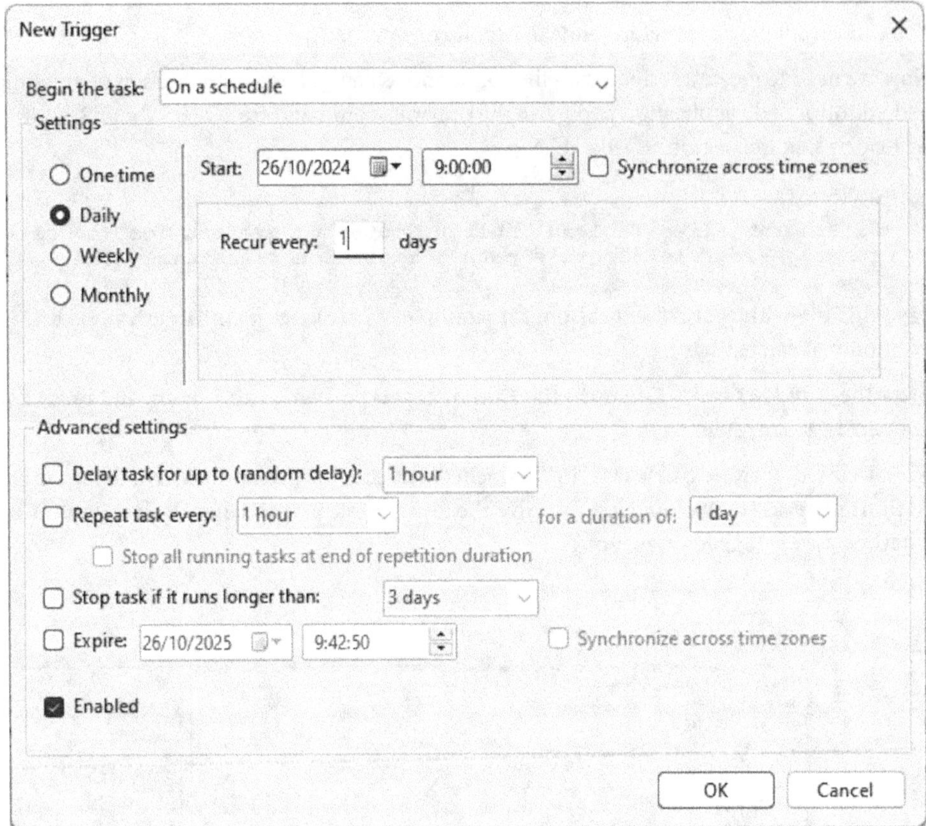

Figure 3.7 – Creating the task trigger

10. Next, we need to tell the Task Scheduler app what we want to execute. Go to the **Actions** tab and click **New**.

11. Choose **Start a program** as the action and use the **Browser...** button to find and select the `.bat` file we created before. The full path of the file location and filename should appear in the **Program/Script** section – for example, `C:\Scripts\backup_workbooks.bat`. Click **OK** when you are ready.

12. Go to the **Settings** tab and check **Run task as soon as possible after a scheduled start is missed** to ensure the backup runs if the computer is off at the scheduled time.

13. Click **OK** to create the task. You may be prompted to enter your Windows account password to grant the necessary permissions for the task to run.

Congratulations! You have just learned how to schedule a Tableau CMT migration plan to run on a daily basis and back up your most relevant Tableau workbooks.

Updating data source connection details at scale to change from development to production databases

The CMT we covered in the previous recipes of this chapter is not just useful for performing actions on workbooks. We can also perform actions and tasks on **data sources** and save significant amounts of time for our Tableau administration and data steward teams.

A very common scenario in big corporations is to have different database environments and separate testing, development, and production. This approach normally causes higher maintenance to Tableau administrators as you might need to change the connection details or credentials of the published data source manually, which is very time-consuming.

With the CMT, we can do this at scale, transforming the connection information of our published data sources to swap test or development databases to production and even archive the test/development versions as a version control mechanism.

Let's learn how we can achieve this.

Getting ready

If you have Advanced Management as part of your Tableau deployment, you can download the CMT for Windows and Linux at `https://www.tableau.com/support/releases/advanced-management`.

Use the preceding link to download and install the CMT before continuing with this recipe.

If you need additional information about how to use the CMT to log in to your Tableau environments, check *Steps 1* to *3* of the *How to do it...* section in the *Using the CMT to back up content at scale* recipe.

How to do it...

Let's learn how we can update a data source connection details at scale with the CMT.

1. After logging in to our **Source** and **Destination** Tableau environments, we will click **Next** in the CMT to go to the **Projects | Selection** tab. Here, we can decide to use all our projects or just work with a sub-group of them. For this recipe, I'll select **All Projects**.

2. Click **Next** in the CMT until you reach the **Published Data Sources | Selection** tab, as highlighted in *Figure 3.8*.

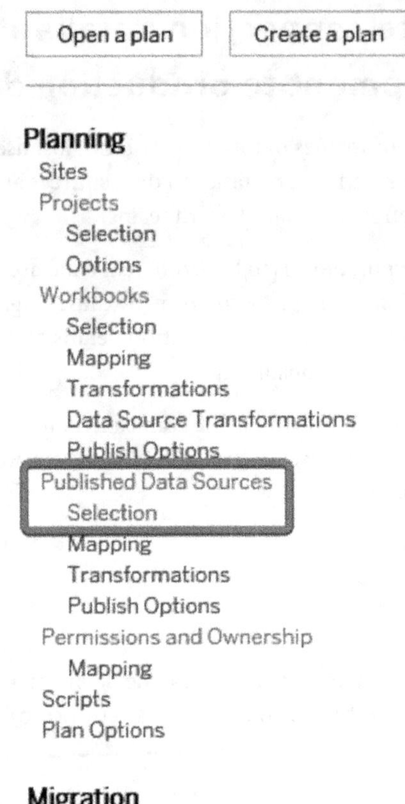

Figure 3.8 – Published Data Sources Selection in the CMT

3. This tab should show you a list of published data sources in the projects selected in *Step 1* – in my case, all my Tableau projects. Select the published data source or data sources for which you want to update the database connection information, such as the name of the database, schema, and table. Click **Next** until you reach the **Published Data Sources | Transformations** tab.

4. Click the **Add Transformation** drop-down menu and select **Set Connection Info**, as shown in *Figure 3.9*, to modify the connection information.

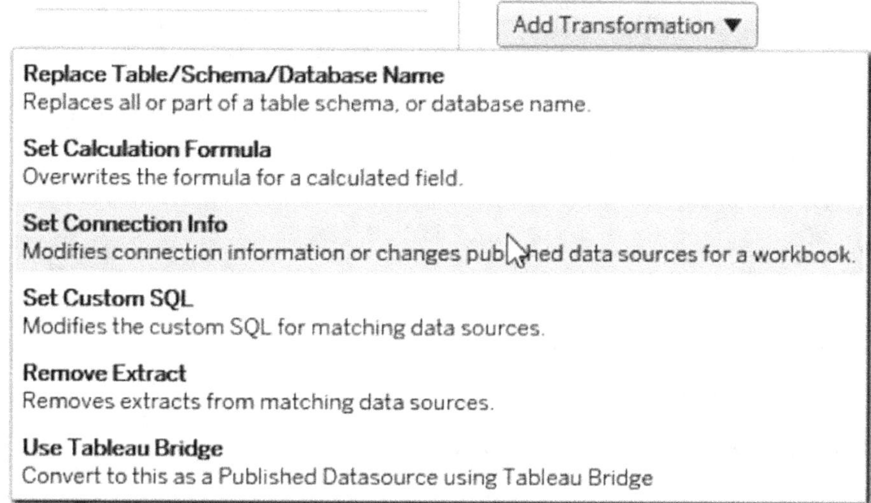

Figure 3.9 – Adding Set Connection Info transformation to our data sources with the CMT

5. The **Edit Transformation** window will appear to set the current and new connection information for our published data source in two different tabs: the **Match Criteria** tab and the **New Connection Values** tab.

    These tabs allows us to match published data sources based on certain criteria and then update them based on the information provided in the **New Connection Values** tab.

6. In our example, as we want to update the connection details of just one published data source, we can configure **Match Criteria** as follows:

    - **Data Source Name** and **Project**: Select from the drop-down menu the data source we want to update and the project where it's located.

    - **Connection Type**: Here, we need to specify the type of connection or database the data source has, such as Snowflake, PostgreSQL, or any other type. In my case, it's a Snowflake database. We can also specify **With or without an extract** if we are not sure whether our published data source has an extract or not.

    - **Server**: The database server we want to look for in our published data sources. In my case, it is my Snowflake URL, which looks something like `<orgname>-<account_name>.snowflakecomputing.com`.

    - **Port**, **Warehouse**, and **Role**: These three options allow us to be more specific in the published data source matching criteria, but we could keep them blank too.

    - **Database**: In my case, the specific Snowflake database I want to use to match and update data sources.

    - **Schema**: The Sschema we want to match and update.

7. In the **New Connection Values** tab, we need to specify the new connection values we want to use for our connection, as in *Figure 3.10*. Here, we can update information such as the following:

- **Tableau Authentication**: We can specify whether we want the user to be prompted for the database credentials or whether we want to embed them in the connection

- **Server**: The updated server we want to connect to

- **Port**: The server port we want to use

- **Warehouse**: The name of the Snowflake warehouse we want to use

- **Database**: The name of the database

- **Schema**: The schema name we want to connect to

- **Role**: The Snowflake role to be used for the connection

- **Username**: The username for the credentials

- **Password**: The password associated with the username above it

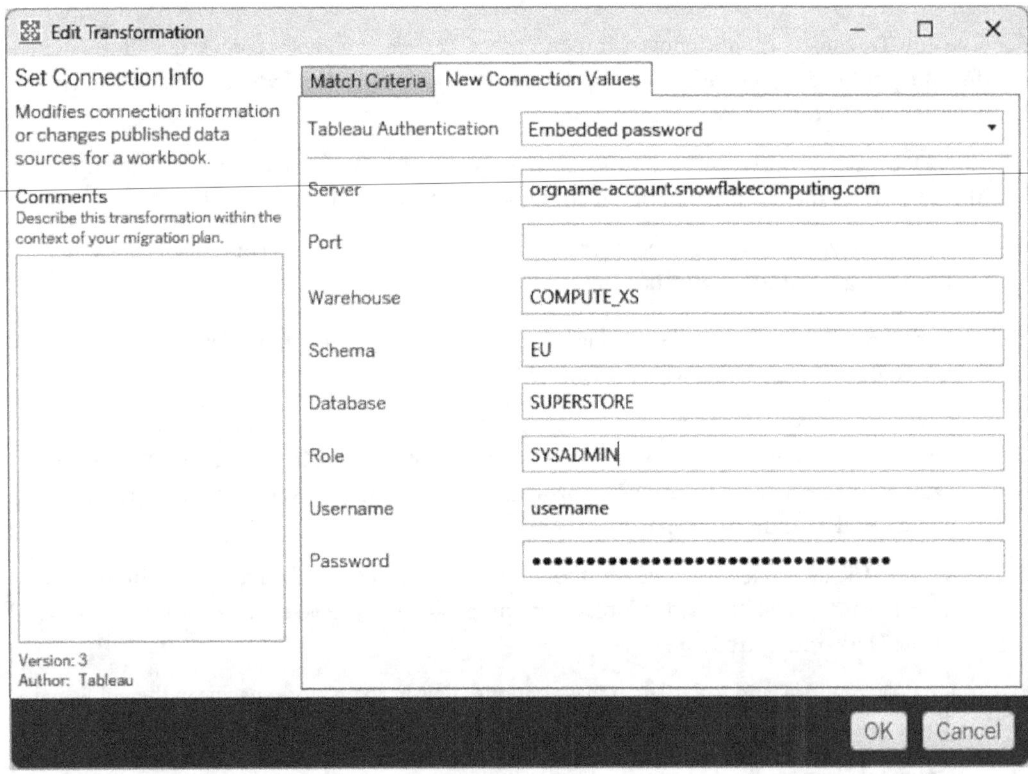

Figure 3.10 – New connection values for our matching published data sources

8. Click **OK** to close the **Edit Transformation** window when you are ready. The transformation should appear in the list of transformations added to the published data sources. We could add more transformations if needed, but in this case, we are done, so click **Next** to go to the **Publish Options** tab.

9. In this tab, we can specify some additional criteria for our tasks, such as whether we want to overwrite data sources, update more recently, copy the data source permissions, or extract refresh schedules. In our case, we can just click **Next** and continue until we reach the **Plan Options** tab.

10. In the **Plan Options** tab, it might be useful to check the **Enable** option under **Version Control** and **Archive Published Data Sources**. Then, we can select a specific project to archive the current published data sources. This basically will allow us to create archive copies in the selected project of our published data sources. It's a great way to keep a copy of the current data source in case we need it in the future.

11. Finally, click **Review** and then click **Run**.

It's as easy as that! By following these steps, you can avoid the pain of updating the data source connection information of data sources manually and do it in a more automated and scalable way.

As we mentioned in the previous recipe, we can also save our migration plan and run these tasks automatically through the scripting and command-line capabilities of CMT.

How it works...

In this case, the CMT finds all the data sources matching the criteria we defined in *Step 6* and updates them with the connection details from *Step 7*.

Then, the CMT will download all the published data sources locally, update the connection info, and republish them.

Additionally, if we enable **Version Control** during *Step 10*, it will also store a copy of the original data sources before the update in the specified project.

As you can probably already guess, there are tons of possible useful use cases for the CMT tool.

Keeping data curated and user's trust – data certification and quality warnings with Data Management

Data quality warnings are fundamental pillars of effective BI because they directly impact an organization's ability to make sound decisions.

When data is incomplete, inaccurate, or outdated, it can lead to costly mistakes, lost opportunities, and damaged credibility. Quality warnings serve as a crucial safeguard by alerting users to potential issues before they make important decisions on problematic data, helping maintain trust in the analytics process, and ensuring that insights derived from the data are reliable.

Data quality warnings are a feature of Tableau Catalog, part of Data Management, and allow Tableau administrators and data stewards to set data quality warnings on data assets and make users aware of specific issues.

Moreover, quality warnings act as an early warning system that enables organizations to address data issues proactively rather than reactively. By flagging problems such as stale information, these warnings help organizations maintain regulatory compliance and ensure that resources are focused on analyzing trustworthy data.

More specifically, you can set data quality warnings on data sources, databases, tables, flows, virtual connections, virtual connection tables, and columns. Let's learn how.

Getting ready

For this recipe, you will need a Tableau Data Management license active and running in your Tableau environment. Tableau Data Management comes with the following licenses:

- Tableau Enterprise
- Tableau+

How to do it...

For this recipe, we will add a data quality warning to a published data source to let users know the data source is **deprecated**, that is, no longer maintained and not to be used:

1. First, locate the data source to which you want to add the data quality warning in your Tableau Server or Tableau Cloud environment.

2. Once you have your data source located, click on the three dots (...) under the **Actions** menu and look for **Data Labels | Data Quality Warning…**, as shown in *Figure 3.11*.

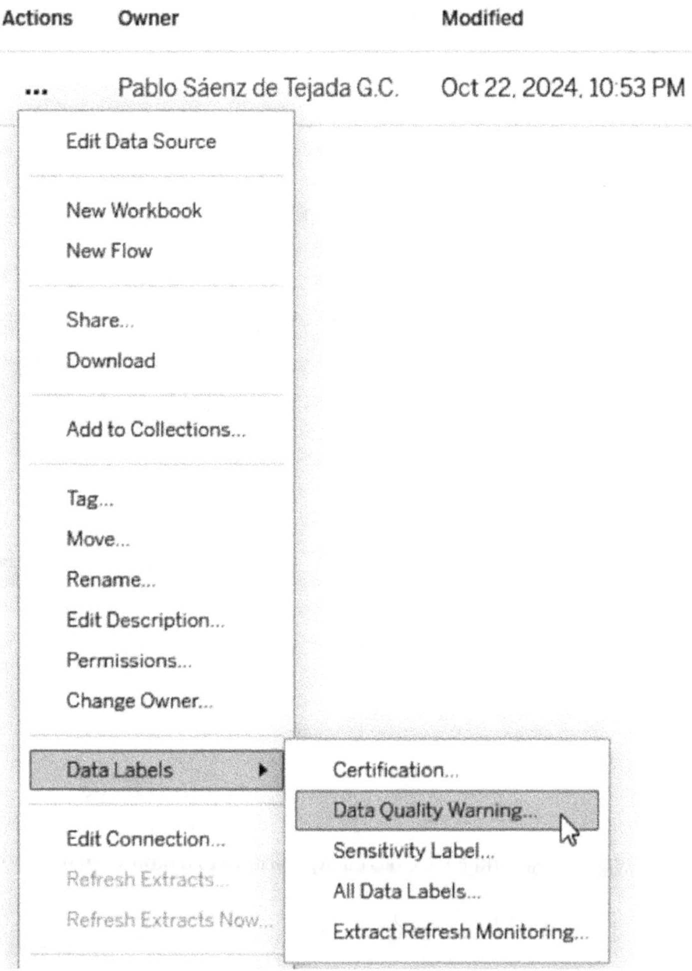

Figure 3.11 – Adding a data quality warning label to a data source

3. A new **Data Label** window will pop up for the selected data source. On the left side, you should see all the available label categories. Select **Quality Warning**.

4.   Click the **Deprecated** checkbox, as shown in *Figure 3.12*, or the specific quality warning you prefer.

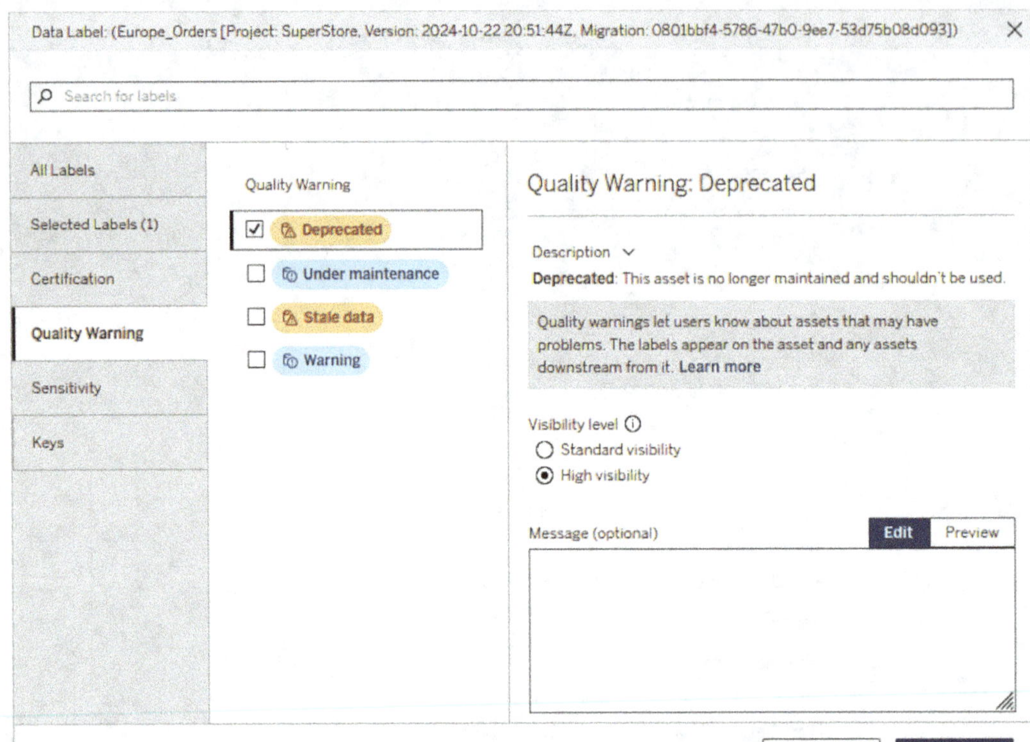

Figure 3.12 – Adding a specific quality warning to a data source

5.   Select the preferred **Visibility level** option for the quality warning.

A **High visibility** warning appears in more places than a **Standard visibility** one. For example, a **High visibility** warning on a data source, as in this recipe, will generate a notification when anyone opens a view that it's connected to that data source. This can be especially useful for users that might not have access to the data source directly, and only to workbooks and views.

You can also add an optional message to the quality warning for users to have more details about why the data source is deprecated. This might be a good place to point to the certified or non-deprecated data source, for example.

6.   To remove a data quality warning or any other data label in Tableau, you can uncheck the data quality warning opening again the corresponding data label through the **Actions** menu, as we did in *Step 2*.

There's more...

You might want to add your own custom data labels and quality warnings. Doing so nowadays is much easier in Tableau with the **Data Labels** capabilities of Tableau Cloud and Tableau Server available with Data Management from mid-2023.

You can add labels to several Tableau assets such as databases, tables, columns, data sources, or virtual connections. To create add, remove, and manage your data labels, follow these steps:

1. Go to the **Data Labels** menu on the sidebar menu on Tableau Cloud or Tableau Server. It's important to remember the following:

    *   Appropriate permissions for the asset are required to add, remove, or update labels

    *   For certification labels, you must be a Tableau administrator, project leader, or the owner of the content you want to add, remove, or update the certification label

2. On the **Data Labels** main page, click on the **New Label** button.

3. On the **New Label** window that appears, you can create a new category using the button at the bottom or select a specific label category in the drop-down menu and add a new label value, description, and visibility level.

    For example, we might want to create a new label that identifies content as from a non-production database or use data from a non-production environment to let users know they should be careful with the data and conclusions they might extract from it, as in *Figure 3.13*.

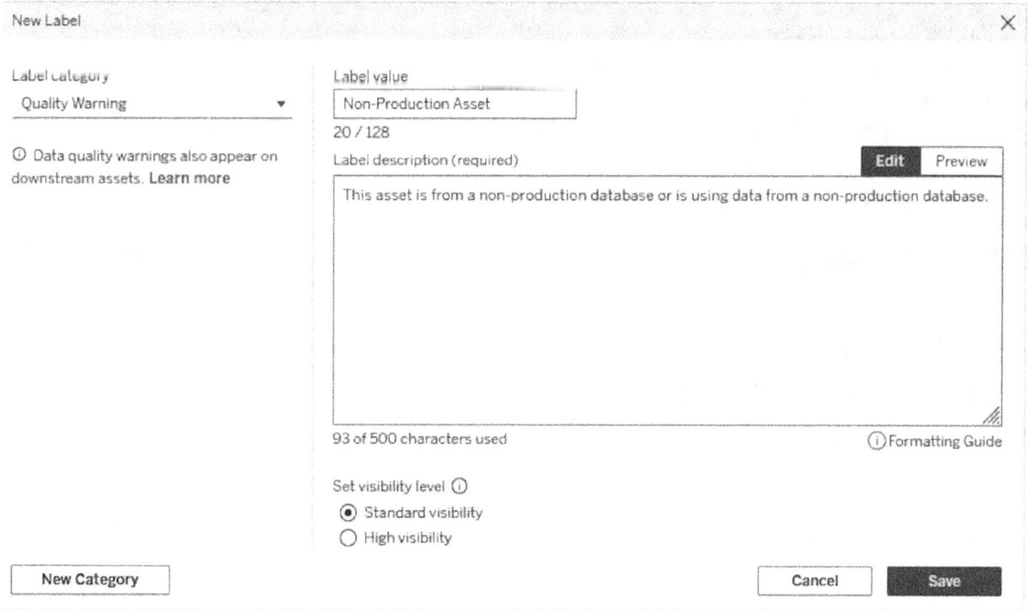

Figure 3.13 – Creating new labels in Tableau Cloud

As we just saw, Tableau is not just a very powerful tool for data visualization, analysis, and BI but also a complete platform to manage and administer all your data assets and facilitate making better decisions with data in a secure and trusted way.

Adding column description metadata from a data dictionary to Tableau Cloud with the Metadata API

One of the main benefits of Tableau Data Management is it allows us to add, query, and provide metadata to Tableau's end users through Tableau's user interface and also through **Metadata API** methods. Having the appropriate context to understand the business definition of data assets is key for developing a data-driven culture, and putting the business definitions of databases and table columns where users analyze their data is a common request.

In this recipe, we will learn how we can use Tableau's Metadata API to add column descriptions to Tableau Cloud using a data dictionary in CSV format as a source.

Getting ready

For this recipe, we will need the following:

- Python installed on our computer

- An IDE or code application such as Visual Studio Code, PyCharm, Sublime, or similar

- The data dictionary CSV file and sample dataset to upload to Tableau Cloud are available at `https://github.com/PacktPublishing/Tableau-Cookbook-for-Experienced-Professionals/tree/main/Chapter_03`

Let's learn how we can leverage Tableau's Metadata API to enrich our data column descriptions.

How to do it...

To add column descriptions to a Tableau table programmatically through the Metadata API, we will need to go through the following steps:

1. Authenticate into Tableau Cloud and get an authentication token to use in the following requests.

2. Find the ID of the table to which we want to add descriptions.

3. Query the columns of that table.

4. Match the column names from Tableau's table with the columns in our data dictionary.

5. Update the column descriptions in Tableau Cloud based on the descriptions in our data dictionary.

Let's go:

1. Open Visual Studio Code, PyCharm, or your Python IDE of choice.

2. Create a new Python file (with the extension `.py`) and give it a meaningful name, for example, `add_column_descriptions_tableau_cloud.py`.

3. Import the different packages we will need – `requests`, `json`, and `pandas` – like this:

```
import requests
import json
import pandas as pd
```

4. To sign in to Tableau Cloud using Tableau's **REST API**, we will need some details, such as our URL, our site name, Tableau's REST API version to use, a PAT name, and a PAT secret. For more information about how to create a PAT, follow the steps in the *Authenticating in Tableau's REST API* recipe in *Chapter 9*.

5. Store those values in different variables. For example, if, when I sign in to my Tableau Cloud site, the URL in my browser looks like `https://10ax.online.tableau.com/#/site/pablosite/home`, then my site URL will be `https://10ax.online.tableau.com` and my site name will be `pablosite`. Add those variables to your Python file:

```
token_name = 'pat-name'
token_secret = 'paste-here-your-pat-secret'
my_tableau_url = 'https://10ax.online.tableau.com/'
api_v = '3.24'
site = 'pablosite'
```

6. Those variables store the information we will need to try to authenticate on our Tableau Cloud site. Now, we need to create a function that sends an API request. The request should include the type of response we want to get and the type of content (`json` or `xml`), the URL to sign in to the REST API, and so on. This Python function should do the job:

```
def sign_in (server, api, tokenname, tokensecret, sitename):
    uri = server + 'api/' + api + '/auth/signin'
    headers = {
        'Content-Type': 'application/json',
        'Accept': 'application/json'
    }
    payload = {
        'credentials': {
            'personalAccessTokenName': tokenname,
            'personalAccessTokenSecret': tokensecret,
            'site': {'contentUrl': sitename }
        }
    }
    request = requests.post(uri, headers=headers, json=payload)
    response = json.loads(request.content)
    siteid = response['credentials']['site']['id']
    userid = response['credentials']['user']['id']
    token = response['credentials']['token']
    return token, siteid, userid
```

7. The function will return three values: a token to be used in future requests, the ID of our Tableau site, and the user ID of our user. We could run our function and check how those three values look by adding the following code to our file. As you can see, in the `sign_in` function, we will use the variables we created in *Step 5*:

```
my_token, my_siteid, my_userid = sign_in(
    my_tableau_url, api_v, token_name, token_secret, site)
print('My API token: ',my_token)
print('My Site ID: ', my_siteid)
print('My User ID: ', my_userid)
```

8. If something goes wrong, check that your variables are correct. If you see those three values printed on the console, then congratulations! You just built a Python function to sign in to your Tableau Cloud.

9. Now, we need to upload our sample dataset for the recipe. Log in to Tableau Cloud and publish a new data source using the `Superstore_Orders.csv` file from the GitHub repository shared at the beginning of the recipe.

10. The next step is to find Tableau's unique ID associated with the `Superstore_Orders.csv` table we just used. It's important to remember that we don't want to find the data source ID but the table ID. With Data Management, Tableau stores information about all the assets used in our Tableau Cloud environment, including databases and tables. Column descriptions can only be added to tables, and that's why we can only perform this action if we have Data Management.

11. We will create a new function that using similar credentials from before, performs an API Get request, and returns the table ID searching for a table name we will specify:

```
def find_table (token, siteid, server, api, tablename):
    uri = server + 'api/' + api + '/sites/' + siteid + '/tables'
    headers = {
        'Content-Type': 'application/json',
        'Accept': 'application/json',
        'X-Tableau-Auth': token
    }
    request = requests.get(uri, headers=headers)
    response = json.loads(request.content)

    for table in response['tables']['table']:
        if table.get('name') == tablename:
            return table['id']
    return None
```

12. To check the function and return the table ID of the `Superstore_Orders.csv` table, we can run the following code afterward:

```
my_tableid = find_table(
    my_token, my_siteid, my_tableau_url,
    api_v, 'Superstore_Orders.csv'
)
print("Table ID: ", my_tableid)
```

13. With our table ID, it's time to query all the columns from it to get the column names and column IDs. How? With another function that runs an API Get request to the table ID we just stored in my_tableid, like this:

```python
def query_columns (token, siteid, server, api, tableid):
    uri = (server + 'api/' + api + '/sites/' + siteid +
            '/tables/' + tableid + '/columns')
    headers = {
        'Content-Type': 'application/json',
        'Accept': 'application/json',
        'X-Tableau-Auth': token
    }
    request = requests.get(uri, headers=headers)
    response = json.loads(request.content)

    columns = []
    for i in response['columns']['column']:
        columns.append({'id': i['id'], 'name': i['name'] })
    return columns
```

14. The previous function will return a list with all the column IDs and column names of our table ID. Again, we could check the results by adding a few lines of code:

```python
table_columns = query_columns(
    my_token, my_siteid, my_tableau_url,
    api_v, my_tableid
)
print('Table Columns: ', table_columns)
```

15. We managed to get all our relevant metadata from our Tableau Cloud table. Now, it's time to read the data dictionary CSV file and merge both lists. Let's create a new function to read column_descriptions.csv, also available at the GitHub repository, and check the results by pointing to the location in our hard drive where we downloaded the file:

```python
def read_file(file_path):
    df = pd.read_csv(file_path)
    data_dictionary = df.to_dict('records')
    return data_dictionary

path = r'D:\Downloads\column_descriptions.csv'
my_dictionary = read_file(path)
print('Data dictionary: ',my_dictionary)
```

16. Now, we will use DataFrames to compare both lists, merge them based on the name/column, and create a new list that contains the column name and column ID from the table_columns list and the description from the my_dictionary list:

```python
df1 = pd.DataFrame(table_columns)
df2 = pd.DataFrame(my_dictionary)
```

```python
combined = df1.merge(
    df2, left_on='name', right_on='column', how='left')
combined = combined[['id','name','description']]
columns_with_descriptions = combined.to_dict('records')
print(columns_with_descriptions)
```

17. We are almost there. Now, we finally have the most important data in a single list that includes the name, ID, and description of each column. It's time to create our last function – in this case, one that adds the description to an individual column providing the table ID, the column ID, and the description we want to add. In this case, we will return just the `status_code` as the response. A code of 200 means the Put request was successful:

```python
def update_column_description (token, siteid, server, api,
                               tableid, columnid, description):
    uri = (server + 'api/' + api + '/sites/' + siteid +
           '/tables/' + tableid + '/columns/' + columnid)
    headers = {
        'Content-Type': 'application/json',
        'Accept': 'application/json',
        'X-Tableau-Auth': token
    }
    payload = {'column': {'description': description } }
    request = requests.put(uri, headers=headers, json=payload)
    response = request.status_code
    return response
```

18. The last step is to send the Put request to each individual column in our `columns_with_descriptions` list:

```python
for column in columns_with_descriptions:
    update = update_column_description(
        my_token, my_siteid, my_tableau_url, api_v,
        my_tableid, column['id'], column['description']
    )
    print(update)
```

If everything goes well, we should get a code of 200 for each call to the REST API to update the column description.

Congratulations! You've just added column descriptions programmatically to Tableau Cloud based on a data dictionary on a CSV file.

How it works...

By adding the column descriptions to the table using Tableau's Data Management capabilities the descriptions are also inherited to the published data source.

This is especially useful if you start planning and managing your published data sources to make sure the underlying tables aren't duplicated in Tableau. That way, you can add a table only once in Tableau, and no matter how many published data sources are connected to that table, all the relevant column descriptions will be inherited without requiring additional effort.

To achieve this, virtual connections, which we'll investigate in the next recipe, are very useful.

Centralizing data access with virtual connections

Data replication in BI has been one of the most common challenges for administrators and data stewards. That's one of the reasons why Tableau's **virtual connections**, available with Data Management, are a powerful feature not available in Tableau's standard licensing. A virtual connection is a shareable resource that provides a central access point to data in a governed and secure way, allowing database administrators or data stewards to create unified connection points to databases that multiple users and workbooks can access.

The main benefits of virtual connections include the following:

- Enhanced data security

- Reduced maintenance as connection credentials and access permissions are managed in one place

- Improved data consistency since all users access the same connection settings and policies

   This means that when a database is updated, administrators only need to update the virtual connection rather than individual data sources or workbooks with the waste of time this implies.

Virtual connections differ from standard connections. When you create a published data source in Tableau, normally, you will embed the credentials of your database so that users don't need to enter those credentials to see the data. The challenge in large deployments comes when the database credentials are updated. As the credentials are normally embedded at the data source level, you will need to update the credentials for every published data source using the database.

Virtual connections provide a central access point to your database so you don't need to embed credentials per published data source. Instead, you embed the credentials in the virtual connections, and then multiple published data sources can be created from the virtual connection, centralizing access to your data.

In this recipe, we will learn how to create virtual connections and how we can use this new Tableau resource to help us keep a central access point to our data.

Getting ready

For this recipe, we will use several tables available in the GitHub repository of this book. Go to `https://github.com/PacktPublishing/Tableau-Cookbook-for-Experienced-Professionals/tree/main/Chapter_03` and download the following files:

- `ch3_visits.csv`

- `ch3_specialties.csv`

- `ch3_patients.csv`

- `ch3_invoices.csv`

- `ch3_hospitals.csv`

- `ch3_doctors.csv`

You will need to also to publish those tables to a virtual connection. In version `2025.1` of Tableau, virtual connections support a lot of different databases such as Amazon Athena, Amazon Redshift, Azure SQL Database, Azure Synapse Analytics, Databricks, Google BigQuery, Microsoft SQL Server, Oracle PostgreSQL, or Snowflake, and file repositories such as Box, Dropbox, Google Drive, or OneDrive connectors.

You will need to upload those files to the database or file repository of your choice to create a virtual connection.

How to do it...

Let's learn how to create a virtual connection that includes those tables:

1. Sign in to your Tableau Cloud or Tableau Server site that includes Data Management.

2. Go to the **Explore** menu on the left sidebar, click on the **New** drop-down menu, and select **Virtual Connection**, as in *Figure 3.14*.

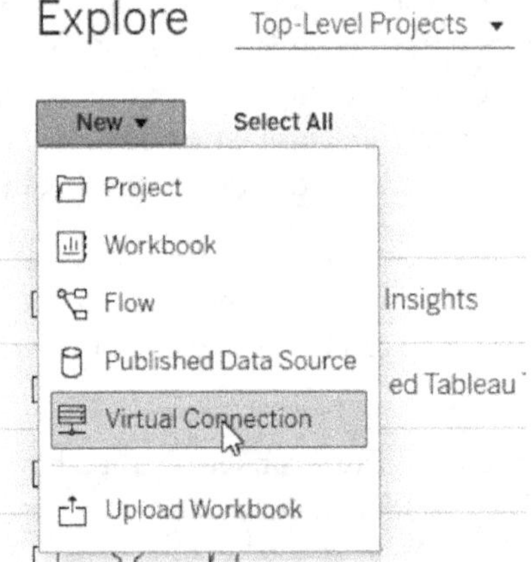

Figure 3.14 – Creating a new virtual connection

3. Select the database or file repository where you have loaded the tables, as explained in the *Getting ready* section.

4. On the left-side menu bar of the **Virtual Connections** window, you should be able to see the six tables you uploaded. Select the six tables and drag and drop them into the canvas where it says **Add Tables**.

5. You should see the six tables on the canvas, as in *Figure 3.15*.

	Alert	Table name	Visibility...	Database	Schema	Data is ⓘ	Data policy	Original table na...
☑	⊞	Hospitals ...	⬤✓	DUMMY	HOSPITAL	Extract – O...	None	HOSPITALS...
☑	⊞	Visits ...	⬤✓	DUMMY	HOSPITAL	Extract – O...	None	VISITS (DU...
☑	⊞	Doctors ...	⬤✓	DUMMY	HOSPITAL	Extract – O...	None	DOCTORS (...
☑	⊞	Invoices ...	⬤✓	DUMMY	HOSPITAL	Extract – O...	None	INVOICES (...
☑	⊞	Patients ...	⬤✓	DUMMY	HOSPITAL	Extract – O...	None	PATIENTS (...
☑	⊞	Specialties ...	⬤✓	DUMMY	HOSPITAL	Extract – O...	None	SPECIALTIE...

Tables (6)   Data Policies (0)

Select All   Clear All   6 items selected   Actions ▾   ↻ Refresh All Extracts

Table Details - Hospitals ▱ ⊞ ▤   ☐ With policy applied   Preview as User ▾   Columns used in connection: 2 of 2 ▾

Alert	Type	Column name		Original column name	Changes ⓘ	Linked keys ⓘ
	Abc	Hospital Id	...	HOSPITAL_ID	▱	
	Abc	Hospital Name	...	HOSPITAL_NAME	▱	

Figure 3.15 – An overview of the configured tables in the virtual connection

There are several tasks you can perform for each individual table:

- Update the metadata such as the table name, column names, and column types for every single table. Updating the metadata will make sure every single user sees table names and column names in the same and meaningful way.

- Turn off the **Visibility** toggle of a table, which can be useful if you want the data from that particular table to not be available for a while due to maintenance reasons for instance.

- Switch between **Live** or **Extract** for each individual table. This is an interesting capability of virtual connections, as it will allow us to mix extracts and live connections in data models, even with incremental extract refreshes.

- You can also create **row-level security** data policies, as virtual connections can be used to set up and centralize row-level security directly in Tableau. See the *Setting up centralized row-level security with virtual connections* recipe in *Chapter 2* to learn how to do this and its benefits.

6. Once you are ready to save and publish your virtual connection, click on the **Publish** button in the top-right corner and choose a name for the virtual connection and the project you want to save it at. In my case, I saved my virtual connection with the name `Patient Visits and Invoices`.

Congratulations! You just created and published a virtual connection. As you have probably noticed, we haven't created any data model. This is because the virtual connection is just a centralized access point to your data.

Let's learn how users with a Creator license can then use the virtual connection and those six tables to create new data models.

How it works…

1. Go to the main Tableau Cloud or Server site and click on **New** | **Published Data Source** to build a new data model and Tableau data source.

2. Instead of looking for those tables again in your database or file store, we can connect directly to our virtual connection. Again, the main benefit of this approach is to avoid users connecting to the same data several times, which might require maintaining a lot of different connections and credentials. From the **On This Site** tab on the **Connect to Data** window, filter for **Virtual Connections** or just search for the virtual connection name you just published before, as shown in *Figure 3.16*.

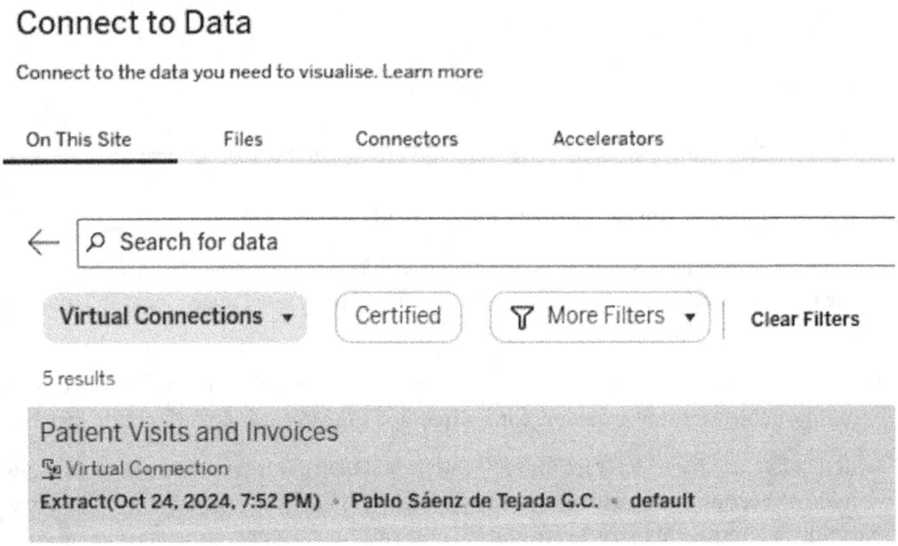

Figure 3.16 – Using a virtual connection

3. Now, we can create our data model in the same way we normally do in Tableau, with the benefit that any user who might need to connect to the tables in our data source doesn't need to have the data source credentials. Additionally, there's a single access point to the data, with unique metadata that we can enrich with column descriptions, as we learned in the previous recipe, *Adding column description metadata from a data dictionary to Tableau Cloud with the Metadata API*.

Part 2: Optimizing Performance and Mastering Complex Calculations

In this part, you will explore essential strategies for overcoming common performance issues in Tableau by improving calculation efficiency, reducing rendering delays, and optimizing slow data sources. You will gain hands-on experience with tools such as the **Workbook Optimizer** and **Performance Recorder**, and learn how to fine-tune workbook performance. This part also introduces advanced calculation techniques, such as secondary table calculations and nested **Level of Detail (LOD)** expressions, and provides guidance on using **Tableau's Order of Operations** framework to resolve filter and calculation related challenges.

This part includes the following chapters:

- *Chapter 4, Maximizing Workbook Performance*
- *Chapter 5, Mastering Advanced Calculations to Answer Complex Business Questions*

Maximizing Workbook Performance

In the modern landscape of data dependency, the ability to quickly and accurately analyze data is paramount. Inefficient data access can impair an organization's agility when responding to market fluctuations and industry pressures, directly affecting its competitiveness.

This chapter aims to provide you with a comprehensive framework for optimizing workbook performance in Tableau. This framework will introduce you to essential strategies and best practices to transform your dashboards into efficient, high-performing tools. The collection of practical recipes included in this chapter will help enhance your understanding of how to address performance bottlenecks, refine data structures, and implement efficient calculation methods, to deliver maximum performance and user adoption.

In this chapter, we'll be covering the following recipes:

- Getting started with workbook optimization
- Enhancing performance through data source and modeling strategies
- Reducing complexity and rendering time
- Optimizing filter performance
- Improving calculation efficiency
- Designing efficient workbooks
- Utilizing the Workbook Optimizer
- Using View Acceleration
- Assessing workbook performance

Technical requirements

The following are required to complete the recipes in this chapter:

- Tableau Desktop version `2025.1` or higher

- Tableau Cloud version `2025.1` or higher

You can download a free 14-day trial if you don't have a licensed version of Tableau Desktop/Cloud:

- Tableau Desktop: `https://www.tableau.com/support/releases`

- Tableau Cloud: `https://www.tableau.com/products/cloud-bi`

Getting started with workbook optimization

Optimizing Tableau dashboards is both an art and a science, rooted in mastering four fundamental elements: data, calculations, worksheets, and dashboard layout. Understanding how these components work is key to ensuring efficiency and good performance. We will explore these aspects in detail in subsequent recipes. To begin, we'll go through some general recommendations and tips for how to approach workbook optimization. We'll focus on the essential considerations related to three main components of Tableau workbooks: **data volume**, **connections**, and **dashboard design**. Optimizing these elements at a high level should be prioritized before exploring more specific methods, as they often resolve common performance issues affecting many Tableau workbooks.

How to do it...

Let's review some core principles and important considerations you need to keep in mind, as you plan your optimization strategy:

- **Reduce data volume**: One highly effective strategy for instantly improving performance is limiting the volume of data you bring into your workbooks. When you limit the amount of data processed to only what's necessary, you significantly decrease the time it takes for Tableau to retrieve and render the data. This leads to faster load times and a more responsive user experience, which is crucial in environments where quick access to insights is necessary. Smaller datasets reduce the computational burden on both Tableau and the underlying data architecture, which can improve overall system stability and efficiency.

  To effectively reduce data volume, start by connecting only to the data you need for your analysis. Avoid connecting to entire databases or data warehouses when a smaller subset will suffice. Use filters to narrow down the dataset to the most relevant records. This approach not only speeds up query execution but also minimizes the memory footprint of the workbook. Aggregating data at a higher level before bringing it into Tableau can also be beneficial, as this will reduce the overall number of records.

- **Optimize data connections**: The aim of optimizing data connections in Tableau is to reduce latency and enhance data retrieval speed. A widely recommended approach is to utilize Tableau's data extracts, which significantly boost performance by reducing reliance on live database queries. This is particularly beneficial when handling large datasets or complex queries, as live queries can be slow and resource-intensive. Additionally, Tableau supports the use of aggregated extracts, which condense data to the necessary level of detail, further decreasing the volume of data that Tableau needs to handle in real time. Further optimization can be achieved through efficient data modeling and data management practices; for instance, scheduling extract refreshes during off-peak hours will ensure that the data remains current without impacting performance during peak usage times. By focusing on these aspects, one can promote a more effective and productive Tableau environment.

- **Simplify dashboard design**: A well-designed dashboard layout can reduce rendering time, making the dashboard quicker to display and interact with, leading to a smoother, more responsive user experience. Efficient layouts can also simplify maintenance and updates, whereas cluttered or overly complex dashboards can make changes or debugging challenging and time-consuming.

  To simplify your dashboard design, begin by reducing the number of views included in your dashboard. Busy dashboards with too many views can take a while to render. Focus on the most essential views that convey key insights and use layout containers to maintain a structured and visually appealing design. Employ guided analysis by incorporating things such as action filters and drop-down menus to guide users through the data, rather than displaying everything at once. This approach will allow users to drill into details as needed, thereby reducing the initial load time. By simplifying your dashboard design and focusing on user interactions, you can significantly enhance the overall usability and performance of your dashboards.

There's more...

Keep in mind that performance tuning is highly specific to your environment, data, analysis, and workbooks. What proves effective in one case may not be suitable in another. Each use case is unique and demands careful evaluation and a tailored approach. It will often involve multiple iterations, which will be directly influenced by the complexity of your data, the intricacies of your calculations, and the design of your worksheets and dashboards. So, once you identify the root cause of performance issues, you can focus your optimization efforts where they will have the most significant impact.

Enhancing performance through data source and modeling strategies

Tableau's versatility allows you to connect to a wide variety of data sources, offering both live connections and extracts. Live connections receive real-time updates, while extracts provide a static snapshot of your data at a specific point in time. Extracts are particularly beneficial as they enable faster query processing by minimizing the need for constant database access. In this chapter, we will explore how to effectively use live connections and extracts, and how to fine-tune each for maximum performance.

Getting ready

This recipe requires the `Sample-Superstore` data source, which can be found in the **Saved Data Sources** section under the **Connect** pane of the **Home** page. Additionally, you can use any Tableau workbook of your choice.

How to optimize extracts

Using extracts is typically recommended for most production environments due to their substantial performance advantages. Let's look at the steps required to set up your extract effectively and fully leverage its capabilities:

1. To create an extract, first, connect to your desired data source and set up your data model. In the **Data Source** window, under **Connection** details in the top-right corner, select **Extract** and choose **Edit** to open the dialog box.

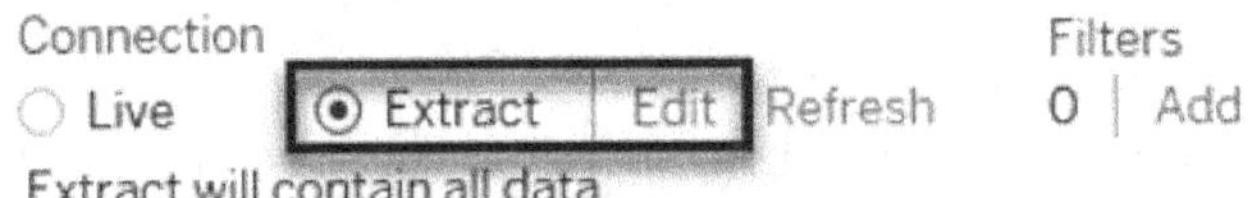

Figure 4.1 – Setting the connection type to Extract in the Connection settings

2. In the dialog box, under **Data Storage**, specify your preferred storage method for your extract by expanding the menu options. Here, you want to make sure you choose the **Logical Tables** option if you think you can benefit from using additional extract settings such as aggregating your fields to visible dimensions or applying extract filters.

Extract Data

Expand All

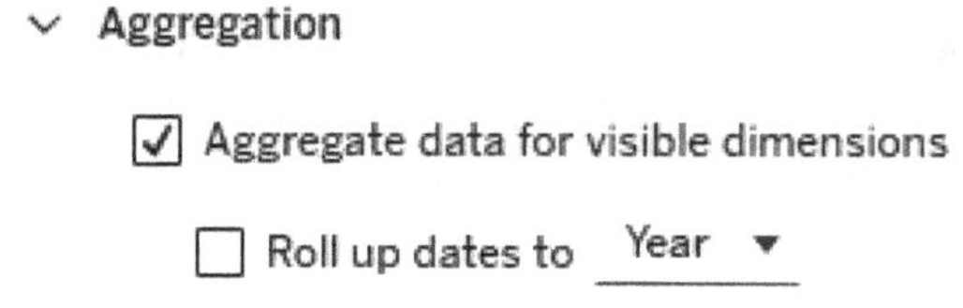

∨   **Data Storage**

⦿ Logical Tables

Store data using one table for each logical table.

Use this option if you need to use extract filters, aggregation, or other extract settings.

○ Physical Tables

Store data using one table for each physical table.

Figure 4.2 – In the Extract dialog box, specify your preferred data storage option

3. Next, you can set up your extract filters to reduce the amount of data that will be saved in the extract, which will reduce the overall size of your extract. Choose **Edit | Add Filter** under the **Filters** section of the dialog box and select **Order Date**. Choose **Years | Next** and select 2023 and 2024, then click **OK** to save the changes (*Figure 4.3*).

∨   Filters

Abc   YEAR(Order Da...   keeps 2023 and 2024   ✎   🗑

Add Filter   ▾

Figure 4.3 – Adding an extract filter to keep both years (2023 and 2024) in our dataset

4. If you don't need row-level records, you can pre-aggregate your extract by choosing the **Aggregate data for visible dimensions** option under **Aggregation**. This option will aggregate your measures into a single row and help in further reducing the size of your extract. You can also roll up your dates to a different level, such as **Year**, **Quarter**, **Month**, or **Day**.

∨   Aggregation

☑ Aggregate data for visible dimensions

☐ Roll up dates to   Year   ▾

Figure 4.4 – Selecting additional aggregation options will group the data for visible dimensions instead of extracting every row in your underlying dataset

5. You can also reduce the size of your extract by restricting the number of rows included in the extract. To achieve this, select either the **Top** or **Sample** option under **Number of Rows**. Both options allow you to select a specified number or **percent** of **rows** from your dataset, which can be useful for testing or exploratory data analysis.

6. To refresh your records, you can choose **Incremental Refresh** in the **Incremental Refresh** section. This option will only add new rows based on the chosen database column and the minimum date range, as opposed to rebuilding the entire extract from scratch (*Figure 4.5*). **Incremental Refresh** will typically perform faster and require fewer resources in Tableau Server, so it's recommended that you use this option when you can. Please note that this option is not available if aggregation is enabled.

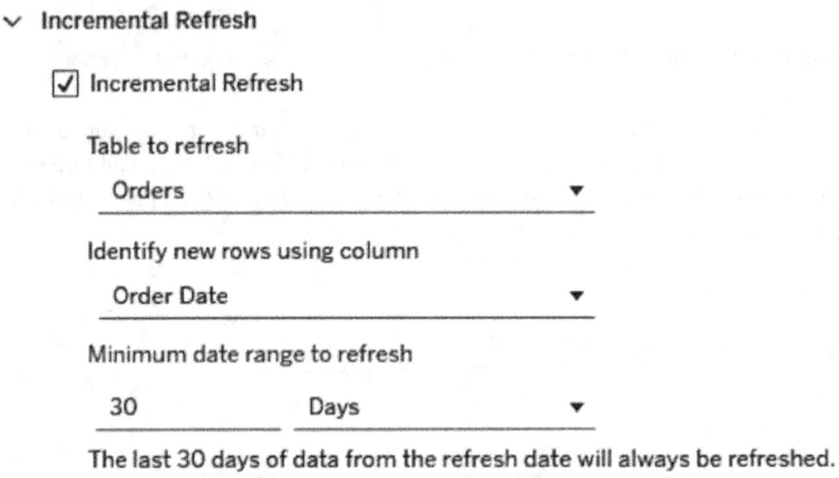

⌄ **Incremental Refresh**

☑ Incremental Refresh

Table to refresh

Orders ▼

Identify new rows using column

Order Date ▼

Minimum date range to refresh

30   Days ▼

The last 30 days of data from the refresh date will always be refreshed.

Figure 4.5 – Adding new records with an Incremental Refresh

7. The **Advanced Settings** can be used to define how Tableau handles updates to the extract. **Replace the last rows added** option will completely replace existing rows with the last recorded values. This setting may take longer for large datasets. **Don't replace the last rows added** option will append new rows to the existing extract without overwriting the current data, it is useful for incrementally updating the extract, without the need to reprocess the entire dataset, which will save time and resources. These settings are particularly important for maintaining the consistency and performance of your extract, depending on how frequently your data changes and how you intend to use the extract.

8. For optimal results, ensure your production workbook is free of any unused fields such as calculations, parameters, dimensions, or measures before generating the extract. To remove unnecessary fields, select **Hide All Unused Fields** at the bottom of the dialog window and click **Save Settings**.

Figure 4.6 – Selecting Hide All Unused Fields before generating your extract

9. Additional calculations created in the extract after it has been generated can be materialized and precomputed to speed up future queries. To materialize new calculations within your extract, navigate to the **Data** menu, select the name of your extract, **Sample - Superstore**, and choose **Extract | Compute Calculations Now**. Please note that this option should only be used when the query performance of your extract is degraded, as a result of complex calculations or regular expressions that involve string manipulations.

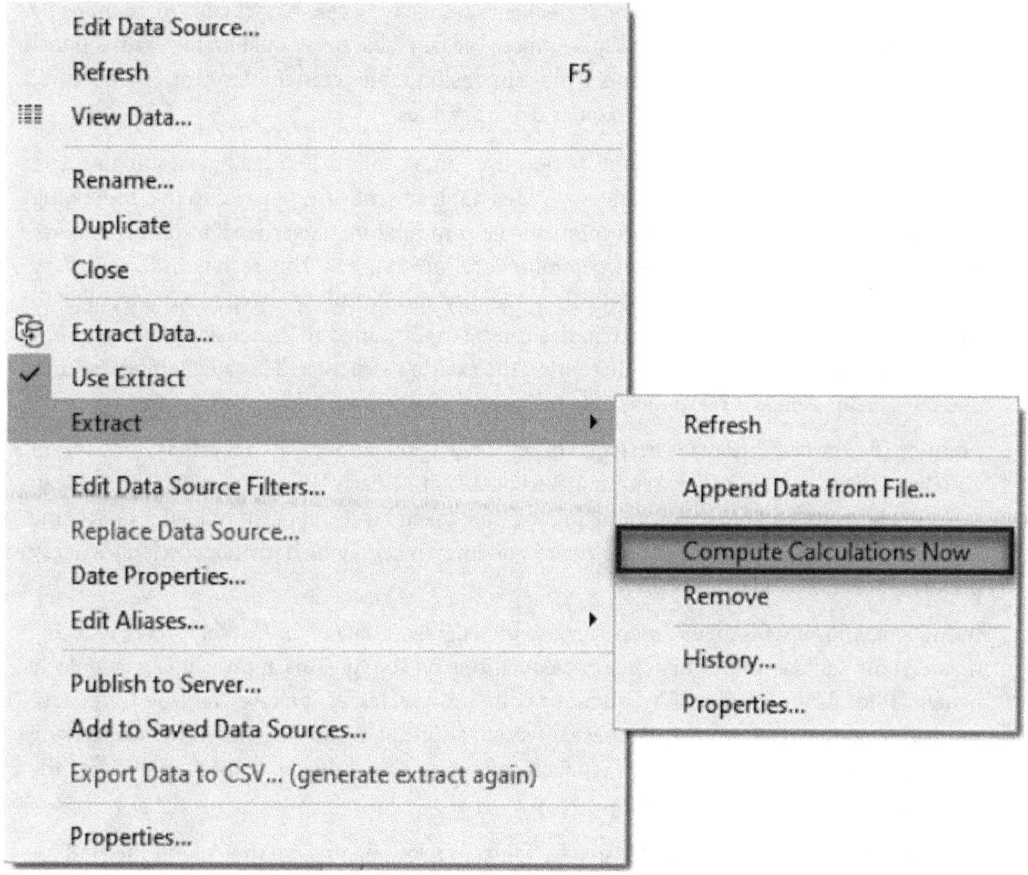

Figure 4.7 – Newly created calculations can be materialized within
an extract by choosing Compute Calculations Now

How to optimize live connections

When working with live data connections in Tableau, it's crucial to remember that the speed and efficiency of your Tableau workbooks are directly influenced by the performance of the underlying data source. If the data source is slow or inefficient, it can significantly impact the responsiveness of your visualizations. Let's discuss several best practices and recommendations for working with live connections, which are essential to maintaining optimal performance and more responsive user experience:

- **Implement star schema design**: The star schema is a robust and efficient data modeling technique that simplifies data organization, improves query performance, and supports flexible reporting and analytics. At its core, the star schema consists of a central fact table surrounded by dimension tables, forming a star-like appearance. The fact table stores quantitative transactional data, such as sales figures or revenue, while dimension tables contain descriptive attributes, such as product names, dates, or customer demographics.

  The star schema can significantly optimize slow live connections in Tableau by streamlining data structure and enhancing query efficiency. When Tableau sends live queries to the underlying database, this simplified structure minimizes the computational overhead, as fewer joins are required and the relationships between tables are more direct. This results in faster query execution, especially for large datasets. Its scalability and flexibility also make it adaptable to changing business needs, as new attributes can be easily added to dimension tables, or new rows can be incorporated without disrupting the existing structure. This adaptability ensures that the schema remains relevant as data grows and evolves over time.

  Additionally, the star schema is designed for efficient aggregation, which is crucial for Tableau visualizations that often require summarized data. With clearly defined dimensions, Tableau can quickly group and filter data, reducing the time taken for dashboards to load. The schema also supports the use of indexing on primary and foreign keys, which further accelerates query performance in live connections.

  By implementing a star schema, users can also pre-aggregate data at the fact table level, reducing the need for Tableau to perform heavy calculations on the fly. This approach is particularly beneficial for dashboards with frequent or complex queries, as it allows Tableau to retrieve results more quickly from the database. Overall, adopting a star schema in the underlying data source ensures a cleaner, more efficient foundation for Tableau, helping to mitigate the challenges of slow live connections.

- **Opt for relationships instead of joins**: In Tableau, relationships are the default method for combining data from multiple tables. They allow you to establish logical connections based on related fields without physically merging them into a single flat table, as is typically done with joins. This architecture reduces data redundancy and improves query performance by allowing Tableau to fetch only relevant data based on user interactions. Additionally, Tableau's query optimization techniques such as query fusion and intelligent caching, are particularly effective with relationships. In essence, the technical benefits of leveraging relationships in Tableau lie in their ability to dynamically query relevant data, reduce record duplication, and improve scalability, while maintaining data integrity through context-aware joins.

- **Cast accurate data types**: It's very common to see data being converted from one type to another for proper display or calculation use in Tableau. Performing these types of conversions directly in Tableau can lead to unnecessary processing overhead. On the other hand, casting correct data types within your underlying data sources can help streamline your data operations and accelerate query performance.

- **Index commonly used dimensions**: Indexing commonly used dimensions in the underlying database can significantly optimize the data retrieval process, by helping the database quickly locate and access relevant records. This technique improves the speed of filtering, sorting, and aggregation operations in Tableau, ensuring that queries are executed efficiently.

- **Use custom SQL sparingly**: Custom SQL in Tableau allows users to write SQL queries directly to their data sources, facilitating data transformation and complex logic for rapid prototyping. However, Tableau treats custom SQL as subqueries within its queries, potentially leading to less optimized execution. It's generally recommended to minimize the use of custom SQL in favor of Tableau's native connectors and functionalities whenever possible.

There's more...

Using embedded extracts can offer additional performance benefits. Embedding an extract directly within a workbook can minimize the dependency on external data sources. This reduction in network roundtrips can significantly enhance dashboard load times and responsiveness, as data retrieval is expedited from the local extract rather than over the network.

Embedded extracts enable Tableau to employ advanced optimization techniques such as creating temporary tables and pre-aggregating data, which can help streamline complex queries, especially those involving extensive calculations and filtering operations.

However, it's essential to consider the trade-offs involved in using embedded extracts – they can significantly increase the workbook size and require periodic updates to ensure data freshness, impacting server storage and maintenance efforts. Despite these considerations, the performance gains achieved by embedding extracts make it a preferred choice for high-impact dashboards, where speed and responsiveness are paramount.

See also

- To learn more about the Tableau data model, visit the following link: `https://help.tableau.com/current/pro/desktop/en-us/datasource_datamodel.htm`

- For information on how to create a star schema and examples, refer to the *What Is the Star Schema Data Model? An Explanation with 3 Examples* blog post by Radu Gheorghiu: `https://vertabelo.com/blog/star-chema-data-model/`

- For more information on working with relationships, visit the following link: `https://help.tableau.com/current/server/en-us/datasource_multitable_normalized.htm`

- To learn more about database indexing, read the following blog post: `https://www.codecademy.com/article/sql-indexes`

- Here is another great blog post, titled *Optimizing Custom SQL for Tableau*, by Sanam Zahedi at phData: `https://www.phdata.io/blog/optimizing-custom-sql-for-tableau/`

- For more information on best practices for published data sources, visit the following link: `https://help.tableau.com/current/pro/desktop/en-us/publish_datasources_about.htm#publishing-data-separately-or-embedded-in-workbooks`

Reducing complexity and rendering time

In the context of Tableau workbooks, rendering refers to the process of generating and displaying visualizations based on the underlying data queries and applied calculations. While Tableau offers powerful rendering capabilities, the complexity and number of visualizations can significantly impact performance, especially when combined across multiple worksheets within a dashboard. Worksheets are crucial for managing much of the rendering workload in Tableau; by optimizing elements within worksheets, users can effectively control and enhance rendering efficiency.

How to do it...

Let's look at some specific best practices and recommendations that can help maximize rendering efficiency in Tableau worksheets:

- **Reduce the mark count**: In Tableau, a mark is a basic element of data visualization. It represents a single data point and can take various forms such as a bar, line, shape, or text. The number of marks rendered within a worksheet can be found in the bottom-left corner under the **Data Source** tab (*Figure 4.8*). The more marks there are, the more processing Tableau must do. Although it's tempting to show every data point in your dataset, and Tableau can handle millions of marks, often, it's not necessary to display every detail. Instead, you can aggregate your data, filter, or separate results into different worksheets, which will reduce the mark count and provide better clarity and faster rendering.

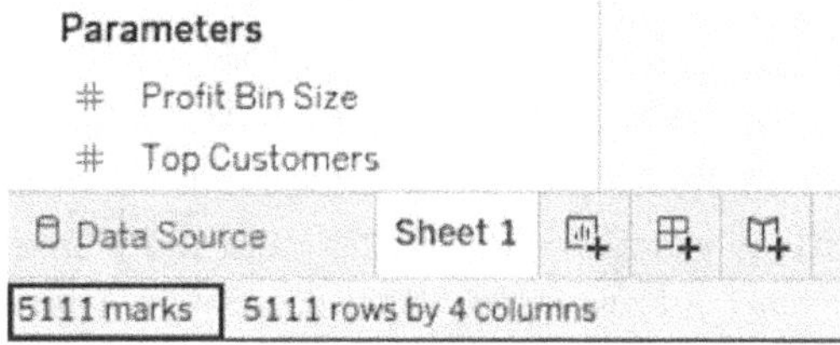

Figure 4.8 – Shows an example of where the mark count is displayed within a worksheet

- **Choose visuals over text**: When you create large text tables in Tableau, each individual text element is treated as a separate mark, which can become cumbersome with large datasets as more and more processing will be required to format, align, and display the text. In contrast, Tableau's internal data engine is optimized for rendering visual elements such as bars, lines, and shapes more efficiently. By minimizing the use of large text tables and leveraging more efficient visualization techniques, you can reduce additional overhead and achieve quicker response times.

- **Utilize built-in custom formatting options**: At times, you may want to represent a numeric value with a KPI indicator, such as ▲(surplus) or ▼(shortage), or a simple text description such as Surplus or Shortage. A handy method to implement this is to use Tableau's built-in custom number formatting options to directly incorporate these elements into your worksheets without creating extra calculations.

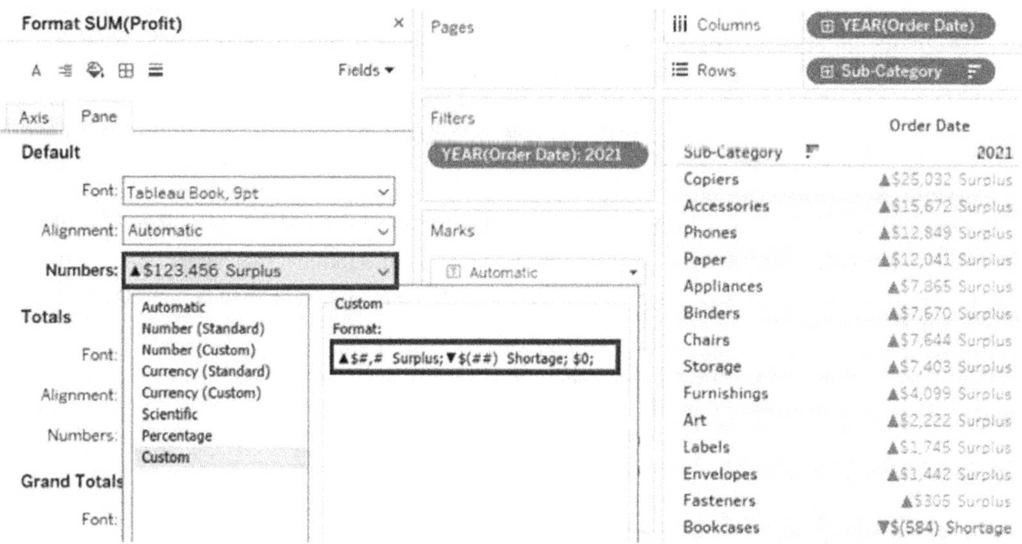

Figure 4.9 – Custom number format settings can be used to control
how numeric values are displayed in your visualizations

To access the custom number format settings, right-click on a measure in the view and choose **Format | Numbers | Custom**, as shown in *Figure 4.9*. From there, you can choose various format options for your values.

- **Reduce chart complexity**: Thoughtfully reducing chart complexity ensures your visualizations are clear and easily interpretable. Advanced chart types, while visually impressive, can significantly increase rendering time and slow down performance due to complex calculations and inefficient layering of various graphical elements. These charts can also be challenging for users who are unfamiliar with them, leading to confusion and misinterpretation of the data. To ensure your charts remain simple and effective, focus on using basic chart types such as bar charts, line charts, or scatter plots. By prioritizing simplicity, you can enhance the overall performance and usability of your Tableau dashboards, which is extremely important in a business context.

- **Leverage Dynamic Zone Visibility or Show/Hide containers**: Dynamic Zone Visibility and **Show/Hide** containers in Tableau are both techniques used to control which elements are displayed in a dashboard, but they differ in how they affect performance. Dynamic Zone Visibility is generally better for performance when the goal is to optimize rendering by only showing elements that are needed based on user interactions. It allows Tableau to conditionally hide components without removing them from the layout entirely. This means that only the necessary elements are processed and rendered, reducing the computational load for hidden elements. However, all components are still loaded when the dashboard first opens, and the Boolean calculation used to control visibility can introduce additional processing overhead, especially if complex logic is involved. Dynamic Zone Visibility is often the better choice for optimizing performance in complex dashboards that feature numerous interactive elements, as it efficiently controls rendering without compromising responsiveness.

  Using **Show/Hide** containers involves switching visibility of entire layout containers, which can contain multiple sheets or objects, such as quick filters, legends, menus, and information buttons. While this method can give you better performance from the get-go, as it prevents hidden elements from rendering on the initial load, it can lead to performance degradation because the hidden elements are still present in the layout and require Tableau to maintain their positions, which can impact rendering speed. **Show/Hide** containers may be more effective for simpler dashboards where the primary concern is layout control.

  To create a **Show/Hide** button, follow these steps:

  I. First, add an empty layout container to your dashboard.

  II. Next, place the elements you want to hide within this container. Select the container, expand the drop-down menu in the top-right corner, and choose **Add Show/Hide Button** as shown in *Figure 4.10*. You can edit the button style and appearance in the **Edit Button** settings once the button is added and then test its functionality in **Presentation Mode**. This button will now control the visibility of the container, allowing you to streamline your dashboard by minimizing the number of elements Tableau needs until a user request is made.

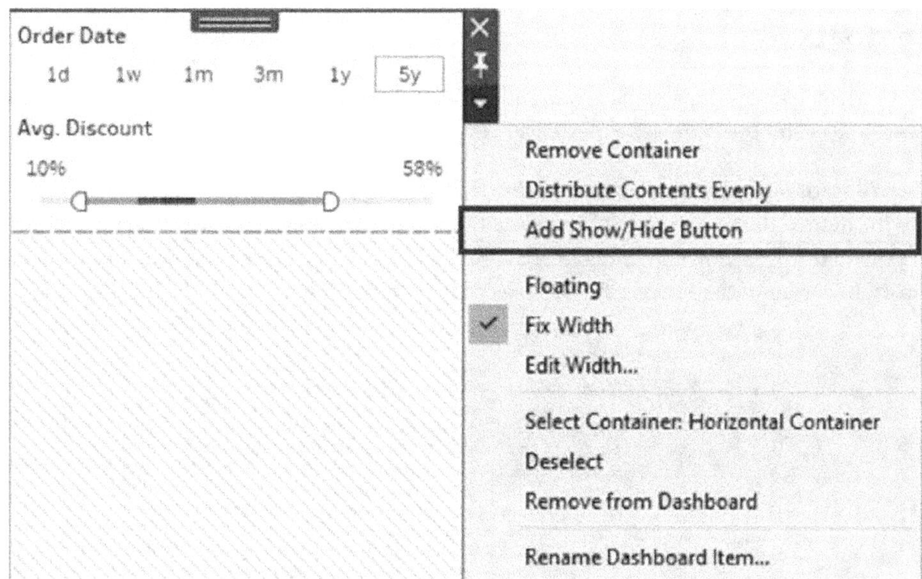

Figure 4.10 – The Show/Hide Button can be added to control the visibility of dashboard elements

- For information on how to use custom number formatting options, visit this link: `https://help.tableau.com/current/pro/desktop/en-us/formatting_specific_numbers.htm#define-a-custom-number-format`

- To learn about supported custom date formats, visit this link: `https://help.tableau.com/current/pro/desktop/en-us/dates_custom_date_formats.htm`

Optimizing filter performance

Filters play a crucial role in Tableau, significantly impacting performance for better or worse. They can be applied at various levels, including the data source, worksheet, and dashboard, making them versatile tools in Tableau. A thoughtful filter strategy can greatly enhance query performance, making your visualizations faster and more responsive. However, an overabundance of filters or inefficient filter design can often lead to sluggish workbooks. This section will explore specific filter types and their performance impact to help you make intelligent choices when building your dashboards.

Getting ready

Before focusing on specific filter-type optimization techniques, I would encourage you to go through some general filter best practices, which can often make significant efficiency improvements. They include reducing the number of filters, limiting filters with large lists, and avoiding calculation-based filters, as they can be resource-intensive with increasing levels of granularity.

How to do it...

Let's look at certain filter customization choices and recommendations that can enhance the performance of your workbooks and the end user experience:

- **Use Wildcard Match and custom value lists**: To customize your filter functionality for dimensions, add the desired dimension to the **Filters** shelf and select **All | OK**. Right-click on the dimension to expand the drop-down menu and select **Show Filter**. Click on the drop-down menu in the top-right corner of the **Filter** card and select the preferred **Filter Card Mode** option.

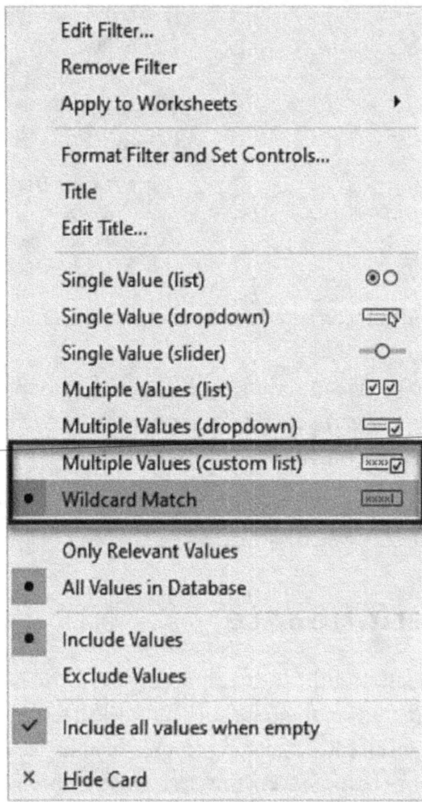

Figure 4.11 – The Multiple Values (custom list) and Wildcard Match filter options

- **Customize with Show Apply Button**: The **Show Apply Button** option can be used to allow dashboard users control the application of filters. When working with **Multiple Values** lists, you can pause the underlying queries from running until filter selections have been finalized. To use the **Show Apply Button** feature, click on the drop-down menu in the top-right corner of the **Filter** card and select **Customize | Show Apply Button**.

Figure 4.12 – The Show Apply Button option adds a button to the filter interface, allowing users to make multiple filter selections before applying them all at once

- **Filter with Range of Values**: To customize your filter functionality for continuous measures, drag your measure to the **Filters** shelf and choose how you want to filter your measure, then save the changes in the **Filter** dialog box. Right-click on the measure to expand the drop-down menu and select **Show Filter**. Once the filter is displayed, use the drop-down menu in the top-right corner of the **Filter** card to select **Range of Values**.

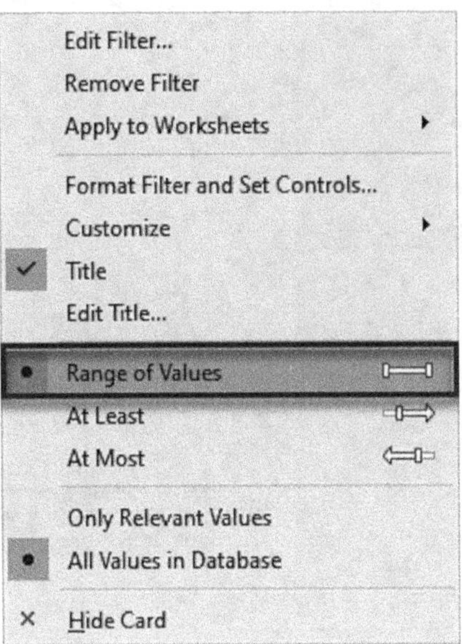

Figure 4.13 – Filtering with Range of Values allows users to select a
specific range of numeric values to include in a view

- **Use Only Relevant Values sparingly**: The **Only Relevant Values** option is a commonly used setting that dynamically displays a unique subset of values based on other filter selections. It improves clarity and usability by streamlining available choices in each filter context. It can be implemented by configuring your dimension filter first and then choosing **Only Relevant Values** in the **Filter** dialog box. Using this option selectively and thoughtfully can help balance the benefits of a streamlined user interface with the potential drawbacks related to performance.

- **Use Continuous Date filters**: **Continuous Date** filters can streamline query logic by treating dates as a continuous timeline rather than discrete categories, which minimizes computational overhead and speeds up visualization rendering. To create a **Continuous Date** filter, drag your date field of choice to the **Filters** shelf and select your preferred filter choice: **Relative Date** or **Range of Dates**. Click **Next** to apply the changes.

- **Leverage Exclude all values for filter actions**: The **Exclude all values** filter action can enhance dashboard performance by limiting the volume of data processed and displayed at any given time. When this action is applied, it filters out all data from the selected view until a specific interaction, such as clicking a filter or selecting a mark, triggers the inclusion of relevant data. To implement this functionality, first, configure the filter action by specifying the **Name, Source** and **Target Sheets**, and the trigger (**Select, Hover,** or **Menu**) in the **Add Filter Action** dialog box. Then, choose the **Exclude all values** option under the **Clearing the selection will** filter action setting, and save the changes. When this option is enabled, clearing the selection will exclude all data from the view, essentially leaving it blank.

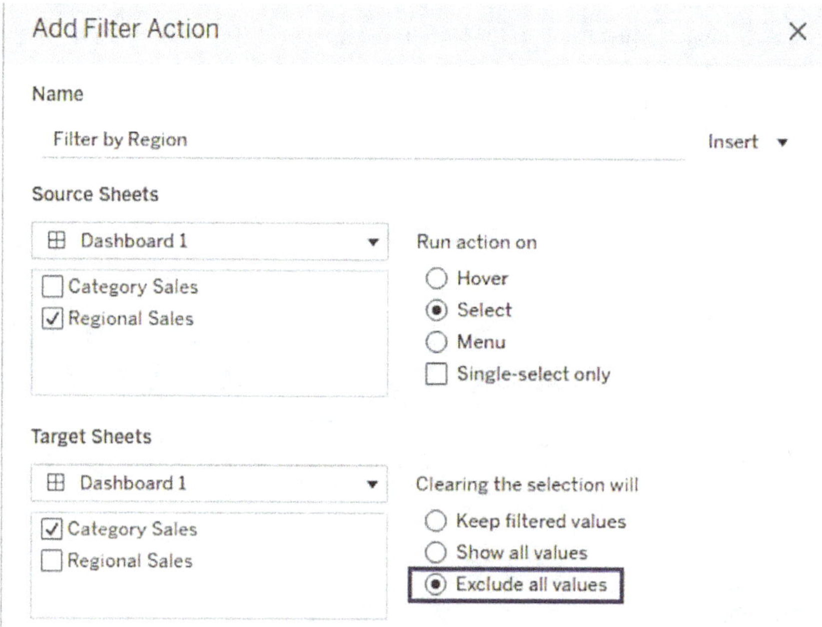

Figure 4.14 – The Exclude all values option determines what happens
when a user clears the selection of data points

- **Include target fields in the Detail shelf**: When configuring your filter actions, make sure to include the target field of the filter in the target view when possible. Let's say we have created a dashboard filter action on **Category Sales**, which targets the **Sub-Category Sales** bar chart, as shown in *Figure 4.15*.

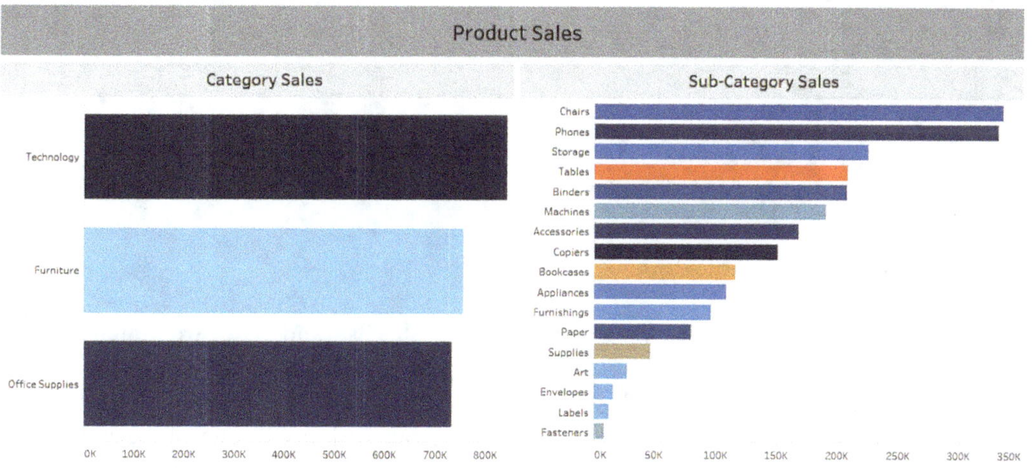

Figure 4.15 – Sample dashboard with filter action that targets a list of sub-categories

- If we add the **Category** dimension to the **Detail** shelf (*Figure 4.16*), we can significantly improve the query performance. Without the **Category** field on **Detail**, Tableau will query the data to determine which Sub-Categories belong to the selected **Category**, which can slow down the filtering process when working with a large number of discrete values.

Figure 4.16 – Adding the Category dimension to the Detail shelf will reduce the time required to query related Sub-Categories

How it works...

- **Wildcard Match and custom value lists:** Custom value lists and **Wildcard Match** filters offer notable performance benefits. They simplify query complexity by avoiding the need for extensive lists of discrete values. These filters also optimize data retrieval speed by specifying precise values or patterns, which reduces unnecessary data fetching. Additionally, these filters enhance usability by allowing users to directly specify values or patterns, reducing the need for manual selection and minimizing the risk of errors.

- **Show Apply Button**: The **Show Apply Button** feature in Tableau can improve user control over data filtering while promoting a more intuitive and reliable user experience. Its main functionality allows users to make multiple filter selections before applying them at once. This reduces the number of queries sent to the data source by batching them together, and reduces the wait time caused by multiple refreshes, giving the appearance of better response times.

- **Range of Values**: Using a **Range of Values** filter enhances data selection efficiency and performance in several ways. It simplifies the filtering process by allowing users to specify a range (for example, sales between $1,000 and $5,000), rather than selecting individual items from a potentially extensive list. This filter type offers flexibility by letting users dynamically adjust their criteria based on analysis needs and without the complexity of updating multiple selections from a dropdown of **Include** and **Exclude** values. When possible, refrain from using filters with numerous discrete value options, as they can generate unnecessary queries and contribute to degraded performance.

- **Only Relevant Values**: It is advisable to limit the use of the **Only Relevant Values** option for several reasons. While it can help users by displaying applicable values based on their current selections, it requires Tableau to query the data each time an upstream filter is applied. This dynamic filtering can become resource-intensive and slow down your dashboard, particularly when multiple filters are involved. This performance degradation occurs because each filter control must repeatedly fetch and process the underlying data to update the list of relevant values, resulting in numerous, potentially complex queries being executed against your data source.

- **Continuous Date filters**: Date fields in Tableau represent unique dimensions that require special handling, particularly when creating date filters. These filters fall into three categories: **Discrete Date**, **Relative Date**, and **Range of Dates**. Each type offers distinct functionalities with varying performance impacts on workbooks.

- **Discrete Date** filters, though useful for specific selections, can generate complex queries and slow down performance. Therefore, they should be limited to scenarios where specific date selection is crucial, and consideration should be given to the potential performance impact, particularly with large datasets. Understanding and utilizing date truncation (reducing a date to a specified part such as year or month) can optimize the underlying queries by simplifying date calculations and leveraging database partitioning, resulting in faster query execution and improved performance. Materializing truncated date parts in data extracts can further enhance query efficiency and overall performance.

- **Relative Date** filters, which allow selections based on dynamic, rolling periods (for example, last 6 months), frequently re-evaluate data to stay current. This dynamic nature results in inefficient caching and can degrade performance due to the continual need for fresh data queries. **Relative Date** filters should be used sparingly and only when dynamic, up-to-date data is essential.

- The **Range of Dates** filters, on the other hand, are typically the most efficient as they can make full use of database indexing properties, making queries simpler and faster. It is recommended to use continuous date range filters whenever possible, as they offer flexibility in data exploration without significant performance overhead.

- **Filter actions and parameters**: Leveraging filter actions in Tableau dashboards offers a dynamic and powerful alternative to traditional filters. When users interact with filter actions – by clicking on marks in visualizations, for example – the relevant data updates instantly, creating a seamless and engaging way to explore insights. This method drastically reduces the complexity and number of database queries, as filter actions capitalize on Tableau's efficient caching mechanisms. The result is not just faster data retrieval but a more fluid, interactive experience that keeps users engaged and focused on analysis rather than waiting for data to load. By consolidating multiple filtering operations into a single, intuitive action, dashboards can become more responsive and visually compelling.

  Utilizing **Exclude all values** offers additional performance benefits. By default, this setting excludes all data from the worksheet view when no relevant values are selected, effectively minimizing the data that needs to be processed and rendered when the dashboard is loaded. This can significantly enhance performance, particularly in dashboards with large datasets or complex visualizations.

  Furthermore, using parameters instead of static filters can significantly reduce the query load on the database. Unlike static filters, which generate new queries each time they are updated, parameters typically issue a single query when the workbook opens or when the parameter is changed.

There's more...

It's important to keep in mind that each type of filter has a unique impact on performance. With various levels and options available, each filter type is processed in a specific sequence known as the **Order of Operations** (we look at how to manipulate this processing in more detail in *Chapter 5*). This sequence not only affects how quickly your dashboard processes data, but it also influences the outcome of your calculations.

For instance, filters are typically evaluated in the following order: **Extract Filters**, applied first, limit data volume right from the start, which can significantly speed up processing. **Data Source Filters**, applied next, further reduce the data before it reaches the worksheet. **Context Filters** limit the data that subsequent filters operate on. **Dimension Filters** and **Measure Filters** affect how the data is filtered and aggregated in the worksheet. **Table Calculation Filters** are applied last, impacting only the data displayed in the final visualization (*Figure 4.17*). Familiarizing yourself with the **Order of Operations** is essential, as it allows you to strategically place filters to optimize dashboard performance, minimize processing time, and ensure that your data is accurately represented and calculated.

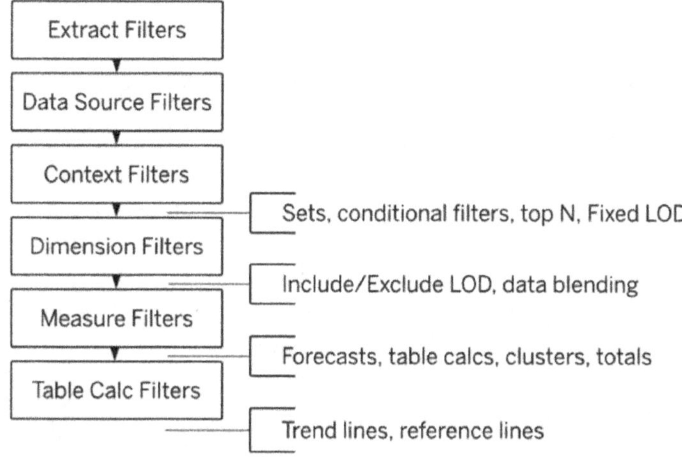

Figure 4.17 – Tableau's Order of Operations defines the sequence in which different filters and calculations are applied to data

See also

- To learn more about Tableau's Order of Operations, see the following: `https://help.tableau.com/current/pro/desktop/en-us/order_of_operations.htm`

- For additional information on how each filter type works, see the following:

  `https://help.tableau.com/current/pro/desktop/en-us/filtering.htm`

Improving calculation efficiency

Calculations in Tableau offer the benefit of unparalleled customization and flexibility, allowing you to tailor analyses to specific business needs. They can be used to create customized metrics and complex data transformations that go beyond predefined options. Calculations can enhance analytical depth and ultimately drive more informed decision-making.

Properly defined calculations can significantly influence the processing time of the underlying queries. Understanding how to apply calculation best practices can help ensure your Tableau dashboards run efficiently and load quickly. This recipe will cover general and specific calculation optimization techniques for improving the performance of parameters, aggregations, and logical calculations.

Getting ready

This recipe requires the `Sample-Superstore` data source, which can be found in the **Saved Data Sources** section under the **Connect** pane of the **Home** page. Additionally, you can use any Tableau workbook of your choice.

How to do it...

Let's look at a few sample calculation examples and syntax, designed to help achieve maximum performance:

- **Use integer values for lists in parameters**: When creating parameters in Tableau, remember that numerical calculations often perform faster than string calculations. So, if you utilize integer values within your parameter settings, it will help speed up the evaluation of the calculation logic. Let's create a parameter control that allows the user to choose a specific measure such as **Sales** or **Profit**. The goal is to define your value as an integer and leverage the **Display As** feature to show the appropriate text labels. So, instead of using `Sales` and `Profit` string values, we can use 1 and 2 integer values for each measure.

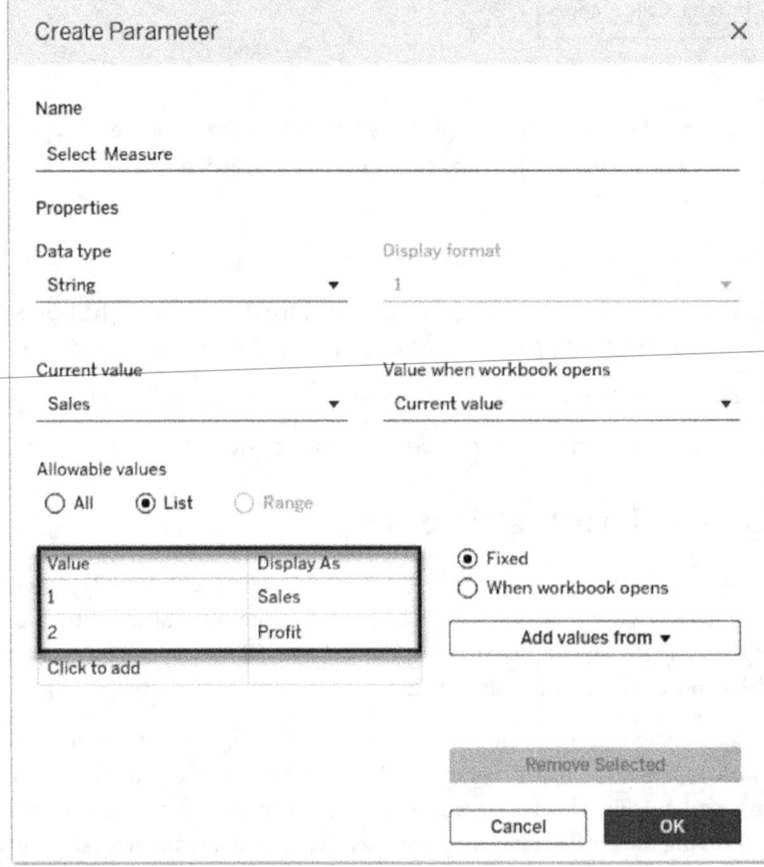

Figure 4.18 – The Display As option can be used to create
user-friendly or descriptive labels for parameter values

- **Define aggregation within calculations**: Logical calculations with undefined aggregation will force Tableau to reference row-level records, which can greatly impact the performance of your calculation. Let's create a calculated field for our `Select Measure` parameter shown in the preceding figure. We will define aggregation directly within our calculated fields to aggregate the records first before performing the logical checks. This will limit the number of records being processed.

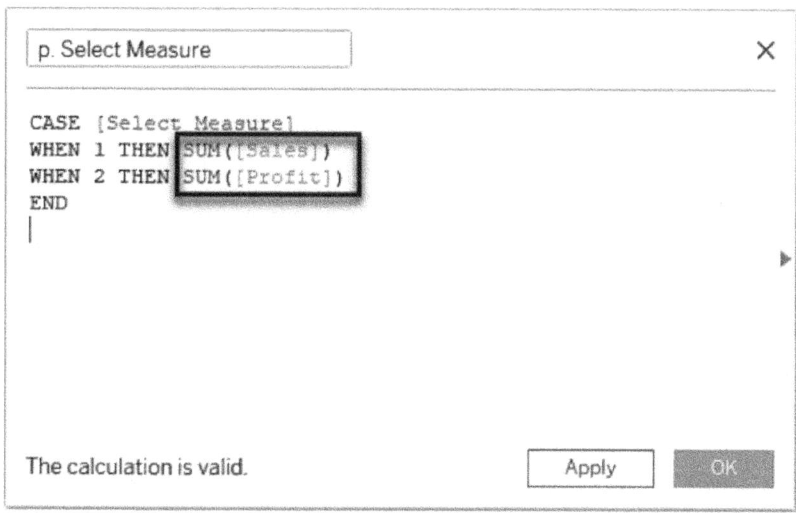

Figure 4.19 – Defining aggregation for each measure within a calculation will result in more efficient performance when evaluating calculation logic

- **Use CASE instead of IF/ELSEIF statements to create logical calculations**: Let's create a calculated field that assigns numeric codes to different regions. We can define the logic of our calculation in several ways, as depicted in *Figure 4.20*. When comparing performance, `CASE` statements will generally perform faster than `IF/ELSEIF` statements, especially with many conditions or complex logic. It's important to mention that the `IF` expression references the `Region` dimension at least three times, in comparison with the `CASE` statement.

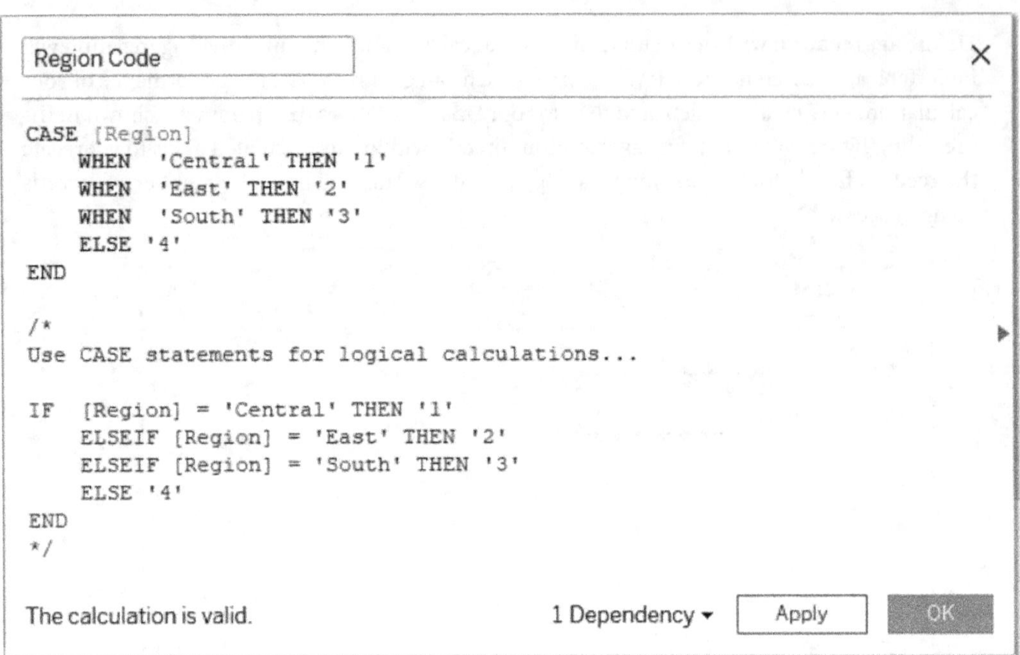

Figure 4.20 – Comparing a CASE statement with IF/ELSEIF logic

If, on the other hand, this expression was referencing a calculated field instead, as seen in *Figure 4.21*, it will most certainly cause degraded query performance, since the calculation will be performed at every reference, creating additional overhead.

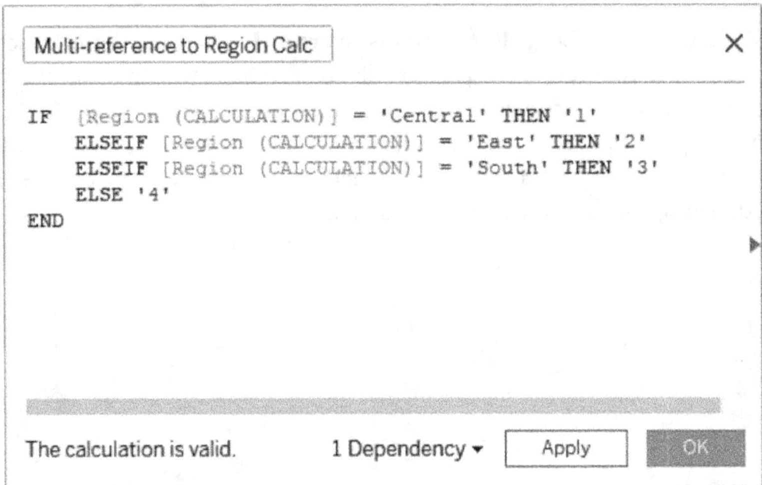

Figure 4.21 – Multi-referencing a calculation within a calculation

as seen here can result in degraded performance

- **Use Boolean logic**: Boolean calculations are the most performance-efficient, compared to numeric or string calculations. The Boolean data type has two outcomes, `True` and `False`, which makes them much faster for Tableau to process. Let's create a simple calculation to answer the following question: `Is Profit greater than 0`? We can apply this logic to evaluate the profitability of a specific branch or product line. If we create a simple Boolean calculation as shown in *Figure 4.22*, instead of creating an `IF` statement, we can significantly improve the calculation performance.

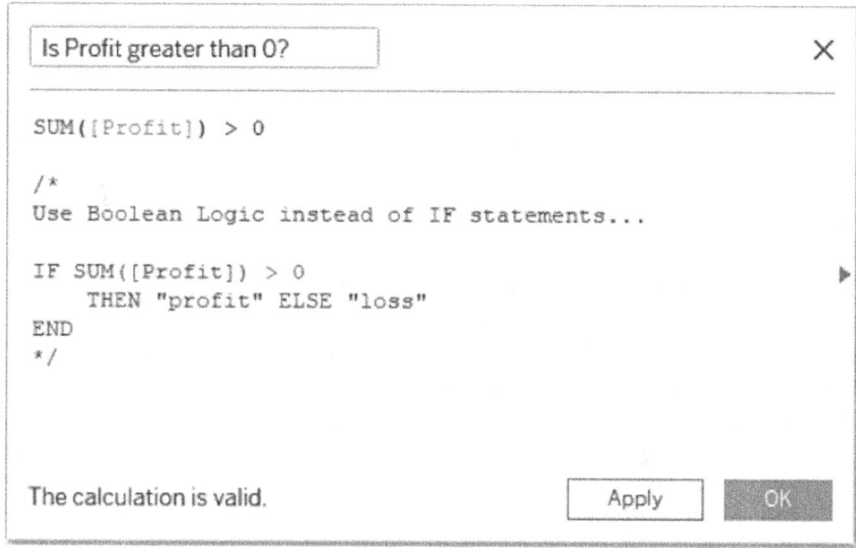

Figure 4.22 – Boolean data types can be used in calculations and filters to simplify logic

- **Test high-frequency matches first**: When Tableau evaluates conditional statements, it terminates processing when the first matching condition is found. To optimize performance, order each condition with the most probable outcomes at the top. This strategy enables Tableau to evaluate high-frequency cases more efficiently, by processing higher record volumes quicker.

Let's create a conditional statement that will classify `Ship Mode` into two categories: `Standard Shipping` and `Priority Shipping`. We'll assume that `Standard Class` is the most common shipping mode. In *Figure 4.23*, we have placed `Standard Class` at the top, since it is the most common shipping mode. This helps Tableau quickly resolve most cases, without having to evaluate the less common conditions first. This logic improves the overall performance of the conditional statement evaluation.

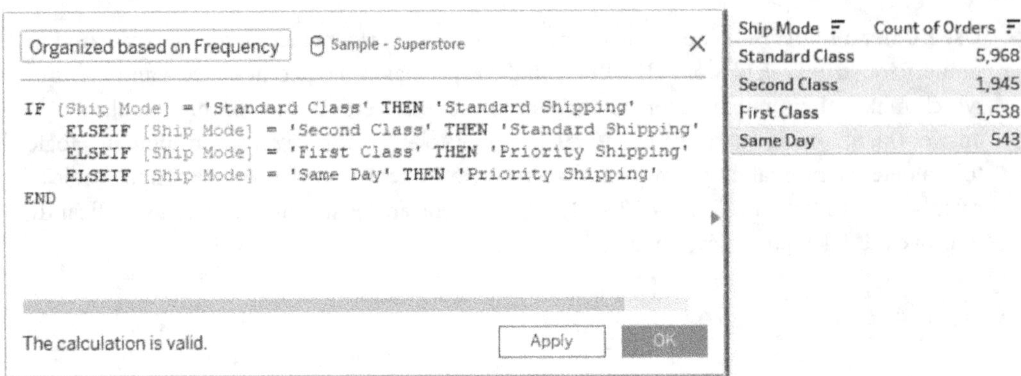

Figure 4.23 – Listing high-frequency matches first allows the query to return results more efficiently

There's more...

It's important to note that, in some instances, better performance can be achieved by precomputing and storing complex calculations in the underlying database. This is especially true for row-level calculations that need to process conditional logic for each record. Calculations that require real-time updates based on user interactions should be handled within Tableau. It is also advisable to limit the use of dynamic calculations such as NOW() and TODAY(), as well as parameter references within your calculations, as they will not be materialized in a Tableau extract due to their changing nature.

Materializing calculations within a Tableau extract is another great strategy that ensures that your calculations are handled efficiently, particularly when the query performance of your extract is slow due to complex calculations. This process involves precomputing and storing calculation results in advance, which allows Tableau to quickly retrieve the values instead of recalculating them on the fly, which reduces the computational load. If you want to materialize calculations created after the initial extract, navigate to the **Data** menu in Tableau Desktop and select **Extract | Compute Calculations Now**. If you're working with a published data extract, you will need to download the extract to your local machine first, open it in Tableau Desktop, and then use the **Compute Calculation Now** option, before republishing it back to the Server.

In some rare instances where you have many nested calculations, the previous method may degrade extract performance instead of improving it. The problem with nested calculations often stems from increased levels of complexity, which are added with each subsequent layer. Multiple layers increase processing demands, particularly when using IF statements or other resource-intensive functions. In most cases, materializing calculations or pushing them upstream will resolve most performance issues related to nesting. Calculations should be carefully categorized based on their frequency and nature to leverage the strengths of both your databases and Tableau. Always evaluate your specific use case to strike a balance and achieve maximum performance.

See also

- Check out the following documentation to learn more about additional guidelines for creating efficient calculations: `https://help.tableau.com/current/pro/desktop/en-us/calculations_calculatedfields_bestpractices.htm`

- There is a great blog post titled *Boolean in Tableau – TRUE or FALSE?* by Andrew Watson at TAR Solutions: `https://tarsolutions.co.uk/blog/tableau-boolean-data-type/#:~:text=%28Note%20in%20some%20software%20True%20is%20represented%20as,Tableau%20performance%20compared%20to%20numeric%20or%20string%20calculations`

- For a handy guide on choosing the right calculation, see the following: `https://www.tableau.com/blog/guide-choosing-right-calculation-your-question-53667?_gl=1%2A189uvki%2A_ga%2AMzc3NDQ2NzMyLjE3MTI5NjY0ODU.%2A_ga_8YLN0SNXVS%2AMTcyMjI5Nzc0My4yNy4xLjE3MjIyOTg2NjUuMC4wLjA.&_ga=2.163397877.836540406.1722297744-377446732.1712966485`

Designing efficient workbooks

Workbook speed in Tableau is closely linked to factors discussed in the previous recipes, such as best practices for calculations, filters, and other performance-enhancing techniques. Each of these elements plays a crucial role in the overall efficiency of a workbook. This section will explore additional workbook-level performance factors that can help ensure your workbooks perform optimally.

Getting ready

This recipe requires the `Superstore` **Sample Workbook**, which can be found in the **Quick Start** section of the **Home** page.

How to do it...

- **Close unnecessary connections**: You should develop the habit of closing unnecessary data source connections within your workbooks if they aren't being used. This practice not only improves performance but also simplifies data management within the workbook. Unused connections can consume system resources and increase load times, impacting the overall responsiveness of the workbook. To close a workbook connection, navigate to the **Data** menu, select the data source, and choose **Close**.

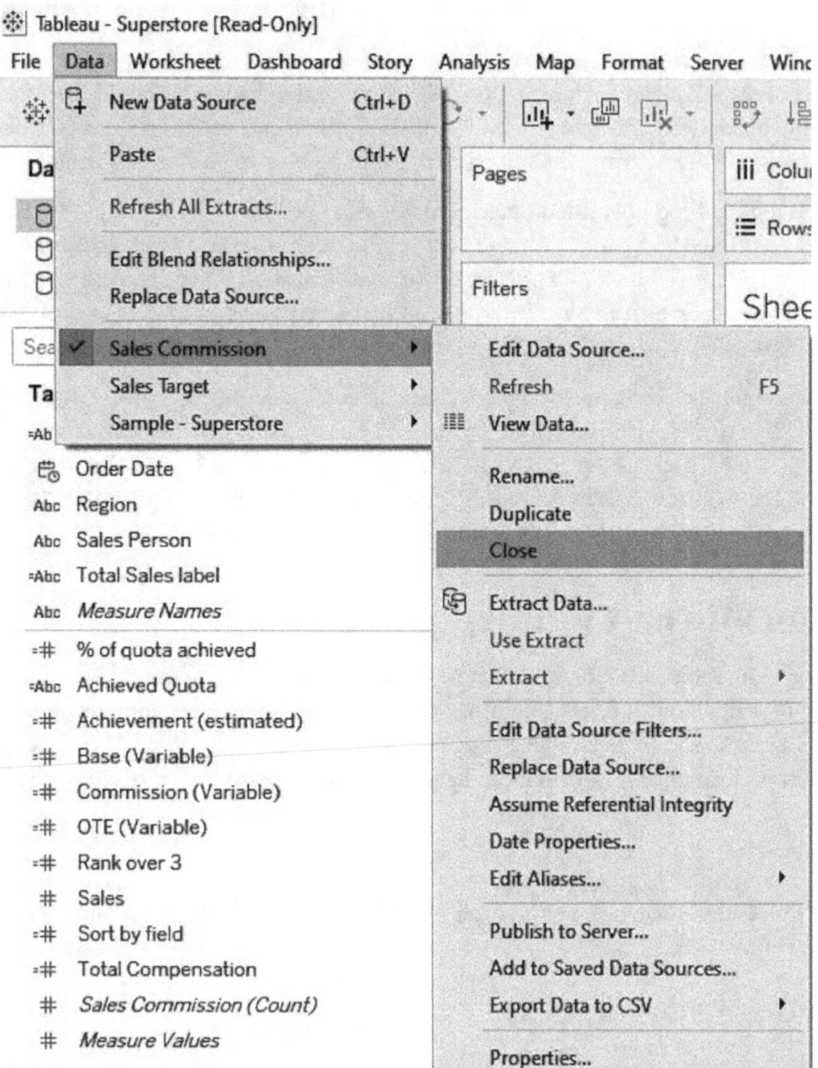

Figure 4.24 – Closing unused data sources helps reduce memory usage and processing overhead

- **Remove unused elements**: Removing unused elements such as calculations, worksheets, and dashboards from a Tableau workbook is important for two reasons. Firstly, it reduces the overall size of the workbook and simplifies the workbook structure, making it easier to manage, share, and load the contents. Secondly, it improves performance by eliminating unnecessary processing and rendering tasks, which can consume additional memory.

- **Hide unused fields**: Hiding unused fields in Tableau offers several performance and usability benefits. It simplifies navigation and management of relevant fields within the **Data** pane. This feature also helps prevent the accidental use of irrelevant data in calculations or visualizations, ensuring that your analysis remains focused and accurate. By hiding fields that are not necessary for your analysis, you can significantly reduce the amount of data Tableau has to process, which leads to improved workbook performance. To hide unused fields within a data source, select **Hide All Unused Fields** from the **Data** pane menu.

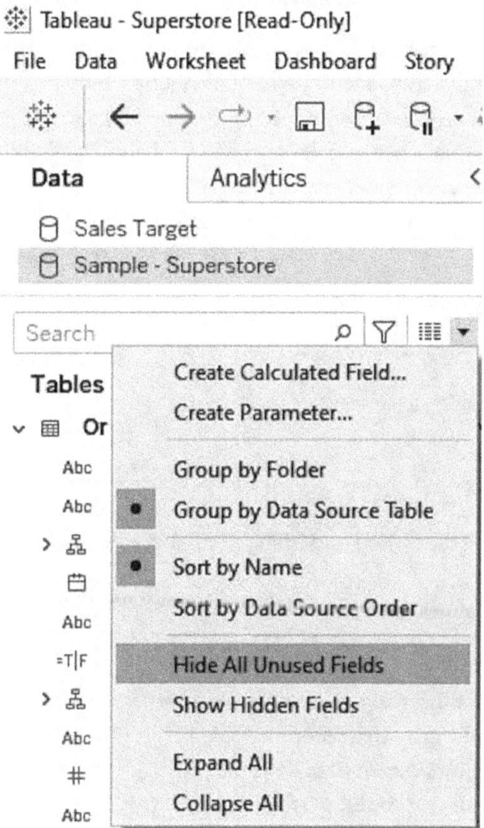

Figure 4.25 – To hide unused fields, Tableau will automatically identify and hide fields not used in the current worksheet

- **Limit the number of views in each dashboard**: Having too many views in a dashboard can lead to longer load times and a sluggish interface. To approach this, focus on consolidating multiple views into fewer, more comprehensive visualizations that convey the necessary information without redundancy. Sometimes, by splitting up your dashboard into multiple more focused dashboards that target a specific aspect of the data, you can reduce complexity and improve performance.

- **Adopt fixed-size dashboards**: Fixed-size dashboards in Tableau offer significant performance advantages by providing a consistent layout that avoids the complexities associated with dynamic resizing. When a dashboard size is fixed, Tableau can generate and store a consistent, optimized layout of the dashboard in its cache. This allows for faster retrieval and display of data, as Tableau can leverage the pre-rendered version rather than recalculating and re-rendering the layout for each user session or screen size. To set your dashboard size to fixed, navigate to the **Size** section on the right-hand side of the **Dashboard** pane, click on the drop-down menu, and select **Fixed size** from the available options.

- **Publish your dashboards tab-free**: When publishing a workbook in Tableau, you can choose to include or exclude tabs. Tabs facilitate easy navigation between views within dashboards. However, you need to be careful when using this option as performance can suffer when showing sheets as tabs; this is because Tableau will load additional information simultaneously. To improve performance, consider using alternative navigation methods such as buttons or URL actions, which can streamline the experience without relying on tabs.

Figure 4.26 – To exclude tabs when publishing a workbook, uncheck Show sheets as tabs

Utilizing the Workbook Optimizer

The **Workbook Optimizer** is a powerful tool that checks whether a workbook follows a list of standard performance best practices and provides recommendations highlighting specific areas that require further action. This feature allows developers to seamlessly identify and fix issues that can improve load times and enhance overall workbook performance. In this recipe, we will demonstrate how to run the Workbook Optimizer from Tableau Desktop.

Getting ready

This recipe requires Tableau Desktop version 2025.1 or higher, and the World Indicators sample workbook, which can be found in the **Quick Start** section of the **Home** page. Alternatively, you can use any Tableau workbook of your choice.

How to do it...

1. In Tableau Desktop, the Optimizer feature can be accessed from the **Server** tab of the menu bar. To run the Optimizer, select **Server** and choose **Run Optimizer**.

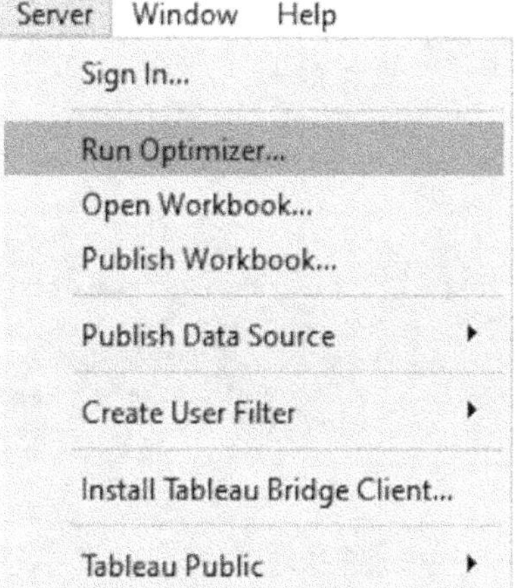

Figure 4.27 – Running the Workbook Optimizer

2. Once your current workbook is evaluated, Tableau will display a report, as shown in *Figure 4.28*. The overall score at the top right will show the total number of items that passed the evaluation. These guidelines are displayed as three unique categories: **Take action**, **Needs review**, and **Passed**.

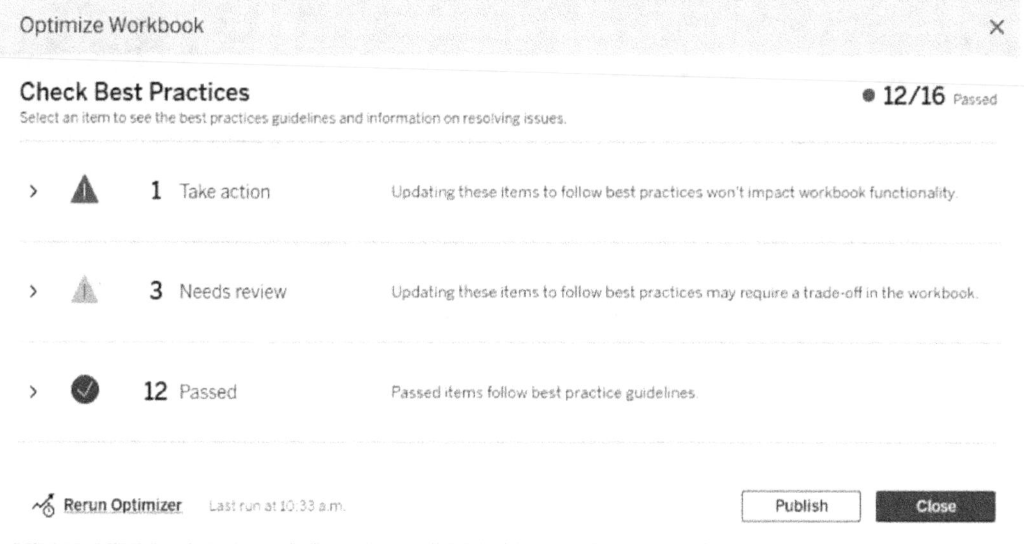

Figure 4.28 – The final output produced after running the Workbook Optimizer

3. Expand each category to further review the guidelines and recommendations. Each guideline will provide additional insights into how specific rules impact workbook performance.

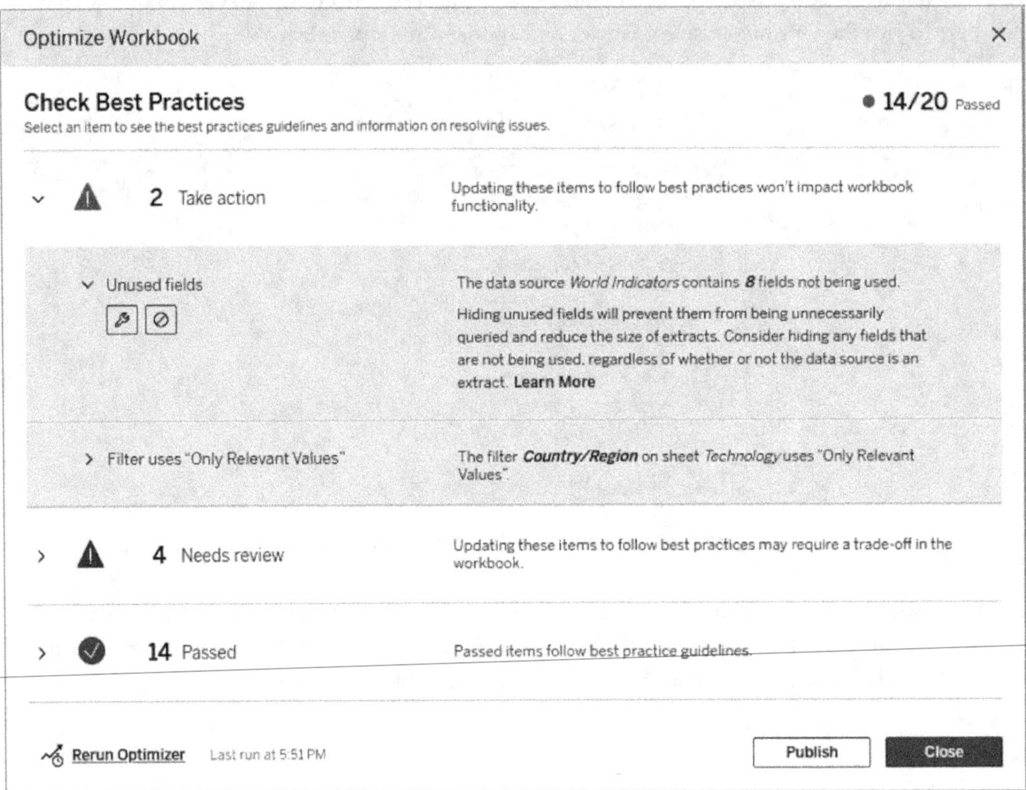

Figure 4.29 – Expanding each category to view the guidelines and recommendations

4. You can choose to address specific recommendations by **auto-fixing** the rules. To auto-fix the rule, click on the **Auto-fix** button in the guidelines section. Once the suggested action runs successfully, the guideline will be placed in the **Passed** section. If **auto-fix** fails to run or the button isn't visible, you will need to address the issue manually.

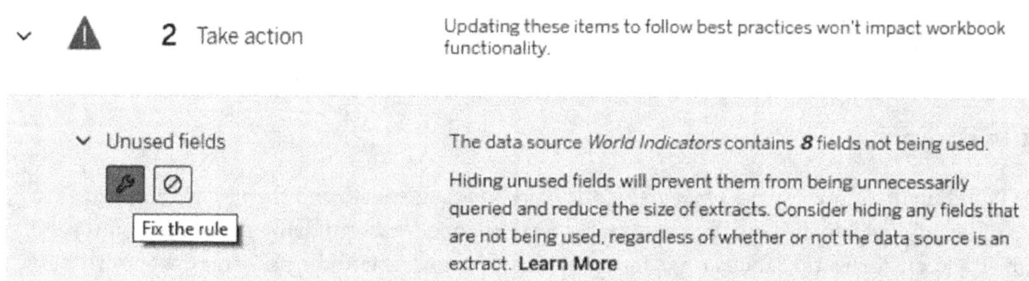

Figure 4.30 – Auto-fixing a suggestion will automatically apply a suggested rule

5. If the rule doesn't apply to your workbook or is not possible to implement with your specific data structure, then you can simply ignore it by selecting the **Ignore this rule** button.

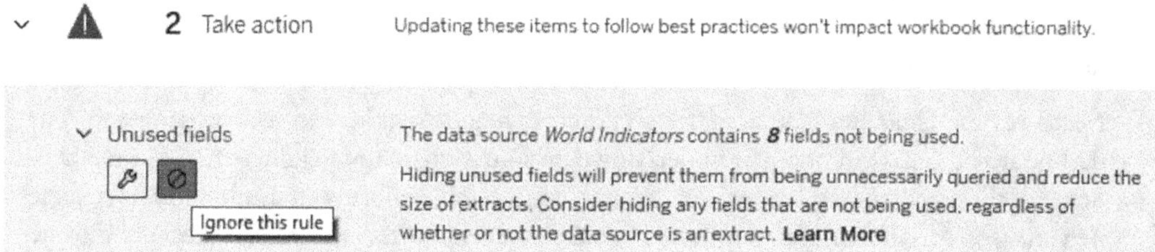

Figure 4.31 – Ignoring a suggestion will remove it from showing up in the recommendations section

6. You can choose to address specific recommendations and rerun the Optimizer, if the suggestions are applicable to your case, or simply ignore the suggestions and proceed to publish the workbook.

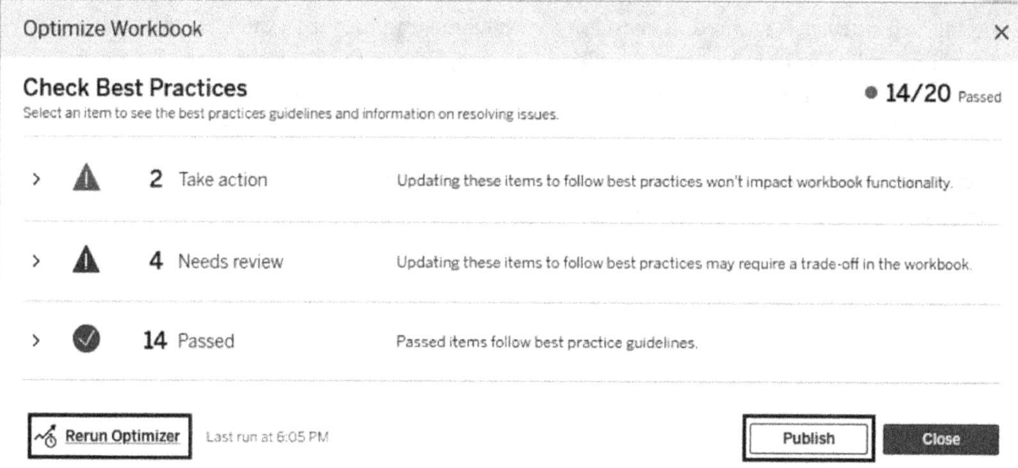

Figure 4.32 – Rerunning the Optimizer or proceeding to publish
your workbook directly from the Optimizer output

7. To close the dialog box and return to your existing workbook, click **Close** in the bottom-right corner of the Optimizer output.

How it works...

The Workbook Optimizer works by parsing the workbook's metadata and then evaluating it against a set of twenty guidelines that affect workbook performance. These guidelines are based on several high-level categories that focus on calculations, data sources, workbooks, and dashboard best practices. The total score breaks down each of these guidelines based on their performance impact and functionality of the workbook: **Take action**, **Needs review**, and **Passed**. You can read a detailed explanation of each guideline in the following list:

- **Take action**: Generally, this section is reserved for best practices that have very minimal impact on workbook functionality, such as hiding used dashboard sheets or unused fields, so it is highly recommended to implement these changes unless, of course, there is a specific need to bypass them.

- **Needs review**: Guidelines found in this section may require making significant changes to your dashboard design, workbook, or underlying data source structure to adhere to best practices. Some of these recommendations will demand considerable effort with minimal performance benefits, so you need to use your best judgment to decide what's practical, especially if some of these choices were made deliberately.

- **Passed/Passed and ignored**: Some suggestions from the workbook optimizer may not be applicable to your situation. For instance, if you're using a live data source connection to monitor incoming patient data in a hospital environment and you need to receive real-time updates, you may want to ignore a guideline notification related to extracting the data source.

  Once a guideline is ignored, it is no longer evaluated and moves to the **Passed and ignored** section of the Optimizer output. It will no longer appear in the **Take action** or **Needs review** sections. To continue evaluating an ignored guideline, you need to find it in the **Passed and ignored** section and click the **Ignore** button again to resume the evaluation.

This section will typically contain all the guidelines that are in line with the best practices, as well as specific ignored guidelines that aren't applicable.

There's more...

It's important to keep in mind that this process has limitations, as many aspects of performance will not be captured by the Workbook Optimizer. If you're facing significant performance bottlenecks, you may want to consider troubleshooting the performance of your workbook using the **Performance Recording** feature discussed in the *Assessing workbook performance* section.

See also

- The full list of guidelines and their descriptions can be found here: `https://help.tableau.com/current/pro/desktop/en-us/wbo_overview.htm`

- For detailed information on how to create performant workbooks, download the following whitepaper: `https://www.tableau.com/learn/whitepapers/designing-efficient-workbooks`

Using View Acceleration

View Acceleration in Tableau advances caching mechanisms to drastically reduce initial load times and enhance dashboard responsiveness for views with long-running queries. At its core, View Acceleration works by generating and storing query results in advance, thereby minimizing the computational load during live user interactions. The primary benefits include improved responsiveness, reduced server load, and smoother experience for end users. In this recipe, we will demonstrate how to leverage this feature to accelerate your views on Tableau Cloud.

Getting ready

The **View Acceleration** feature isn't available in Tableau Desktop. To follow along, you can download a trial version of Tableau Cloud using the following link: `https://www.tableau.com/products/online/thanks-dl`.

How to do it...

1. You can turn on **View Acceleration** for specific views or accelerate all existing views within a workbook. To enable **View Acceleration** for all views, navigate to the `Superstore` sample workbook and choose **More Options...** | **Acceleration** | **On**.

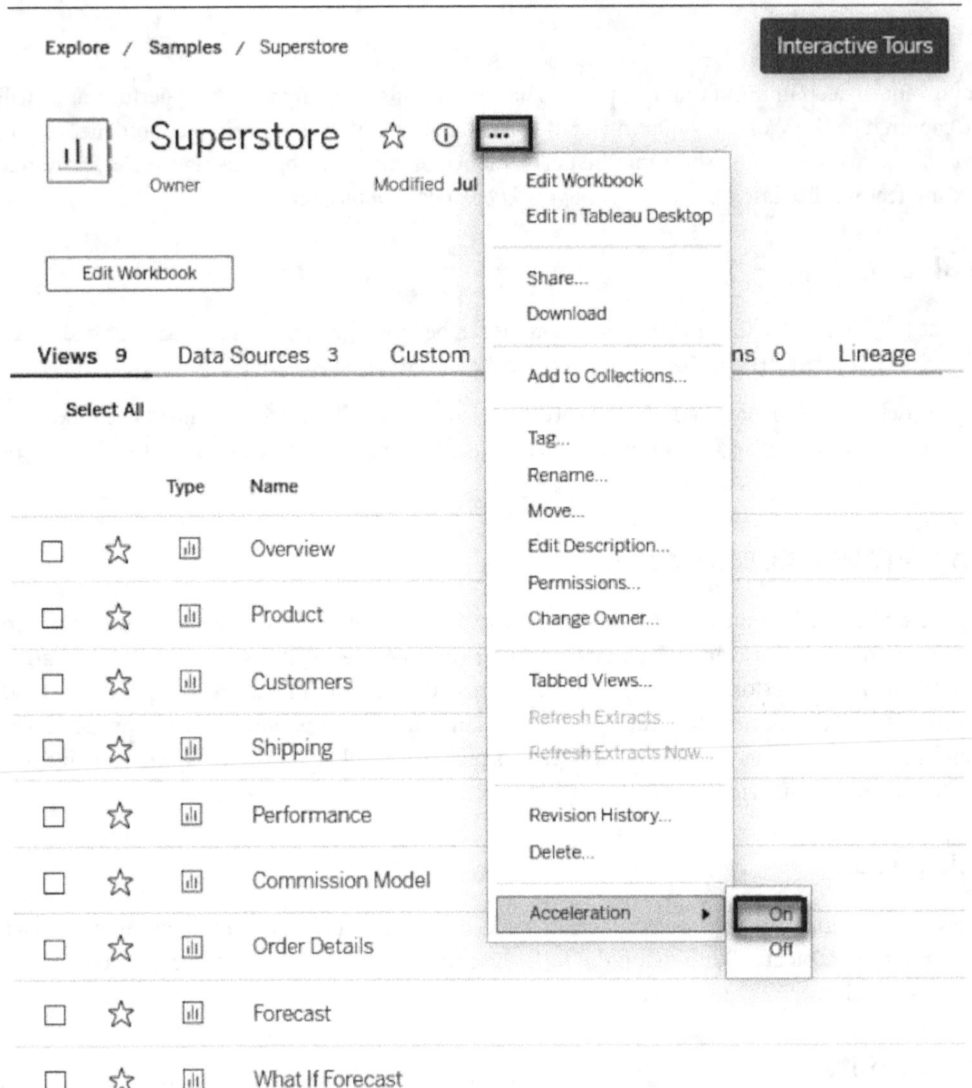

Figure 4.33 – Turning on View Acceleration for all views within the Superstore workbook

2. To accelerate a specific view, select the desired view, click on **Actions**, and choose **Acceleration | On** from the workbook page. Additionally, you can also enable View Acceleration by choosing **More Options…** for a preferred view and selecting **Acceleration | On** (as shown in *Figure 4.33*). If your view is open in **Edit** mode, you can use the **Accelerate** icon to switch on **View Acceleration**.

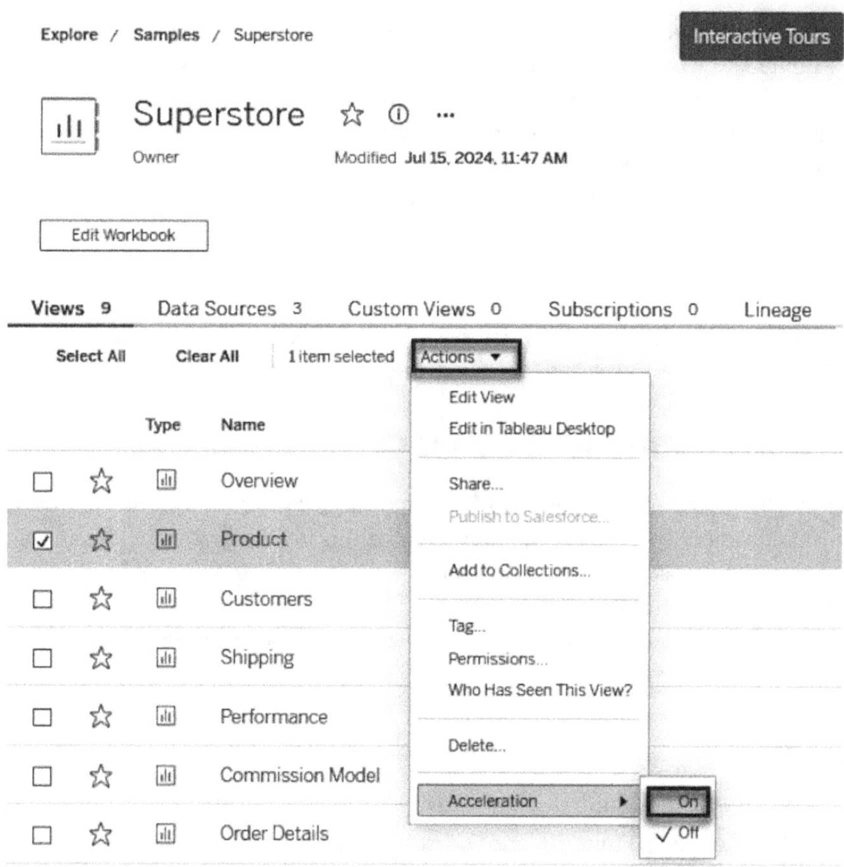

Figure 4.34 – Accelerating a specific view within a dashboard – for example, Product

How it works...

Tableau administrators with *Creator* or *Explorer* licenses can enable or completely disable **View Acceleration** for their organization's site, directly from the **View Acceleration** section in the **Settings** menu. If **View Acceleration** is enabled, Tableau will recommend accelerating specific views based on usage patterns and performance metrics. The process begins with Tableau monitoring the interaction history of all views, identifying those that are frequently accessed and exhibit slower load times. Using these insights, Tableau suggests which views would benefit most from acceleration.

Users can also flag specific views for acceleration. Once a view is flagged, administrators and workbook owners are alerted to these recommendations within the Tableau interface. It's important to remember that if your views are loading slowly for reasons other than querying, this option wouldn't be effective in improving the workbook's performance.

Disabling **View Acceleration** on the server can be beneficial when real-time data is critical, server resources are limited, or when testing and debugging performance. For instance, in environments where dashboards and reports are highly dynamic and frequently updated, maintaining cached views could add unnecessary complexity. In this case, disabling **View Acceleration** ensures that each view reflects the latest dataset without the system managing cached versions. The decision will often depend on your specific use case, with a focus on balancing data freshness with system performance.

See also

For more information on how to manage accelerated workbooks, check out the following link: `https://help.tableau.com/current/online/en-gb/data_acceleration.htm`.

Assessing workbook performance

In this section, we'll introduce you to Tableau's **Performance Recorder**, a powerful tool that captures detailed information about specific user actions, highlighting areas that may be causing slow load times or inefficient data processing. Understanding how to use this tool is crucial for any Tableau user aiming to create fast and responsive visualizations. By leveraging the insights provided by the Performance Recorder, you can identify and address the root cause of poor performance, so you can focus your optimization efforts toward high-impact areas.

Getting ready

This recipe requires Tableau Desktop version `2025.1` or higher, and the `World Indicators` sample workbook, which can be found in the **Quick Start** section of the **Home** page. Alternatively, you can use any Tableau workbook of your choice.

How to do it...

To implement this recipe, open a sample workbook and follow these steps:

1. In Tableau Desktop, the **Performance Recording** feature can be accessed from the **Help** tab of the menu bar. To start the performance recorder, select **Help | Settings and Performance** and choose **Start Performance Recording**.

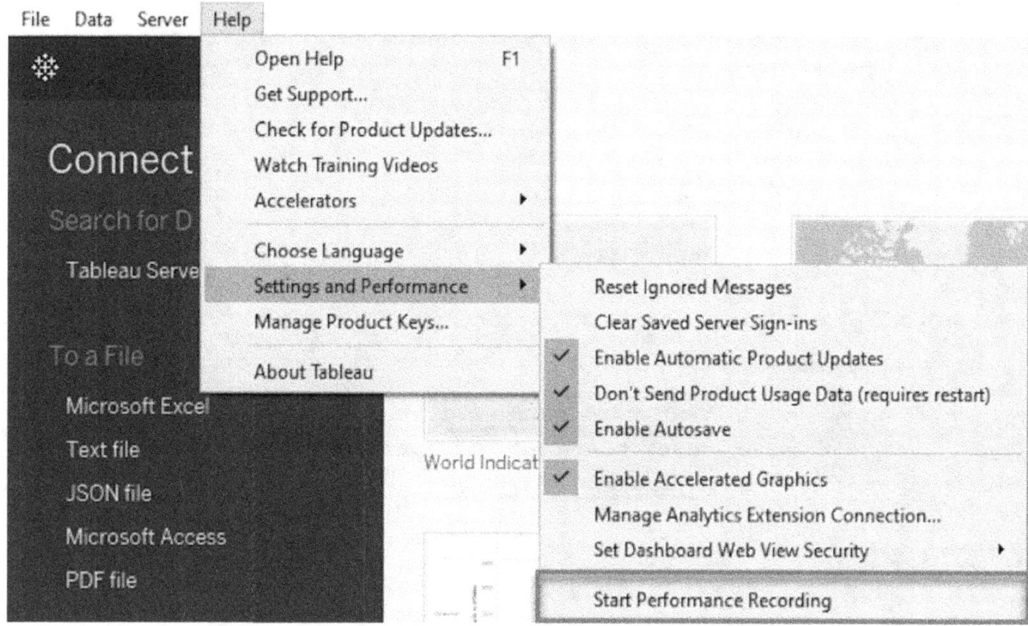

Figure 4.35 – How to run the performance recorder

2. To stop the **Performance Recording** session, you can navigate back to the **Help** menu and
    select **Settings and Performance | Stop Performance Recording**.

3. Once the session has ended, Tableau will automatically generate the output in the form of a
    Tableau dashboard, as seen in *Figure 4.36*, which can then be used to diagnose type-specific
    performance issues.

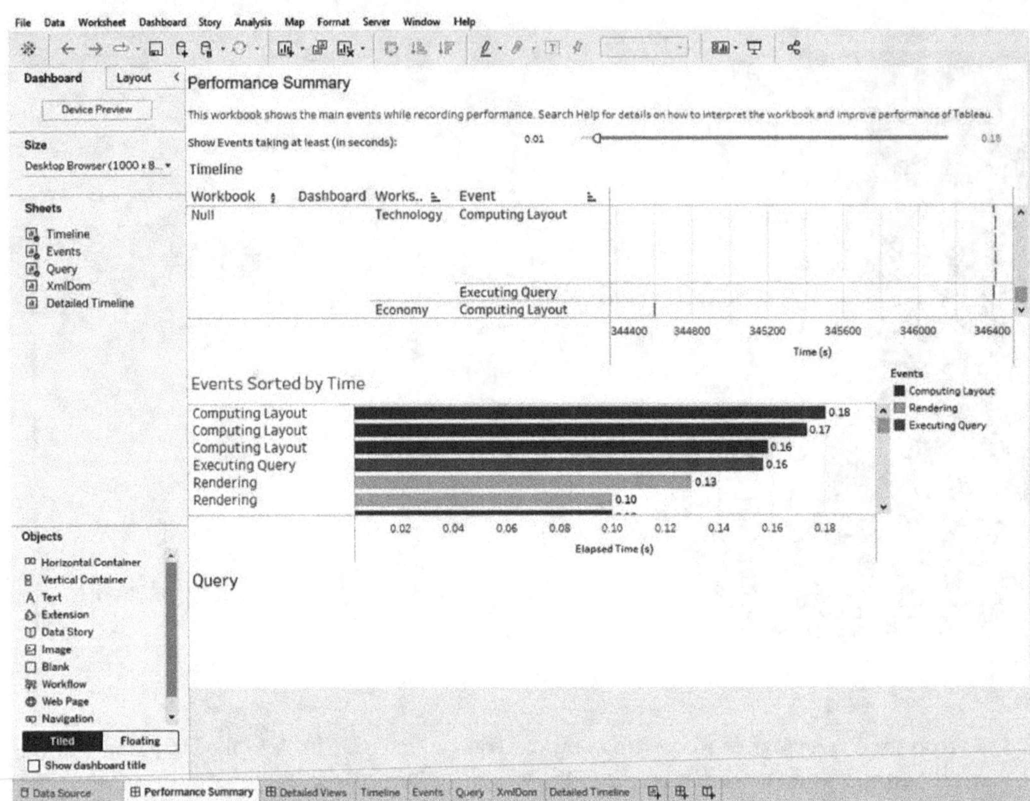

Figure 4.36 – Performance Summary dashboard

4.   To save the **Performance Recording** output, choose **File | Save**.

How it works...

The **Performance Recording** workbook includes two main dashboards: **Performance Summary** and **Detailed Views**. The **Performance Summary** dashboard provides a quick overview of the most time-consuming events, and **Detailed Views** contains a more granular view of the high-level information displayed in the **Performance Summary** dashboard. Let's examine various elements of the **Performance Summary** dashboard.

Performance Summary is broken down into three main sections: **Timeline, Events,** and **Query**. The **Timeline** section at the top shows all the events that happened during the recording – an event can be thought of as a unit of work required to carry out a specific action such as applying a filter or loading a view. All the events are listed from left to right in the order in which they were carried out by the user. The **Event** column describes what each event is, and the last column shows how much time was required to execute each event in seconds and how it lines up with other events. The **Workbook, Dashboard,** and **Worksheet** columns provide additional context for where the event was executed.

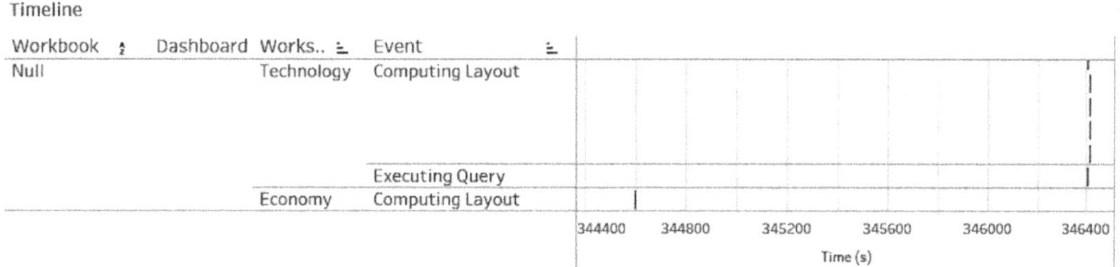

Figure 4.37 – Performance Summary and its elements – Timeline

The next section of **Performance Summary** displays different types of events sorted by their duration in seconds, from the longest events at the top to the shortest events at the bottom. Each event is color-coded to help you visually differentiate the nature of the event type. This section will give you a good idea of where to start; you want to begin by cutting down events with the longest durations.

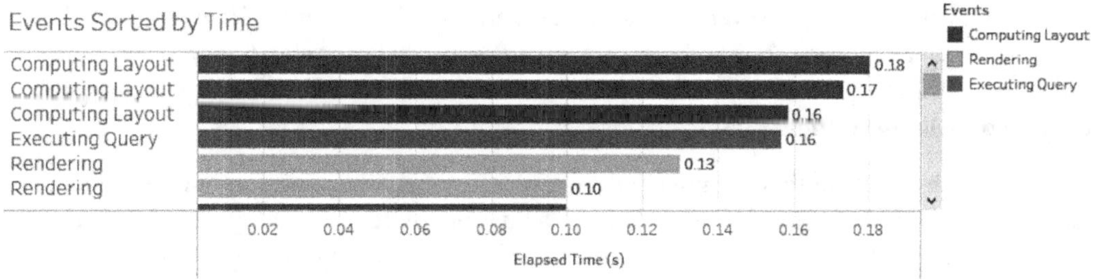

Figure 4.38 – Performance Summary and its elements – Events Sorted by Time

The **Query** section at the bottom of the **Performance Summary** dashboard can be used to display specific query text of the **Executing Query** event. This information can be used to further optimize your queries in the underlying data source. To display the **Query** text, select the **Executing Query** event in the **Timeline** or **Events** section.

```
Query

SELECT "Orders"."Category" AS "Category",
 SUM("Orders"."Profit") AS "TEMP(Calculation_740560695314231303)(1796823176)(0)",
 SUM("Orders"."Sales") AS "TEMP(Calculation_740560695314231303)(3018240649)(0)"
FROM "TableauTemp"."Orders$" "Orders"
WHERE ("Orders"."State/Province" = 'Wyoming')
GROUP BY 1
```

Figure 4.39 – Performance Summary and its elements – Query

There's more...

There are several other tools that Tableau developers and administrators can use when they need to evaluate and improve Tableau server performance under different levels of user load. One such open-source tool is TabJolt, which works by executing a series of automated user actions such as loading dashboards, applying filters, and interacting with views while measuring response times, resource utilization, and potential bottlenecks. It is particularly useful in scenarios where real-world performance testing is required before deploying dashboards to a large audience. This helps identify whether the server can handle the expected load and if optimizations are needed before going live. It's worth noting that TabJolt runs independently of Tableau Server and does not introduce additional load on the server during testing. However, it does have limitations-TabJolt is not officially supported by Tableau, meaning organizations must rely on community resources for troubleshooting and setup. It also requires technical expertise to configure, as it operates via command-line execution and requires scripting knowledge to customize test scenarios.

Wiiisdom for Tableau is another commercially available automated testing solution that extends beyond performance testing to include dashboard validation, regression testing, data consistency checks, and security audits. It offers a user-friendly, no-code interface and supports both Tableau Server and Tableau Cloud, making it a more comprehensive choice for organizations that need end-to-end Tableau governance and quality assurance. While TabJolt is useful for evaluating server load under heavy usage, Wiiisdom for Tableau provides a broader set of features for ensuring dashboard accuracy, stability, and performance in production environments.

Here's a table comparing TabJolt, Wiiisdom for Tableau, and Tableau Performance Recorder based on their capabilities, use cases, and limitations.

Feature	TabJolt	Wiiisdom for Tableau	Tableau Performance Recorder
Primary Purpose	Load testing and stress testing Tableau Server	Automated testing, governance, and performance monitoring	Analyzing query execution and rendering performance for dashboards
Performance Testing	☑ Yes (load testing with simulated users)	☑ Yes (load testing + dashboard validation)	☑ Yes (measures query execution and load time)
Security & Governance Audits	✗ No	☑ Yes	✗ No
Data Accuracy Checks	✗ No	☑ Yes	✗ No
Automation	✗ No	☑ Yes	✗ No
User Interface	✗ No (Command-line tool)	☑ Yes (No-code UI)	✗ No (Built into Tableau Desktop)
Compatibility with Tableau Cloud	✗ No	☑ Yes	☑ Yes
Works with Tableau Server	☑ Yes	☑ Yes	☑ Yes
Works with Tableau Desktop	✗ No	☑ Yes	☑ Yes
Setup Complexity	⚠ Requires installation, scripting, and a separate server	☑ Easy setup with UI-based workflows	☑ Simple (built into Tableau Desktop)
Ideal Use Case	Simulating high user traffic to test server performance	Comprehensive testing for dashboards, performance, data consistency, and security	Troubleshooting slow dashboard performance
Best for	Tableau Server admins testing scalability	Organizations needing full Tableau quality assurance	Developers debugging dashboard performance

See also

To learn more about specific event types, see the following documentation: `https://help.tableau.com/current/pro/desktop/en-us/perf_record_create_desktop.htm`.

For more information on getting started with TabJolt, refer to the following resources:`https://www.tableau.com/blog/introducing-tabjolt-point-and-run-load-testing-solution-tableau-server-38604`

To learn more about Wiiisdom for Tableau, visit the official webpage: `https://wiiisdom.com/`

Join our community on Discord

Join our community's Discord space for discussions with the authors and other readers:

`https://packt.link/ds`

5

Mastering Advanced Calculations to Answer Complex Business Questions

Calculated fields in Tableau are the key to unlocking the true potential of your data. They enable you to move beyond simple data points, crafting personalized solutions that directly address your business challenges. Whether you're designing custom metrics, implementing advanced logic, or refining data for deeper insights, calculated fields offer the flexibility to tailor your analysis to your exact needs, driving more informed and strategic decision-making.

This chapter isn't just about formulas and syntax-it's about understanding the logic that powers Tableau and how to manipulate it to your advantage. By understanding how to implement **Table Calculations**, **Level of Detail (LOD) Expressions**, and Tableau's **Order of Operations**, you will unlock the tools needed to build accurate, dynamic, and high-performing dashboards. The hands-on techniques and strategies presented here will empower you to handle complex data scenarios and maximize the impact of your Tableau visualizations in real-world applications.

In this chapter, we'll be covering the following recipes:

- Understanding Tableau's Calculation Framework
- Explore Table Calculation uses and learn to optimize their scope
- Create advanced table calculations
- Implement LOD Expressions
- Working with and creating advanced LOD expressions
- Manipulate Processing using Tableau's Order of Operations

Technical requirements

The following are required to complete the recipes in this chapter:

- Tableau Desktop version `2025.1` or higher
- Tableau Cloud version `2025.1` or higher

You can download a free 14-day trial if you don't have a licensed version of Tableau Desktop/Cloud from:

- Tableau Desktop: `https://www.tableau.com/support/releases`
- Tableau Cloud: `https://www.tableau.com/products/cloud-bi`

Understanding Tableau's Calculation Framework

Tableau offers three distinct types of calculations to empower data analysis: **basic expressions**, **table calculations**, and **LOD expressions**. Basic expressions perform row-level or aggregated calculations using simple arithmetic or logic, transforming data at its source or within the visualization. Table calculations, on the other hand, operate solely on the aggregated results in the view, allowing for comparative analyses like rankings and moving averages. LOD expressions go beyond these capabilities by enabling calculations at a custom level of detail, either independent of or adjusted to the granularity of the visualization. This recipe will review each calculation type, highlighting their unique applications and best use cases.

How it works...

- **Basic Expressions**: Basic expressions are created in Tableau using the calculation editor, which allows you to compute your values using Tableau's calculation syntax and functions. These calculations can range from simple arithmetic operations, such as calculating profit margins, to more advanced string manipulations or logical comparisons and classifications.

  Basic expressions can be applied at two distinct levels: *row* and *aggregate*, which is based on the level of detail of the visualization. **Row-level calculations** operate on individual rows of data in the original data source. These calculations are computed before any aggregation occurs. For example, consider the following expression, which calculates the discount amount for each order:

  This calculation is applied to each transaction, multiplying the sales amount by the corresponding discount value for that specific row, or in this case for each order individually. For instance, if an order has sales equal to `16.45` and a discount of `0.20`, the **Discount Amount** will be `3.29` (*Figure 5.1*). Row-level calculations are ideal for deriving metrics at the transaction level, or for transforming or cleaning raw data.

Abc	#	#	#	≠#
Orders	Orders	Orders	Orders	Orders
Order ID	**Quantity**	**Discount**	**Sales**	**Discount Amount**
US-2021-103800	2	0.200000	16.45	3.29
US-2021-112326	2	0.800000	3.54	2.83
US-2021-112326	3	0.200000	11.78	2.36
US-2021-112326	3	0.200000	272.74	54.55
US-2021-141817	3	0.200000	19.54	3.91

Figure 5.1 – Determining the discount amount for each order using a row-level calculation

Aggregate calculations, on the other hand, operate on data that has been grouped and summarized. These calculations are performed after aggregation and are dependent on the structure of the visualization. For instance, the following calculation computes the **Profit Ratio** and performs a check for each item to see if the aggregate **Profit Ratio** is less than five percent for each dimension in the view, in this case its by **Sub-Category** (*Figure 5.2*).

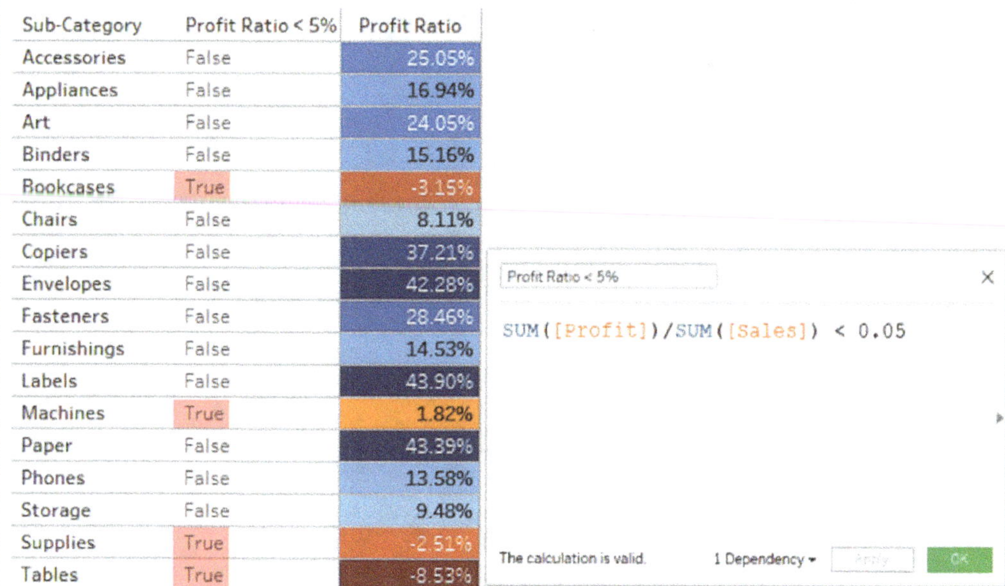

Figure 5.2 – Applying an aggregate calculation based on the current view's level of detail

Aggregate calculations are commonly used for summarizing data at higher levels or performing computations on aggregated metrics such as calculating percent of total.

It's important to remember that row-level calculations occur before aggregation, while aggregate calculations happen afterward, once each metric has been aggregated to the level of detail of the visualization. The outputs also differ, with row-level calculations producing one result per row and aggregate calculations producing one result per group.

Basic expressions can be reused across multiple sheets and dashboards, making them highly adaptable. Furthermore, they can be referenced in subsequent calculations, allowing users to build complex logic incrementally.

- **Table Calculations**: Table Calculations in Tableau are uniquely suited for comparing data points within the context of visualization. Unlike basic or LOD calculations, which operate on the data source level, table calculations dynamically adjust to the dimensions and structure of the view. This capability allows users to gain insights by examining relationships, trends, and differences directly within their charts and tables.

At a high level, table calculations can be applied in two ways, predefined table calculations, which are also known as **quick table calculations** and **custom table calculations**. Quick table calculations provide ready-to-use options for common scenarios, such as **Running Total**, **Rank** and others (*Figure 5.3*). Alternatively, you can write your own table calculation formulas inside the calculation editor using LOOKUP, WINDOW or INDEX functions for more tailored requirements.

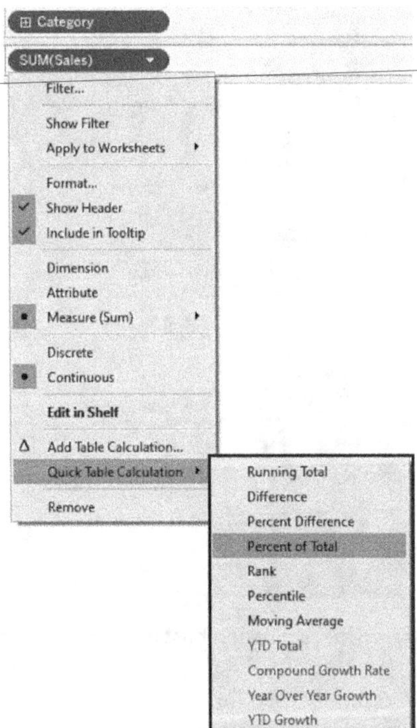

Figure 5.3 – Using a quick table calculation with built-in functions

It's important to remember that Table calculations are inherently tied to the structure of your visualization. Adding or removing dimensions, changing sorting orders, or altering the scope can significantly impact the insights drawn from these comparisons. This flexibility makes table calculations indispensable for interactive and exploratory data analysis, where dynamic adjustments are critical.

Finally, quick table calculations that are applied within worksheets are not stored as standalone fields in the data source or workbook. They exist only within the context of visualization, where they are computed. However, they can be reused across multiple sheets or dashboards if duplicated or recreated using the calculation editor (*Figure 5.4*).

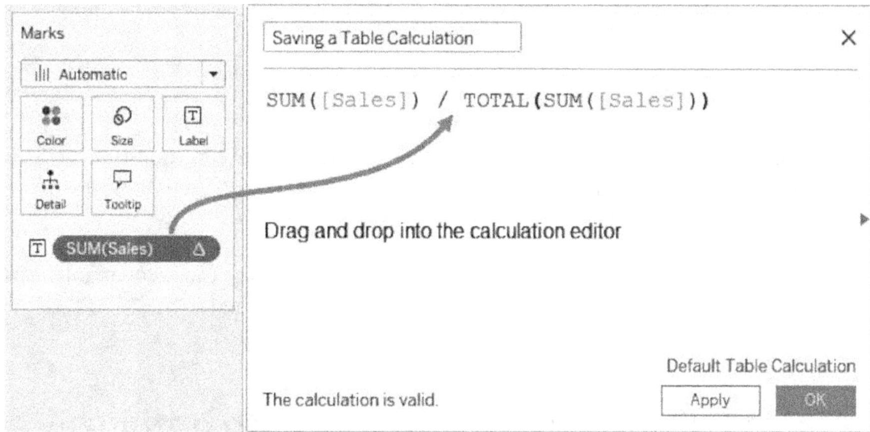

Figure 5.4 – Converting a quick table calculation into a reusable field

- **Level of Detail Expressions**: LODs provide a way to control the granularity of calculations independently from the structure of the view. This unparallel flexibility allows precise control and customization when you need to calculate metrics across specific dimensions or compare aggregated data at varying levels of detail. They can accommodate scenarios where you need calculations at levels different from the visualization's structure. They particularly stand out in scenarios where maintaining consistency across various views or working with multi-granular datasets is critical.

LODs are created in Tableau's calculation editor using one of three keywords: **FIXED, INCLUDE,** or **EXCLUDE**. These keywords define the scope of the calculation. The `FIXED` keyword allows users to calculate a value at a fixed level of detail, independent of the dimensions in the view. The `INCLUDE` keyword ensures that additional dimensions are included in the calculation's context, while the `EXCLUDE` keyword removes specified dimensions from the calculation's context. For example, to calculate the average sales per customer across all regions, the following FIXED expression can be used: `{FIXED [Customer ID] : AVG([SALES]) }`. After creating the expression, it can be used like any other calculated field. This means they can be reused across multiple visualizations and referenced in other calculations, offering flexibility and consistency in analysis.

It's important to keep in mind that LODs can increase query complexity, especially with large datasets or if used in nested calculations. Unlike table calculations, LOD expressions are static and do not adapt dynamically to filters unless explicitly accounted for inside the expression.

When deciding whether to use level of detail expressions, table calculations, or basic expressions, specific guidelines can help. LOD expressions should be chosen for calculations requiring specific granularity, complex aggregations or date calculations containing partial data. On the other hand, table calculations are better for dynamic contexts and metrics that compare relationships within the view, such as ranking or running totals. The distinction is essential because choosing the appropriate calculation type ensures both accuracy and efficiency. When combined with other calculation types, they form a robust toolkit for extracting actionable insights from data.

See also

- Here is a handy guide to help you choose the right calculation for your question: `https://www.tableau.com/blog/guide-choosing-right-calculation-your-question-53667`

- For an overview of the different types of calculations in Tableau, see the following: `https://help.tableau.com/current/pro/desktop/en-us/calculations_calculatedfields_understand_types.htm`

Explore Table Calculation uses and learn to optimize their scope

Table calculations in Tableau are dynamic, powerful tools that adapt to the structure of your visualizations, enabling advanced analytical capabilities. We'll delve into the technical underpinnings of table calculations, focusing on partitioning and addressing - fundamental concepts that dictate how Tableau organizes and computes data across your view. By understanding and controlling these mechanisms, you can tailor calculations to answer complex business questions with precision.

Getting ready

This recipe uses the `Sample-Superstore` dataset, which can be accessed in a new workbook from the **Data Connection** pane of the **Home Page** under the **Saved Data Sources** section.

How to do it...

Suppose your organization wants to analyze changes in regional sales performance over the past four years, with a particular focus on identifying each region's yearly rankings. This analysis will provide valuable insights into how competitive dynamics have shifted over time. For instance, has the historically strong West region maintained its top position, or has another region, like the South or East, taken the lead? Similarly, are there regions that consistently rank lower and struggle to improve their performance?

For this scenario, we'll be creating a bump chart that visualizes changes in regional rankings over time, this will allow us to focus on relative performance trends without using absolute sales figures, making it easier for stakeholders to grasp insights at a glance.

1. Let's begin by placing **Region** on the **Rows** shelf and **Order Date** on the **Columns** shelf. Drag **Sales** to text and then apply a quick table calculation to calculate the ranks in each year. Right-click on **Sales** and select **Add Table Calculation**. Set the **Calculation Type** to **Rank** in **Descending** order (*Figure 5.5*). We'll use the **Competition** rank type. Various options displayed under **Competition** define how Tableau assigns ranks to values that are tied. The choice between these methods will depend on how you want to handle ties and whether preserving the gap in ranks will add clarity to your analysis.

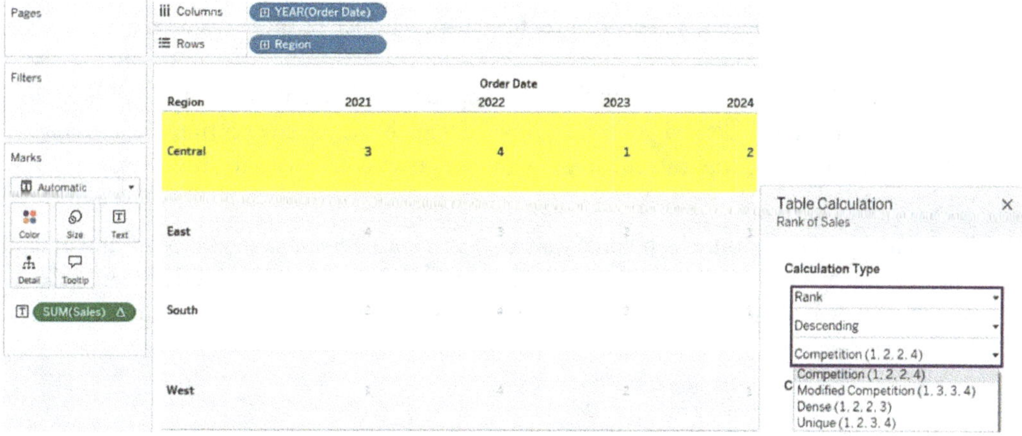

Figure 5.5 – Applying a table calculation to rank regional sales over time

2. The current setup assigns ranks by the year within each **Region**. However, we want to assign ranks by **Region** for each year. To achieve this, first select **Specific Dimensions** in the **Compute Using** section, then uncheck the **Year of Order Date** and select **Region** (*Figure 5.6*).

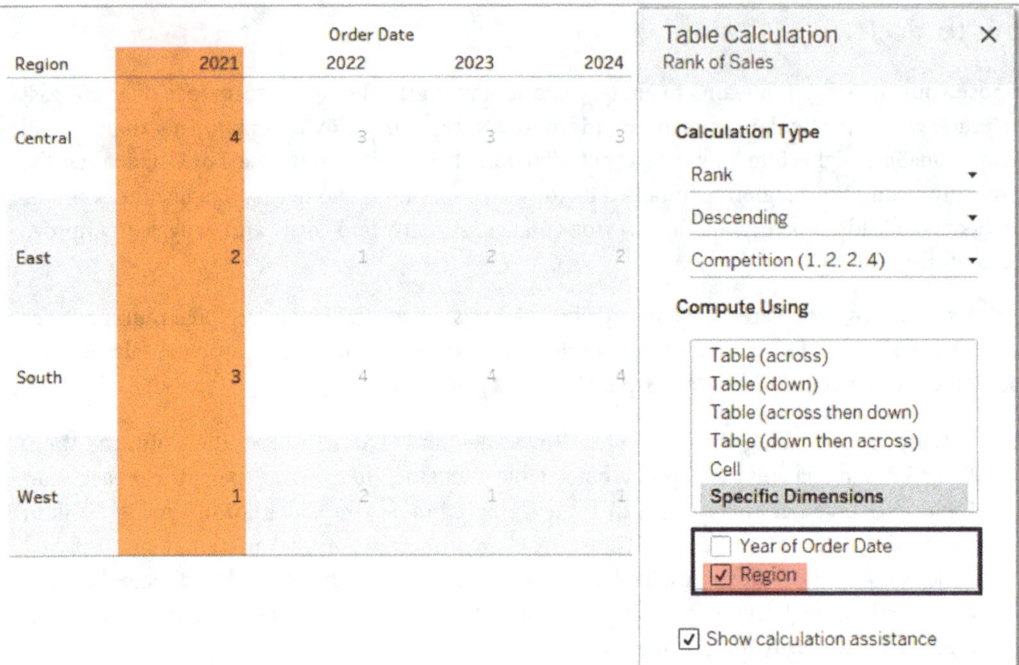

Figure 5.6 – Setting the scope and direction of the table calculation by specific dimensions

3. After setting the scope and direction for the computation, drag **Sales** from the text field to **Rows** to visualize the ranks and observe how each region has changed over time. To add color coding for each region, duplicate the **Region** dimension and place it on the **Color** shelf in the **Marks card**.

4. Duplicate the **Sales** measure by holding down the *Ctrl* key (*Command* key on Mac) and drag it next to the original pill on the **Rows** shelf. In the **Marks card**, select the duplicate **Sales** measure, change the mark type to **Circle**, and adjust the **Size** shelf to set the circles to the desired size (*Figure 5.7*).

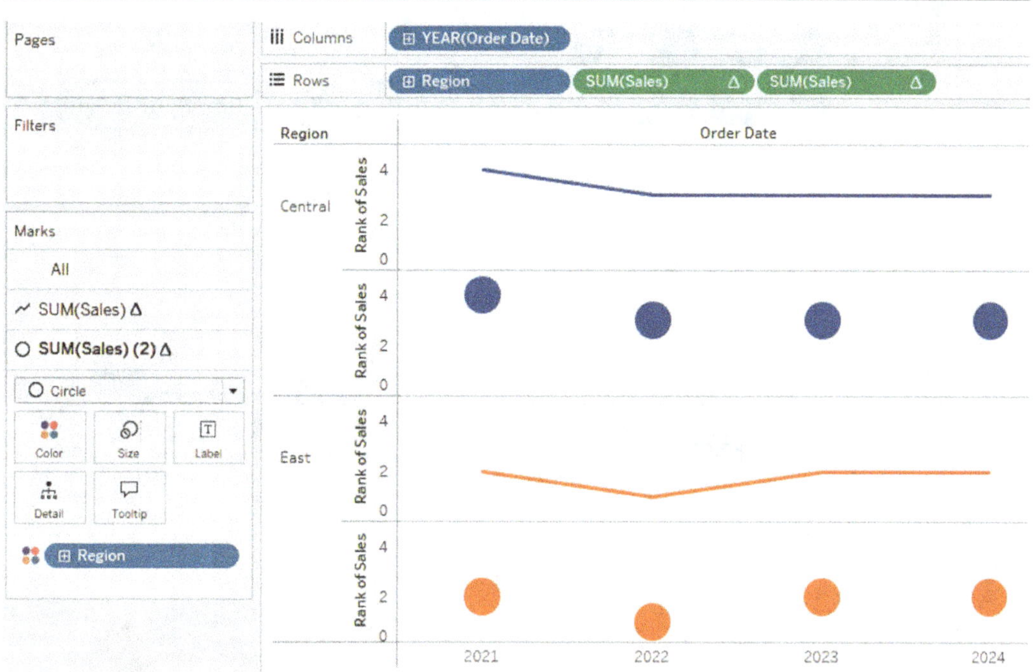

Figure 5.7 – Replicating the table calculation and assigning a different mark type configuration

5. Right-click on the duplicated **Sales** measure on the **Rows** shelf and merge the two charts by selecting the **Dual Axis** option. Ensure the axes are synchronized to align both metrics in the same view. To display the best ranks at the top, right-click on the rank axis, choose **Edit Axis**, and select **Reversed** under the scale options as shown in *Figure 5.8*.

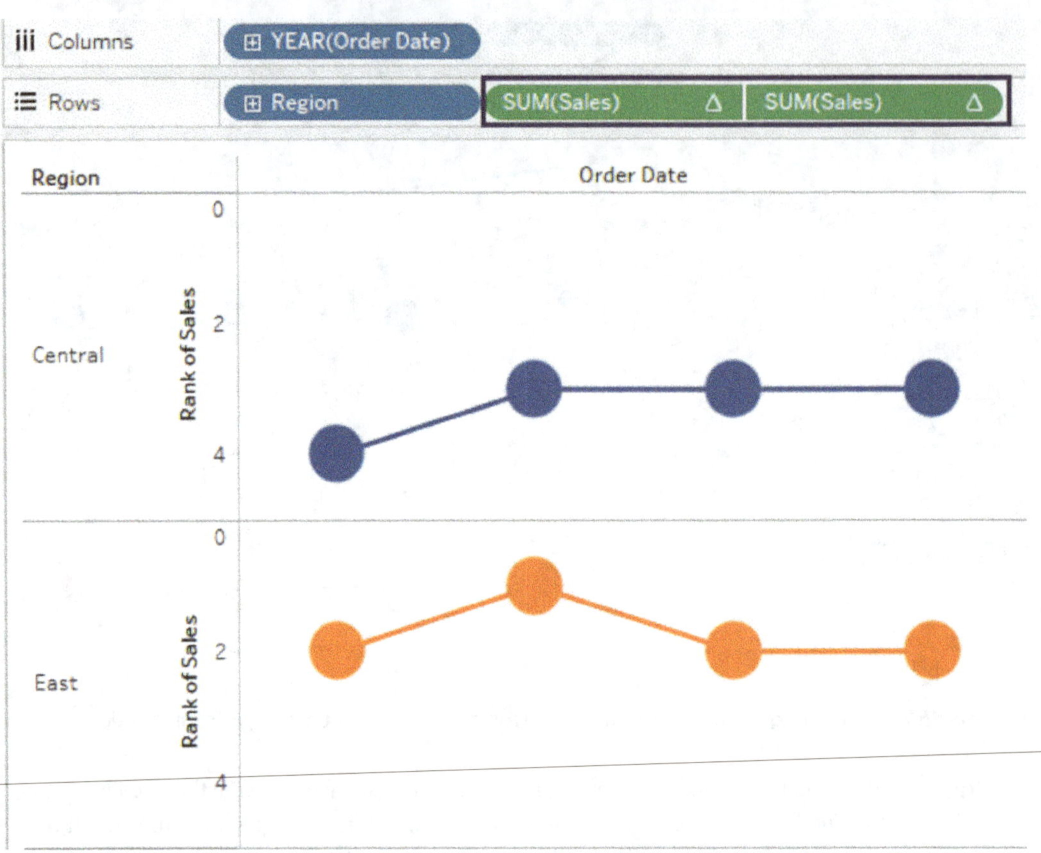

Figure 5.8 – Reversing the rank axis to display the best ranks at the top

6. To format the final bump chart, enable mark labels for the **Sales** (copy) in the **Marks card** and align the rank labels in the middle. Remove the axis headers by right-clicking on the rank axis and unchecking **Show Header**.

7. Remove the **Region** dimension from the **Rows** shelf to display a single line for each region over time (*Figure 5.9*).

Figure 5.9 – Excluding the region dimension from the rows shelf
to display a single line for each region by year

There's more...

In the **Table Calculation** window under **Compute Using | Specific Dimensions**, the fields you select define the **addressing dimensions**, while the unchecked fields act as the **partitioning dimensions**.

Partitioning defines the groups or so-called partitions that Tableau creates in the dataset to compute the table calculation independently for each group. For instance, if you partition by **Region**, Tableau treats each region as a separate group and calculates the table computation within each.

Addressing, on the other hand, specifies the direction of the calculation within each partition, such as computing across rows, columns, or a combination of both. For example, if addressing is set to **Month**, Tableau computes values sequentially across months within each region. These settings are crucial for ensuring that the calculation aligns with the intended analysis, whether you're computing running totals, rankings, or percent differences. Customizing partitioning and addressing allows you to tailor the computation to different scenarios, such as comparing metrics within categories or over specific time periods.

When using **Quick Table Calculations** in Tableau, the scope and direction of the computation can be adjusted directly within the visualization, making it easy to refine how the calculation is applied. After adding a quick table calculation such as rank or percent difference, you can set the scope and direction by selecting **Compute Using** options in the dropdown menu when right-clicking on the measure used for table calculation. Here, Tableau provides several options to define how the calculation will be applied to the current view:

- **Table (Across)**: The calculation moves horizontally across the rows of the table.

- **Table (Down)**: The calculation moves vertically down the columns of the table.

- **Table (Across then Down)** or **Table (Down then Across)**: The calculation follows a nested direction, completing one dimension before moving to the next.

- **Specific Dimensions**: Allows precise customization by specifying addressing and partitioning dimensions discussed above.

These settings control both the **scope** (which dimensions define partitions) and the **direction** (the flow of calculations within those partitions).

See also

- For a comprehensive guide on working with table calculations, refer to the following Tableau documentation: `https://help.tableau.com/current/pro/desktop/en-us/calculations_tablecalculations.htm`

- To explore different table calculation types, uses and examples, see the following: `https://help.tableau.com/current/pro/desktop/en-us/calculations_tablecalculations_definebasic_runningtotal.htm`

- For guidance on applying quick table calculations, see the following: `https://help.tableau.com/current/pro/desktop/en-us/calculations_tablecalculations_quick.htm`

Create advanced table calculations

In this recipe, we provide a deep dive into advanced table calculation techniques that offer greater flexibility and precision in data analysis. We will examine secondary table calculations, which enable the application of multiple calculations within the same view to generate more nuanced insights. Additionally, we will explore custom table calculations using window functions and lookup functions, which allow for the calculation of relative positioning across data sets.

Getting ready

This recipe uses the `Sample-Superstore` dataset, which can be accessed directly from the **Data Connection** pane on the **Home Page** under the **Saved Data Sources** section.

How to do it...

For this scenario, the goal is to gain insights into how each product segment contributes to the overall sales performance over the past year. Specifically, you need to calculate the running total for each segment and then determine the percentage contribution to the total sales, broken down by quarter. This will help identify trends and show the relative impact of each segment on the company's sales throughout the year.

Let's start with our **Secondary Table Calculations**.

1. Create a line chart to display **Segment Sales** for the year 2024, broken down by quarter. Apply a table calculation to compute the running total for each **Segment**. Set the scope to compute using **Order Date** (*Figure 5.10*).

Figure 5.10 – Applying a table calculation to compute the running total by segment

2. Next, let's add a secondary calculation to compute the cumulative percentage of total. Right-click on the **Sales** measure in the **Rows** shelf and select **Edit Table Calculation**. In the **Table Calculation** window, check the box for **Add secondary calculation**. Set the **Secondary Calculation Type** to **Percent of Total**, then choose **Compute Using Specific Dimensions** and ensure that only **Segment** dimension is selected. This will calculate the percentage of total Sales by Segment for each quarter (*Figure 5.11*).

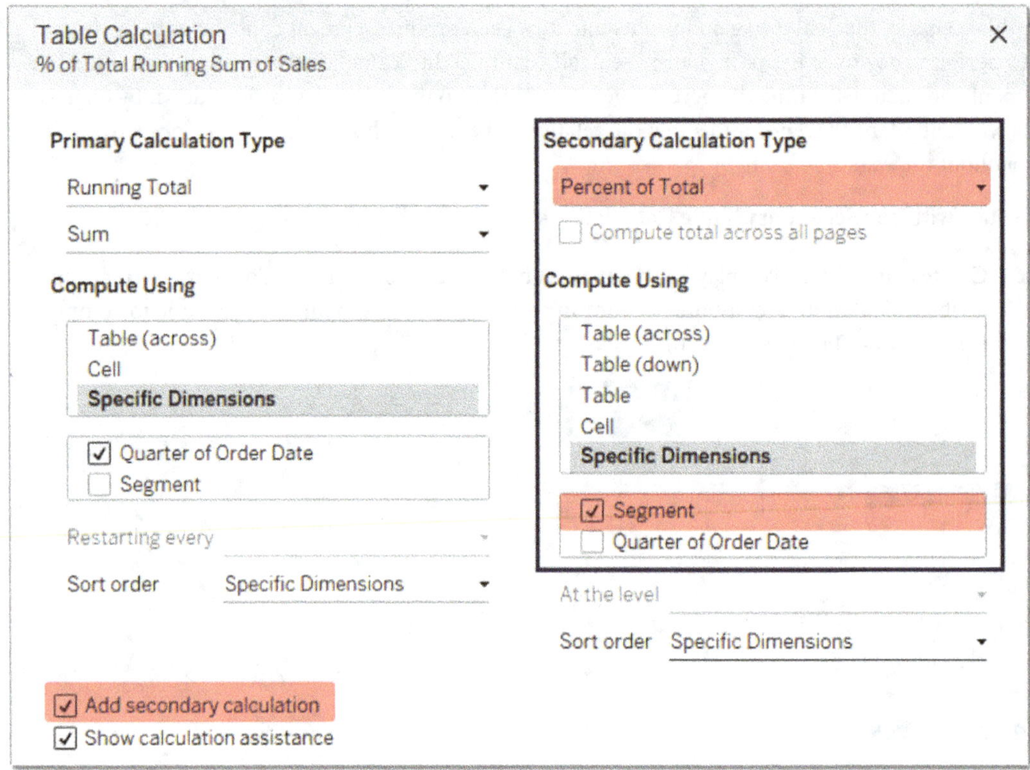

Figure 5.11 – Adding a secondary calculation to calculate the
cumulative percentage of total sales by segment

3. Change the **Mark** type from **Line** to **Bar** to display the total as hundrerd percent and show how it's distributed across segments. This reveals that the **Consumer Segment**, which accounted for 51.4% of total sales at the beginning of the year, saw a decline, contributing only 44.9% by the end of the year. This shift highlights changing trends in segment performance.

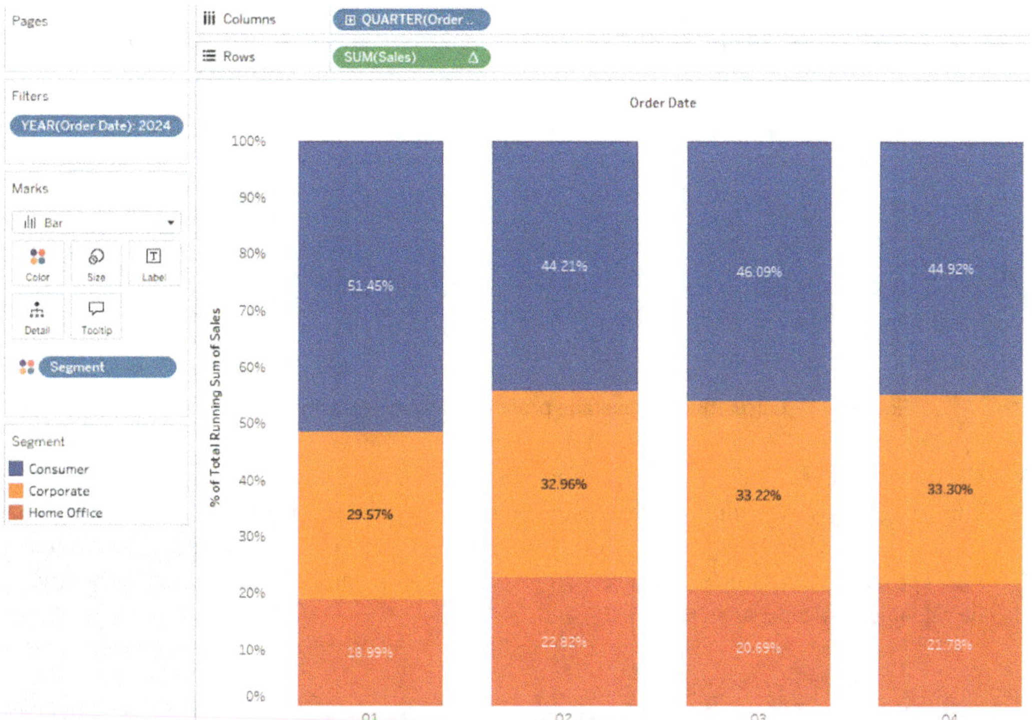

Figure 5.12 – A bar chart displaying the cumulative percentage contribution of total sales by segment

4. Next, we'll look at **Window Functions**.

For our next use case, our task is to determine which states are exceeding or falling short of the average profit of their region. This will help us highlight regional outliers where states either outperform or underperform relative to their peers.

Create a calculated field to calculate the average profit for each state (*Figure 5.13*).

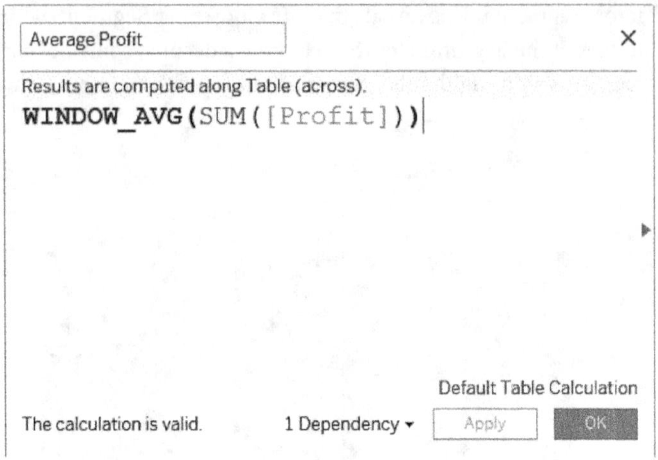

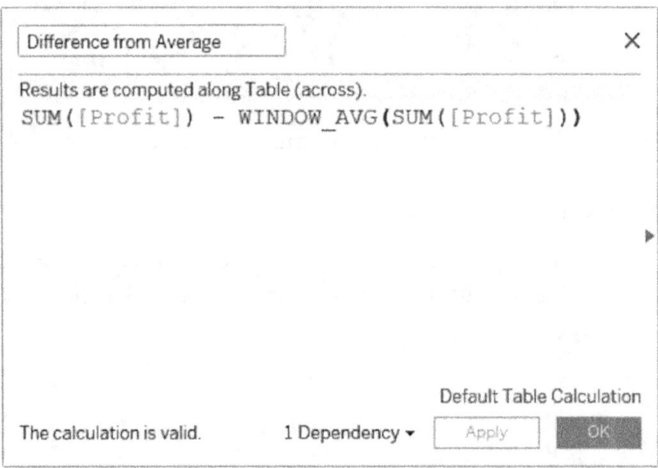

Figure 5.13 – Calculating the average profit by state using a window function

5. Create a calculated field to compare each state's profit to its regional's average (*Figure 5.14*). This will give positive values for states exceeding their regional average and negative values for those below it. Calculating the difference from profit (rather than just classifying whether a state's profit is above or below the average) provides more granularity and context, which can be valuable for deeper analysis.

Figure 5.14 – Determine the variance in profit from the regional average

6.   Create a State map by double clicking on the **State/Province** dimension in the **Data** Pane. Set the mark type to **Map** under **Marks** card and add a dimension filter to exclude **Canada** from the view using **Country/Region** field. To show the difference from regional average by State, place the **Difference from Average** calculation on the **Color** shelf and adjust the scope to compute using **State/Province**. You can modify the color palette to utilize the full range and set 0 as the central point of divergence (*Figure 5.15*).

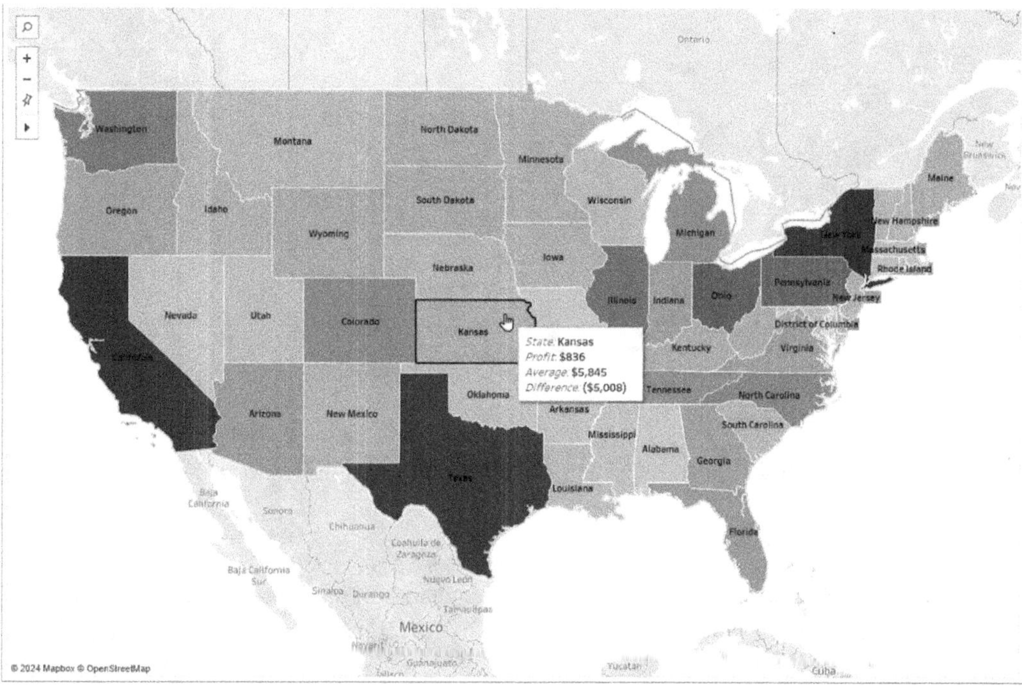

Figure 5.15 – A state map displaying the deviation from the regional average profit

7.   You can enhance the map further, by adding relevant details to the tooltip, as shown in the map image above. Drag additional measures, such as **Profit**, **Average Profit**, and **State/Province**, from the **Data** Pane to the **Tooltip** on the **Marks card** (*Figure 5.16*). Ensure the computation scope for **Average Profit** is set to compute using **State/Province**. Since this is a custom table calculation, always verify the calculation's scope. Format the tooltip text to present the information clearly and effectively.

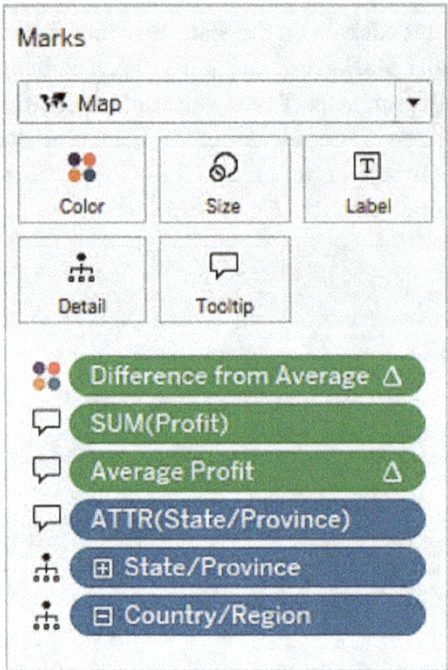

Figure 5.16 – Including extra details in the tooltip under the Marks card

Finally, let's look at **Lookup Functions**.

In this scenario, you'll calculate the quarter-over-quarter change in profit ratio to analyze quarterly trends and monitor profit ratio shifts by region. This will provide valuable market insights, guiding you to take appropriate action.

1. Create a text table displaying the quarterly profit ratio values by region for 2024, as illustrated in *Figure 5.17* below.

Figure 5.17 – A text table showing the quarterly profit ratio values by region for 2024

2. Create a custom table calculation to calculate the profit change from the previous quarter within each region (*Figure 5.18*).

Figure 5.18 – Using the LOOKUP function to retrieve the value from the previous quarter

3. Create a second calculation to categorize values as `Stable` or `Significant decline` if the profit ratio decreases by more than seven percent (*Figure 5.19*).

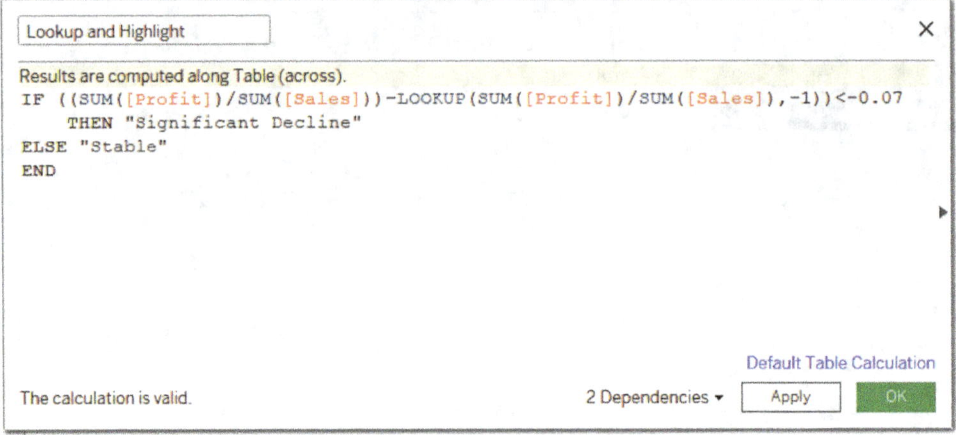

Figure 5.19 – Applying conditional logic to mark values with a significant decline

4. Double-click the **QOQ Change in Profit Ratio** calculation in the **Data** Pane to add it to the text table. Then, edit the calculation by setting the scope to **compute using Specific Dimensions**, ensuring **Quarter of Order Date** is selected, as we want to calculate the quarterly difference within each **Region** (*Figure 5.20*).

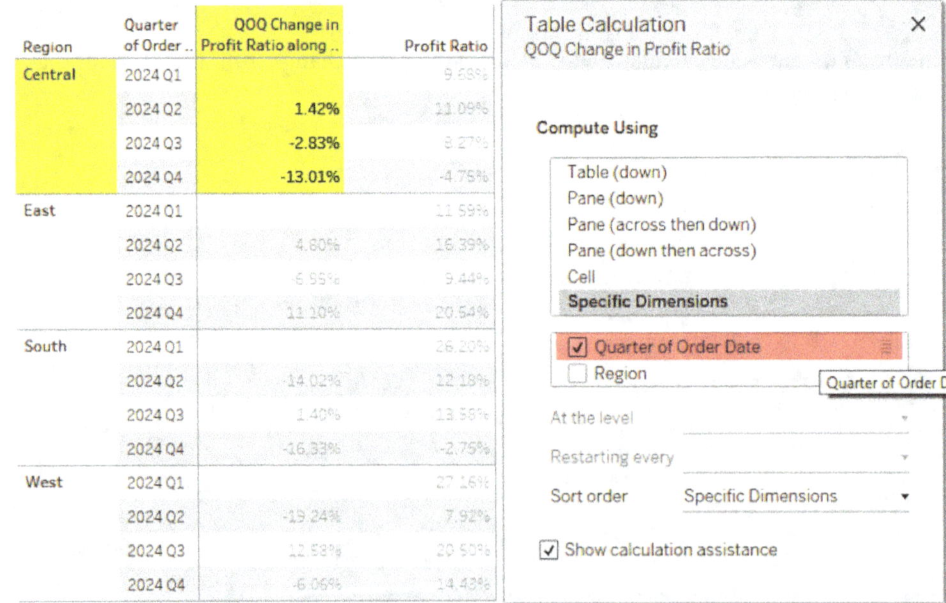

Figure 5.20 – Defining the scope and direction of the table calculation by using specific dimensions

5. To highlight quarters with significant decline, add the **Lookup** and **Highlight** calculation to the **Color** shelf, assigning *red* for significant decline and *grey* for stability and remove the **Profit Ratio** measure from the view. Make sure the scope is applied across the entire table of values (*Figure 5.21*).

Region	Quarter of Order Date	QOQ Change in Profit Ratio along Quarter of Order Date
Central	2024 Q1	
	2024 Q2	1.42%
	2024 Q3	-2.83%
	2024 Q4	**-13.01%**
East	2024 Q1	
	2024 Q2	4.80%
	2024 Q3	-6.95%
	2024 Q4	11.10%
South	2024 Q1	
	2024 Q2	**-14.02%**
	2024 Q3	1.40%
	2024 Q4	**-16.33%**
West	2024 Q1	
	2024 Q2	**-19.24%**
	2024 Q3	12.58%
	2024 Q4	-6.06%

Figure 5.21 – The final report showing quarterly stability in the East region

How it works...

- **Secondary Table Calculations** in Tableau allow you to apply multiple table calculations to the same table structure. These calculations work alongside the primary table calculation, providing an additional layer of analysis. When setting up a secondary table calculation, it's crucial to understand its scope and how it interacts with the primary calculation to ensure accurate results. Secondary calculations enhance flexibility by allowing multiple levels of aggregation and comparison within a single view.

- **Window Functions** enable the calculation of values over a specified range or "window" of data, providing powerful tools for performing calculations across specific records. Window functions consider the order and partitioning of the data to provide accurate calculations, making them ideal for time-series analysis or any scenario where the relationship between consecutive or grouped data points is critical. By using window functions, you can perform complex calculations without altering the underlying data structure. It's important to note that in our earlier example, excluding one of the states from the view would alter the `WINDOW_AVG()` calculation. Since window functions are calculated based on the data points currently present in the view, removing a state would reduce the number of data points considered. This change would directly impact the calculated average and, as a result, affect the difference from average values for the remaining states. Understanding this behavior is crucial when interpreting results, especially when filtering or excluding data from the view.

- **Lookup Functions** are used to retrieve values from a different row in the data set, based on a specified offset or relative position. These functions are particularly useful for calculating relative positioning, such as comparing values between consecutive rows or between different time periods. The `LOOKUP()` function allows you to reference data from a previous or next row in the dataset, enabling the calculation of differences, percentage changes, or shifts in data over time. By using lookup functions, users can create dynamic analyses that adjust automatically to changes in the data context, such as calculating month-over-month growth or comparing a current value to a previous reference point.

Implement LOD expressions

In this section, you will explore the powerful functionality of **Level of Detail** (**LOD**) expressions, a key feature that allows you to perform complex calculations at different granularities within the same view. You will learn about each of the three main types of LOD expressions-Fixed, Include, and Exclude, and explore practical use cases for each. By the end of this section, you will be able to confidently choose the right type of LOD expression for your specific business scenario, understand how each affects the granularity of your calculations, and see the impact of these expressions on the structure of your data. You'll also gain hands-on experience in applying these expressions to solve real-world business challenges.

Getting ready

This recipe uses the `Sample-Superstore` dataset, which can be accessed directly from the **Data Connection** pane on the **Home Page** under the **Saved Data Sources** section.

How to do it...

Let's start with **FIXED LOD**.

Suppose your organization's logistics manager wants to analyze how different ship modes contribute to regional sales and compare these contributions to the total sales for each region. A basic aggregation would fail here because the sales for **Region + Ship Mode** and the sales for the **Region as a whole** require different levels of granularity in the same view.

1. We can use a **FIXED LOD** expression (*Figure 5.22)* to calculate the total sales for each region. This expression ensures that the total sales value is calculated solely based on the region, regardless of the breakdown by ship mode or other dimensions in the view.

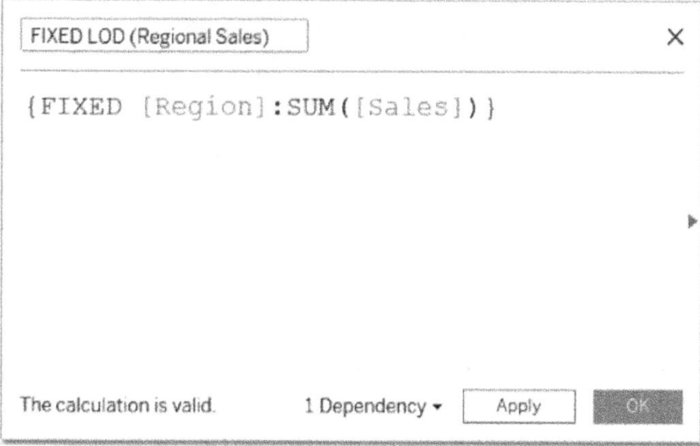

Figure 5.22 – Creating a fixed LOD expression to calculate regional sales

2. Let's create a text table that displays both the sales and FIXED LOD measures as illustrated in *Figure 5.23*. Without the FIXED LOD expression, the total regional sales calculation would be influenced by **Ship Mode** or other dimensions in the view. By fixing the calculation at the **Region** level, the FIXED LOD ensures that the total sales value is consistent and can be used for comparison against the breakdown by ship mode.

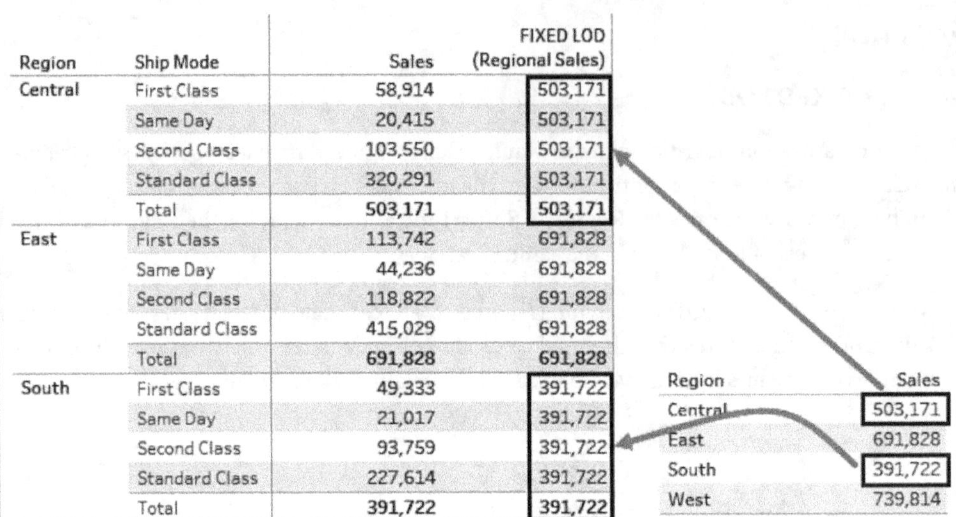

Figure 5.23 – Displaying the results of a fixed LOD that sets the granularity
according to the dimensions defined in the expression

Now, we'll look at **INCLUDE LOD**.

For our next use case, we'll calculate the number of unique orders returned by each customer, even though the customer information is not included in the current view and the current level of detail is set to Region and Ship Mode.

1. We can use an **INCLUDE LOD** expression (*Figure 5.24*) to get a count of unique returned orders for each customer.

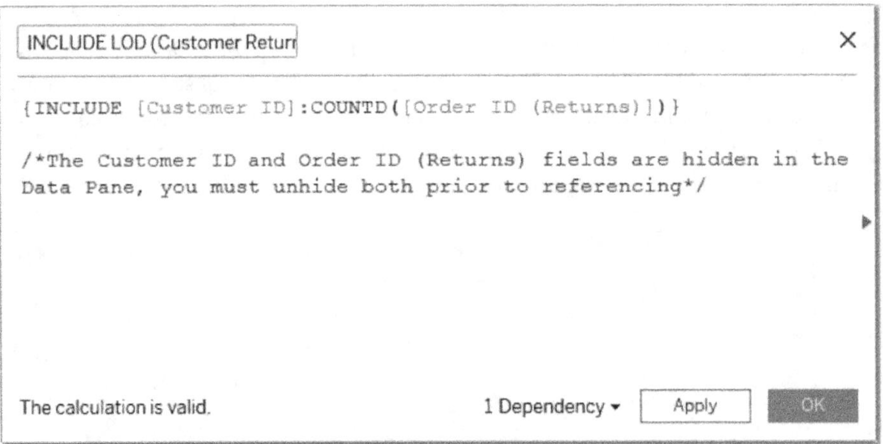

Figure 5.24 – Using an include LOD expression to incorporate customer-
level detail when calculating the number of returned orders

2. Add the new calculation to the previously created text table. This expression ensures that the distinct count of returned orders is calculated at the customer level (by including the **Customer ID** in the calculation) *Figure 5.25*. In this case, simply including the order ID of returned products and taking the unique count would yield the same result because the granularity of the dataset is at the individual order level which implicitly accounts for **Customer ID**, since each row represents an individual order, and each order is associated with a customer.

Region	Ship Mode	Sales	FIXED LOD (Regional Sales)	INCLUDE LOD (Customer Returns)
Central	First Class	58,914	503,171	6
	Same Day	20,415	503,171	6
	Second Class	103,550	503,171	5
	Standard Class	320,291	503,171	22
	Total	503,171	503,171	39
East	First Class	113,742	691,828	7
	Same Day	44,236	691,828	2
	Second Class	118,822	691,828	
	Standard Class	415,029	691,828	
	Total	691,828	691,828	
South	First Class	49,333	391,722	
	Same Day	21,017	391,722	
	Second Class	93,759	391,722	
	Standard Class	227,614	391,722	
	Total	391,722	391,722	
West	First Class	129,762	739,814	
	Same Day	43,604	739,814	
	Second Class	150,541	739,814	

Region	Ship Mode	Customer ID	Order ID (Returns)	Distinct count of Order ID (Returns)
Central	First Class	BM-11650	US-2024-102519	1
		CP-12085	US-2024-144064	1
		LS-17200	US-2024-131618	1
		MM-18280	US-2022-132941	1
		MN-17935	US-2021-123225	1
		TC-20980	US-2021-123498	1
	Same Day	AG-10495	US-2022-111948	1
		JE-15745	US-2022-139731	1
		JH-15910	US-2023-115952	1
		LS-16975	US-2024-108294	1
		NB-18655	US-2024-107825	1
		SC-20800	US-2022-155761	1

Figure 5.25 – Showing the results of an include statement at view's current level of detail

Finally, we'll explore **EXCLUDE LOD**.

Let's consider another scenario where we want to compute the overall sales contribution by **Ship Mode** and **Region**. Essentially, you want to calculate total sales at the country level and exclude the **Ship Mode** and **Region** dimensions from the calculation.

1. We can use an **EXCLUDE LOD** expression to remove **Ship Mode** and **Region** from the calculation, ensuring that total sales are computed only at the **Country** level (*Figure 5.26*).

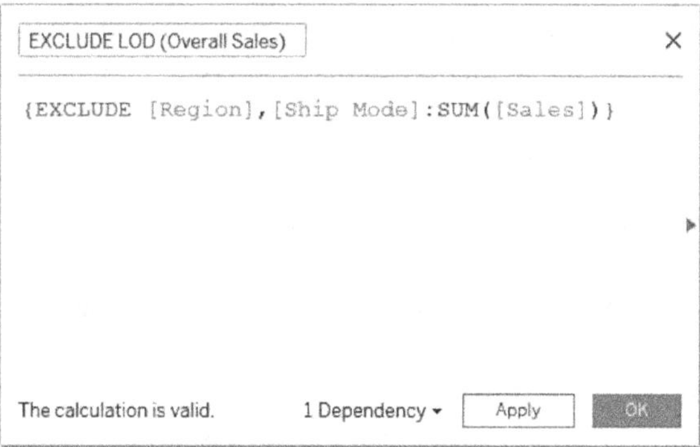

Figure 5.26 – Excluding selected dimensions from the view with an exclude LOD to compute overall sales

2. Drag the calculation into the text table. Now you can see that the EXCLUDE statement ignores the dimensions listed in the expression, while calculating the total sales at the country level.

Region	Ship Mode	Sales	FIXED LOD (Regional Sales)	INCLUDE LOD (Customer Returns)	EXCLUDE LOD (Overall Sales)
Central	First Class	58,914	503,171	6	2,326,534
	Same Day	20,415	503,171	6	2,326,534
	Second Class	103,550	503,171	5	2,326,534
	Standard Class	320,291	503,171	22	2,326,534
	Total	503,171	503,171	39	2,326,534
East	First Class	113,742	691,828	7	2,326,534
	Same Day	44,236	691,828	2	2,326,534
	Second Class	118,822	691,828	10	2,326,534
	Standard Class	415,029	691,828	25	2,326,534
	Total	691,828	691,828	44	2,326,534
South	First Class	49,333	391,722	4	2,326,534
	Same Day	21,017	391,722	0	2,326,534
	Second Class	93,759	391,722	3	2,326,534
	Standard Class	227,614	391,722	17	2,326,534
	Total	391,722	391,722	24	2,326,534
West	First Class	129,762	739,814	37	2,326,534
	Same Day	43,604	739,814	11	2,326,534
	Second Class	150,541	739,814	37	2,326,534
	Standard Class	415,907	739,814	104	2,326,534
	Total	739,814	739,814	189	2,326,534

Figure 5.27 – Showing the results of the exclude statement at the current level of detail

3. Once the total sales at the country level are computed, you can calculate the sales contribution for each Ship Mode using the following expression: . This will give you the proportion of total sales contributed by each ship mode at the country level, regardless of the regional breakdown.

How it works...

Each LOD expression type provides flexibility in how calculations are performed, allowing you to control granularity and customize how Tableau processes your data.

- **FIXED**: A Fixed LOD expression allows you to calculate an aggregate value at a specific level of detail, regardless of the dimensions currently present in the view. This means that the calculation is "fixed" to a defined level of granularity, and any filters or dimensions in the view will not impact the results. Fixed LOD expressions are useful when you need consistent calculations that do not change based on the current view's level of detail.

- **INCLUDE**: An Include LOD expression allows you to calculate an aggregate value at a more detailed level than what's currently displayed in the view. This is useful when you want to include additional dimensions in your calculation that aren't part of the view itself. This allows you to expand the granularity of the calculation beyond the view, bringing in additional dimensions that may be necessary for accurate analysis. Include LOD expressions are beneficial when you need to bring in detail from dimensions that are not displayed, but still want to control the level of aggregation in your results.

- **EXCLUDE**: An Exclude LOD expression allows you to remove specific dimensions from the calculation, effectively lowering the level of detail and ignoring certain dimensions when performing your aggregation. This is useful when you want to calculate an aggregate at a higher level than what is present in the view. Exclude LOD expressions are ideal when you need to remove certain dimensions from your aggregation to simplify the analysis or provide a clearer comparison across dimensions.

See also

- To learn more about creating LOD expressions in Tableau, check out the following: `https://help.tableau.com/current/pro/desktop/en-us/calculations_calculatedfields_lod.htm`

- For examples of top 15 LOD use cases and scenarios, refer to the following blog: `https://www.tableau.com/blog/LOD-expressions?_gl=1%2A1bq067%2A_ga%2AMTU2OTIxNTI3Mi4xNzIzNTA5MzQ3%2A_ga_8YLN0SNXVS%2AMTczNTA1NzM2MS4xODcuMS4xNzM1MDYwOTI4LjAuMC4w`

- To learn more about how level of detail expressions are calculated and their functionality, see the following: `https://help.tableau.com/current/pro/desktop/en-us/calculations_calculatedfields_lod_overview.htm`

Working with and creating advanced LOD expressions

In the previous recipes, we explored different types of LOD expressions and saw how to manipulate the granularity inside our calculations. These techniques are powerful and solve many common challenges, but there are times when we need to go further. In such cases, we may need to create even more complex calculations, such as nesting one LOD expression within another, to tackle more advanced data scenarios. Here, we will delve into two advanced techniques: nested and conditional LOD expressions, each offering unique ways to solve data challenges.

Getting ready

This recipe uses the `Sample-Superstore` dataset, which can be accessed directly from the **Data Connection** pane on the **Home Page** under the **Saved Data Sources** section.

How to do it...

Let's start with **Nested LOD Expressions**.

Imagine that your organization's regional manager wants to assess how each state's sales stack up against the best-performing state within its respective region. For example, if California has $458,000 in sales in the West region, while Washington has $139,000, the manager is interested in comparing the sales of each state to the top-performing state in that region.

1. Let's create a fixed LOD expression to calculate the maximum sales for any state within a given region *Figure 5.28*. The inner part of the expression computes the total sales for each state, while the MAX function identifies the highest state-level sales within each region.

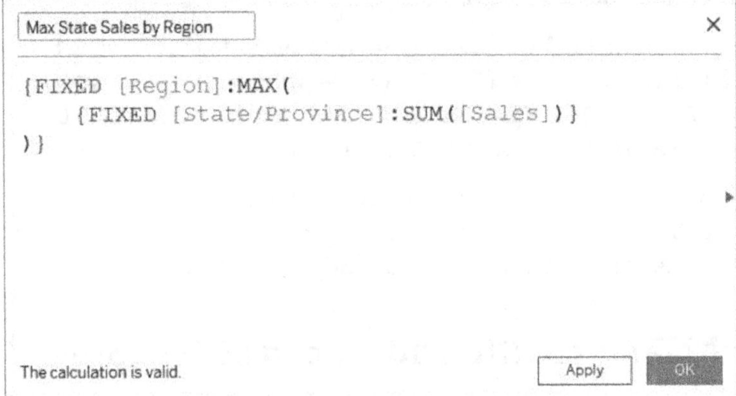

Figure 5.28 – Creating a nested LOD expression to calculate the highest sales at the state level within each region

2. To build the text table, drag **Region** and **State/Province** to the **Rows** shelf, and place **Sales** on **Label** in the **Marks Card**. Then, include the **Max State Sales by Region** calculation in the view, by double clicking on the field in the **Data** Pane *Figure 5.29*.

Region	State/Province	Sales	Max State Sales ..
West	California	457,688	457,688
	Washington	138,641	457,688
	Arizona	35,282	457,688
	Colorado	32,108	457,688
	Oregon	17,431	457,688
	Nevada	16,729	457,688
	Alberta	11,460	457,688
	Utah	11,220	457,688
	Montana	5,589	457,688
	New Mexico	4,784	457,688
	Idaho	4,382	457,688
	British Columbia	2,763	457,688
	Wyoming	1,603	457,688
	Saskatchewan	132	457,688
South	Florida	89,474	89,474
	Virginia	70,637	89,474
	North Carolina	55,603	89,474
	Georgia	49,096	89,474
	Kentucky	36,592	89,474
	Tennessee	30,662	89,474
	Alabama	19,511	89,474
	Arkansas	11,678	89,474
	Mississippi	10,771	89,474
	Louisiana	9,217	89,474
	South Carolina	8,482	89,474

Figure 5.29 – Displaying the maximum state sales for each region using a nested LOD expression

3. To simplify the comparison, you can reference your LOD expression in a separate calculation to determine the difference between a state's sales and the top-performing state in its region (*Figure 5.30*).

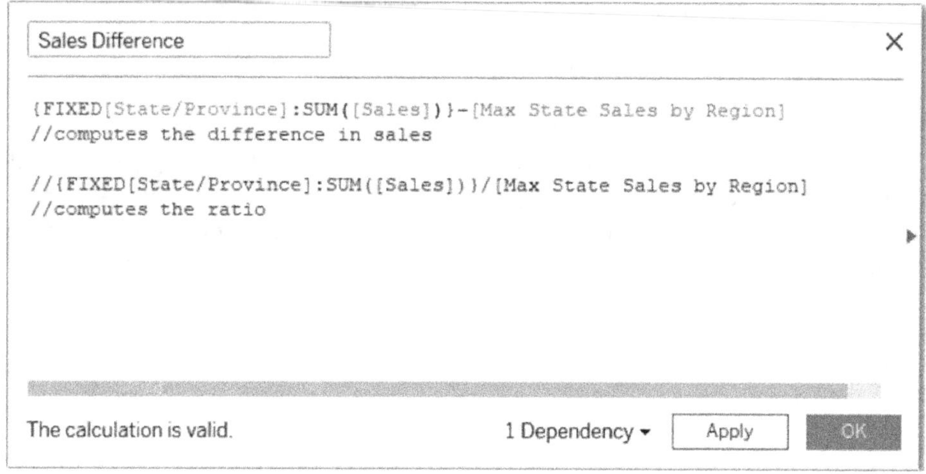

Figure 5.30 – Calculating the sales difference between each state
and the maximum state sales within each region

Next, we'll explore **Conditional LOD expressions**.

For this scenario, our goal is to identify unprofitable orders in each Sub-Category. An order is considered unprofitable if its Profit is less than 0. For each Sub-Category, we'll calculate the total Profit across all orders and flag those with a negative Profit as unprofitable.

1. Let's create an LOD expression to calculate the total profit for each order, based on the Sub-Category, and use conditional logic to determine whether an order is unprofitable. The following expression uses the FIXED LOD to calculate the profit for each Order ID within each Sub-Category. If the Profit is less than 0, the order is flagged as unprofitable (1), otherwise it is marked as profitable (0) (*Figure 5.31*).

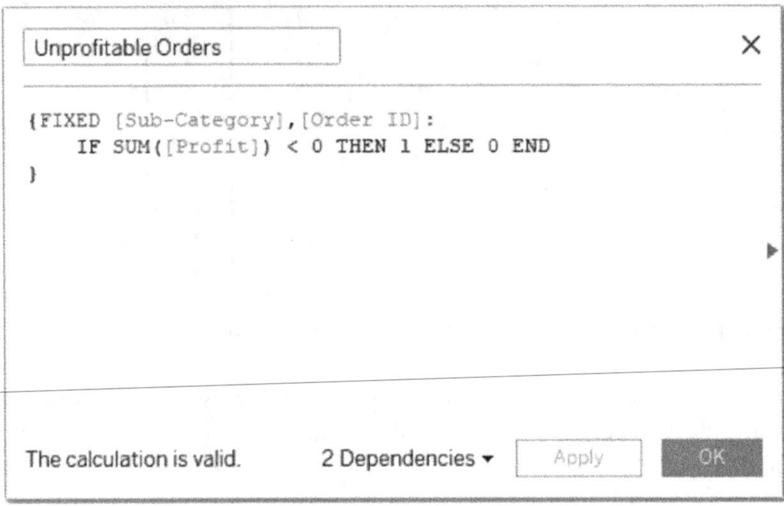

Figure 5.31 – Using a Nested LOD expression to flag unprofitable orders

2. Let's visualize the results as a bar chart by placing **Category** and **Sub-Category** on the **rows** shelf and Unprofitable Orders on the **columns** shelf. The calculated field aggregates the orders flagged as Unprofitable at the **Sub-Category** level, displaying the total count of unprofitable orders for each **Sub-Category** (*Figure 5.32*). For additional clarity, you can color-code each category and sort the items in descending order.

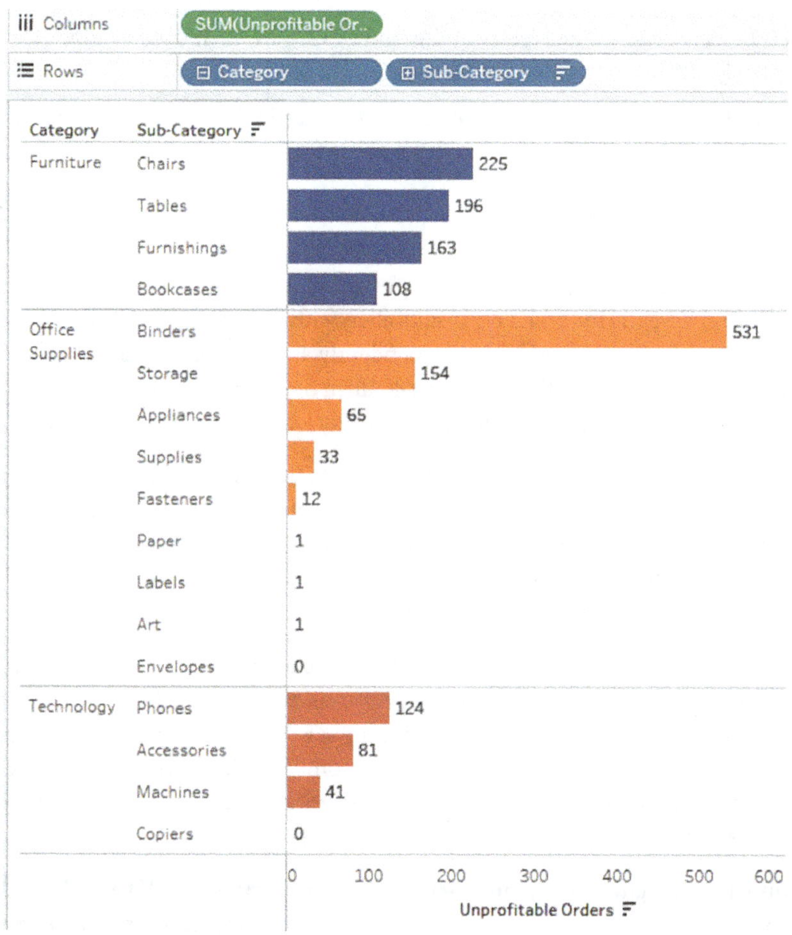

Figure 5.32 – Displaying unprofitable orders across Sub-Categories using a bar chart

How it works

A nested LOD expression in Tableau works by combining one LOD calculation inside another, allowing you to perform calculations at multiple levels of detail step by step. It's important to understand the order in which the calculations are evaluated. Nested LOD expressions are processed from the innermost to the outermost layer. This means that the inner LOD expression is calculated first, and its result is then used as the input for the outer expression. Let's break it down:

1. **Inner LOD Expression**: Tableau starts by evaluating the innermost LOD expression. This calculation is performed at the specified granularity defined by the FIXED, INCLUDE, or EXCLUDE keyword. Once the inner calculation is complete, Tableau returns a value for the expression.

2. **Outer LOD Expression**: The results of the inner LOD are then used as input for the outer LOD expression.

3. **Final Output**: After evaluating both the inner and outer LOD expressions, Tableau produces the final aggregated result at the granularity defined by the outer LOD.

There's more...

When working with nested LOD expressions, it's important to understand how each layer contributes to the final output to ensure the intermediate results align with your desired outcome. To verify this, you should test each layer of the nested LOD independently. By isolating and checking the results of individual expressions before nesting them, you can confirm that each one behaves as expected before combining them into a more complex calculation.

Another important consideration when working with nested LODs is simplicity. If the goal of the nested LOD expression can be achieved with a single LOD or a simpler calculation, it is generally better to use the simpler approach. Overly complex nested LODs can introduce errors, reduce performance, and make the calculation difficult to maintain. Simplifying your approach not only improves clarity but also enhances the efficiency of your Tableau workbook.

Proper alignment of granularity across layers is another critical aspect. LOD expressions function at specific levels of granularity, and when you nest expressions, the granularity of the inner and outer layers must align logically. For instance, if you're using a FIXED LOD expression at the product level within an outer LOD expression that operates at the customer level, this could cause discrepancies because the two levels are not directly comparable. Therefore, ensure that the granularity of each nested expression is consistent and meaningful for your analysis.

Additionally, understanding how filters interact with different types of LOD expressions is key to getting accurate results. As we will see in the next recipe, FIXED LOD expressions are independent of filters-they are calculated based on the entire data set before any filters are applied. This can lead to discrepancies if you expect the filter to affect the calculation. In contrast, INCLUDE and EXCLUDE LOD expressions respect filters and are calculated based on the subset of data defined by those filters. If you don't account for these differences, the results of your nested LOD expressions may not match your expectations. Being mindful of how filters impact each layer of your nested expressions will help ensure that your results are accurate and that your analysis reflects the data you intend to focus on.

LOD expressions can be combined with other calculation types to expand their functionality and address a wide range of analytical scenarios. By integrating LOD expressions with other calculations, you can unlock deeper insights and perform advanced analysis tailored to specific needs.

One common limitation of combining LOD expressions with other calculations in Tableau is the challenge of mixing aggregate and non-aggregate functions within a single expression. Tableau restricts the use of these two types of functions together, which can lead to errors when trying to combine them in complex calculations. Specifically, if an LOD expression involves an aggregate function, such as SUM() or AVG(), and is combined with a non-aggregate field reference, Tableau will throw an error, as it does not know how to reconcile the two different types of calculations.

This limitation can be frustrating when trying to build more sophisticated calculations or when you need to combine the results of an LOD expression with other aggregations or table calculations. To avoid this issue, it's important to either ensure that all parts of the calculation are aggregated at the same level or adjust the logic to keep aggregate and non-aggregate functions separate. A common workaround is to first apply the necessary aggregation to non-aggregate fields before using them in the LOD expression or to structure the calculation so that the non-aggregate fields are handled outside of the LOD expression itself.

Finally, since nested LODs can be computationally intensive, test their performance with large datasets and optimize by pre-aggregating data or using extracts where needed.

Manipulate Processing using Tableau's Order of Operations

Tableau's **Order of Operations** plays a critical role in determining how data is processed and displayed, especially when working with various filter types and calculations. This recipe explores how to manipulate processing to overcome common challenges, such as ensuring FIXED LOD calculations respond to **Dimension Filters** or how to use **Table Calculation Filters** to control which data appears in the view without impacting the underlying data used for computations. Through detailed examples, you'll learn how to adjust your approach strategically to align with Tableau's evaluation sequence, enabling accurate and optimized visualizations.

Getting ready

This recipe uses the Sample-Superstore dataset, which can be accessed directly from the **Data Connection** pane on the **Home Page** under the **Saved Data Sources** section.

Before diving into specific examples, let's briefly recap how the **Order of Operations** works in Tableau. When Tableau processes a query, it follows a specific order to evaluate filters, calculations, and other visual elements. This order is important because the results of one step can impact the behavior of subsequent steps. Understanding this sequence is essential for diagnosing problems related to improper filtering, or inaccurate calculation results.

The order starts with **Extract Filters** and **Data Source Filters** which limit the data as it enters Tableau, helping to improve performance by reducing the size of the dataset. Next, **Context Filters** are applied. Context Filters are crucial in determining the order in which other filters are processed. When you use context filters, you create a temporary dataset that subsequent filters work within, which ensures that they don't conflict with one another. **Top N and Conditional Filters** help narrow down data to a subset before dimension filters are applied. **Dimension Filters** reduce the data based on specific dimensions, like **Region** or **Category**, and work after context filters. **Measure Filters** further restrict the data, but they act after dimension filters have already been processed. Finally, **Table Calculation Filters** are executed last, after all other filters have been applied.

How to do it...

We'll first look at **Context Filters**.

Let's revisit our earlier example in section *[Implement LOD Expressions]* recipes 1 through 6, where we created three different types of LOD expressions. This time, we'll modify the table by adding a Category filter and examine how it affects the three types of LOD expressions in our text table.

1. Drag the **Category** dimension to the **Filters** shelf and filter to include only the **Technology** category *Figure 5.33*.

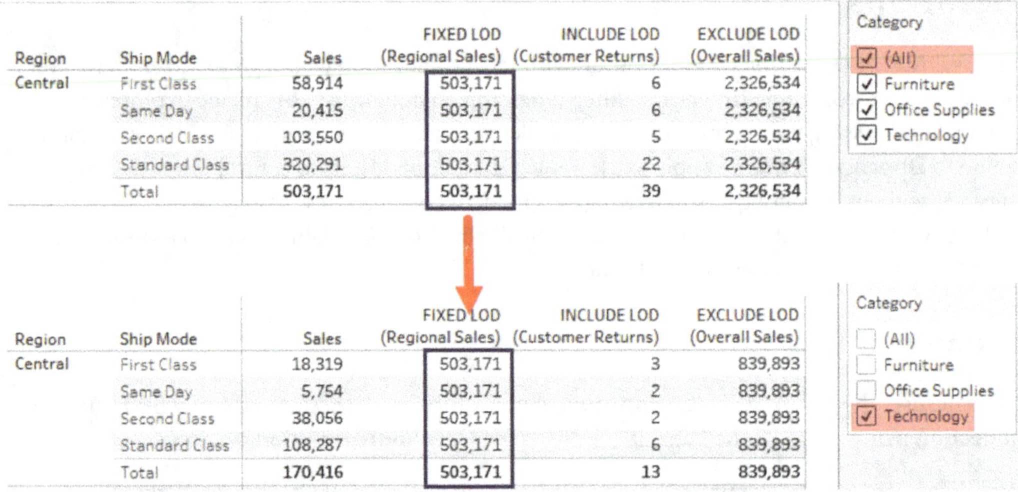

Region	Ship Mode	Sales	FIXED LOD (Regional Sales)	INCLUDE LOD (Customer Returns)	EXCLUDE LOD (Overall Sales)
Central	First Class	58,914	503,171	6	2,326,534
	Same Day	20,415	503,171	6	2,326,534
	Second Class	103,550	503,171	5	2,326,534
	Standard Class	320,291	503,171	22	2,326,534
	Total	503,171	503,171	39	2,326,534

Region	Ship Mode	Sales	FIXED LOD (Regional Sales)	INCLUDE LOD (Customer Returns)	EXCLUDE LOD (Overall Sales)
Central	First Class	18,319	503,171	3	839,893
	Same Day	5,754	503,171	2	839,893
	Second Class	38,056	503,171	2	839,893
	Standard Class	108,287	503,171	6	839,893
	Total	170,416	503,171	13	839,893

Figure 5.33 – Using a dimension filter to observe the impact on each LOD type

2. From the results above, you'll notice that the table values for the fixed LOD expression remain unchanged, even after applying the dimension filter. However, the other two LOD calculations respond to the addition of this filter. To understand why, refer to the Order of Operations table in *Figure 5.34*. It shows that fixed LOD expressions are calculated before dimension filters are applied, which means the dimension filter is ignored. This explains why the **Regional Sales** values remain static. **Include** and **Exclude** calculations are evaluated after dimension filters, which is why applying the **Category** filter also updated the table values for **Customer Returns** and **Overall Sales**. To ensure the filter is applied before the fixed LOD expression, we can promote it to a context filter. When a dimension filter is set to context, it is processed upstream of sets, conditional filters, Top N and Fixed Level of Detail expressions.

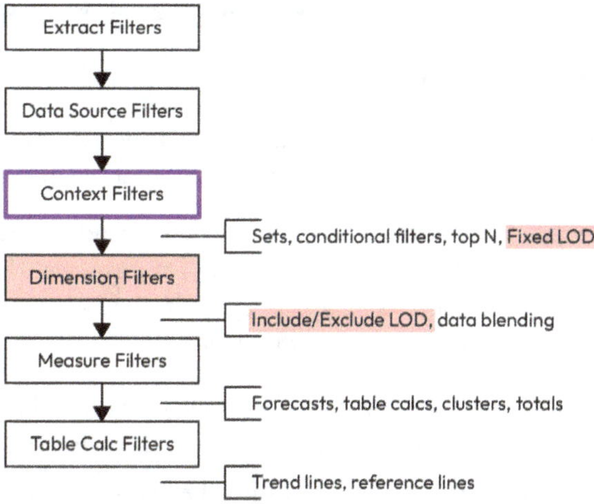

Figure 5.34 – Tableau's order of operations table that outlines the sequence in which various filter types and calculations are evaluated

3. To promote the **Category** dimension filter to context, right-click on the filter and select **Add to Context** (*Figure 5.35*).

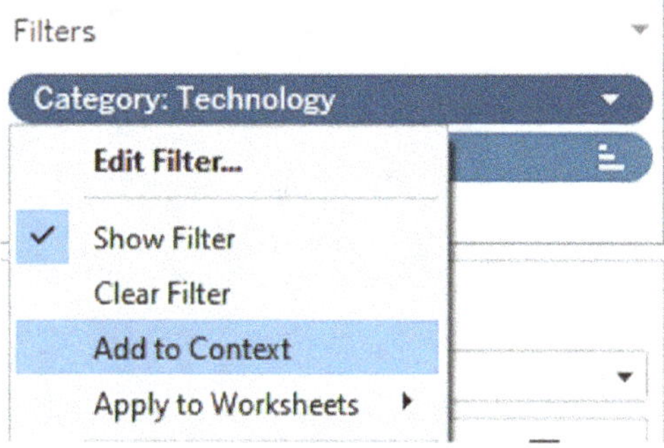

Figure 5.35 – Promoting a dimension filter to a context filter

4. This action resolves the issue mentioned earlier, updating the **Regional Sales** values as shown in *Figure 5.36*. Alternatively, you can modify the LOD type to an Exclude calculation, such as {. This approach still computes **Regional Sales** while making the expression responsive to dimension filters applied in the worksheet.

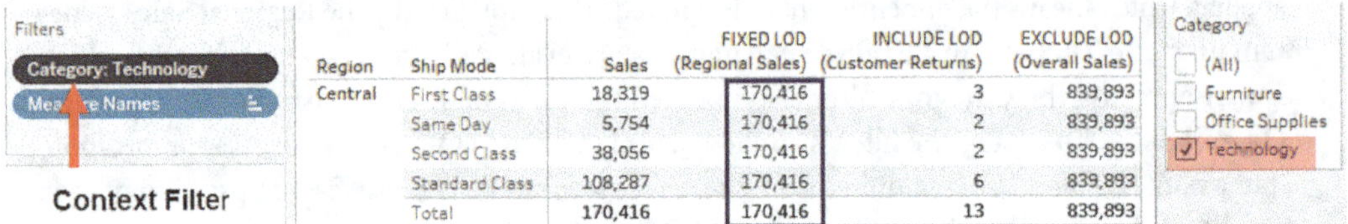

Region	Ship Mode	Sales	FIXED LOD (Regional Sales)	INCLUDE LOD (Customer Returns)	EXCLUDE LOD (Overall Sales)
Central	First Class	18,319	170,416	3	839,893
	Same Day	5,754	170,416	2	839,893
	Second Class	38,056	170,416	2	839,893
	Standard Class	108,287	170,416	6	839,893
	Total	170,416	170,416	13	839,893

Figure 5.36 – Resolving the fixed LOD issue using a context filter

Finally, we'll look at **Table Calculation Filters**.

Let's explore another common scenario that requires a thoughtful approach and a basic understanding of how various calculations and filters are evaluated within the Order of Operations framework.

Suppose the sales team at Superstore wants to examine daily sales trends for each product category (Furniture, Office Supplies, and Technology) using a 30-day moving average. This approach smooths short-term sales fluctuations while emphasizing longer-term trends. The focus is on recent performance, so they're only interested in showing the last 12 months of data.

1. To visualize daily sales for each category, place **Order Date** on the **Columns** shelf and set it to **Exact Date** to display daily records. Then, drag **Category** and **Sales** to the **Rows** shelf.

2. Apply the moving average calculation by duplicating the **Sales** measure and placing it next to the original field on the **Rows** shelf. Right-click on the duplicated **Sales** field, then select **Quick Table Calculation | Moving Average**.

3. Add a date filter by dragging **Order Date** from the **Data** pane to the **Filters** shelf. Choose **Relative Date | Next**, select **Months** and set the filter to display **Last 12 months**. Check off the **Anchor relative to** option and set it to **12/31/2024 | OK** (*Figure 5.37*).

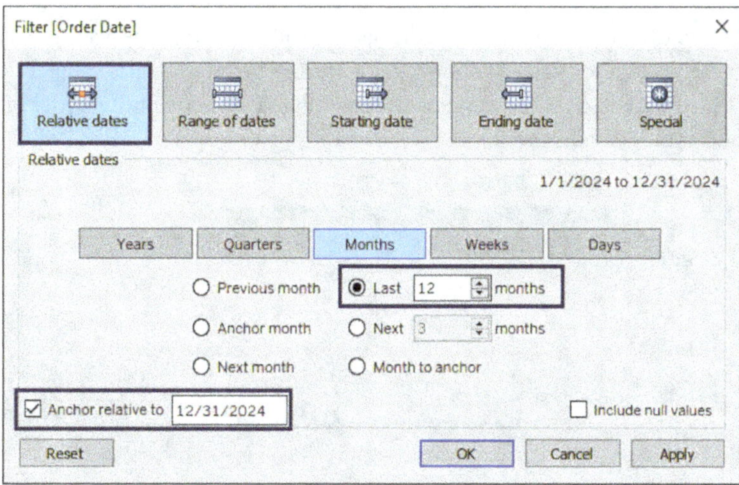

Figure 5.37 – Applying a relative date filter to show the last 12 months of data in the visualization

4. Right-click on the table calculation and choose **Edit Table Calculation**. Modify the calculation to use the 29 previous values along with the current value to calculate the 30-day moving average. Ensure that **Order Date** is selected under the **Specific Dimensions** section (*Figure 5.38*).

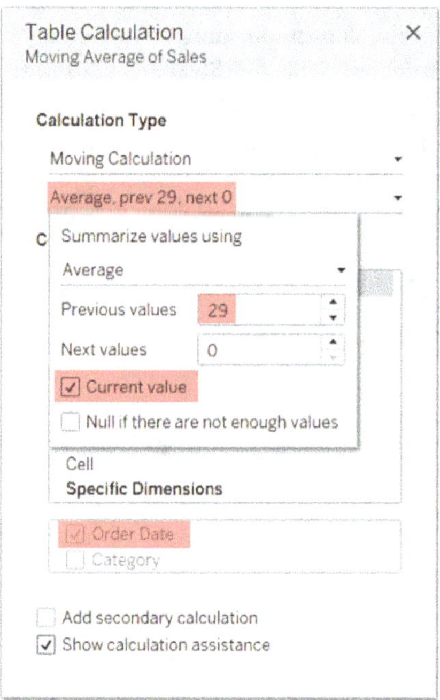

Figure 5.38 – Modify the table calculation to calculate the 30-day
moving average and define the scope and direction

5. Adding labels to display the first value in the dataset will reveal that the averages are inaccurate due to the absence of prior data. As shown in *Figure 5.39* below, the sales value for the first data point is 975, which matches the moving average value. Let's consult the Order of Operations table to understand why this occurs.

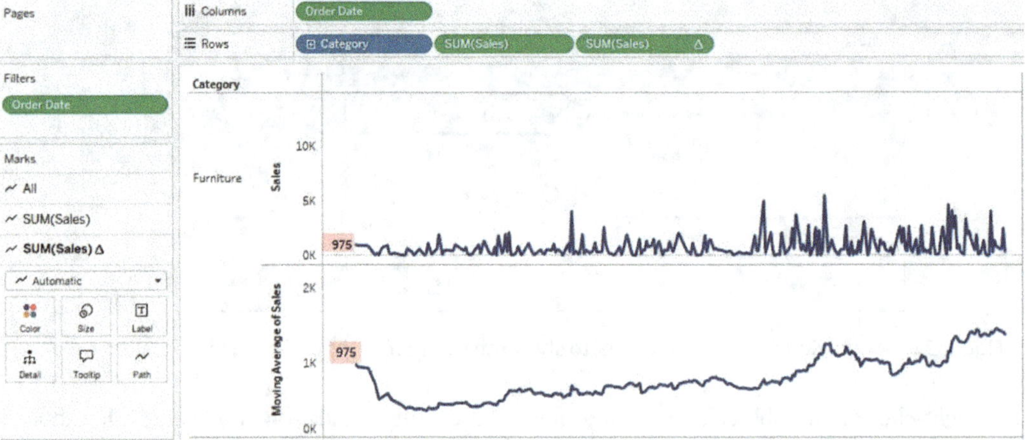

Figure 5.39: Checking the initial value to ensure the moving average calculation is accurate

6. In Tableau's order of operations, continuous dimensions are applied before table calculations, which excludes prior data from the calculation. To address this, we can create a **Table Calculation Filter**, which is evaluated last in the query pipeline (*Figure 5.40*). This will include the prior data in the calculation while keeping it hidden from the view.

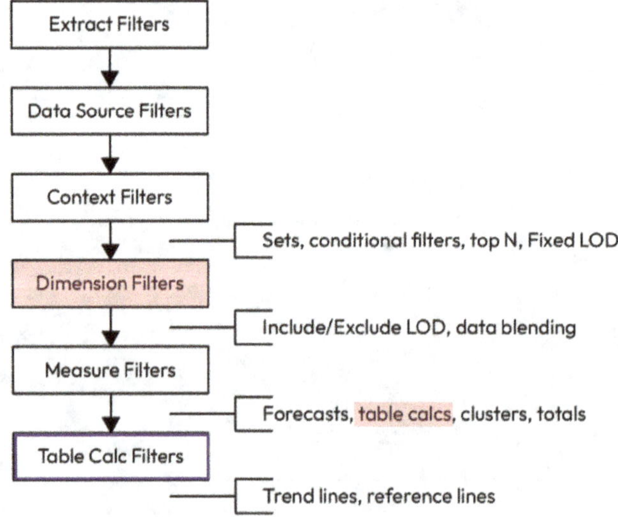

Figure 5.40 – Utilizing Tableau's Order of Operations table to determine the appropriate filter type

7. Open the calculation editor and create the following calculated field:

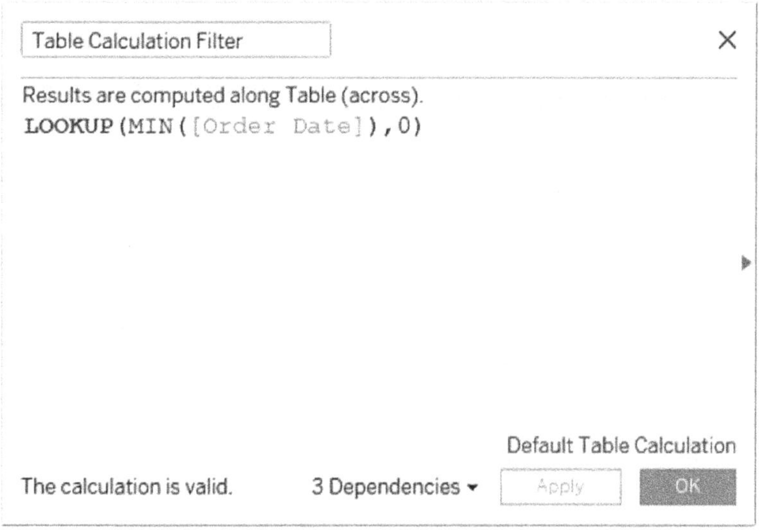

Table Calculation Filter   ✕

Results are computed along Table (across).
LOOKUP (MIN([Order Date]),0)

Default Table Calculation

The calculation is valid.   3 Dependencies ▾   Apply   OK

Figure 5.41 – Using a Lookup function to create a table calculation filter

This calculation works by using the LOOKUP function to reference the minimum order date, starting from the current row (indicated by 0). By doing this, it ensures that all prior data is included in the table calculation, allowing for accurate computation of the moving average. This method effectively addresses the issue of missing prior data, which is crucial for maintaining the integrity of the calculation.

8. Replace the **Order Date** filter in the **Filters** shelf with the newly created **Table Calculation Filter**. Right-click on the calculated field and select a continuous format. Use the **Relative Date** option and set it to **Last 12 Months**. Adjust the **Anchor relative to** date to **12/31/2024** and adjust the scope to compute using **Order Date**. Now, the moving averages will include some of the prior data, even though it is hidden from view. The **Table Calculation Filter** ensures that these hidden data points are still part of the calculation, as illustrated in *Figure 5.42*.

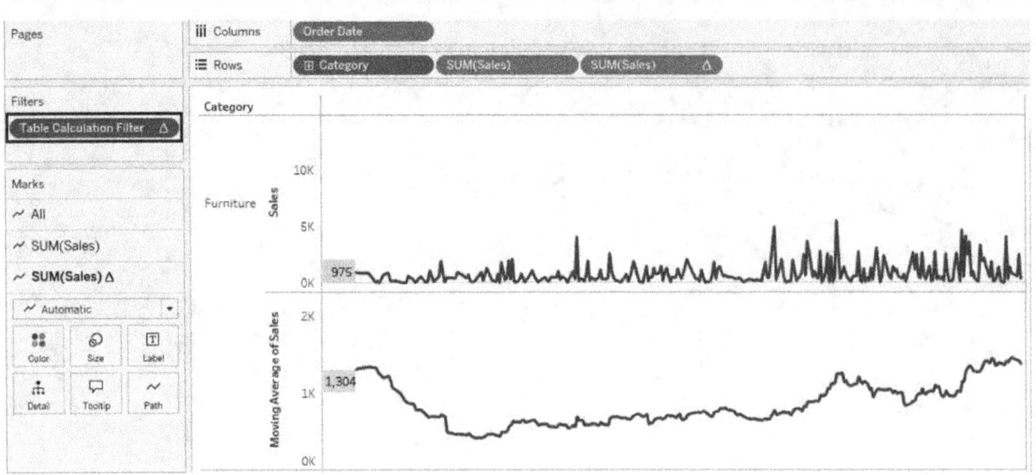

Figure 5.42 – Updated view with a table calculation filter that displays
the correct values for the 30-day moving average

9. Finally, create a dual axis chart and tweak it for better presentation. Right-click on the duplicated **Sales** field in the **Rows** shelf and select **Dual Axis**. To synchronize the axis scales, right-click on the **Sales** axis and choose **Synchronize Axis**. Then, format the labels, line width, and colors to your preference (*Figure 5.43*).

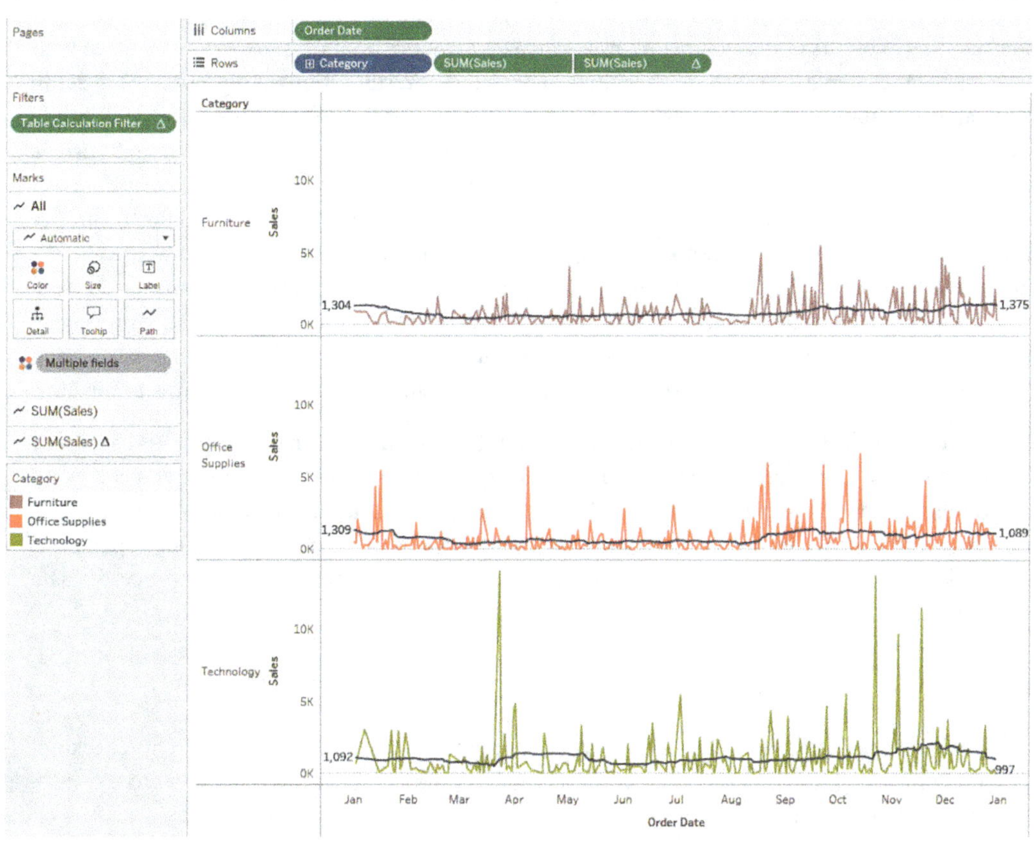

Figure 5.43 – Final chart displaying daily sales and the 30-day moving average by category

How it works...

The exact order in which different types of calculations are executed depends on their nature. **Fixed LOD Expressions** are computed before any filters are applied, meaning they ignore the filters (except for data source and context filters). This can be useful if you need a fixed value regardless of the filters applied in the view. **Include and Exclude Expressions** are calculated after dimension filters but before table calculations, meaning they respect dimension filters but not the final visualizations' table calculations. **Table Calculations** are evaluated last and are based on the data that remains after all filtering and aggregation have been performed. These calculations, such as running totals or moving averages, are applied at the very end of the query pipeline, just before the data is displayed. **Aggregated Calculations**, such as SUM(), AVG(), and COUNT(), are performed as part of the query and are impacted by the order of operations. These are calculated after dimension and measure filters have been applied but before table calculations.

Understanding Tableau's Order of Operations is crucial for troubleshooting unexpected results in your workbooks. For example, if you are not seeing the correct filter results, it might be due to the order in which Tableau is applying the filters. If a dimension filter isn't working as expected, check if it should be moved to the context filter or if its precedence needs adjustment. Table calculations might not be behaving as expected if they are not accounting for certain filter conditions. You may need to revisit the order in which the calculations are executed and whether they need to be adjusted for the proper context. Similarly, if a Fixed LOD expression is ignoring certain filters, recall that it is computed before dimension filters are applied. You can use `INCLUDE` or `EXCLUDE` LOD expressions if you need them to respect specific filters or use context filters to control the order in which filters are processed. Additionally, if your workbook is running slowly, consider revisiting your filters. Using extract and data source filters effectively can improve performance by limiting the data early in the query pipeline.

Understanding Tableau's Order of Operations can significantly improve the efficiency and accuracy of your analyses. By knowing how and when Tableau applies filters and calculations, you can avoid common pitfalls, optimize performance, and ensure that your results are accurate. Whether you're troubleshooting unexpected behavior or designing more efficient workbooks, the order of operations framework provides a powerful tool for understanding and controlling how Tableau processes data and visualizations.

See also

- For a complete overview of Tableau's order of operations and processing hierarchy, check out the following blog: `https://www.salesforceben.com/tableau-order-of-operations-an-overview/`

- For additional examples of order of operations issues, refer to the following blog: `https://www.flerlagetwins.com/2020/09/order-of-operations.html`

Part 3:
Building Interactive Dashboards and Data Apps

In this part, you will gain a comprehensive understanding of the six types of actions that can be integrated into worksheets and dashboards to enhance interactivity. You will explore when and how to use these actions effectively, with a specific focus on how to leverage Parameter and Set actions to tackle complex data questions. Additionally, you will apply specialized techniques such as proportional brushing to deliver deeper insights and added value to your analysis. Lastly, you will discover how to utilize Dynamic Zone Visibility to build interactive data applications that prioritize user needs and drive actionable results.

This part includes the following chapters:

- *Chapter 6, Creating Interactive Dashboards*
- *Chapter 7, Interactivity and Zone Visibility: From Dashboards to Data Apps*

6

Creating Interactive Dashboards

Interactivity is one of the key differentiators of modern data visualizations, graphs, and dashboards, allowing users to engage with the data and find answers to their questions.

When we think about interactivity, filtering is most commonly what comes to our minds. But Tableau has different interactivity types for different use cases, allowing us to develop much more advanced tools, closer to analytical apps, to solve more complex scenarios, adding more value to our analysis and answering more advanced questions.

In Tableau, the different types of interactions between sheets or dashboards are called **actions**. Currently, there are six types of actions – **Filter**, **Highlight**, **Go to URL**, **Go to Sheet**, **Change Parameter**, and **Change Set Values** – and understanding when to use them and how to have full control of each one will open a new world of possibilities in our visualizations. This is especially true for **parameter actions (Change Parameter)** and **set actions (Change Set Values)**, to which we will devote most of this chapter, with practical examples and recipes.

The key recipes covered in this chapter are as follows:

- Adding interactivity with Tableau actions

- Setting up filter actions to navigate through dashboards

- Creating an interactive temporal analysis with parameter actions

- Creating interactive sheets to switch between different measures with parameter actions

- Building part-to-whole and proportional brushing analysis with set actions

- Analyzing different levels of granularity with sets and set actions

By the end of this chapter, you will have learned how to have full control of all Tableau action types and how you can use parameter and set actions to allow end users to interact with the data in new ways, answering more advanced questions and engaging with data in new ways that were not possible before with traditional actions, such as filtering and highlighting. This will provide you with the knowledge and inspiration to use dashboards to answer more advanced questions and provide more value.

Technical requirements

For this chapter, you will need to have Tableau Desktop version `2025.1` or higher or Tableau Desktop Public Edition.

The starter and solution dashboards we will use can be found at `https://github.com/PacktPublishing/Tableau-Cookbook-for-Experienced-Professionals/tree/main/Chapter_06`.

Adding interactivity with Tableau actions

This first recipe will be a bit less practical, just as an introduction to explain how to create actions in Tableau and the most common configuration options available. If you are familiar with Tableau actions, feel free to move on to the next recipe.

How to do it...

There are two main action categories in Tableau: **worksheet actions** and **dashboard actions**.

The main difference between them is the scope of the interactivity. Worksheet actions operate within a specific worksheet and apply changes directly to that sheet without affecting other sheets. Dashboard actions are more global and can affect multiple sheets within the same workbook.

Based on my experience, dashboard actions are more common and, personally, I prefer to set actions at the dashboard level, keeping individual sheets not actionable. But of course, this is just my personal preference.

What is important to have in mind is that to create a worksheet action, you need to be in a concrete sheet of a workbook or first select one if you are in a dashboard.

There are two ways to create a **dashboard action**:

1. Click on the **Dashboard** menu at the top and then **Action**.

    You can also use shortcuts instead:

    - On Windows: *Ctrl + Shift + D*

    - On Mac: *Shift + Command + D*

2. In both cases, a new window appears where you can add new actions using the **Add Action** button and edit or remove existing ones (see *Figure 6.1*).

Actions   ✕

Actions let you create interactive relationships between data, dashboard objects, other worksheets and the web.

Show actions for

◉ This workbook   ◯ This sheet

Name	Run On	Source	Fields

| Add Action ▼ | | Edit | Remove |

| Cancel | OK |

Figure 6.1 – The Actions menu

3. Click on the **Add Action** button. Let's briefly review each of the action types. The setup of each action type is slightly different, but they all have a lot in common. Once you understand one of them, it's easy to understand the rest.

    As mentioned at the beginning of the chapter, filter actions are probably the most common type of action. Filtering allows us to show just part of the data based on the user's action. To create a filter action and have full control of how it works and behaves, just go to the **Actions** menu from a dashboard, as shown before, and then click on **Add Action | Filter**.

A new **Add Filter Action** menu should appear, like in *Figure 6.2*.

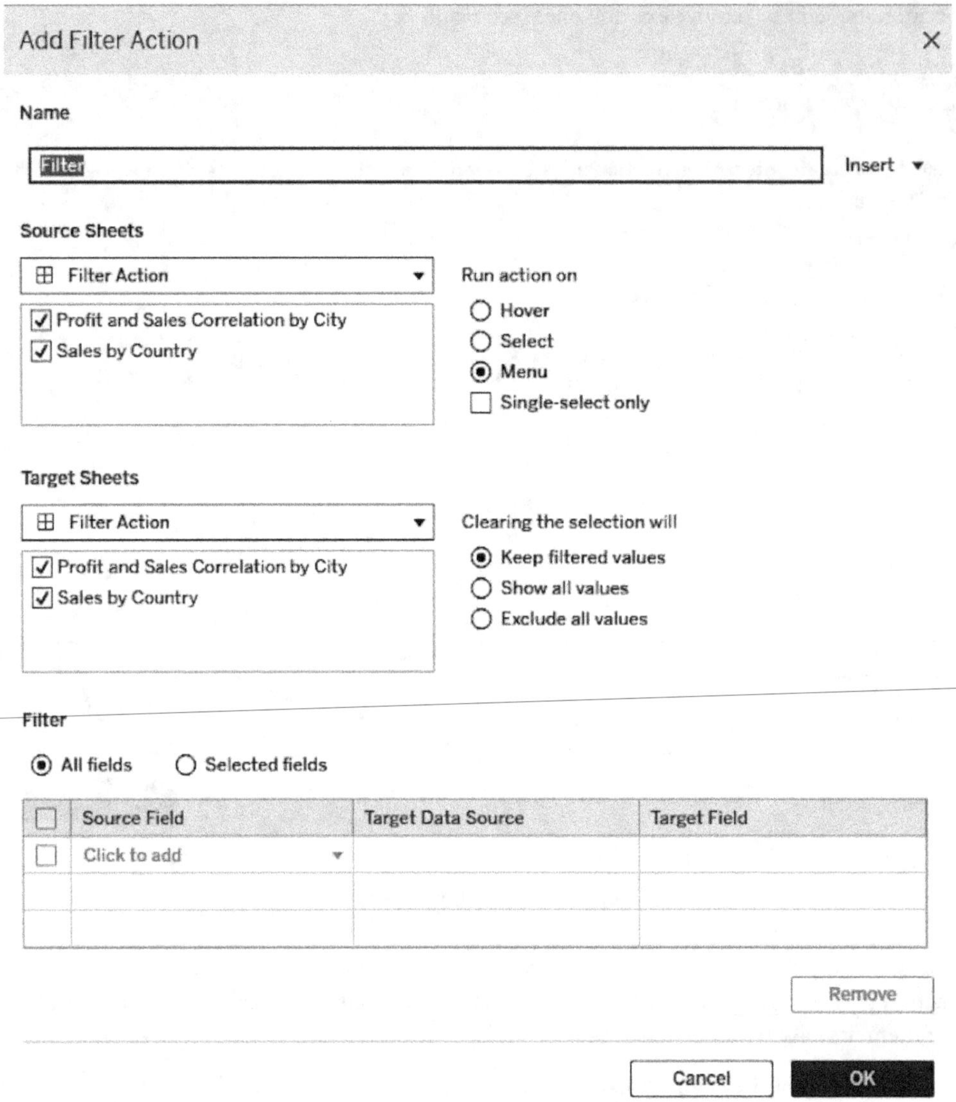

Figure 6.2 – Filter action configuration menu

Let's review and explain the different sections and options in detail.

- **Name**: This allows you to give the action you are creating a specific name. This might not sound very useful or important, but in complex dashboards with a lot of actions, it will simplify your work a lot if you can identify each action easily to modify or remove them and understand what each action does.

- **Source Sheets**: Here, you specify the sheet or sheets you want to launch the action from.

- **Run action on**: Defines when the action will be triggered. There are three alternatives:

  - **Hover**: Runs when you mouse over marks in the source sheets.

  - **Select**: Runs when you click marks in the source sheets.

  - **Menu**: Runs when you click an option that will appear in the tooltip menu of the marks hovered over or selected in the source sheets.

  Run action on has an option to avoid running the action when multiple marks are selected by checking the **Single-select only** option.

- **Target Sheets**: Defines which sheet or sheets will be affected by the action.

- **Clearing the selection will**: This allows you to control what happens when the selection is cleared. There are three options:

  - **Keep filtered values**: The filter will still be applied even if the user clears the selection.

  - **Show all values**: The filter will be cleared, showing the data as it was before the action was triggered.

  - **Exclude all values**: All data will disappear, excluding the values. This is very useful when we want to follow a guided analytics approach and only show data in a sheet if a value in another sheet is selected.

- **Filter**: Gives you full control over what dimensions and variables you want to filter by when the action is triggered.

  - **All fields**: This is the default option. If selected, all the dimension values of the source sheet will be passed to the target sheets to filter the data.

  - **Selected fields**: This allows you to specify the dimensions you filter by. This gives you more control over what fields to filter by, and in some cases, it can improve performance.

4. Once you have configured the action as needed, just click **OK** to confirm the action created and go back to the **Actions** menu.

Tip: Name your actions in a meaningful way

Always give your actions a meaningful name to make them easy to identify. This will improve your productivity when you create a lot of actions, it will make it much easier to apply changes and understand what each action does in the future and will also help other people learn how you built your dashboard.

Now that you understand how filter actions work, you will find that the rest of the action types are very similar in terms of configuration. Let's put into practice what we have just learned.

See also

- For more information about additional types of actions, see `https://help.tableau.com/current/pro/desktop/en-us/actions.htm`.

- You can also read this article from Peter Gilks for a quick review of basic action use cases: `https://www.tableau.com/blog/rough-guide-dashboard-actions`.

Setting up filter actions to navigate through dashboards

Sometimes, filtering data inside a dashboard is not enough and we need to navigate between different dashboards while filtering the data. Imagine the following scenario:

We have a global sales workbook analyzing the performance of an international company. The workbook has two different dashboards:

- The first dashboard is a global view of the company across all countries and some key metrics for each country

- The second dashboard shows detailed data by city of a specific country of interest

We want the user experience to be as smooth as possible, allowing users to click on a specific country in the global dashboard and then navigate to the detailed view, but filtering the detailed view for the country the user clicks on at the same time.

Some benefits of this approach are as follows:

- Giving a better experience to our users

- Saving some time by pre-filtering the second dashboard we navigate to

- Potentially, saving some database resources by avoiding showing all the data in the second dashboard and just showing the country the user is interested in instead

Getting ready

For this scenario, just filtering a dashboard is not enough because we want to navigate to a different one. Using the **Go to Sheet** action doesn't work either as we don't want to just navigate between dashboards, but also apply a filter based on the user's selection.

The good news is that you can use a **filter action** to only filter data on the dashboard the user is currently at but also navigate to a different dashboard of the same workbook.

For this recipe, we will start from the `Chapter 6. Recipe 2. Global Dashboard` sheet in the `Chapter 6 - Starter` workbook. The dashboard should look as shown in *Figure 6.3*.

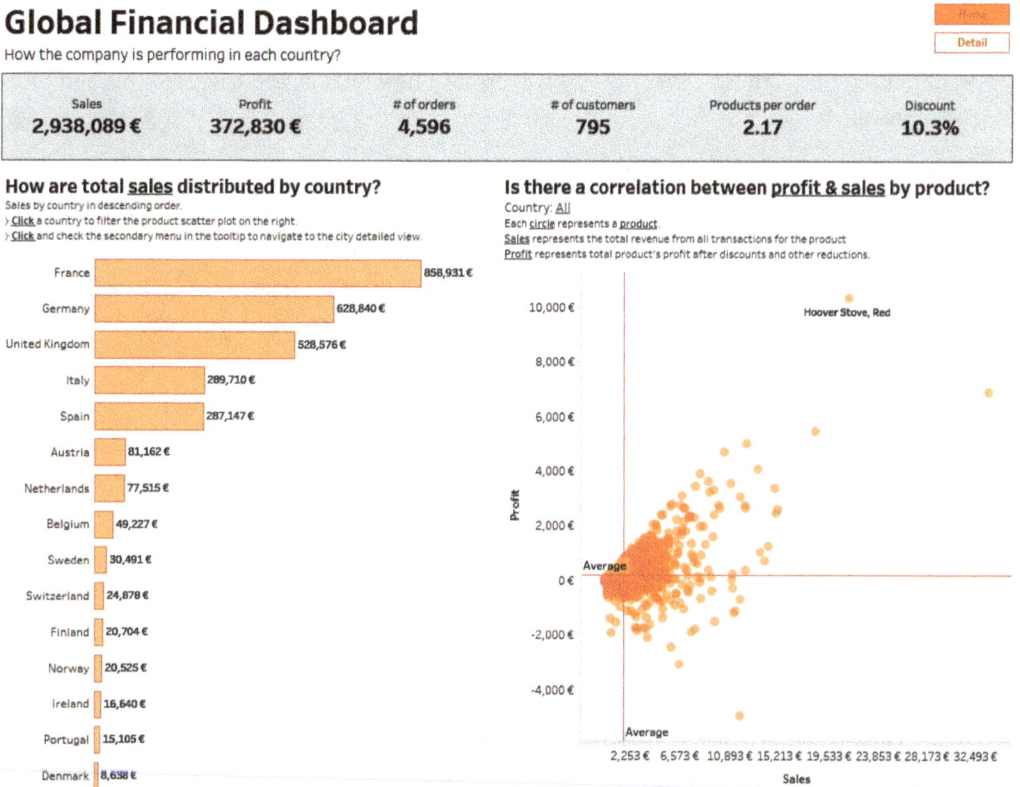

Figure 6.3 – An overview of Global Financial Dashboard

The objective is to allow users to click on a country on the bar chart of that dashboard and navigate to `Chapter 6. Recipe 2. Detailed Dashboard`, filtering at the same time to show only the details for the selected country. Let's see how to achieve this with filter actions.

How to do it...

1. Open `Chapter 6 - Starter Workbook` and go to the sheet called `Chapter 6. Recipe 2. Global Dashboard`.

2. Access the **Actions** menu: Go to the **Dashboard** menu at the top of the screen and then click **Actions**.

3.   Select **This sheet** in the section *Show actions for* at the top of the menu to only see actions for the dashboard we are currently on, instead of actions of the entire workbook. You will see there is already an action configured on this dashboard.

     This action filters the data for a country when you click on a country in the bar chart. We want to keep that action as it is. Now we will create a new filter action triggered through the tooltip menu.

4.   In the **Actions** menu, click on **Add Action** and then **Filter....**

5.   Let's set up when the action will run. Select **Menu** as the *Run action on* and check also the **single-select only** check box to avoid the action running if multiple countries are selected.

6.   We want the action to only be triggered when the bar chart is selected, so make sure only the `6.2. Sales by Country` sheet from `Chapter 6. Recipe 2. Global Dashboard` is selected as the source sheet.

7.   Now comes the important part. We don't want the action to act on this dashboard. Instead, we want to filter `Chapter 6. Recipe 2. Detailed Dashboard`. To achieve this, in **Target Sheets**, use the drop-down menu and select `Chapter 6. Recipe 2. Detailed Dashboard`. Then mark all the sheets, as we want the filter to apply to all the sheets of this second dashboard.

8.   Select **show all values** once the user clears the selection to see all the data in the second dashboard if no country is selected.

9.   In the **Filter** section at the bottom, we could leave it as **All fields,** but in case we add more dimensions to the bar chart, let's make sure the only dimension filtered by is the **Country/Region** field. Choose **Selected fields** and **Country/Region** for **Source Field** and **Target Field**.

10. Finally, give the action a meaningful name. At the top, name it `Click here to see details for cities in `, and then use the **Insert** drop-down menu at the top right and select **Country/Region**, typing `cities` at the end. The name should then be **Click here to see details for cities in <Country/Region>**. This is a very nice tip, especially for actions triggered in the menu as users will see the name of the action in the tooltip, showing a dynamic value replacing the *<Country/Region>* string for the name of the country they click on.

11. Click **OK** to confirm the action and **OK** again to close the **Actions** menu.

That's it! You can check also *Figure 6.4* to make sure the action is set up as we just explained.

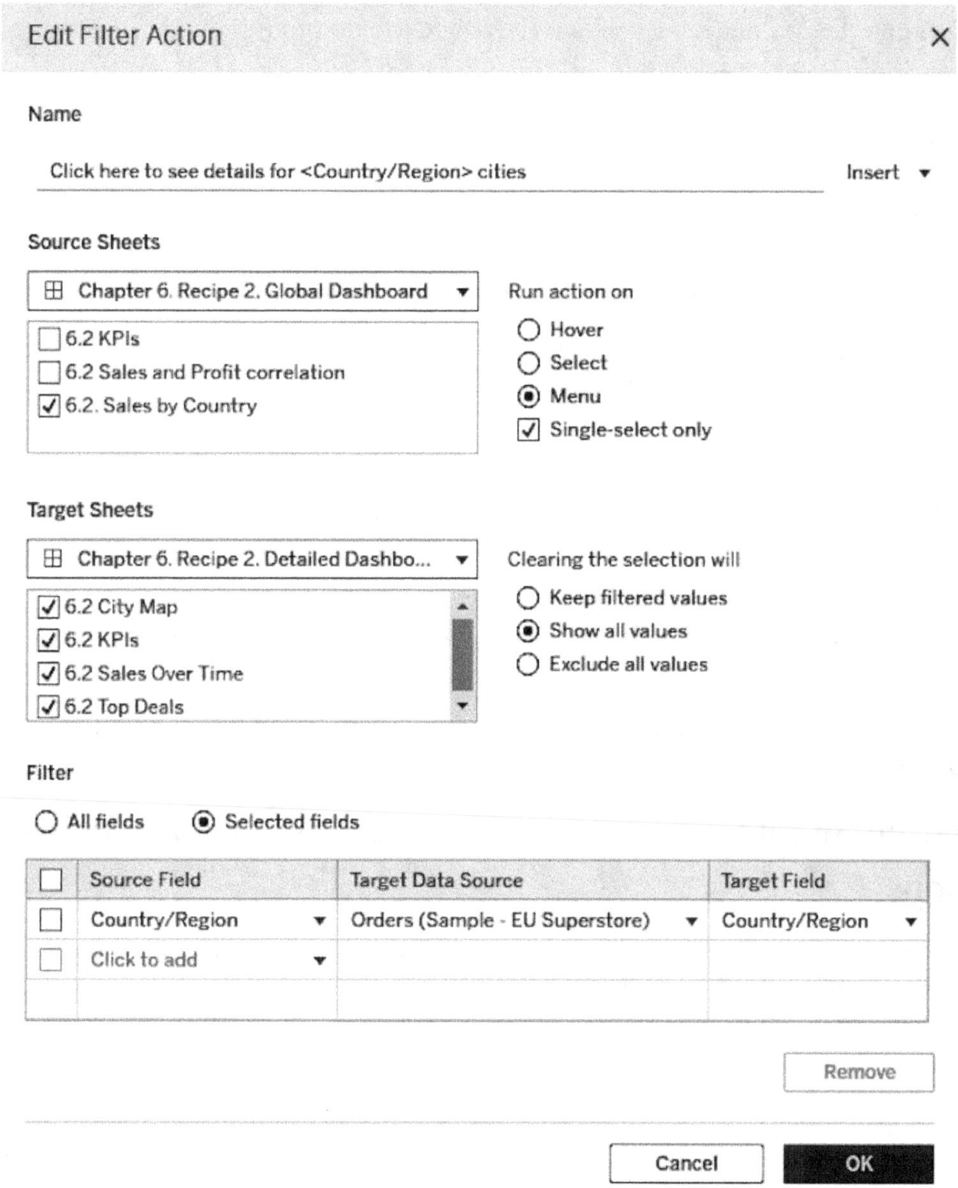

Figure 6.4 – Full filter action configuration

How it works...

1. It's time to make sure the action runs correctly. Go to the `Chapter 6. Recipe 2. Global Dashboard` sheet.

2. Click on one of the countries of the *How are total sales distributed by country?* bar chart. You should see the tooltip with the total sales in that country and an additional message that says **Click here to see the details for <country> cities** and the name of the country selected instead of *<country>*.

3. If you click on the text, the action will be triggered. The dashboard will navigate from the global view to the detailed dashboard and filter the data for the country you selected.

Good job! You just learned how you can have total control of your analytical flow to navigate and filter between different dashboards with filter actions.

There's more...

When filters and other actions are applied, Tableau can animate the transition for a smoother transition between the original view and the filtered or new view. You can turn on/off those animations or even define their duration for the entire workbook or even sheet by sheet.

To customize the duration of workbook animations, go to **Format** at the top menu of Tableau Desktop and then **Animations**.

Setting up longer durations can make transitions more appealing to end users and provide a greater feeling of movement and dynamism.

Creating an interactive temporal analysis with parameter actions

Parameter actions were released in Tableau version 2019.2, allowing you to change a parameter value through direct interaction with a visualization.

Because parameters can be used in reference lines, calculations, filters, and even SQL queries, parameter actions opened new possibilities to engage your audience, making dashboards more dynamic and interactive.

In this recipe, we will learn how we can use parameter actions to create an interactive temporal analysis that allows users to interact with a bar chart that shows the percentage profit difference across quarters to dynamically change the quarter that is used as a baseline.

This will allow users to answer different questions based on their needs just by clicking on different periods of time, such as the following:

- How is the company profit in the latest quarter compared to the same quarter of the previous year?

- How has the company performed each quarter compared to the most profitable quarter in the company's history?

- How has the company profit changed compared to the first quarter of the current year?

Getting ready

For this exercise, we will start from the `Chapter 6. Recipe 3. Creating an interactive temporal analysis with Parameter Actions` sheet in the `Chapter 6` workbook (*Figure 6.5*).

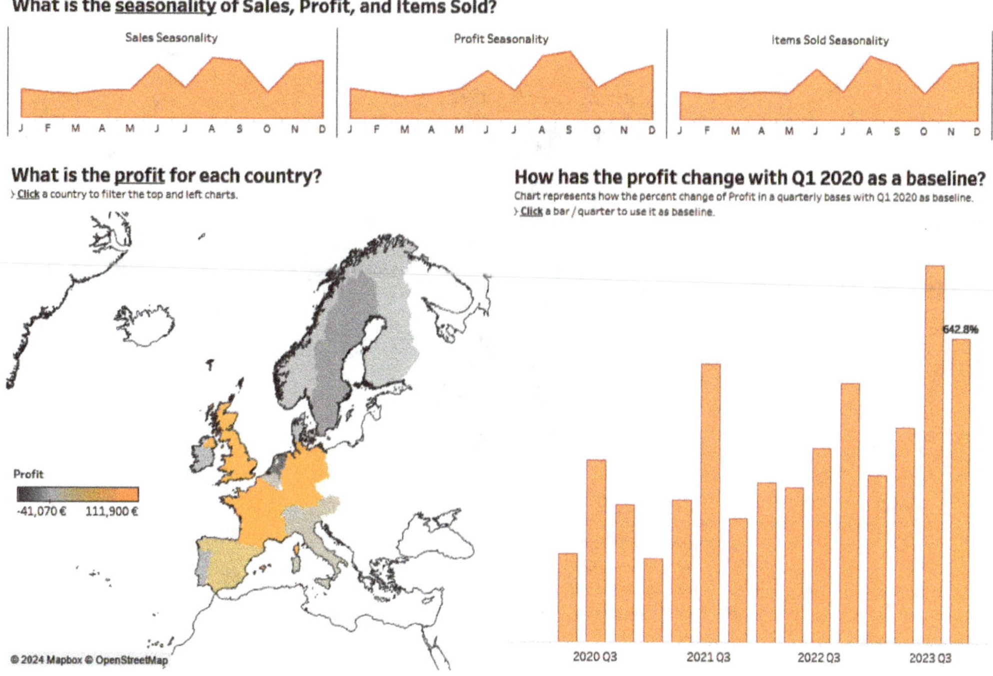

Figure 6.5 – An overview of the seasonality and profit percent difference dashboard

The objective is to add interactivity to the bottom-right chart currently showing the profit percent difference from the first quarter (Q1 2020) and update the quarter baseline for the percent difference calculation by clicking on a specific bar. This will encourage user exploration and allow them to better understand the company's performance at different moments in time.

How to do it...

1. First, go to the 6.3. Profit Percent Change worksheet and right-click on the **Sum(Profit)** measure in the **Rows Shelf**. Check the **Quick Table Calculation** and **Relative to** submenus. As you can see, the chart shows the profit change percentage relative to the first value. This means that, compared to Q1 2020, in 2023 Q4 the profit was 642.8% higher. Now, it's time to make this more interactive. But to create a parameter action, first, we need a parameter.

2. Creating a parameter is easy: click the drop-down arrow in the upper-right corner of the **Data** pane and select **Create Parameter** (*Figure 6.6*).

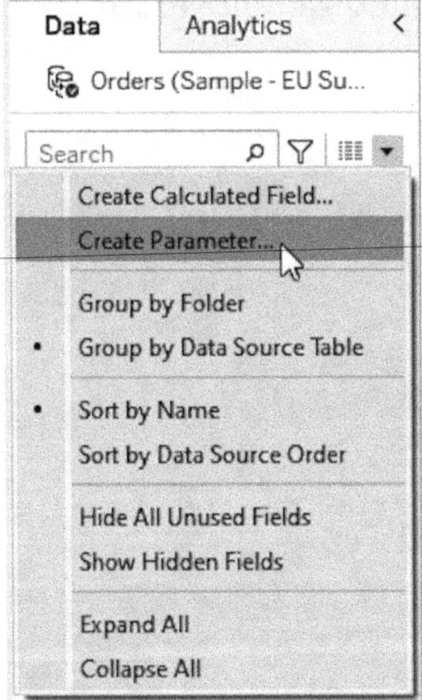

Figure 6.6 – Creating a parameter from the Data pane

3.   A new **Create Parameter** menu should appear. Parameters need to be of a concrete data type (**Integer**, **Float**, **String**, **Boolean**, **Date**, or **DateTime**). We want to allow users to select the quarter they want to compare the profit to, so we need a **DateTime** parameter. Choose **DateTime** from the **Data type** drop-down menu. We will not need to limit the values allowable for the parameter, so we can leave the other options as the default. Just remember to give the parameter a meaningful name, such as **Reference date** (see *Figure 6.7*).

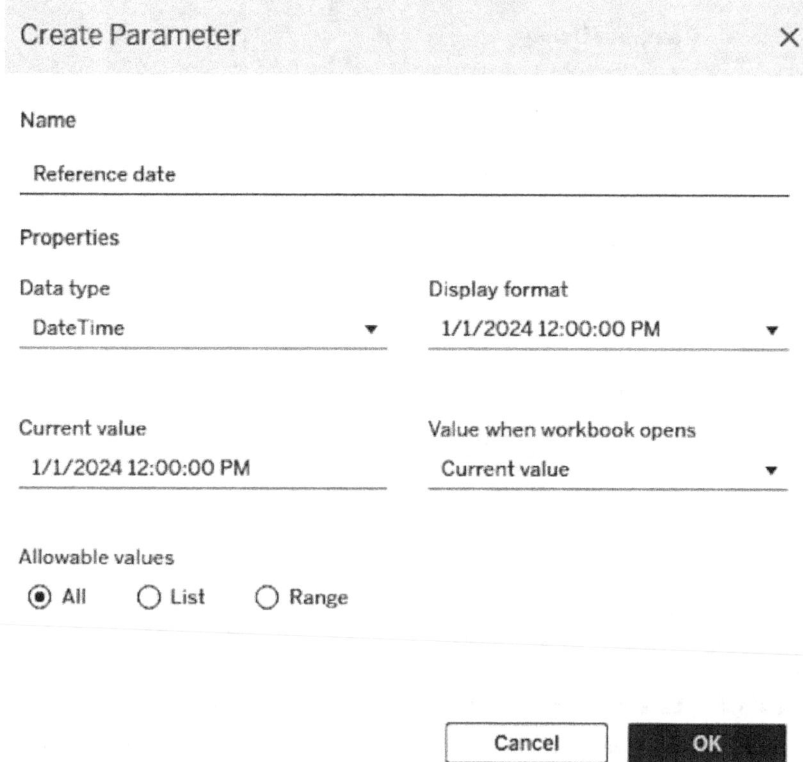

Figure 6.7 – Reference date parameter configuration

4.   Click **OK** once you are done to close the **Create Parameter** menu. The parameter should appear at the bottom of our **Data** pane.

5.   Now it's time to update how the **Percent Difference From** table calculation for profit is calculated. Right-click on **SUM(Profit)** in the **Rows Shelf** and select **Edit Table Calculation....** In the **Table Calculation** menu, we need to compute **Percent Difference From** using **Specific Dimensions**: **Quarter of Order Date**, and to compute it relative to the **Reference date** parameter created (*Figure 6.8*).

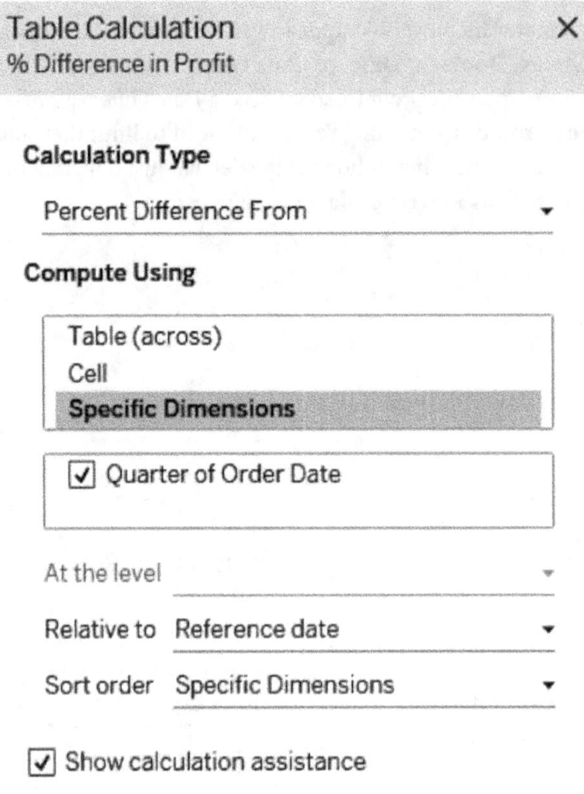

Figure 6.8 – Updated Table Calculation configuration

> **Tip: If all data disappears, use the Show data at default position option**
>
> Depending on the default value of the parameter when creating it, you might see all data disappearing after updating the quick table calculation. If that happens, you should see a label in the bottom-right corner of the chart that says, **16 nulls**. Click on that message and then on **Show data at default position**. This will show all the bars for every quarter at the zero position. Everything will work once we create our parameter action in the next step.

6. Now it is time to create the parameter action. Go back to the `Chapter 6. Recipe 3. Creating an interactive temporal analysis with Parameter Actions` dashboard worksheet and open the **Actions** menu from **Dashboard** > **Actions** in the top menu.

7. Click on **Add Action** at the bottom right and select **Change Parameter....**

8. Now, let's configure the parameter action. As always, give the action a meaningful name such as `Update Reference Date Parameter`. What we want is to click on a bar of the `6.3 Profit Percent Change` bar chart and update the **Reference date** parameter, keeping the new value after the selection. With this in mind then, set the action as follows:

    - **Source Sheet**: Just select the `6.3 Profit Percent Change` sheet.

    - **Run action on**: Choose **Select**.

    - **Target Parameter**: Select **Reference date**.

    - **Clearing the selection will**: Select the **Keep current value** option.

    - **Source Field**: Select the **QUARTER (Order Date)** field in the drop-down menu.

    - **Aggregation**: We don't need to aggregate, so select **None**.

    - Click **OK** to confirm the parameter action and **OK** again to close the **Actions** menu.

How it works...

Now it's time to test it. Click on any of the bars of the bar chart, for example, the one corresponding to 2022 Q4. The bar chart should be updated, showing 0% in 2022 Q4 as this becomes our new baseline for the percentage difference analysis, and showing that our profit in 2023 Q4 increased by 14.6% compared to that period.

Well done! You have created a dynamic temporal analysis with parameter actions.

There's more...

Let's improve the visualization a bit more by adding a dynamic title, a dynamic tooltip, and a reference line showing the current baseline:

1. Go to the `6.3. Profit Percent Change` worksheet and select the **Analytics** pane instead of the **Data** pane.

2. Drag and drop a reference line on the canvas. From the Analytics pane, click and drag **Reference Line** to the canvas, and drop it in the **Table** of the **QUARTER (order Date)** field. Make sure the reference line value is the **Reference date** parameter. You can also format it to your preferences. For example, I like a red dotted line and edit the label to appear at the top of the bar chart showing the quarter baseline with the **YYYY QQ** format.

3. Edit the chart's title to show the **Reference date** parameter values instead of the default **Q1 2020**.

4. Next, navigate from the **Analytics** pane back to the **Data** pane and create a new calculated field named **Reference Date Quarter** to truncate the parameter value to the quarter using the following formula:

```
DATE(DATETRUNC('quarter', [Reference date]))
```

5. Drag and drop the new **Reference date quarter** field from the **Data** pane to the **Detail** shelf of the **Marks Card**. Right-click on it and change it to a continuous quarter format.

6. Feel free to also edit the tooltip to give a more meaningful message to your audience.

    Did you notice that now, when you click on a quarter, the selected bar chart stays highlighted, and all the other bars are dimmed? There's a little trick you can use to automatically unhighlight the bar selected. Here's how you can do it.

7. Go to the dashboard and create a new action, but in this case, a **Highlight action**, and configure the action as follows:

    *   **Name**: No dimmed bars

    *   **Source Sheets**: `6.3. Profit Percent Change`

    *   **Run action on**: Select

    *   **Target Sheets**: `6.3. Profit Percent Change`

    *   **Target Highlight**: Selected Fields > Quarter (Reference date quarter)

8. Click **OK** twice to confirm the action and close the **Actions** menu.

9. Now, if you select any bar in the chart to update the baseline of your Profit Percent Change analysis, the rest of the bars are not dimmed.

Creating interactive sheets to switch between different measures with parameter actions

Using parameters to change a measure in a chart is one of the most frequent parameter use cases.

The disadvantage of parameters is they can be easily missed by end users. Tableau's default parameter controls are like filters and a bit small, so they can be forgotten or unseen on the dashboard, especially if we have tons of filters and control options.

Instead, parameter actions are a great way to alternatively use worksheets as easy to see and use parameter controls.

In this recipe, we will learn how to use measure names to create a worksheet that will be used as a control parameter, allowing users to choose what measure they want to visualize.

The benefits of this approach compared to regular parameter controls are that it allows us to do the following:

- Improve the user experience with easier-to-use control parameters

- Encourage exploration with a more prominent call to action

- Improve dashboard accessibility

Getting ready

For this recipe, we will start from a very similar dashboard to the one we had in the last recipe: the `Chapter 6. Recipe 4. Creating interactive sheets to switch between different measures with Parameter Actions` sheet in the `Chapter 6 Starter` workbook.

Our objective is to provide the user with the names of three measures in large text – **Sales**, **Profit**, and **Quantity** – at the top of the dashboard, allowing you to click on each of them in order to change the measure displayed on the two worksheets at the bottom: `6.4. Country Map` and `6.4. Percent Difference From`.

Let's see how we can do it.

How to do it...

1. First, we should build the worksheet used to swap between the different measures when clicked. Go to the `6.4. Measure Selection` worksheet. Drag **Measure Names** to the **Filters Shelf** and select only the measures we are interested in: **Sales**, **Profit**, and **Quantity**.

2. In Tableau, **Measure Names** always need to be used with **Measure Values**. In this case, we don't really need to show measure values on our sheet, but still, we need them in the view, so drag **Measure Values** to the **Detail** shelf on **Marks Card**. Additionally, for a second time, drag **Measure Names** from the **Data** pane onto the **Columns** shelf, and for a third time, onto the **Text Shelf** on **Marks** card.

3. Format the text to align text to the center and make it a bit bigger. You can also remove borders and row dividers using **Format** > **Borders** from the top menu and remove the header. Now go back to the dashboard, and make sure the sheet fits the entire view to see the three measure names properly. Your dashboard and worksheet should look similar to *Figure 6.9*.

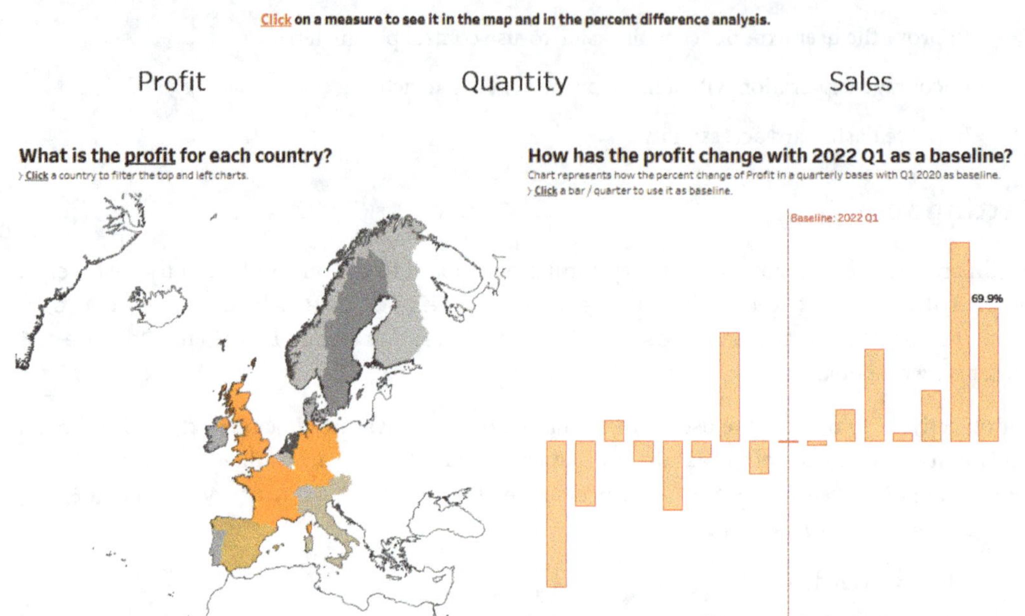

Figure 6.9 – An overview of the dashboard with the new measures sheet included

Now we need to add actions to the new sheet. But first, we need to create a parameter that we can update through a parameter action:

4. Go back to the `6.4. Measure Selection` worksheet and create a new parameter through the **Data** pane. The values of the parameter should match the measure names. In our case, the **Data type** should be **String**, and **Allowable values** should be a **list** of three values: **Sales**, **Quantity**, and **Profit**, as in *Figure 6.10*. Don't forget to give the parameter a meaningful name (I named it **Measure parameter**) and click **OK** once it's ready.

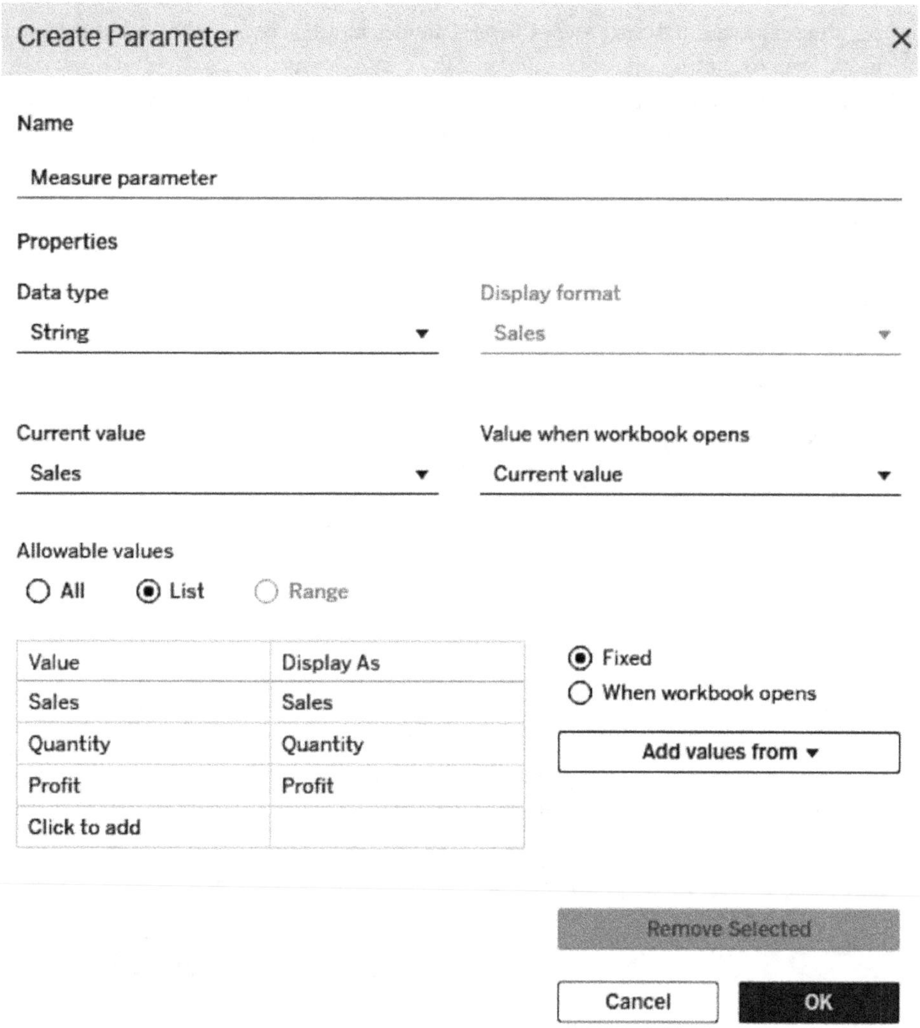

Create Parameter   ✕

Name

Measure parameter

Properties

Data type

String ▼

Display format

Sales ▼

Current value

Sales ▼

Value when workbook opens

Current value ▼

Allowable values

◯ All   ⦿ List   ◯ Range

Value	Display As
Sales	Sales
Quantity	Quantity
Profit	Profit
Click to add	

⦿ Fixed
◯ When workbook opens

Add values from ▼

Remove Selected

Cancel   OK

Figure 6.10 – Creating the measure parameter

5. With the parameter set up, we can now create the parameter action.

6. Go back to the dashboard and create a new **Change Parameter...** action through the **Dashboard > Action** menu. We want to click on one of the marks of the `6.4. Measure Selection` worksheet and update the **Measure parameter** just created based on the measure name. So, after giving the action a name (for example, **Update Measure Parameter**) the configuration should be as shown in *Figure 6.11*:

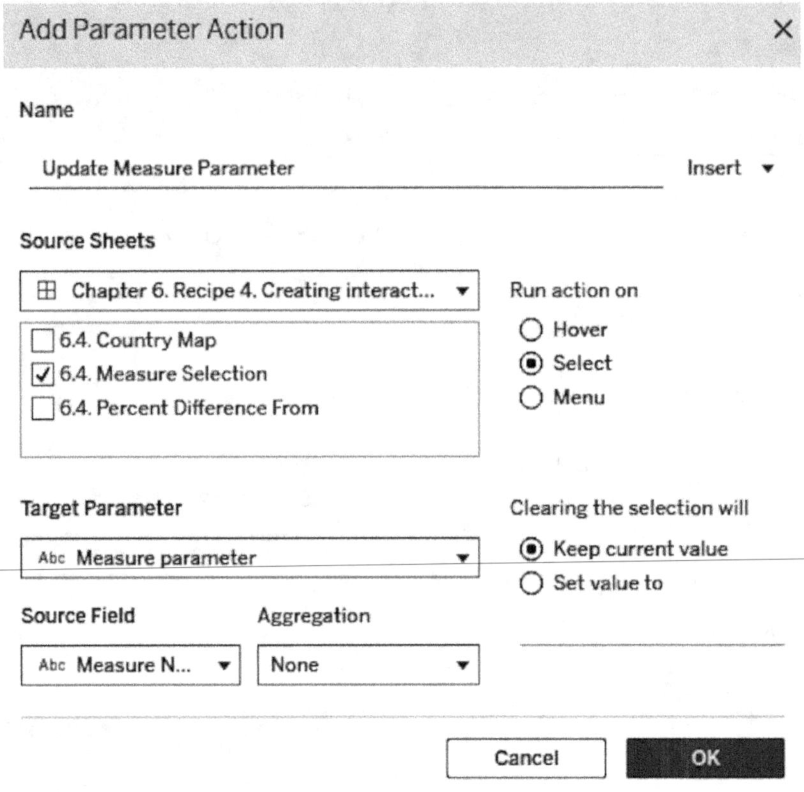

Figure 6.11 – Update measure action configuration

7. Now, go to the sheet `6.4. Country Map` and create a new calculated field named **Measure Selected** like the following:

```
CASE [Measure parameter]
WHEN "Profit" THEN SUM([Profit])
WHEN "Sales" THEN SUM([Sales])
WHEN "Quantity" THEN SUM([Quantity])
END
```

8. Click **OK** to save the calculated field.

9. Now we need to replace the Profit measure in the Color Shelf of the `6.4. Country Map` sheet and also in the Rows Shelf of the `6.4. Percent Difference From` sheet, making sure you edit the **Quick Table Calculation** as a **Percent Difference** and relative to the first value. Update also the tooltips accordingly to show a meaningful text referencing the new measure and the parameter.

10. Last but not least, we can make things a bit easier for the end user. Edit the title of the `6.4. Country Map` and `6.4. Percent Difference From` worksheets, replacing "profit" with the parameter so the title also updates with the name of the measure we are visualizing.

How it works...

Now it's time to test the parameter action. Go to the dashboard and click on the **Profit**, **Quantity**, or **Sales** text at the top of the worksheet. Both charts at the bottom should update accordingly.

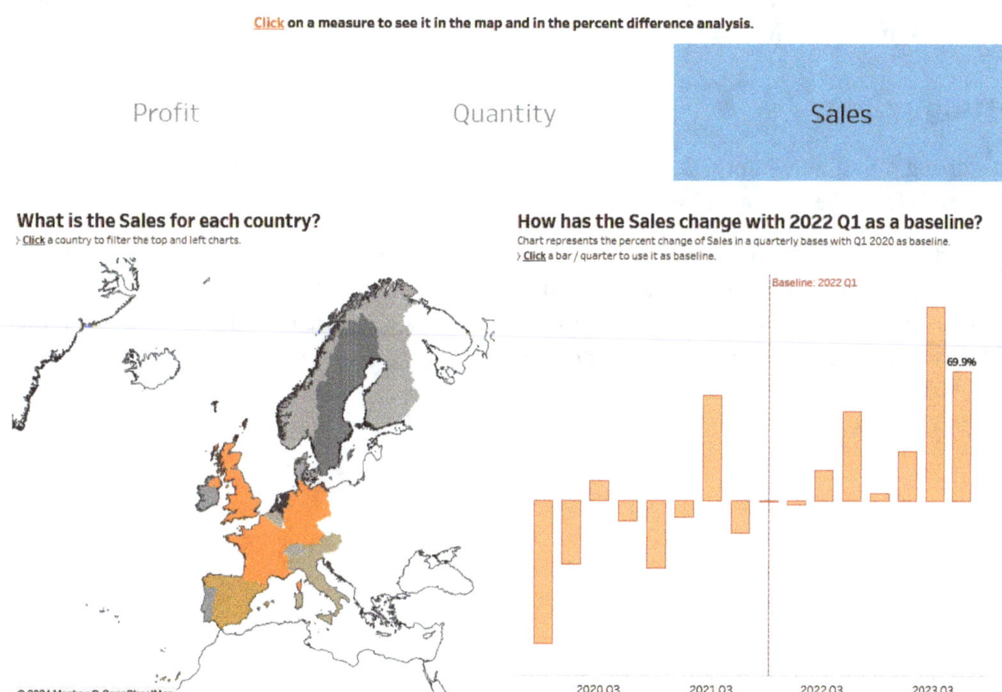

Figure 6.12 – Clicking the Sales measure text for testing

Good job! You have just learned how to use parameter actions to switch a parameter based on a worksheet.

Building part-to-whole and proportional brushing analysis with set actions

Most of the time, when users interact with dashboards they expect to click on the different charts and filter the data based on the selection. This is why filter actions are the most common ones in Tableau and other BI platforms.

Nevertheless, filtering implies some drawbacks. They allow us to focus on the data we want to see but, at the same time, we lose context. Once a filter is applied, we can't see the full picture anymore unless we remove the filter. Wouldn't it be great if we could select the data we want to focus attention on but keep the full picture in context?

This is one of the main use cases of **sets** and **set actions**, allowing us to build more insightful analysis with the easiness of Tableau's actions.

In this recipe, you will learn how you can build a part-to-whole and proportional brushing analysis with set actions, allowing users to keep the context of the full data but also get insights into the parts they are most interested in.

Getting ready

As a starting point, we will use `Chapter 6. Recipe 5. Proportional Brushing` (*Figure 6.13*) from the `Chapter 6 Starter` workbook.

The objective is to allow users to click on a country on the bar chart on the left side of the dashboard and see the proportion of Sales of the selected country or countries of the total sales, items sold, and number of orders in the pie charts on the right. Additionally, compare the sales of the cities in the selected country to all other cities in the bottom-right chart.

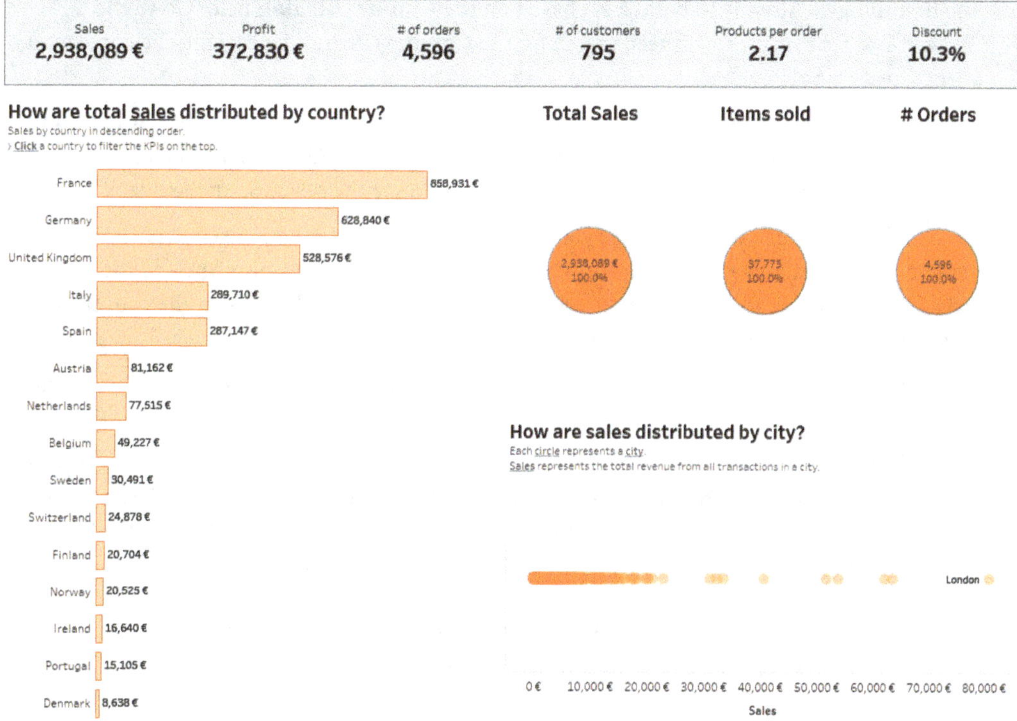

Figure 6.13 – An overview of Global Financial Dashboard for set actions

The benefit of this approach is that users will always keep the context of how much represents the selected country over the total for the different KPIs. At the same time, it will allow users to identify whether there are any cities where sales are concentrated, but again, also comparing them to all other cities of all the other countries.

This is a much more real approach to how we ask business questions and look for insights. Context is key to making good business decisions, so keeping the full picture of our business situation while we dig into the details will allow everyone to make better-informed decisions.

To summarize our goals for this recipe, we want to do the following:

- Allow users to select a country in the left-side bar chart and see how much that country represents total sales, items sold, and the number of orders

- Compare the cities of the selected country to all other cities of the rest of the countries in the bottom chart

Now let's learn how to make this possible.

How to do it...

1. The first thing we need is to build a set based on the **Country/Region** field. Go to the `6.5. Sales by Country` worksheet, search for the **Country/Region** field, right-click on it, and select **Create > Set**.

2. In the **Create Set** window, give the set a relevant name, such as **Country Selection Set**, and select any country you want in the list box. In my case, I selected Germany, but any country will do the job. At the end, we will add the action to change the selection dynamically.

3. Now, in the **Data** pane, you should see your country selection Set. Go to the `6.5 Sales Pie Chart` worksheet and add the **Country Selection Set** field to the **Color Shelf** of the **Marks Card**. The pie chart should update, showing the percentage of total sales that the country you selected in the set represents of the total.

4. Repeat step 3 for the other two pie charts in worksheets `6.5 Quantity Pie Chart` and `6.5 Number of Orders Pie Chart`.

5. Now, add the set to the `6.5 Sales by City` worksheet to allow end users to compare how sales for cities of the country set are doing against all the cities of the rest of the countries. Go to the `6.5 Sales by City` worksheet and add the **Country Selection Set** field to the **Rows Shelf** and to the **Color Shelf** of the **Marks Card** (*Figure 6.14*).

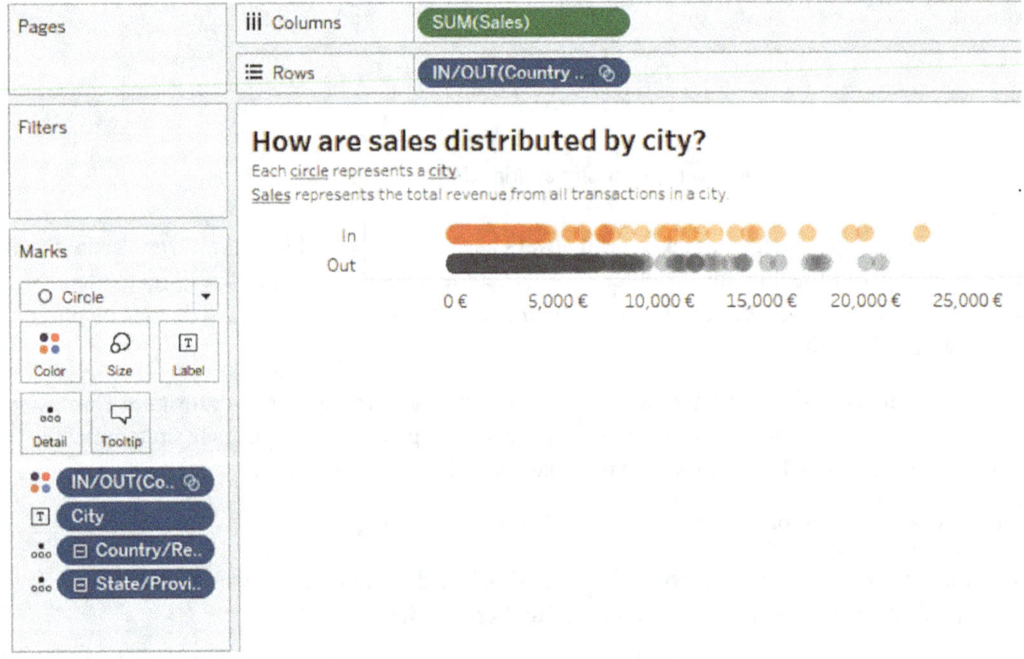

Figure 6.14 – Adding the set to the City sheet

6. Go to the `Chapter 6. Recipe 5. Proportional Brushing` dashboard. You should see something similar to *Figure 6.15*.

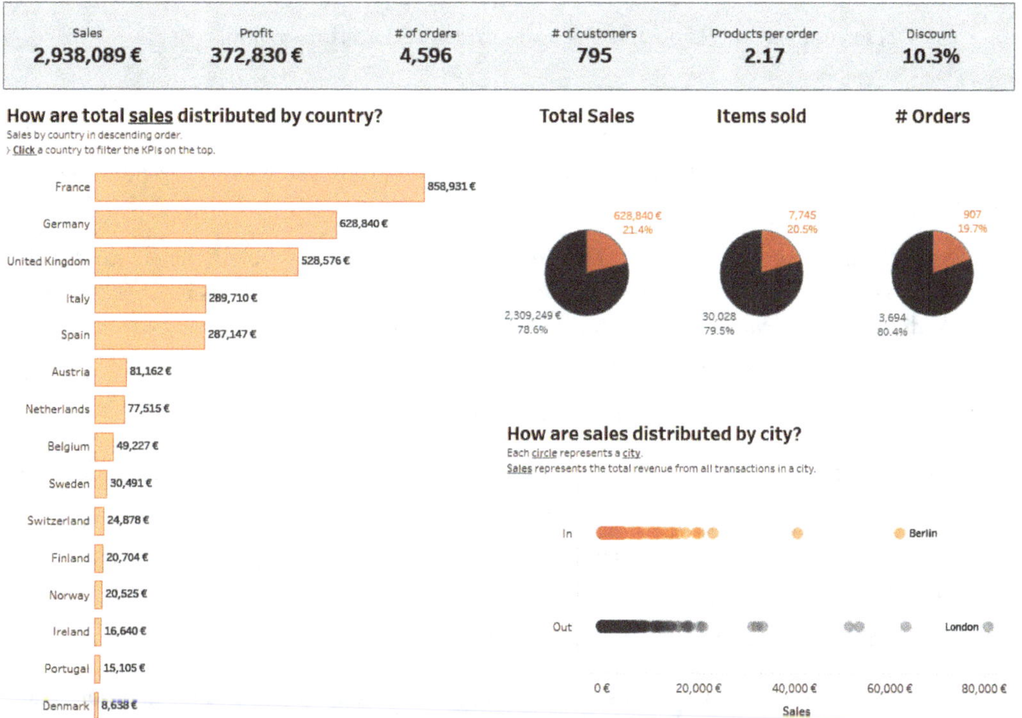

Figure 6.15 – An overview of the dashboard with the set added to the different sheets

7. The set is ready and on all relevant charts, but how can we make it dynamic? Now is when set actions come into play.

8. Go to **Dashboard** in the top menu and select **Actions** to create an action. Click **Add Action** and select **Change Set Values...**.

9. In the **Add Set Action** menu, we will specify how and when we want the set to be updated:

   - **Name**: Give it a meaningful name, such as *Update Country Selection Set*.

   - **Source Sheet**: Select the `6.5. Sales by Country` worksheet.

   - **Run action on**: Choose **Select** so the action runs when users select a mark on the source sheet.

   - **Target Set**: Select the name of the set created previously – in our example, **Country Selection Set**.

- **Running the action will**: We want the set to update the values of selected countries, so choose **Assign values to set** here.

- **Clearing the selection will**: Select **Add all values to set**. That way, when the user unselects the country, all countries will be part of the set by default.

10. Click **OK** to confirm the action and **OK** again to close the **Actions** menu.

How it works...

Done! Our action is ready. You just created a part-to-whole and proportional brushing analysis with set actions.

Now, if you click on any country in the bar chart on the left side of the dashboard, the pie charts will update, showing the proportion of sales, items sold, and the number of products for that concrete country. Additionally, you can see how each city is doing in terms of sales and compare cities of the selected country to all other cities in Europe.

The main benefits of this approach with set actions compared to filter actions are as follows:

- **Keeping context**: Instead of just filtering the data for the selected country, we can analyze the selected country while keeping the overall view

- **Improving the interpretation and communication of data** by allowing users to see how much their selection represents over the total.

- **Enriching the user experience** by providing a more powerful comparative analysis

You have just learned about a powerful use case for sets and set actions. But let's see another great example of how set actions allow us to extend Tableau's interactivity.

See also

- For more information about how to create sets, see `https://help.tableau.com/current/pro/desktop/en-us/sortgroup_sets_create.htm`

- For more information about set actions and the differences from filter actions, read this article from Bethany Lyons: `https://www.tableau.com/blog/8-analytic-concepts-express-tableau-set-actions-99108`

Analyzing different levels of granularity with sets and set actions

We just learned how powerful set actions are and how set actions allow endless compositions in our visualizations and analysis.

For example, we are used to having a fixed level of granularity in a sheet: sales by country, profit by product, salary by role, and so on. But set actions allow us to develop richer analysis, also merging different levels of detail in a single view.

Getting ready

In this recipe, you will learn precisely how we can easily have different levels of granularity in a same chart with set actions. Imagine the following scenario:

Managers want to see the total sales by country, but because some specific regions have such a big weight in our company, they also want to see how much of the total sales represent the provinces or states of a concrete country in Europe.

For this recipe, we will start from the `Chapter 6. Recipe 6. Analyzing different levels of granularity with Sets` sheet in the `Chapter 6 Starter` workbook.

Let's learn, step by step, how we can use set actions to combine different levels of granularity.

How to do it...

1. First, we need to build a set based on the **Country/Region** field. You might have a similar set created if you went through the previous exercise. If that's the case, you can use the same set, skip this step, and go directly to *Step 3*. If you want to create a new set or haven't gone through the *Building part-to-whole and proportional brushing analysis with set actions* recipe yet, then go to the `6.6. Sales by Country` worksheet, search for the **Country/Region** field in the **Data** pane, right-click on it, and select **Create > Set**.

2. In the **Create Set** menu, give the set a relevant name such as *Country Selection Set* and select any country you want from the list box. You should see the set in the **Data** pane. The set will just divide the countries into two groups (in/out) based on whether they are part of the set or not.

3. Now let's go a bit further. For countries that are part of the set, we want to retrieve the states/provinces of that country, and for all the other countries that are not part of the set, we want to just show the country, not the different states/provinces. To do this, we need to create a **Calculated Field** with an `IF` or `IIF` statement. I named this field *State or Country Based On Set*. The calculated field formula should be the following:

```
IIF([Country Selection Set], [State/Province], [Country/Region])
```

4. Now, replace the **Country/Region** field in the **Rows Shelf** with the field we just created.

5. Sort the chart in descending order and add **Country Selection Set** to the **Color Shelf** of the **Marks Card** to make it easier for users to differentiate between the countries of the set.

6. Now it's time to set up our actions. Go back to the `Chapter 6. Recipe 6. Analyzing different levels of granularity with Sets` dashboard. Navigate to **Dashboard > Actions...** from the top menu to create a new action and select **Change Set Values** from the **Add Action** drop-down menu.

7. We want the set to be updated when the user clicks on a country on the bar chart. So, the configuration should be as shown in *Figure 6.16*:

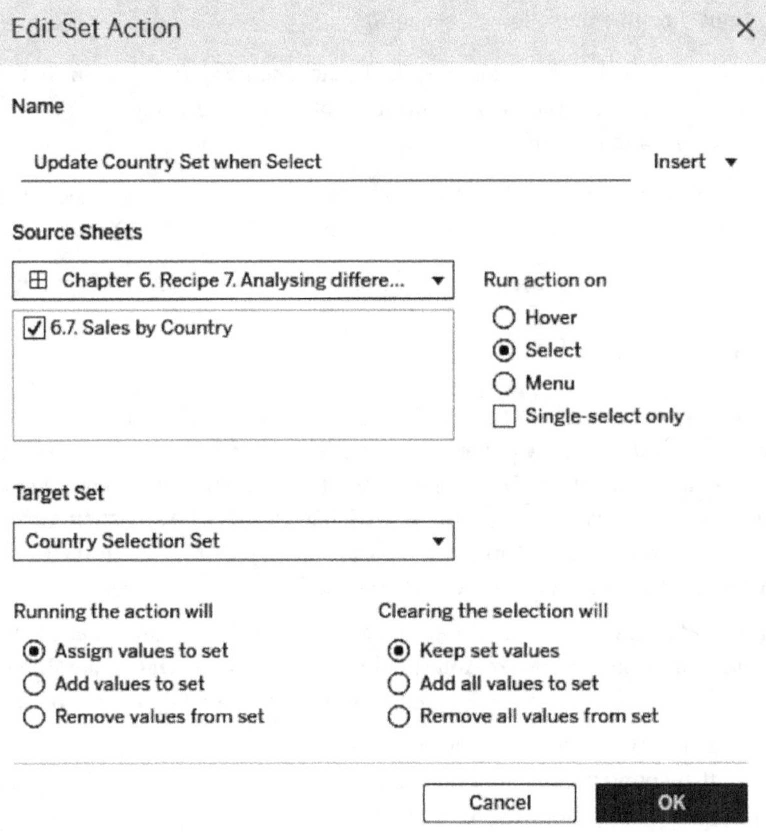

Figure 6.16 – Update Country Set action configuration

8. Click **OK** to confirm the action and **OK** again to close the **Actions** menu.

Now, if you select a country in the bar chart, you should see the different states/provinces for that country and, on the same chart, the rest of the countries. You have just combined different levels of granularity in a single view!

Let's go a bit further to make it easier for the users to go back to the original view using an additional set action through the tooltip.

9. Create a new **Change Set Values** action in the dashboard as you just did, but in this case, the configuration will be slightly different to show users a menu in the tooltip suggesting they click on it to remove all values of the set and show only sales by country:

    - **Run action on**: Choose **Menu.**

    - **Source Sheet**: Mark the `6.6 Sales by Country` worksheet.

    - **Target Set**: Select the same one as before – in my case, **Country Selection Set.**

    - **Running the Action will**: Choose **Remove values from set.**

    - **Clearing the selection will**: We don't want any changes when the user clears the selection, so select **Keep set values.**

    - Finally, give the action a name, such as *Click here to remove State/Province split.*

10. Click **OK** to confirm the action and **OK** again to close the **Actions** menu.

How it works...

Let's test it. Click on a country in the bar chart. The chart should update, showing sales for the states/provinces of that country, and in the same view, the rest of the countries.

Clicking on a different country, split and highlight the state/provinces for the country selected. Clicking on one of the states/provinces shows the message **Click here to remove State/Province split** in the tooltip. If you click on it, all values will be removed from the set, again showing only the country-level data.

There's more...

You might want to make it easier for users to know how to use the dashboard but also make instructions dynamic based on whether the user currently is looking at all countries or they have already split the analysis for a concrete country. To do this, we are going to create a new calculated field and add it to the view:

1. Create a new calculated field named *Country Set Instructions*, as follows:

```
IIF(
    {max([Country Selection Set])} = FALSE,
    "Click a country to see the split by State/Province for that
country",
    "Select a region of the selected country to go back to the
full country view"
    )
```

This calculation uses a Level of Detail expression to check whether the set has a value selected. The first part of the calculated field is as follows:

```
{ max([Country Selection Set]) } = FALSE
```

It checks whether the maximum value of the set is equal to `FALSE` (all the values are out of the set). If that's the case, it will return the `Click a country to see the split by State/Province for that country` text. In another case (if there is at least one country in the set), the calculation will return the `Select a region of the selected country to go back to the full country view` text.

Add this new calculated field to the Detail Shelf on the **Marks Card** on the `6.6. Sales by Country` worksheet.

2. Edit the title of the chart to show the value of the calculation as a subtitle.

This type of instruction helps users understand how to use your dashboards, improves the user experience, and helps adoption across your organization.

Join our community on Discord

Join our community's Discord space for discussions with the authors and other readers:

```
https://packt.link/ds
```

Interactivity and Zone Visibility: From Dashboards to Data Apps

Making dashboards and data applications easy to understand and use is key to user adoption and ensuring they provide real value to your organization.

Traditional dashboards, while interactive, have the risk of becoming busy and overwhelming, making them difficult to understand for users who might not be as proficient at using them as the developers building them.

Data applications are interactive tools for delivering insights and taking action based on those insights. Data apps provide relevant context and reduce the complexity of traditional dashboards.

Interactivity and **Dynamic Zone Visibility (DZV)** are key features that allow you to move from traditional, heavy dashboards to data applications when you are developing your dashboards with Tableau.

Dashboard space is valuable, and DZV allows us to show or hide elements and zones of our dashboards based on user interaction and the values of fields or parameters. This allows you more flexibility in your dashboard designs, while encouraging user interaction and improving how we communicate with data.

In this chapter, we will see how DZV allows us to make visualizations dynamic in more flexible ways, and how we can move from a dashboard approach to a data application approach.

The following recipes are covered in this chapter:

- Understanding containers and why they are important
- Showing and hiding content based on a basic parameter with DZV
- Showing content only to specific users and groups with DZV
- Advanced guided analytics with parameter actions
- Advanced guided analytics with DZV

Technical requirements

All the starter workbooks and solutions for this chapter can be found in our GitHub repository:

```
https://github.com/PacktPublishing/Tableau-Cookbook-for-Experienced-
Professionals/tree/main/Chapter_07
```

Understanding containers and why they are important

As mentioned in the introduction, **DZV** allows you to reveal or hide tiled or floating dashboard elements based on the value of a field or a parameter.

You will see that the configuration of DZV is quite simple, but one topic that becomes important when using DZV and designing more complex use cases is how to organize the different elements in your Tableau workbook.

Tableau allows you to organize all the content in **layout containers** by grouping related dashboard elements together.

Understanding how layout containers work will save you a lot of time when building your dashboards and making DZV work the way you want it to work. Although this chapter is not intended to explain layout containers in detail, it's important to understand the basics.

Getting ready

Basically, layout containers allow you to group related items together to organize them according to your needs.

There are two types of containers:

- **Horizontal layout containers**: Used to align dashboard elements one next to the other
- **Vertical layout containers**: Used to align dashboard elements one on top of the other

The benefit of containers is that you can also add containers inside of each other, allowing you to build complex content structures such as in UI / UX tools.

How to do it...

If you want to add a layout container to your dashboard, just do the following:

1. Make sure you are on a dashboard sheet. On the left side of the dashboard, there's a menu with two different tabs: **Dashboard** and **Layout**.

2. Click on the **Dashboard** tab if you are not already there.

3. Scroll down until you see the **Objects** section. There, you should see both the horizontal and vertical container objects.

4. To add one to the dashboard, just drag one of them and drop it onto your dashboard.

You can then place charts, images, text, or any other dashboard object inside of a container. As mentioned before, you can even put containers inside of containers.

Getting used to containers is very important in Tableau because they allow you to build any layout you want to make the dashboard exactly as you like. Especially when we want to show or hide content dynamically, they allow our dashboards to still look great and all the content with the size we need, no matter the interaction the users have during their analysis.

See also

- Learn more about containers in Tableau's official help guide here: `https://help.tableau.com/current/pro/desktop/en-us/dashboards_organize_floatingandtiled.htm#group-items-using-layout-containers`

- You can master how to organize content with containers with this blog post and video by Andy Kriebel, Tableau Visionary Hall of Fame: `https://www.vizwiz.com/2023/03/containers.html`

Showing and hiding content based on a basic parameter with DZV

Dashboards are a great option to show different types of visual data in a single place, but they can be overwhelming when they include too much information. To improve communication and user experience, it's important to think about how we can make it easier for users to focus on what's important, and show additional information, context, and detail when needed.

Because dashboard space is so valuable, DZV can be of great help, and integrating this feature into your design process can change the way you think about dashboards significantly and transform them into guided data applications.

Getting ready

In this first recipe, we will learn how we can use a Boolean parameter to hide and reveal the zones of a dashboard.

Download the `Chapter 7.1 - Showing and hiding content based on a Boolean parameter using DZV - Starter` workbook and go to the **Quality of life in 85 European cities** dashboard.

This visualization shows the quality of life rankings in 85 cities in Europe based on different KPIs such as education, environment, health, and safety. A section of the dashboard is shown in *Figure 7.1*.

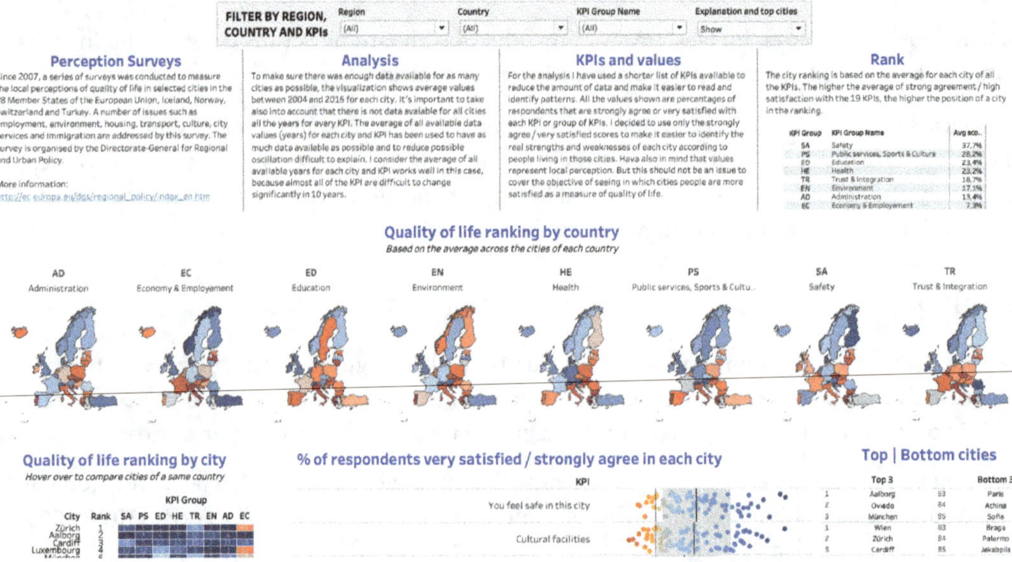

Figure 7.1 – A partial overview of the Quality of life in 855 European cities dashboard

As you can see, the dashboard has a lot of information. In this recipe, we will learn how to use a Boolean parameter to show and hide two areas of the visualization:

- The explanatory text about perception surveys, analysis, KPIs and values, and rank at the top

- The **Top | Bottom cities** area at the bottom right of the dashboard

How to do it...

Let's see how DZV works:

1. Go to any of the workbook sheets – for example, the **City Distribution** sheet, or create a new sheet if you prefer.

2. Look for the **Explanation and top cities** parameter at the bottom of the **Data** pane. Right-click and edit the parameter.

3. You should see the parameter details, as in *Figure 7.2*. The parameter is very simple. It's just a Boolean parameter, with aliases assigned so the **True** value appears as **Show** and the **False** value appears as **Hide** to end users.

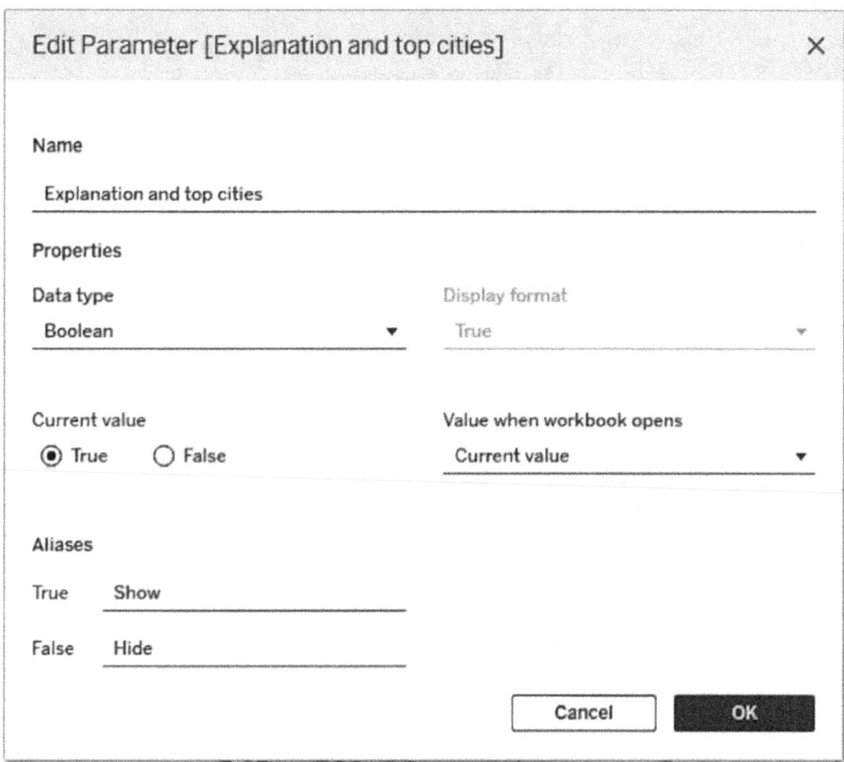

Figure 7.2 – The parameter configuration

4. Click **OK** to close the **Edit Parameter** window. This is the parameter we will use to show and hide the sections that we want.

5. Go to the **Quality of life in 85 European cities** dashboard and on the left menu, click on the **Layout** tab.

6. Expand the elements under the **Item hierarchy** section until you find **Explanation Container**, as shown in *Figure 7.3*.

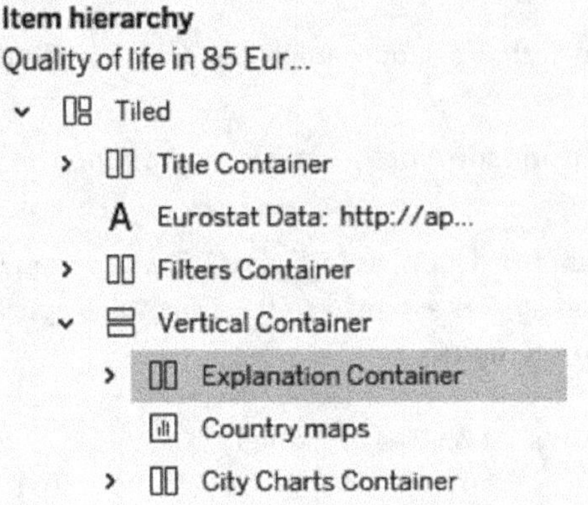

Figure 7.3 – The Item hierarchy section in the Layout tab of the dashboard

7. Click on the **Explanation Container** element in the item hierarchy. This should also highlight that element in the dashboard.

8. At the top of the **Layout** menu, search for the **Control visibility using value** checkbox and activate it.

9. Select the **Explanation and top cities** parameter in the drop-down menu, as shown in *Figure 7.4*.

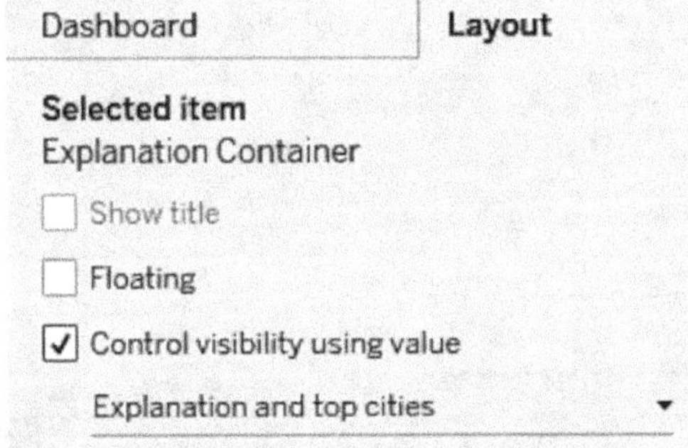

Figure 7.4 – Configuring DZV for the dashboard element

Easy, right? Perhaps you don't see any change, but now, if you change the **Explanation and top cities** parameter at the top of the dashboard, swapping the value from **Show** to **Hide**, the container with the explanation disappears.

10. Repeat steps 6 to 9 but for the **Top/Bottom Cities Container** element in the item hierarchy of the dashboard. This will make the list of top and bottom cities disappear, following the same logic.

11. Now, when you switch the parameter to **Hide**, the dashboard should look as it does in *Figure 7.5*.

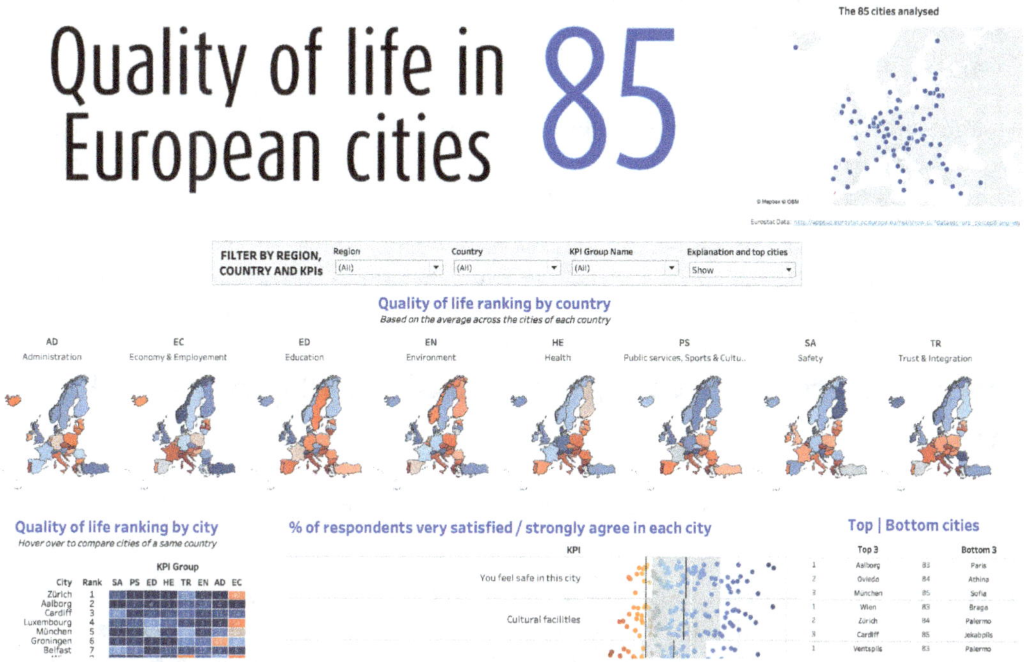

Figure 7.5 – An overview of the dashboard with the two containers hidden using DZV

How it works...

As we just saw, DZV allows you to show and hide any dashboard element automatically or based on user interaction. Before DZV, you could hide sheets using parameters, or show/hide elements using the **Add Show/Hide Button** feature.

The benefit of DZV is it combines the best of both approaches and offers a much wider set of use cases.

One of the key aspects of DZV and how it works is to remember that you can use a parameter or a calculated field, but they need to meet some requirements. As of the time of writing, to be used for DZV, a field or parameter must be the following:

- Boolean

- Single-value

- Independent of the visualization: the field must return a constant value independent of the structure of the sheet, such as a fixed **Level of Detail (LOD)** calculation.

See also

- You can also learn about the **Add Show/Hide Button** feature added to Tableau in version 2012.2 here: `https://interworks.com/blog/2021/07/12/tableau-20212-new-feature-show-and-hide-everything/`

- Learn about the differences between traditional sheet swapping in Tableau and the new approach with DZV by reading this article: `https://playfairdata.com/how-to-do-better-sheet-swapping-with-tableaus-dynamic-zone-visibility/`

Showing content only to specific users and groups with DZV

In the previous recipe, you learned how to use a basic Boolean parameter to show and hide content based on the user's interaction.

As mentioned before, this opens wider creativity options for organizing the content in a Tableau workbook, allowing developers to move away from overwhelming and busy dashboards to data apps where data, visualization, and insights appear based on user interaction using Tableau's DZV.

In this recipe, you will learn how you can leverage Tableau's user and group functions to show different content based on the group the user belongs to.

This can be very useful for different use cases. Here are a couple of examples:

- For companies monetizing their data through analytics, allowing them to present different sections to different users depending on their subscription status or tier

- To show different data based on the area or group the user belongs to in corporate environments, without needing to apply row-level security or maintain independent dashboards.

Getting ready

For this recipe, we will use the `Chapter 7.2 - Showing content only to specific users - Starter` workbook and go to the **Water Reservoirs in Spain** dashboard. It should look as it does in *Figure 7.6*.

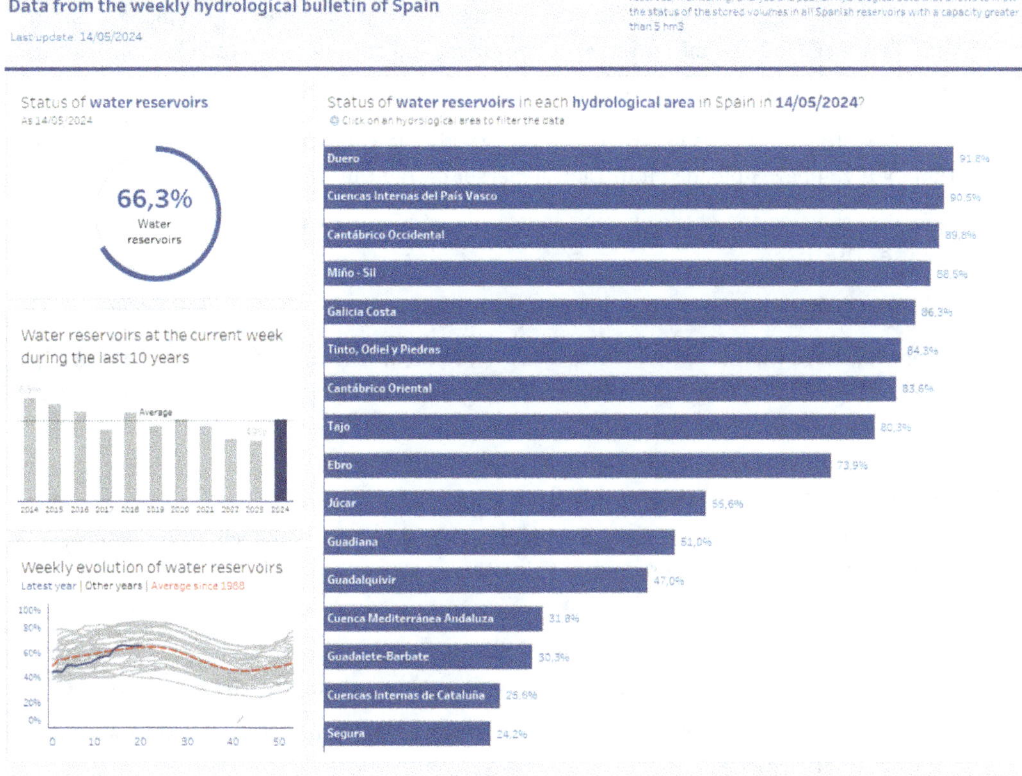

Figure 7.6 – An overview of the Water Reservoirs in Spain starter dashboard

Imagine you are providing this data and analysis as a service for your customers and you have two types of users:

- **Free users,** who can only see the big horizontal bar chart titled **Status of water reservoirs in each hydrological area in Spain**

- **Pro users,** who can also see the three different charts on the left side, and the link at the bottom to access the original data

How can we use DZV to achieve this?

How to do it...

1. First, you need a Tableau group to filter the content based on the membership to that group. Go to your Tableau Cloud or Tableau Server environment and create a group called `Pro Users`.

2. Add your user, and any additional users you want, as members of the group.

3. Now it's time to edit the dashboard. Open the workbook using Tableau Desktop or edit the workbook if you have uploaded it to Tableau Server or Tableau Cloud.

4. Go to a new sheet or any of the existing sheets and create a new calculated field called `Pro License User?`

```
ISMEMBEROF("Pro Users")
```

The calculation will check whether the user that is accessing the workbook is a member of the group "Pro Users", returning TRUE if they are a member of the group and FALSE if they are not a member of the group.

> **Check spelling when using ISMEMBEROF functions**
>
> User functions in Tableau are case-sensitive so always review how you spell group names, usernames, or any other attribute used when using these types of functions in Tableau.

5. Now it's time to use the calculation to control the user's ability to see the elements we want to show or hide. Go to the **Water Reservoirs in Spain** dashboard and switch to the **Layout** tab.

6. Look for the **Left Charts Container** element in **Item hierarchy**, under the **Tiled Container | Main Container** elements.

7. Click on **Left Charts Container** in **Item hierarchy** and then select the **Control visibility using value** checkbox at the top of the **Layout** tab.

8. Use the drop-down menu to select the calculation created in *Step 4* as shown in *Figure 7.7*.

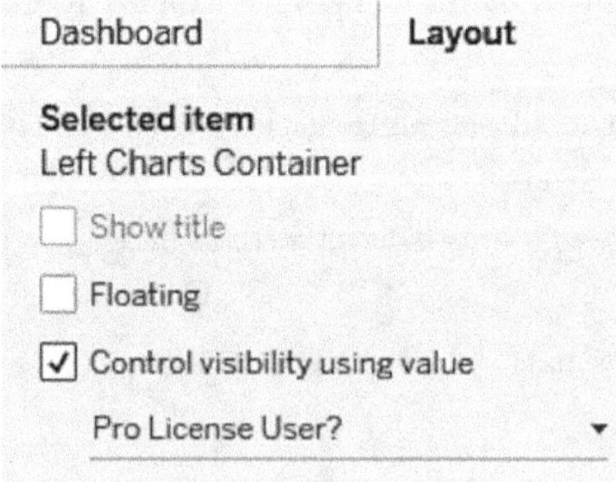

Figure 7.7 – Setting up DZV

9. Repeat *Step 8*, but this time select the **Link to data** element in **Item hierarchy**.

If you have added your user as part of the Pro License group, nothing should happen because, as the user is a member of the group, the calculation returns a **TRUE** value and shows the content using DZV.

If your user is not part of the Pro License group, you should only see the bar chart, as in *Figure 7.8*.

Figure 7.8 – An overview of the dashboard view for users who are not members of the Pro License group

How it works...

DZV combined with user attribute functions allows you to show different elements to different users. To check that the DZV is working as expected, you can do the following:

1. Go to the **Groups** section in Tableau Cloud or Tableau Server.

2. Open the Pro Users group and make sure your user is a member of the group.

3. Open the dashboard and make sure you see all the charts, as in *Figure 7.6*.

4. Go back to Tableau Cloud/Server groups and remove your user from the Pro License group.

5. Open the dashboard again and see the differences. You should the dashboard as shown in *Figure 7.8*.

Now, you can give more value to your paid customers and simplify your data monetization strategy by only needing to maintain the group membership of your users, instead of having multiple dashboards and more complexity in your Tableau environment.

Advanced guided analytics with parameter actions

The key to moving from overloaded dashboards to easier-to-follow and more insightful data apps is to combine what you have learned in this chapter and the previous one.

Think about how you can encourage exploration to engage your audience. One of the benefits of showing data and insights in a more guided way is by encouraging your users to pause, think about what they are seeing, and ask questions before looking for the answers.

The combination of the different action types, and especially parameter actions and set actions, with DZV will open new paths for your creativity and also improve the adoption and usage of your dashboards.

Let's see how.

Getting ready

In this recipe, we will combine parameter actions with DZV to move from a busy dashboard to a guided data app to make it easier for users to go through the data in the way we want to improve insight discovery and data retention.

Download the `Chapter 7.3 - Advanced Guided Analytics with Dynamic Zone Visibility - Starter` workbook and go to the **Product Revenue Insights** dashboard. It should look like it does in *Figure 7.9*.

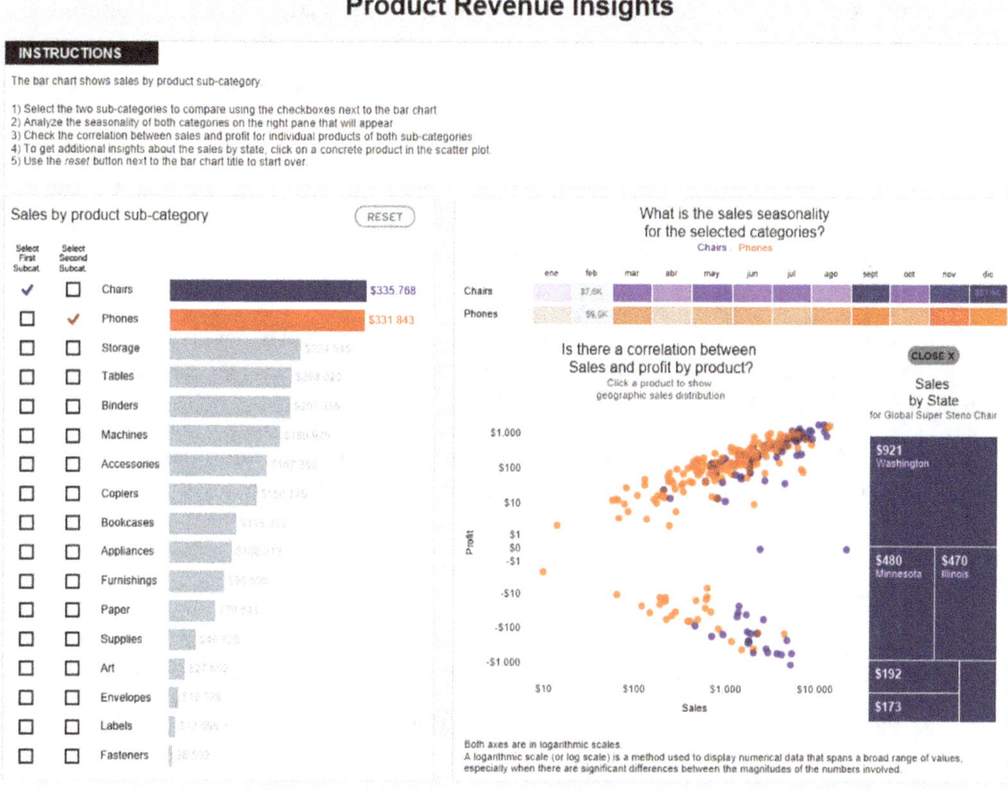

Figure 7.9 – An overview of the starter dashboard

As you can see, there's a lot of information and the dashboard can be overwhelming for users seeing it for the first time. Let's use actions and DZV to make it more interactive, following the instructions provided at the top as a guide to allow users to explore the data and find their own insights more easily.

How to do it...

For this dashboard, we have all the parameters already created, so we will focus on the actions and calculations to make DZV work in the way we want.

1. First, let's use parameter actions to allow users to update the sub-categories analyzed using the checkboxes on the left:

    I.   Go to **Dashboard | Actions** and add a **Change Parameter** action.

    II. Use the **Selection 1** sheet as the only source sheet and run the action on **Select**.

    III. Our target parameter to update is the one called **Sub-Category Selection 1**.

IV.   The source field to use to update the parameter is **Sub-Category**, using **None** as the aggregation, and clearing the selection will keep the current value.

V.   Name the action `Update First Sub-category` and click **OK** once you are ready.

Now, when clicking on one of the checkboxes on the dashboard, the category selected should be highlighted in purple.

2.   Now, create a similar parameter action but use **Selection 2** as the source sheet to update the **Sub-Category Selection 2** parameter and **Sub-Category** as the source field. Name this action `Update Second Sub-Category`.

3.   The reset button next to the bar chart title should serve to start over and remove both sub-category selections. The button is a sheet with a shape created with Figma, but you can use any other tool to create buttons like this to be used in Tableau.

First, we need a parameter action that changes the **Sub-Category Selection 1** parameter to - to clear the sub-category selected. The configuration should be as follows:

- Create a new **Change Parameter** action.

- Use the **Reset parameters** sheet as the source sheet and run the action on **Select**.

- The target parameter should be **Sub-Category Selection 1** and the source field should be - (this is dummy text with the - character added directly to the sheet in the details pane).

- No aggregation is required and clearing the selection should keep the current value.

- Name the action `Reset Sub-Category 1`.

This should look like it does in *Figure 7.10*:

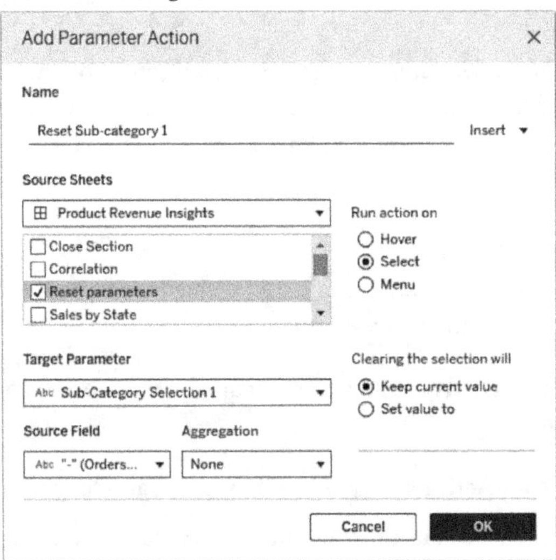

Figure 7.10 – Reset first sub-category parameter action

4. Create a new action that is almost identical to clear the **Sub-Category Selection 2** parameter with the following setup:

   - Create a new **Change Parameter** action, use the **reset parameter** as the source sheet, and run the action on **Select**.

   - The target parameter should be **Sub-Category Selection 2** and the source field should be "-".

   - No aggregation is required and clearing the selection should keep the current value. Name the action `Reset Sub-Category 2`.

Advanced guided analytics with DZV

The dashboard is more dynamic using parameter actions, but let's make it even more dynamic with DZV.

Getting ready

Having a look again at the dashboard from the previous recipe, it will be much easier for users if they don't see all the sections at the bottom right until at least one of the two subcategories has been selected.

We can achieve this very easily with DZV by creating a calculated field that allows us to control when the user has selected a category in the checkboxes, and use it to show or hide a full container accordingly!

How to do it...

Let's start from the last step of the previous recipe:

1. First, create a new calculated field called `Show Right Section`. The formula should be as follows:

    ```
    [Sub-Category Selection 1]!="-"
    OR [Sub-Category Selection 2]!="-"
    ```

    This calculation will return a TRUE value when any of the two `Sub-Category Selection` parameters is not "-" and FALSE when both parameters have the value "-".

2. Go back to the **Product Revenue Insights** dashboard. Look for the container named **Additional Analysis Container** in **Item hierarchy**, under the **Layout** pane.

3.   Select the container and use the **Control visibility using value** option to select the **Show Right Section** calculation, as in *Figure 7.11*.

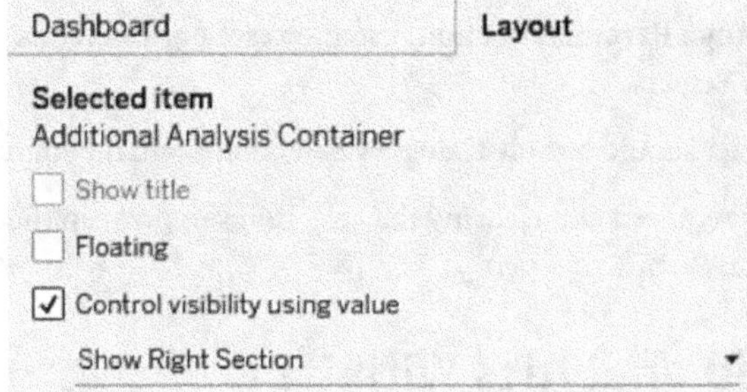

Figure 7.11 – Show/hide the container with additional analysis

4.   This approach can be used to also hide the `Sales by State` analysis until a product is selected in the scatter plot. Let's set it up by following these steps:

- Create a new calculated field named `Show State Container`. The calculation formula should be as follows:

```
[Product Parameter] != "-"
```

- The calculation returns `TRUE` when the product parameter is - and `FALSE` in any other case.

- Go back to the dashboard, and in the **Layout** pane, look for the **State Container** element in **Item hierarchy**, inside **Charts Container** | **Additional Analysis Container** | **Scatter Plot and State Container**.

- Click on that element and use the **Control visibility using value** option in the **Layout** pane. Select the calculated field we just created in the drop-down menu, as in *Figure 7.12*.

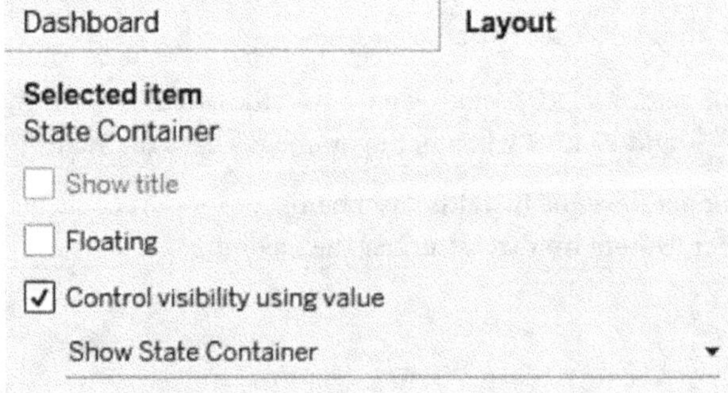

Figure 7.12 – Show/hide the state container

Well done! Now you have everything ready and it's time to check how it works.

How it works...

Let's recap. From a dashboard with basic interactivity such as filtering and highlighting, we used parameter actions and DZV to transform it into a guided data app that encourages exploration and provides insights in a more fluid way.

You can test how it works by downloading the Chapter 7.3 - Advanced Guided Analytics with Dynamic Zone Visibility - Solution workbook and checking the interactivity of the **Product Revenue Insights** dashboard.

When you open the dashboard, or if you build the solution following the *How to do it...* section, if you click on the reset button, you should just see the sales by sub-category.

You can use the checkboxes to select the two categories you are interested in and see the seasonality for both sub-categories and the product correlation between sales and profit, as shown in *Figure 7.13*.

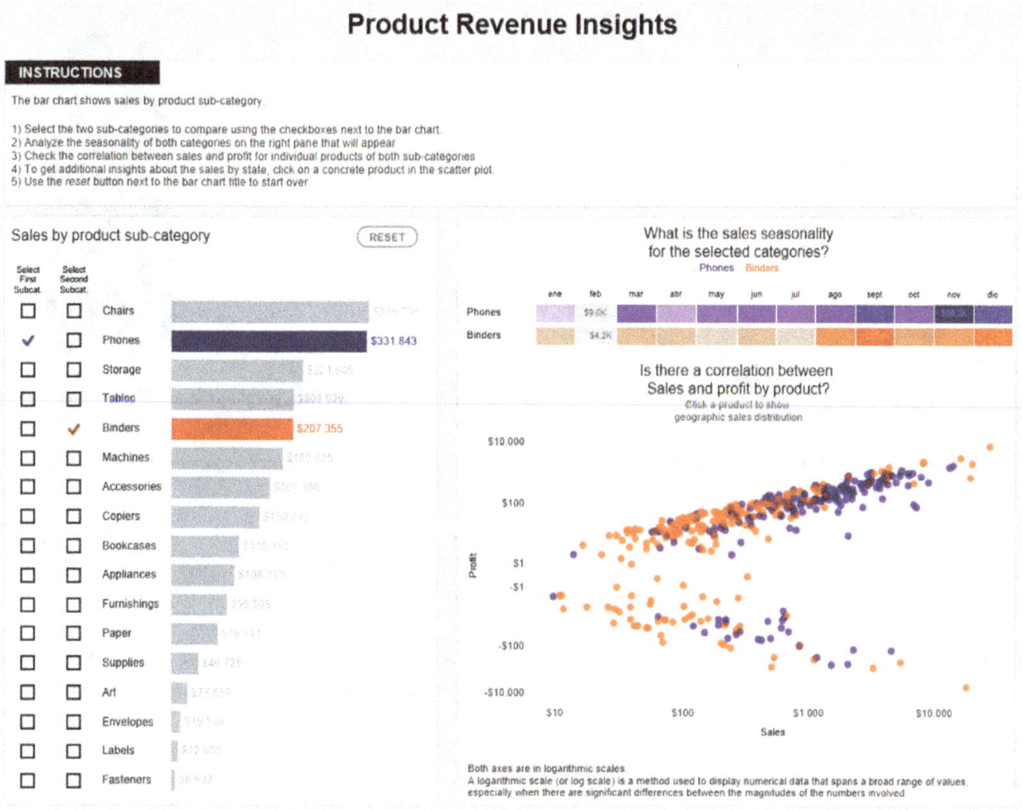

Figure 7.13 – An overview of the dashboard with categories selected

And you can dig into the details even more, by selecting a concrete product in the scatter plot to show the sales by state for the selected product, as in *Figure 7.14*.

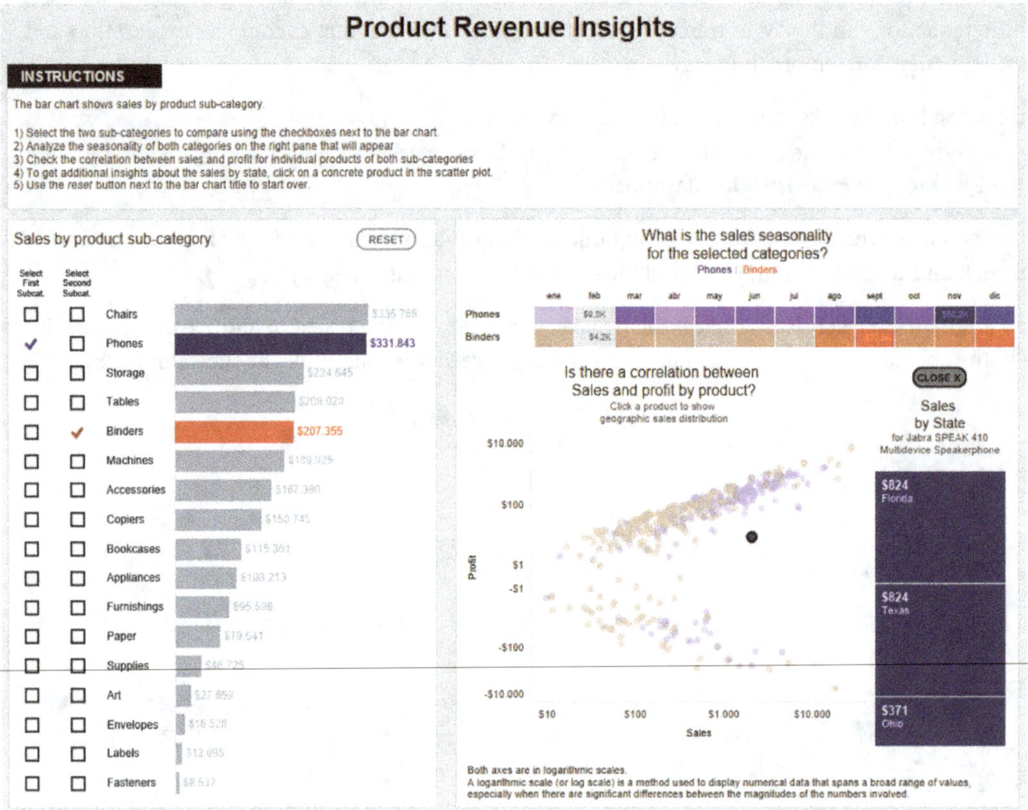

Figure 7.14 – An overview of how you can explore more insights by selecting a product

Finally, you can move one or several steps back, clicking on the close icon to hide the sales by state and reveal them again by clicking on a product in the scatter plot, or you can click on the reset button to start your sub-category selection from scratch and start over again.

As you can see, showing the data in different steps is a much better user experience. This is how we navigate and use applications in our daily life, by interacting with the different options that allow us to make decisions based on the data and insights that we discover.

DZV is a great, simple way to move away from traditional dashboards and transform them into guided data applications.

See also

- Learn about more complex calculations to be used with DVZ in this post from Marc Reid: `https://datavis.blog/2022/10/31/tableau-dynamic-zone-visibility/`

- Additional advanced examples can be learned from Alyssa Huff in this article: `https://playfairdata.com/how-to-do-advanced-dynamic-zone-visibility-in-tableau/`

Part 4:
Exploring Geospatial Solutions, Developer Tools, and Design Best Practices

In this part, you will learn how to leverage Shapefiles and spatial calculations to reveal patterns and relationships that conventional approaches often overlook. You will explore advanced methods for integrating location intelligence to identify optimal store locations and evaluate market influence areas to support business expansion. Additionally, you will dive into Tableau's developer tools and APIs to streamline workflows using the REST API, enhance analytics with Python and R integrations, and manage large-scale deployments with the Metadata API and GraphQL. Finally, you will master audience-centric dashboard design by learning how to maintain visual consistency, design for accessibility, and build advanced tables that effectively communicate trends and outliers.

This part includes the following chapters:

- *Chapter 8, Advanced Geospatial and Mapping Use Cases*

- *Chapter 9, Extending Tableau with Developer Tools and APIs*

- *Chapter 10, Core Techniques for Impactful Data Design*

8

Advanced Geospatial and Mapping Use Cases

Geographic data visualization can reveal patterns and relationships that might otherwise remain hidden. In this chapter, we will introduce some of Tableau's advanced spatial analysis capabilities and use cases. You will learn how to effectively combine traditional data analysis with spatial features to create more insightful and actionable visualizations.

The core objective is to master Tableau's key spatial functionalities, including working with multiple map layers, performing spatial calculations, and handling Shapefiles. Through practical examples, you will learn how to integrate different types of geographic data, customize map visualizations, and apply spatial joins and calculations to answer location-based business questions.

In this chapter, we will use the same files and datasets across different recipes to improve our knowledge of how to work with geospatial data with Tableau and how to build up more complex solutions and answer deeper questions with our geospatial data.

We will cover the following recipes:

- Performing geographic analysis using Shapefile data in Tableau

- Building advanced data models with spatial joins

- Adding multiple layers in Tableau's maps

- Using store and customer location data to run a store influence area analysis

- Using spatial data and clustering to find optimal store locations

By the end of the chapter, you will be equipped to create sophisticated spatial analyses that go beyond basic mapping and troubleshoot common spatial data challenges.

Technical requirements

For this chapter, we will need the latest version of Tableau Desktop or Tableau Desktop Public Edition: `2025.1` or higher.

Additionally, all the files required are available on this chapter's GitHub page at `https://github.com/PacktPublishing/Tableau-Cookbook-for-Experienced-Professionals/tree/main/Chapter_08`.

Performing geographic analysis using Shapefile data in Tableau

A **Shapefile** is a popular format that was developed by the **Environmental Systems Research Institute (ESRI)**. It is used for storing geographic information. When talking about shapefiles, their benefit is based on the collection of files that work together:

- The main `.shp` file stores the geometric shapes themselves
- The `.dbf` file holds the attribute data about those shapes
- The `.shx` file acts as an index to help quickly find specific shapes
- The `.prj` file defines the coordinate system and projection information

Some of the key benefits of Shapefiles are their wide-ranging compatibility across platforms and tools, compact file size, and fast rendering capabilities. This makes them particularly valuable for both analysis and visualization tasks. One of Tableau's main advantages to visualizing geographic data is its native capabilities to easily read and work with this type of file.

In this recipe, we will use election data from the USA with county-level results and combine it with a county-level shapefile to analyze election results with the power of maps to make complex data accessible to diverse audiences and support both expert and general audience needs.

Getting ready

For this recipe, we will use **Tableau Desktop** or **Tableau Desktop Public Edition** and the two main files available at `https://github.com/PacktPublishing/Tableau-Cookbook-for-Experienced-Professionals/tree/main/Chapter_08`:

- The `countypres_2000-2020.csv` file contains USA election results between the years 2000 and 2020 and it's also available at `https://dataverse.harvard.edu/dataset.xhtml?persistentId=doi:10.7910/DVN/VOQCHQ`.

- The `cb_2018_us_county_500k.zip` folder contains USA county-level geographical information and can also be found at `https://www.census.gov/geographies/mapping-files/time-series/geo/carto-boundary-file.html` with the same filename. This file needs to be unzipped to use with Tableau.

Let's start by learning how we can connect to a Shapefile with Tableau:

1. Download and unzip the `cb_2018_us_county_500k.zip` folder.

2. To connect to the Shapefile available in the folder we just unzipped, open Tableau Desktop or Tableau Desktop Public Edition and choose **Spatial File** under **Connect | To a File**. Alternatively, go to the **Data** menu at the top, select **New Data Source**, and select **Spatial File**.

3. Navigate to the folder with the unzipped files; you should see a file named `cb_2018_us_county_500k.shp`. Select the file and then click **Open** to connect to it.

4. You should see the **Data Source** window with the file we have just connected to, and the different columns at the bottom. Everything looks very similar to any other data source you have connected to before, but if you scroll to the right to see all the columns, at the end you'll see a column named `Geometry` with **Polygon** in every row. The column contains information on all the points and their latitude and longitude for each county in the USA.

   How can we visualize each county on a map and combine this Shapefile with the CSV with all the election results data? Let's find out.

How to do it...

Visualizing geographic data from spatial files with Tableau is really easy. Once you have connected to the file, first go to a new sheet in the Tableau workbook. Then, follow these steps:

1. Double-click on the `Geometry` column. As you should see, Tableau automatically places all the required fields to visualize the data on a map as shown in *Figure 8.1*.

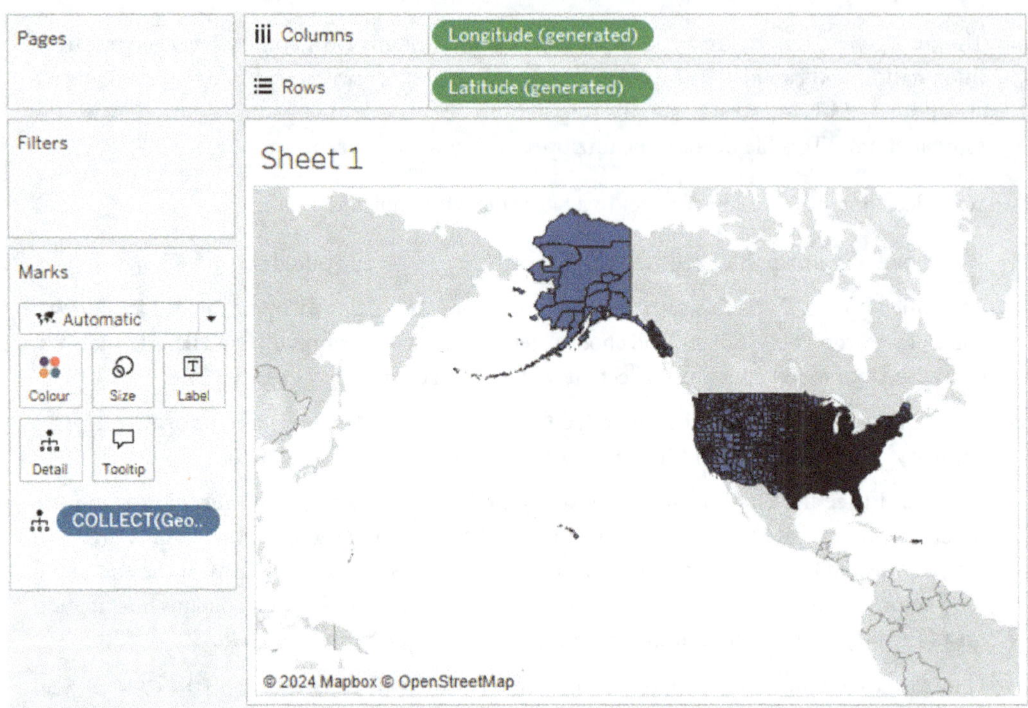

Figure 8.1 – Creating a map from a Shapefile Geometry field

What Tableau is doing automatically for us is adding generated `Longitude` and `Latitude` fields to the **Columns** and **Rows** shelves and the `Geometry` field to **Detail** in the **Marks** card. But, if we hover over any of the polygons plotted, you'll see Tableau highlights all the counties. In fact, if you look in the bottom-left corner to check the number of marks in the view, you'll see there's just one mark. This happens because Tableau is plotting all the county polygons together, but we haven't added any additional details to the view. We need to make sure we visualize each county individually.

2. To do so, we need to add to the **Detail** shelf of the **Marks** card: a field or fields that represent the full granularity of the data. In our case, we can achieve this with the `Geoid` field, which has a unique value for each county. Drag the `Geoid` field to **Detail**, and when you hover over any county, now you should see the Geo ID of each individual county. You can also add the `Name` field to **Tooltip** to see the name of the county when hovering through the map.

3. As you probably have realized already, this data set only has the geographic information for each county in the USA. Now, let's combine our shapefile with the `countypres_2000-2020. csv` file containing all the county results for USA presidential elections between 2000 and 2020.

4. Go back to the **Data Source** pane and add a connection to the file, or right-click on the data source and select **Edit Data Source.** In the Data Source window, click on **Add** at the top left next to **Connections** and select **Text File** as our data is in CSV format. Look for the `countypres_2000-2020.csv` file in your computer and connect to it.

5. On the left sidebar, just under **Connections**, you should now have the Spatial file and the Text file. see the **Files** section with a list of the text files inside the folder where your `countypres_2000-2020.csv` file is located. Drag the file from the left sidebar to the canvas to create a connection between the Shapefile and the CSV.

6. Now, let's define the **relationship** between both files, as we learned in the *Building a basic data model* recipe in *Chapter 1*. Both files have a unique ID for each county: the `Geoid` field in the Shapefile and the `County Fips` field in the CSV. The challenge we have is that each field is of a different data type: a string for `Geoid` and an integer for `County Fips`, so we will need to convert one of them and use a **relationship calculation**.

7. Select the `Geoid` field on the **Relationship Pane** for the `cb_2018_us_county_500k.shp` Shapefile, and for the related field in the CSV file, select **Create Relationship Calculation…** in the dropdown, as shown in *Figure 8.2*.

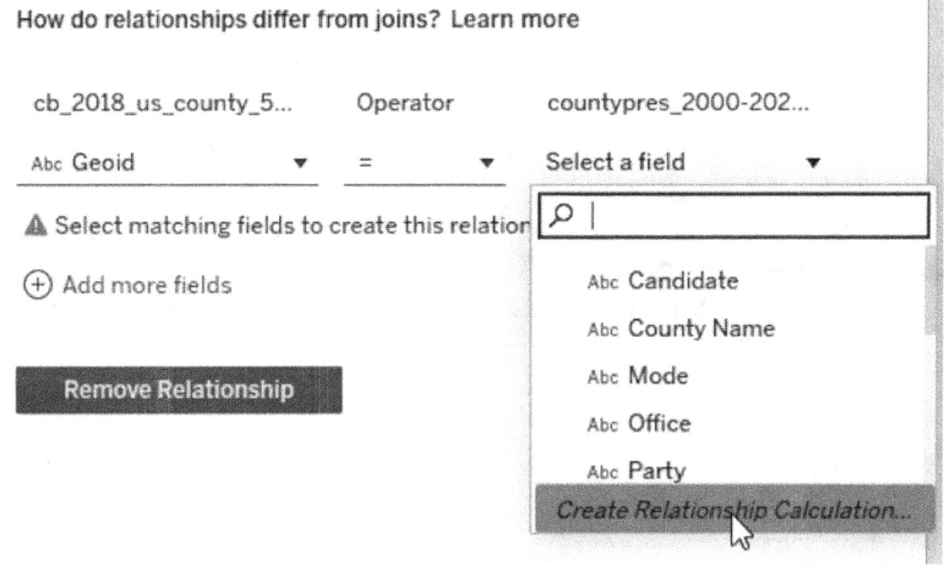

Figure 8.2 – Adding a relationship calculation

8. We need to keep in mind that Geo IDs always have 5 characters, such as `01001`, but in the CSV, the same `County Fip` value will appear as `1001`, so we need to add a leading 0 if the `County Fip` value has 4 characters. To do so, the calculation we need for the relationship is as follows:

```
IIF(LEN(STR([County Fips]))=4,
    "0"+STR([County Fips]),
    STR([County Fips])
)
```

9. Perfect, now both files are related. Let's create a new sheet and visualize which party received more votes in 2020 for all the counties in the USA:

I. On a new sheet, create the following calculated field named `Winner` to flag for each county and each year whether the Democrat or Republican party received more votes:

```
IF
{FIXED [County Fips],[Year] :
SUM(IIF([Party]="DEMOCRAT",[Candidatevotes],0))} >
{FIXED [County Fips],[Year] :
SUM(IIF([Party]="REPUBLICAN",[Candidatevotes],0))}
THEN "DEMOCRATS WON" ELSE "REPUBLICANS WON"
END
```

II. Double-click on the `Geometry` field to visualize all the counties in the USA.

III. Add `Year` to **Filters** and keep only data from 2020. Add also `State` to filters and remove `Alaska` and `Hawaii` to focus on mainland counties.

IV. Add `Winner`, the field we just calculated, to the **Color** shelf and edit the colors so that the DEMOCRATS WON value is represented in blue and REPUBLICANS WON is represented in red.

V. Add the `Geoid` field from the Shapefile to the **Detail** shelf to get an individual mark for every county.

VI. Add the `Name` field (the county name) from the Shapefile and the `State` field from the CSV file to **Tooltip**.

Your visualization should look similar to *Figure 8.3* at the end.

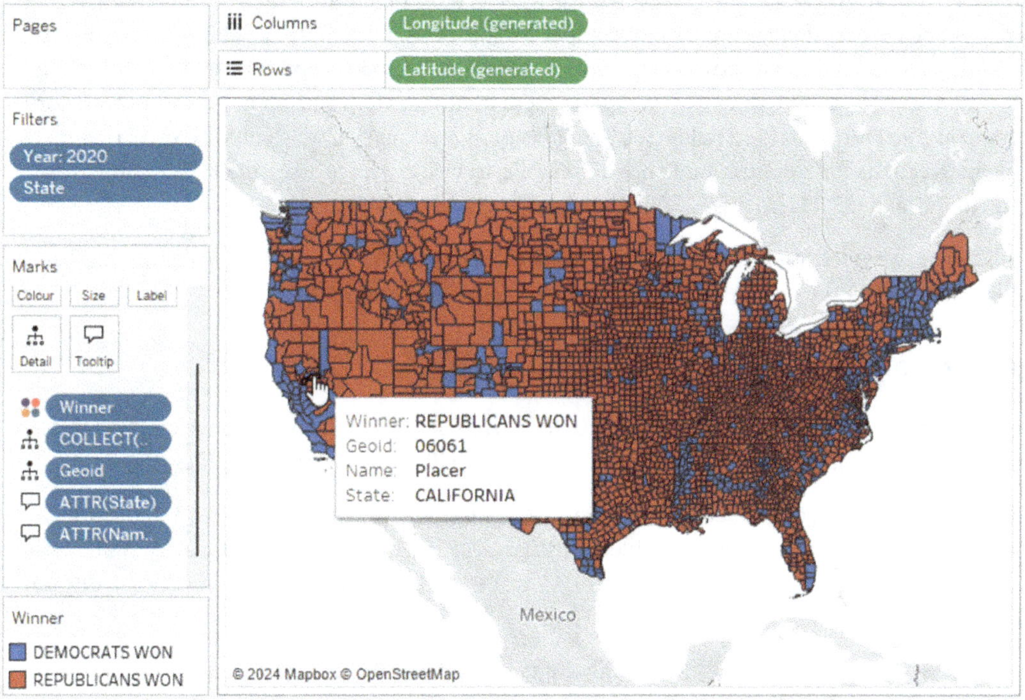

Figure 8.3 – Visualizing election winners in each county in the USA

Nicely done! You have just learned how to connect and use Shapefiles combined with other datasets to analyze your data using geographic fields.

Shapefiles and other spatial files, combined with other datasets, are a great opportunity to make your analysis much more appealing and easier to understand for your audience.

Building advanced data models with spatial joins

As we already mentioned in this chapter, geospatial information is useful because it provides an appealing, easy-to-understand, and intuitive way to unveil insights. Location data also makes data more engaging as people can relate it to places they have visited or lived in.

But geospatial data can also be, in some cases, the only way we can combine and correlate data together. With Tableau, we can use geospatial information to join datasets between them based on an intersection, for example, points that are inside a concrete area, paths crossing a specific polygon, and other scenarios.

These spatial intersections are used across multiple sectors, particularly in retail, real estate, and insurance. In retail and real estate, companies use intersections to optimize site selection by analyzing overlapping customer demographics and competitor locations. In the telecommunication industry, companies use spatial intersections for network coverage optimization and infrastructure planning, while transportation and logistics companies use these techniques for route optimization and territory assignment. Environmental and public sector applications are equally important, with urban planners using intersections for zoning compliance and public service coverage assessment. Marketing firms use them for targeted advertising.

In this recipe, we will learn how to create spatial relationships with Tableau to relate county-level and city-level data when the only relationship available is a spatial relationship.

Getting ready

For this recipe, we recommend following the *Getting ready* section of the previous recipe, *Performing geographic analysis using Shapefile data in Tableau*, as we will use those same two files.

We will build a more advanced model combining logical and physical layers by adding the `cities_florida.xlsx` file, available at `https://github.com/PacktPublishing/Tableau-Cookbook-for-Experienced-Professionals/tree/main/Chapter_08`, to our data model.

The `cities_florida.xlsx` Excel file only contains 6 columns and 56 rows, each row representing a city in the State of Florida:

- `City Id`: A unique ID for each city
- `City Name`: The name of the city
- `Population`: Total population of the city
- `Date`: The date of the population value
- `Latitude`: The latitude of the city
- `Longitude`: The longitude of the city

Apparently, there is no way we can connect or join this dataset with our Shapefile as there is no matching field we can use. We will use Tableau's `MAKEPOINT` function and an **Intersects Spatial Join** to combine both datasets.

How to do it...

For this recipe, we will assume you have gone through at least the *Getting ready* section of the previous recipe, *Performing geographic analysis using Shapefile data in Tableau*. If not, please review it to learn how to connect the Shapefile with the county data with the CSV with election data in the USA. Once you have those two files ready in your data model, we can continue with our current challenge:

1. Go to the **Data Source** tab in your Tableau workbook to see the current data model.

2. Double-click the rectangle representing the shapefile table, named, by default, `cb_2018_us_county_500k.shp`, to access the table's physical layer.

3. On the left-side menu, click on **Add** and add a new connection to the `cities_florida.xlsx` Excel file. Once you have connected to the file, drag the sheet named `data` to the canvas. You should see the default setup to create a join between both tables as in *Figure 8.4*.

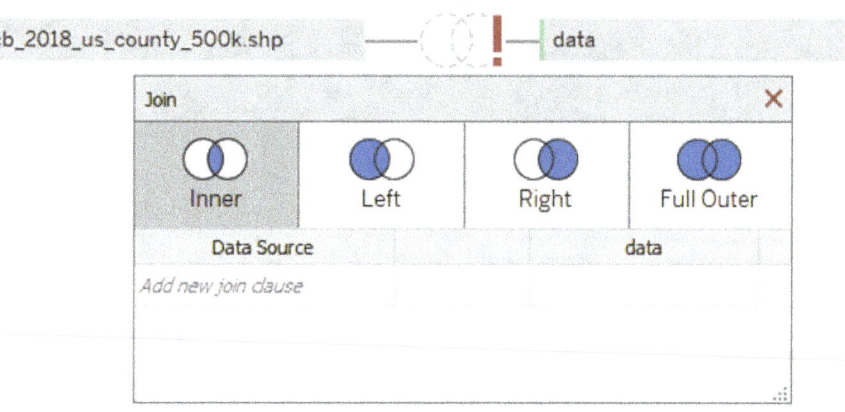

Figure 8.4 – Creating a join between our shapefile and Excel file

Now, we need to define how both files are related. But as we mentioned, there is no common field we can use. What we will need to do is create a geographic field in our Excel file using the `Latitude` and `Longitude` fields, and then use a **Spatial Join** type.

4. First, select `Geometry` as the field to join from the shapefile.

5. For the join field of our `data` sheet of the `cities_florida.xlsx` file, click the dropdown to select a field from the file, and then click on **Create Join Calculation....**

6. A **Join calculation** screen should appear. Now, we will create a spatial point based on the `Latitude` and `Longitude` columns of the Excel file. To achieve this, we will use the `MAKEPOINT` function in Tableau, which allows us to create a spatial point based on `Latitude` and `Longitude` fields. In the screen, type the following calculation:

    ```
    MAKEPOINT([Latitude],[Longitude])
    ```

7. Press **OK** to confirm the calculation.

8. Now, we need to define the join operator between both tables. As our shapefile contains polygons (counties) and our Excel file contains points (cities), the equal operator will not return any valid data. Click the dropdown on the equal sign between both fields and select the new option available, **Intersects**, as shown in *Figure 8.5*. The **Intersects** operator for joins only works with spatial fields and it will match records from both files when the city points from our Excel file intersect with the county polygons from our shapefile.

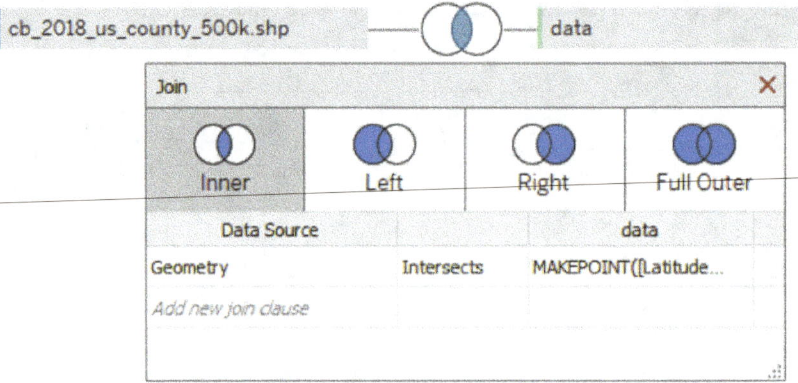

Figure 8.5 – Join configuration to define an intersection between spatial fields

9. Leave the **Join** type as **Inner**, to only keep counties and cities that intersect. Bear in mind that we will only see the counties corresponding to the cities in our Excel file.

10. Close the **Join** configuration window and the physical layer of our table.

11. Create a new sheet in Tableau and create a simple bar chart to see how the data is now combined. Drag the `City Name` field to the Rows shelf., and then the `Population` field to the **Columns** shelf, both from the `cities_florida.xlsx` file.

12. Now, drag the `Name` field from our shapefile, which contains the name of the county, to the **Rows** shelf next to the `City Name` field. You should have a similar visualization as in *Figure 8.6*.

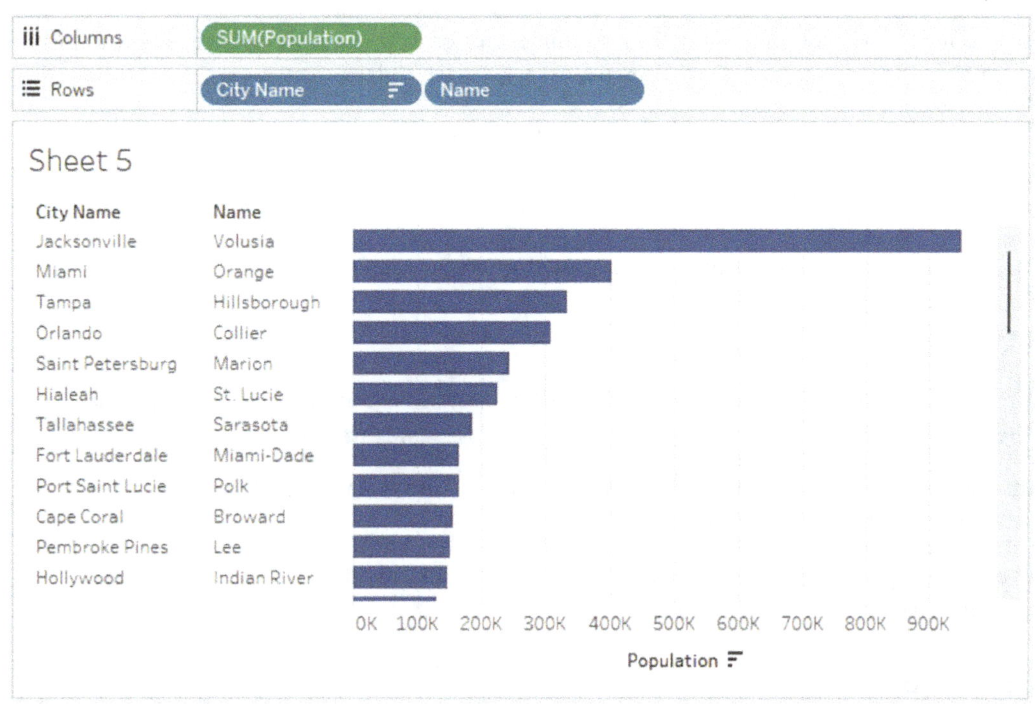

Figure 8.6 – Visualizing data from different sources using a spatial intersects join

Congrats! You have used a spatial join between two fields that apparently didn't have any fields in a column by taking advantage of Tableau's spatial capabilities and functions.

To summarize, we have used a polygon field from a shapefile, already prepared for spatial analysis, and joined it with a point field from an Excel file, created from `Latitude` and `Longitude` fields.

Adding multiple layers in Tableau's maps

During the last few years, Tableau has consistently added additional mapping features to enhance its geospatial analysis capabilities.

With Tableau 2020.4, multiple layer mapping capabilities were added, allowing users to combine different geospatial types, shapes, and analyses together. One of the better things about the multiple-layer capability is how easy it is to implement it.

In this recipe, we will continue using the data model created in the two previous recipes and learn how we can add additional layers to our map to visualize three different data layers:

- Map the different counties in Florida and who won the elections in 2020

- Add points showing the cities we have in our `cities_florida.xlsx` Excel file and locate the main cities of the state

- Make each city point size proportional based on the population

Getting ready

For this recipe, we recommend following the *Getting ready* section of the previous recipe, *Building advanced data models with spatial joins*, as we will use those same three files.

With the data model built in the previous recipe, we can now visualize the Florida counties with intersecting cities from our Excel file.

Let's build a simple map visualization and learn how we can add additional layers as well as use some of the newest spatial functions in Tableau.

How to do it...

Adding additional layers to your maps it's easy. Here's how we can do it:

1. Using the data model created in the previous recipe, go to a new Tableau sheet and double-click the `Geometry` field from the county shapefile dataset called `cb_2018_us_county_500k.shp`. As mentioned in the previous recipe, we defined a spatial intersection between USA counties and the Florida Excel file with the latitude and longitude of a few cities.

2. Filter the visualization by year keeping only data from 2020, the latest election we have data for in the file. Add also the `Winner` calculation created in *Step 9* of the *Performing geographic analysis using Shapefile data in Tableau* recipe. You should now have a map like *Figure 8.7*.

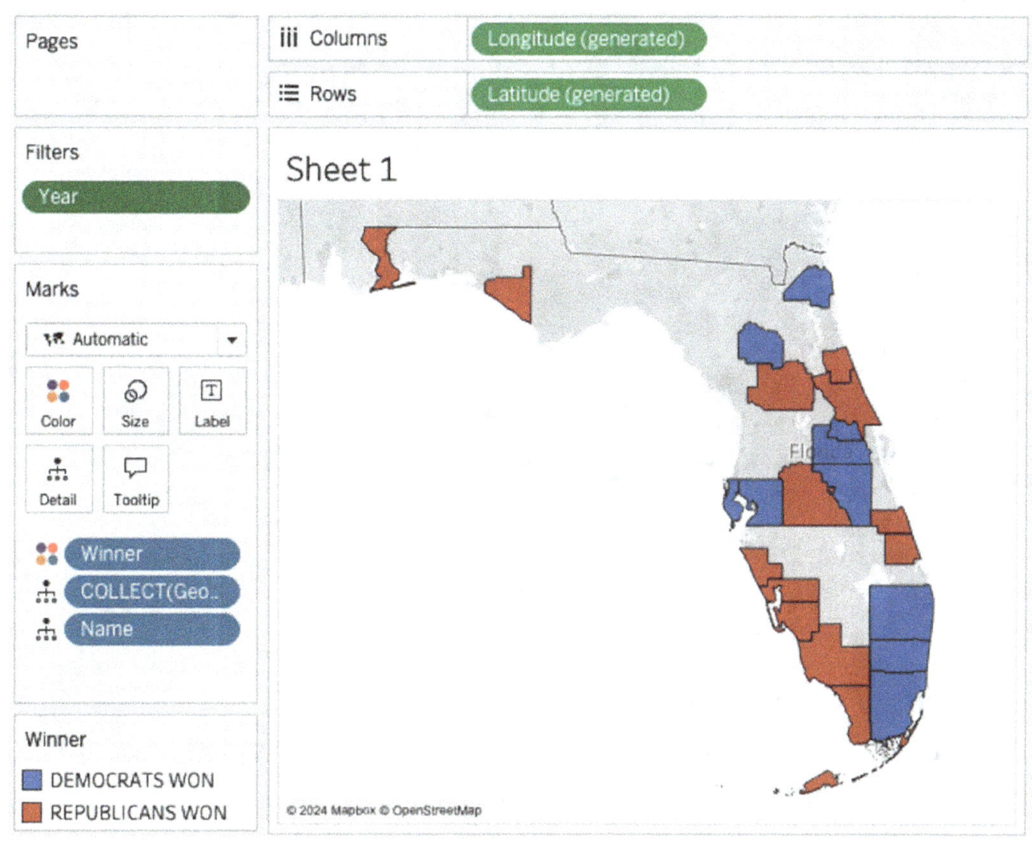

Figure 8.7 – Visualizing Florida counties

3. We only see a few counties from Florida because those are the counties that intersect with the locations of the cities in our Excel file.

4. To add additional layers, we will need to use another spatial field. To do so, we need to use the MAKEPOINT function and create spatial points based on the cities' Latitude and Longitude fields. Create a new calculated field named City Point with this formula:

```
MAKEPOINT([Latitude], [Longitude])
```

5. Drag the new field just created to the canvas; you should see an icon at the top left that says **Add a Marks Layer**. Drop the City Point field there, as in *Figure 8.8*.

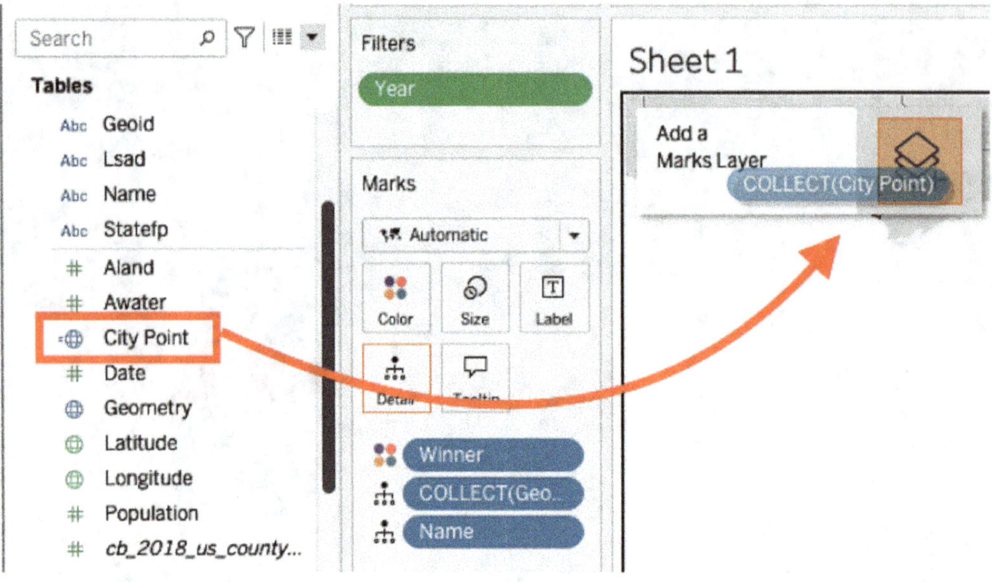

Figure 8.8 – Adding a second layer to a map

Two important things should happen:

- First, the cities should appear on the map as points

- Second, the **Marks** card now should have two subsections, one for each layer

6. Check the two layers of the **Marks** card. You can click on the selector icon of each of them and check additional options for each layer, as in *Figure 8.9*.

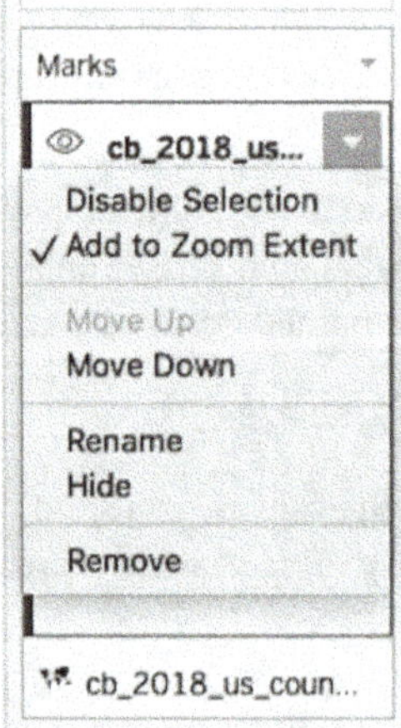

Figure 8.9 – Map layer options in the Marks card

7. Rename each layer so it's easier to identify the **County** layer and the **City** layer. You can also use the **Move Up** and **Move Down** options, or just drag a layer before or after another to change the order of the layers. In this case, it makes more sense to have the **City** layer on top of the **County** layer because in other cases, the shape of the counties will not allow us to show and hover over the cities properly.

8. Add the `City Name` field to the **City** layer to get a single mark for each city.

9. Finally, let's make some additional changes to the **City** layer so it looks a bit nicer:

I.   Change the **Marks** type of the **City** layer from **Automatic** to **Circle**.

II. Add the `Population` field to **Size** in the **Marks** card of the **City** layer.

III. Change the color to black so that cities are easier to identify.

Our visualization should look similar to *Figure 8.10*.

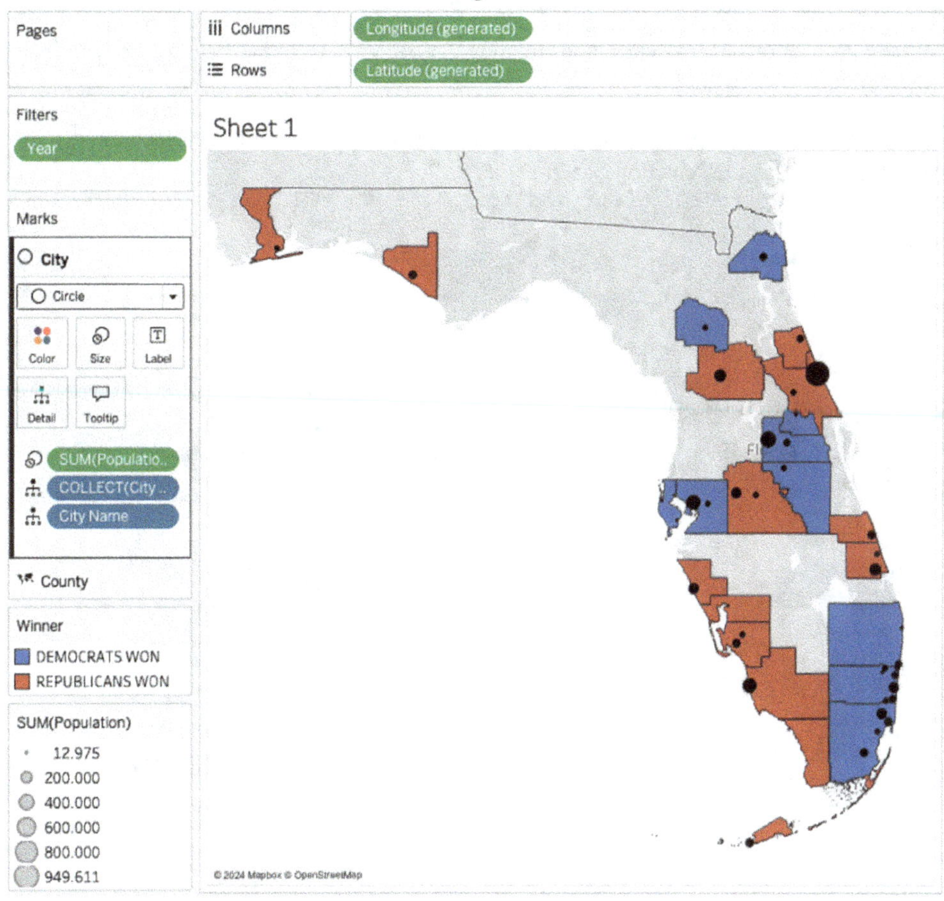

Figure 8.10 – Combining city locations and county election results

That's how you can add additional layers to your maps. Remember that the best and most efficient way is to use additional spatial objects, such as points, polygons, or lines. Also, remember that you can create points if you have `Latitude` and `Longitude` fields.

Of course, we are not limited to two layers. We could add more if we had more spatial data.

There's more...

Tableau keeps adding additional spatial capabilities and functions to the platform. For instance, if you don't want to see all the polygon areas of each county, since Tableau version 2024.3, we can use the `OUTLINE` function to return polygons converted into line strings.

Create a new calculated field named `County Outline` with this formula:

```
OUTLINE([Geometry])
```

In the **County** layer of our **Marks** card, add the new `County Outline` field to the **Detail** shelf and remove the `Geometry` field.

Now, instead of the full county polygon shapes, you should just see the outline of each country, colored by the party that won the 2020 elections, as in *Figure 8.11*.

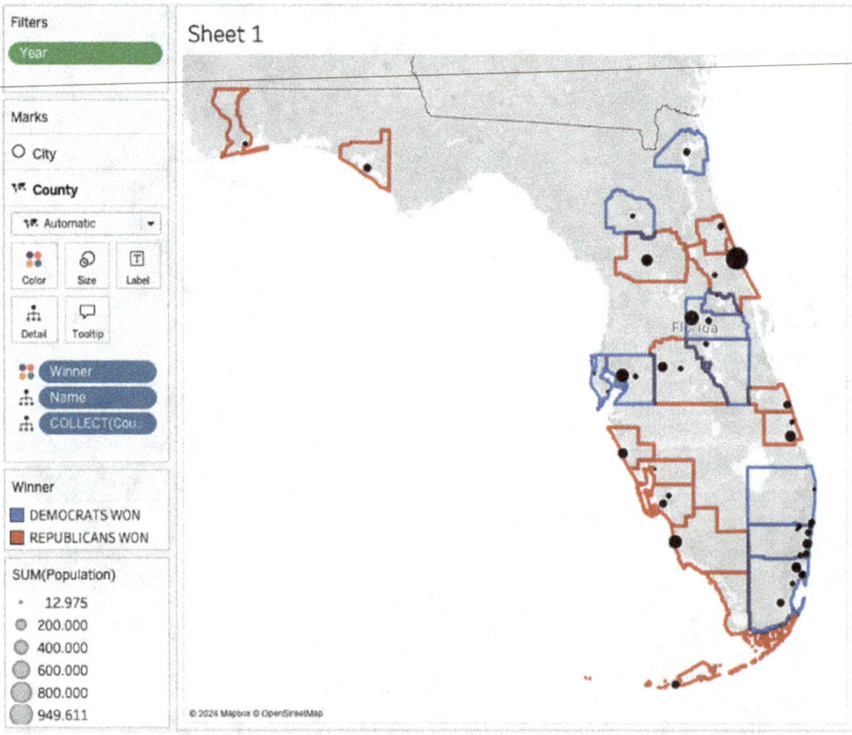

Figure 8.11 – Using the OUTLINE function in Tableau 2024.3

Using store and customer location data to run a store influence area analysis

The techniques we have learned thus far during this chapter are great examples of how we can start using spatial data and get value from it. In this recipe, we will combine different techniques learned already with new ones to showcase the potential of spatial analysis and build a store area analysis.

Imagine we work for a retail company with different stores across the world. We might want to analyze customers close to each store, understand the money each customer has spent with us, and maybe send them a promotion or discount that encourages them to visit our physical stores. To achieve this, we have two different datasets:

- The first dataset is a CSV with a list of store locations: the latitude and longitude of each store in the city of Barcelona.

- The second dataset is another CSV, with the latitude and longitude of each customer who has bought from our physical or online stores in the last year. It also contains data about the total sales, units, and revenue of each customer in Barcelona.

Our objective is to use these two datasets and Tableau's spatial capabilities to learn which stores have more customers in a radius of 600 meters.

Getting ready

Download the `customer_data.csv` and `store_locations.csv` files. You can find both files at `https://github.com/PacktPublishing/Tableau-Cookbook-for-Experienced-Professionals/tree/main/Chapter_08`.

These are the two files we will use for our analysis with Tableau Desktop or Tableau Desktop Public Edition.

1. Once you have both files downloaded, open Tableau and load the `store_locations.csv` as a **Text** file.

2. In the **Data Source** window, make sure you change the data type of the `Geometry` field in the `store_locations.csv` file to **Spatial**, as in *Figure 8.12*.

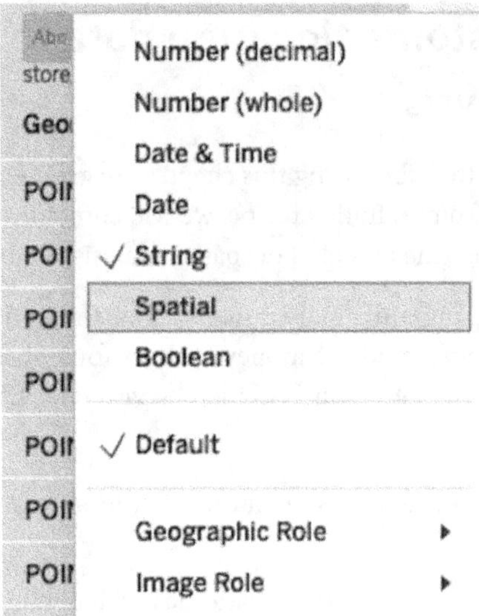

Figure 8.12 – Changing the data type of the Geometry field

3. Add the `customer_data.csv` file and create a relationship between both files based on the `City` field of each file.

Now, we are ready for our spatial analysis.

How to do it...

Let's start by visualizing the 10 stores in our store file:

1. In a new Tableau sheet, double-click the `Geometry` field from the `store_locations.csv` file and add the ID to the **Detail** shelf to be able to hover over and identify each store individually. You should see 10 different marks, one for each store in Barcelona.

2. Change the **Marks** type to **Shape** and update the shape to one that allows you to identify the stores more easily, such as a star shape or any other type you like.

3. Let's add the customer's location based on the latitude and longitude. To do this, we will need to create a new spatial object with a calculated field and a `MAKEPOINT` function. Create a new calculated field named `Customer Location`, as in the following:

```
MAKEPOINT([Latitude],[Longitude])
```

4. Drag the new `Customer Location` field to the map as a new **Marks** layer, as we learned in the previous recipe. Add also the `Customer Id` field to the **Detail Shelf** in the **Marks Card** of the layer to identify each customer individually.

5. Update the **Marks** type to **Circle**, reduce the mark size a bit, and change the color to gray or another one of your choice to make it easier to identify the customer shapes (circles) and the store shapes (stars). Update the names of each to make them easier to identify. At this point, your visualization should look similar to *Figure 8.13*.

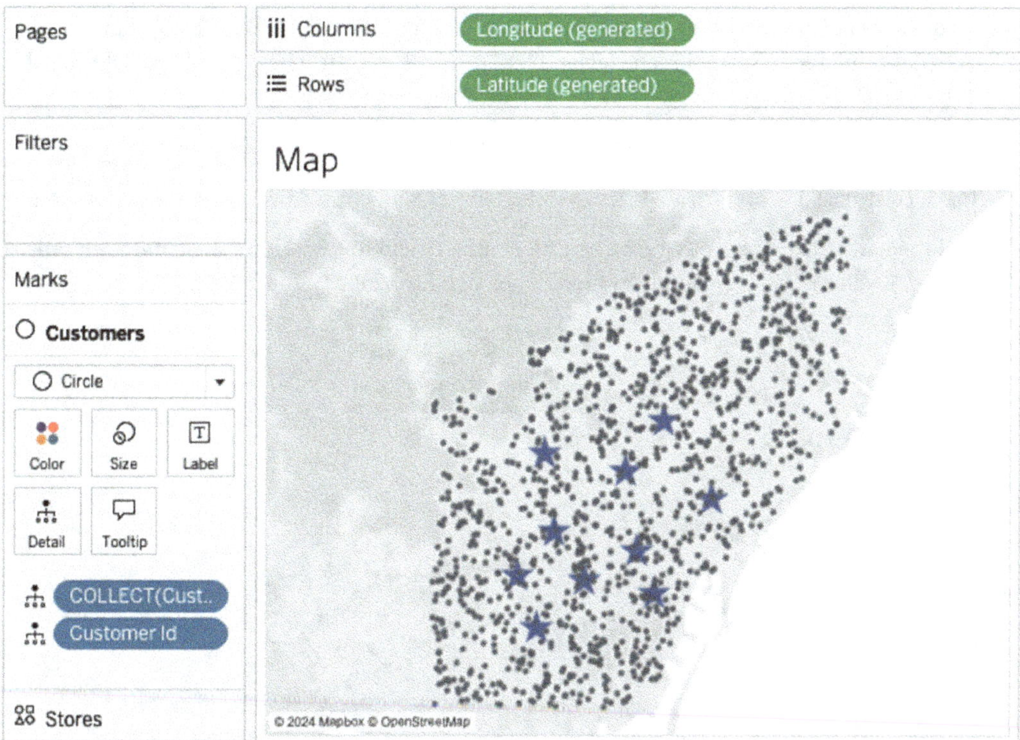

Figure 8.13 – Stores and Customers using Tableau's spatial capabilities

6. Now, we are going to start creating our "store influence area" using Tableau's BUFFER function. A buffer is an area created around a geographical point, in this case, our stores. To add a buffer for each store, follow these steps:

I. Create a new calculated field named `Buffer` of `600` meters around the `Geometry` field of the store locations file using the following formula:

```
BUFFER([Geometry],600,"m")
```

II. Add the new `Buffer` field as a new **Marks** layer to the map in the same way we added the customers in the previous step.

III. Add the `Id` field from the store locations file to the **Detail** shelf to identify each store buffer individually.

IV.   Rename the layer we just added to `Buffer` and move it down so it's the last layer in the **Marks** card. Feel free to adjust the color of each buffer area and add some opacity so the customers inside the area are also visible.

7.   So far so good! But how can we make sure we identify and see only the customers that are inside those buffer areas? Our two datasets only share the `City` field (Barcelona). But we can use a new function to solve this challenge: `INTERSECTS`. Create a new calculated field called `Customer Intersects Buffer` using the following formula:

```
INTERSECTS([Buffer],[Customer Location])
```

The calculated field will return a `TRUE` value when `Buffer` and `Customer Location` intersect.

8.   Add the new `Customer Intersects Buffer` field to the **Filters** shelf and keep only the `TRUE` values. Your visualization should look like *Figure 8.14*.

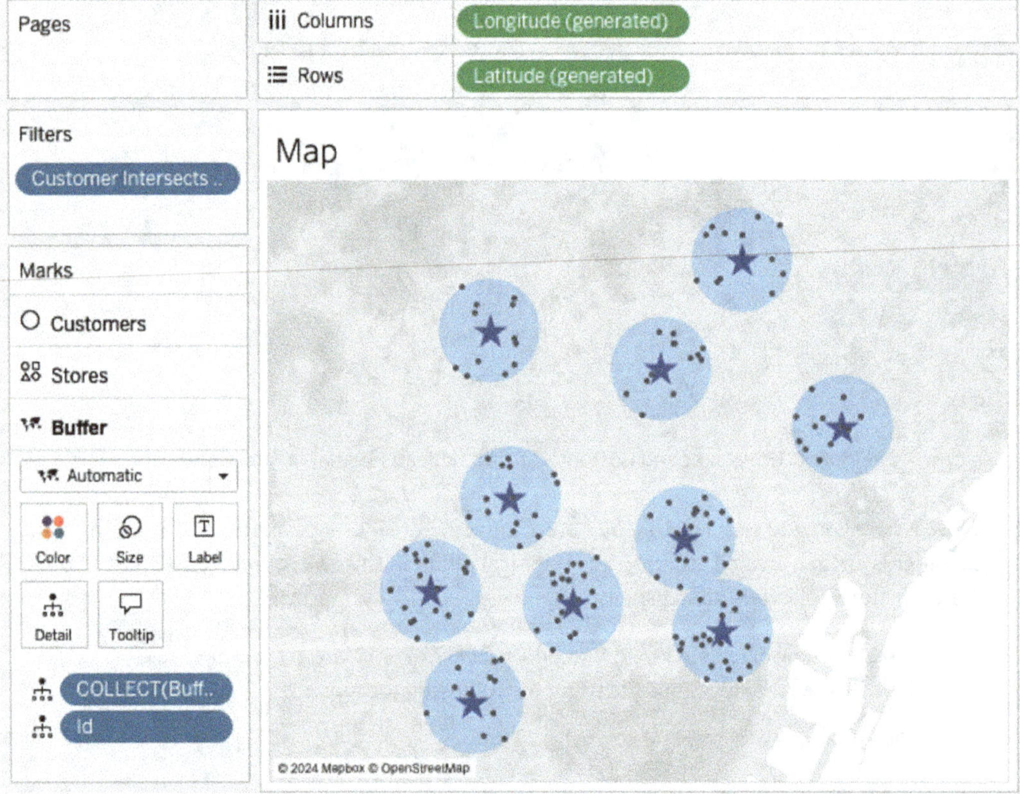

Figure 8.14 – Customers intersecting a 600-meter buffer from store locations

The benefit of this analysis is that we can now use this same filter in any chart or analysis to only analyze customers that intersect with our `Buffer` area. Right-click on the field we just added in the **Filters** shelf and select **Apply to Worksheets… | All Using This Data Source**. Now, the filter will be applied to any new sheet we create.

For example, we can identify the total amount spent by the customers in that radius of 600 meters. To do so, create a new sheet, add the ID from the stores dataset, and add the sales from the customer dataset to columns. Because the previous filter is applied now automatically to all new sheets, we will analyze the sales by the customers in that area of 600 meters. We can perform a similar analysis using the **Profit** measure in our dataset or count the number of customers inside the buffer area of each store.

All these additional analyses together in a dashboard can provide a powerful analysis of each store; for instance, they can identify **Store 7** as the second one in terms of **Profit** with fewer customers in 600 meters, as shown in *Figure 8.15*.

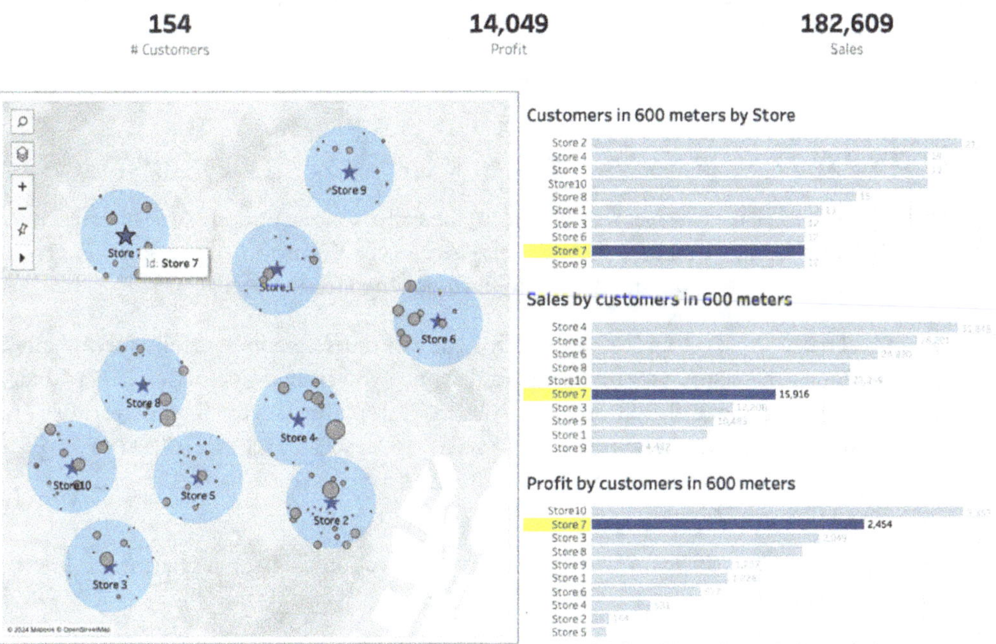

Figure 8.15 – Example of a full dashboard using store and customer locations

We could even identify each customer inside the buffer to identify them as potential customers to send them different marketing campaigns.

You can download the full dashboard called from `Chapter 8. Store and Customer Analysis` at `https://github.com/PacktPublishing/Tableau-Cookbook-for-Experienced-Professionals/tree/main/Chapter_08`.

Using spatial data and clustering to find optimal store locations

Tableau's spatial capabilities can be used in combination with any other functionality. The benefit of Tableau's mapping features is they are of great help when a key part of our analysis and our decision-making process is *where* things are happening.

In this recipe, we will combine Tableau's mapping capabilities with a more advanced analytical technique that not many people use in Tableau: **K-means clustering**.

What we will try to achieve is to find possible good locations to open a pharmacy in the city of Barcelona using real data such as income per household, population, and the official census sections of the Spanish territory. Census sections are the smallest official areas used in Spain for official purposes, such as defining where each citizen has to go to vote during the elections for example.

Let's go.

Getting ready

1. First, let's download all the data files we will need for the analysis. Go to `https://github.com/PacktPublishing/Tableau-Cookbook-for-Experienced-Professionals/tree/main/Chapter_08` and download the following files:

    *   `Barcelona_shapefile.zip`: This file contains census sections for the city of Barcelona. Make sure you unzip the folder once you have downloaded it. The data source is the INE (Spanish National Statistics Institute). The data for the full territory of Spain can also be found here: `https://ine.es/ss/Satellite?c=Page&p=1259952026632&pagename=ProductosYServicios%2FPYSLayout&cid=1259952026632&L=1`.

    *   `Pharmacies_Barcelona.csv`: This contains location data about pharmacies in the city of Barcelona.

    *   `Income_Barcelona_2022.csv`: This contains information about the average income per census section in the city of Barcelona. The data source is the INE (Spanish National Statistics Institute). The data can also be found here: `https://ine.es/jaxiT3/Tabla.htm?t=30896&L=1`.

- `Population_Barcelona.csv`: This contains the official population data for each census section in the city of Barcelona. The data source is the INE (Spanish National Statistics Institute). The data can also be found here: `https://ine.es/jaxiPx/Tabla.htm?tpx=61441&L=1`.

2. Once we have the different files, it's time to create our data model:

    I.   First, connect to the `Barcelona.shp` file inside the `Barcelona_shapefile` folder once unzipped.

    II.   Add a connection to the `Pharmacies_Barcelona.csv` file and create a relationship with the `Barcelona.shp` file based on the Nmun field from the shapefile and the `City` field from `Pharmacies_Barcelona.csv`. Both fields have the value of `Barcelona` for all rows. In this case, we are running this analysis just for a specific city or municipality, but we could perform the same analysis with data from different cities.

    III. On the **Data Source** page, select on the canvas the `Pharmacies_Barcelona.csv` table just added to your data model, and make sure to update the data type of the `Geometry` field to **Spatial**.

    IV.   Add a connection to `Population_Barcelona.csv` and create a relationship with the `Barcelona.shp` file. The relationship must be based on a unique census section ID available in both datasets. This field is called CUSEC in the `Barcelona.shp` file. For the `Population_Barcelona.csv` file, we will need to use a calculation for the relationships, as the file might be loading the `Census Area` field as an integer and not a string, getting read of some leading 0 we need. Create a new calculated field in the relationship for this file. The calculation will check the length of the field and add a leading 0 if it has 9 characters or keep the value as is if not. The calculation we need is as follows:

```
IIF(LEN(STR([Census Area]))=9,
    "0"+STR([Census Area]),
    STR([Census Area])
)
```

    V.   Finally, let's add the last file to the data model. Add a connection to the `Income_Barcelona_2022.csv` file and create a relationship with the `Barcelona.shp` file. In this case, we have a similar problem as with the previous file, so we will create another calculation for the relationship. The related field is also the CUSEC field for `Barcelona.shp`, and the calculation for the relationship in the `Income_Barcelona_2022.csv` file should be as follows:

```
IIF(LEN(STR([Census Area1]))=9,
    "0"+STR([Census Area1]),
    STR([Census Area1])
)
```

3. With the four files in our data model and the relationships created, the final model should look like *Figure 8.16*.

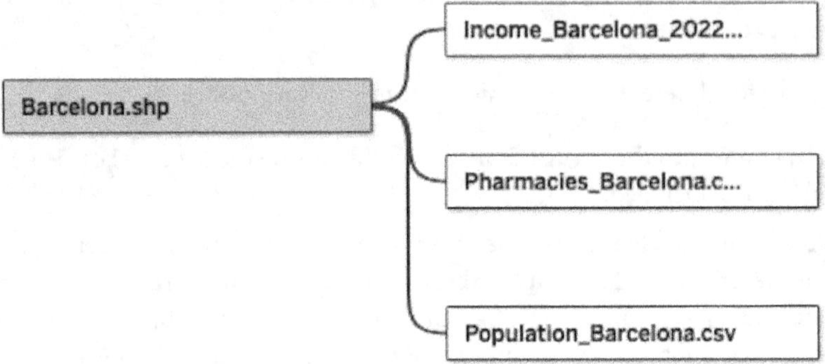

Figure 8.16 – The data model for this recipe

Why don't we clean the files beforehand?

You might be asking yourself why we have provided the files in a cleaner and nicer format to build the relationships. The main reason is that these types of challenges appear on a daily basis in the work of every analyst. Finding solutions that allow us to keep providing value to our stakeholders is key to being successful as an analyst.

With our data model ready, we can move forward and build our analysis to find optimal store locations with spatial data and Tableau.

How to do it...

So, how can we do a clustering analysis to identify census sections that might be more interesting to open a new pharmacy in Barcelona based on the population of each census section and the average income per household? Let's find out:

1. Let's start by visualizing the correlation between population and household income per census section. Create a new sheet in your workbook and follow these steps:

    I.   Add the `Population` field from the `Population` table to the **Columns Shelf**.

    II.   Add the `Average income per household in euros` field from the `Income` table to the **Rows Shelf**. Right-click on it and change the aggregation to an average.

    III. Add the `CUSEC` field from the `Barcelona.shp` table to the **Details Shelf**.

    You should now have a mark for each census section in Barcelona (a bit more than 1,000 marks).

2. Now, we will add our clustering analysis. Tableau has a built-in capability to perform a K-means cluster using **Lloyd's algorithm** with squared Euclidean distances to compute the K-means clustering. To perform the K-means clustering analysis:

I.   Go to the **Analytics** pane on the left menu bar of your sheet.

II. Under **Model**, double-click on **Cluster**.

III. A new **Cluster** window appears with the variables included to calculate the K-means clustering – in our case, just the average Income per household and the population. The number of clusters is by default automatic, but let's update it to 4 to have some more variance between the clusters. Feel free to edit the colors for each cluster. Your scatter plot at the end should look similar to *Figure 8.17*.

Figure 8.17 – Clustering Barcelona census sections

3. One of the most interesting things about Tableau's K-means clustering is that we can save those clusters as a `Group` field and use them in any analysis. Drag the `Clusters` field from the **Marks** card and drop it in the **Data** pane on the left side. You can also change the name of the field to something more meaningful, such as `Section Clusters`. Then, drag and drop the field from the **Data** pane to the **Color** shelf of the **Marks** card to replace the original `Cluster` field created automatically by Tableau.

    As you can see in *Figure 8.17*, it seems like there is a cluster of census sections in Barcelona with an average income above 100K (top of the *y* axis). These areas might be good candidates to open a new pharmacy if our criteria are based on the income of the area.

4. Now, let's use this new `Cluster` field in a map to visualize how the areas and clusters are distributed around Barcelona:

    I.   Create a new sheet and double-click the `Geometry` field from the `Barcelona.shp` table.

    II. Add `CUSEC` to the **Detail** shelf to have a single mark for each census area.

    III. Add the `Section Clusters` field created in *Step 3* to the **Color** shelf in the **Marks** card.

    We will also add the pharmacies' locations as a new layer to the map to see where each pharmacy is located and check whether there are any close pharmacies next to the areas we are interested in.

    IV. Add the `Geometry` field from the `Pharmacies_Barcelona` table as a new layer to the map.

    V.   Add the `Id` field from the `Pharmacies_Barcelona` table to **Detail** to have a mark for each pharmacy. Feel free also to change the **Marks** type and color and to disable the **Add to Zoom Extend** option for the pharmacies layer by deselecting the option from the additional options in the marks card. There's additional information about how to disable this feature and other useful layer options in Tableau's documentation here: `https://help.tableau.com/current/pro/desktop/en-us/maps_marks_layers.htm#add-to-zoom-extent`.

The map should look similar to *Figure 8.18*.

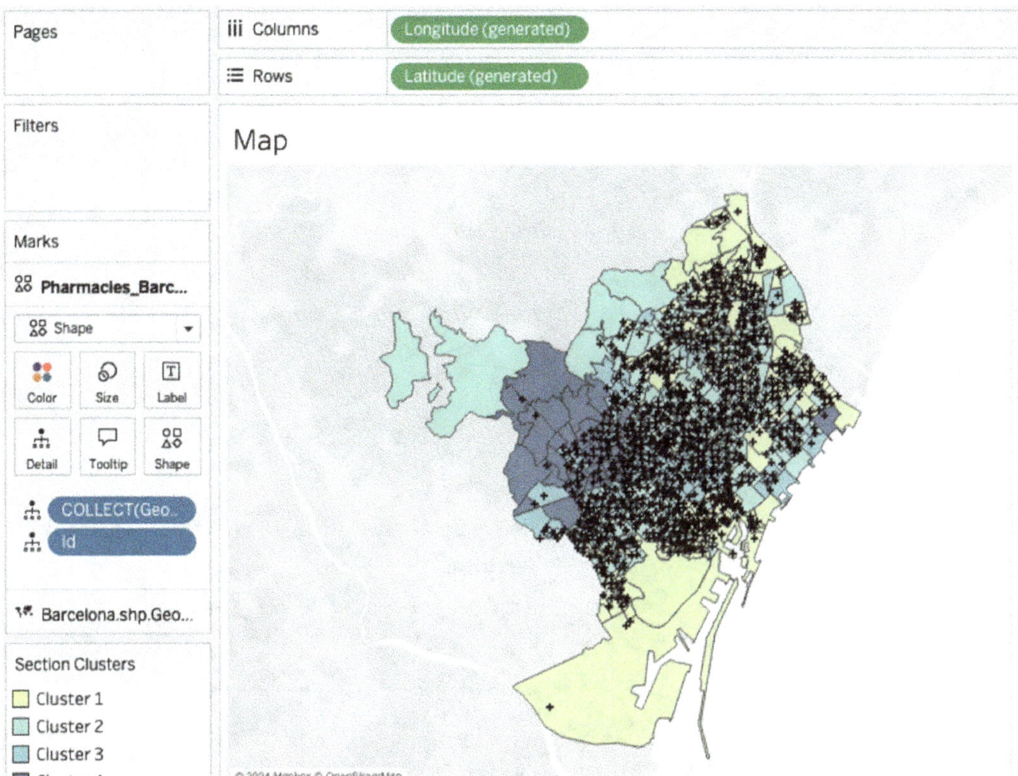

Figure 8.18 – Combining census locations with pharmacies and coloring by clusters

Finally, add both analyses to a new dashboard and use the scatter plot as a filter. We could focus on the census sections from the cluster with higher income and more than 2,000 population, select those, and see those specific census areas. For instance, in *Figure 8.19*, there is a census section in the west of Barcelona, next to the coast with high income, higher population than the average, and only one pharmacy around. This area might be a good potential location to open a new business.

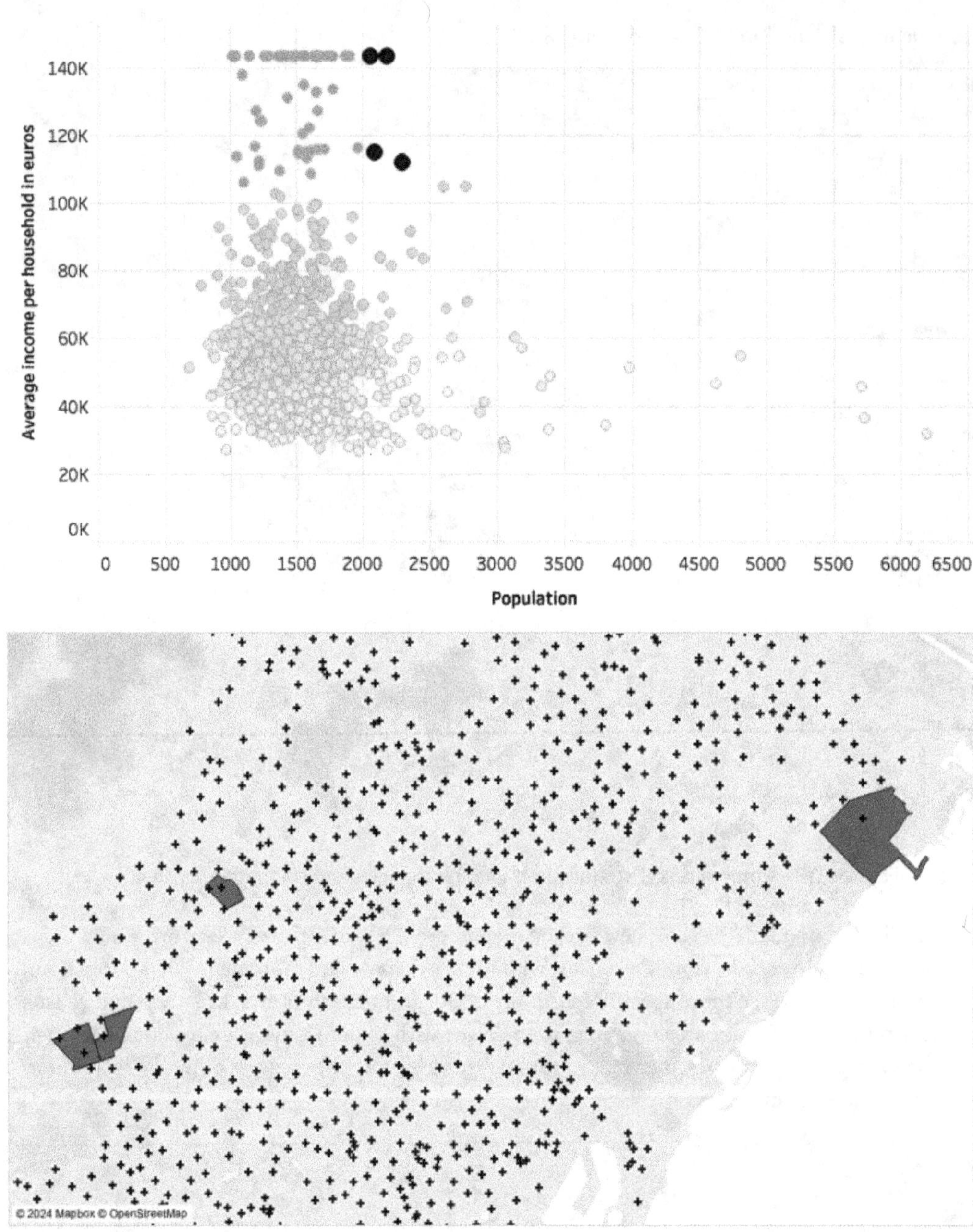

Figure 8.19 – Using our clustering and spatial analysis to identify potential store locations

You can also download the final dashboard example, named `Chapter 8. Find potential store locations with clustering.twbx`, from the GitHub page of the chapter.

Extending Tableau with Developer Tools and APIs

Tableau is a great data visualization tool, but during the last few years, it has become much more than a powerful data visualization tool. As you can see at `https://www.tableau.com/developer`, with Tableau, you can now use the **REST API** to automate your Tableau maintenance tasks, enrich your analytics with Python and R integrations, easily embed and automate analytics everywhere, and increase efficiency with a wide range of APIs.

By utilizing these developer resources, organizations can tailor Tableau to their specific needs, enhancing data-driven decision-making processes and improving overall efficiency.

Some key benefits and advantages of Tableau's developer resources include the ability to extend Tableau's functionality to meet unique business requirements, the incorporation of Tableau into existing workflows and applications, automation of repetitive tasks and processes, saving time and reducing errors, and managing Tableau more efficiently across large organizations.

In this chapter, we will cover the following developer features:

- Authenticating in Tableau's REST API
- Updating a user's role using the REST API
- Updating a workbook's owner using the REST API
- Using your data sources beyond visualizations with VizQL Data Service (VDS)
- Geocoding addresses with TabPy, Tableau Prep, and openrouteservice
- Finding all workbooks connected to a specific database with Metadata API and GraphQL
- Using the Metadata API and GraphQL to document calculated fields created by your users

Technical requirements

During this chapter, we will use many more tools than just Tableau, so for some of the recipes, you will need to install the following software on your computer:

- Python

- Postman

- Tableau Prep Builder

- The openrouteservice API

- Visual Studio Code or another coding application

All the code and data that we will use during the chapter can be found on GitHub: `https://github.com/PacktPublishing/Tableau-Cookbook-for-Experienced-Professionals/tree/main/Chapter_09`

Authenticating in Tableau's REST API

Tableau's REST API is a web-based interface that allows developers to programmatically interact with Tableau Server and Tableau Online. Using standard HTTP requests and JSON for data exchange, it provides access to a wide range of Tableau resources and functionalities. This includes content management (such as publishing workbooks and managing data sources), user and group administration, and site management.

To interact with the REST API, Tableau has developed and made available for everyone a tool called the **Tableau Server Client** (**TSC**).

The TSC is a Python library that simplifies interactions with Tableau's REST API, providing a more user-friendly and Python-friendly interface for developers. It abstracts away many of the low-level details of making HTTP requests and parsing JSON responses, allowing developers to work with Tableau Server or Tableau Cloud using familiar Python objects and methods.

Some of the TSC features include the following:

- Easy authentication and session management

- Object-oriented representation of Tableau resources (workbooks, data sources, users, etc.)

- Simplified methods for common operations such as publishing, downloading, and updating content

- Handling of pagination and other API-specific behaviors

The TSC is particularly useful for Python developers who want to automate Tableau-related tasks or integrate Tableau functionality into their Python applications. It can significantly reduce the amount of code needed to perform complex operations compared to working directly with the REST API.

In this recipe, we will learn how we can start using the TSC, install it, and authenticate to our Tableau Cloud site with it.

Getting ready

The first thing we need to do is to make sure we have the TSC library installed on our computer. You can install the TSC from pip or from the source code.

In our case, we will install it from pip as this is the method recommended by Tableau.

Open a terminal window in your computer and run the following commands to upgrade pip and then install the latest stable version of TSC:

```
pip install --upgrade pip
pip install tableauserverclient
```

With the library installed, we can move forward and start using the TSC to authenticate in a Tableau Cloud or Tableau Server environment. If you don't have a Tableau environment to work with, you can always join the **Tableau Developer Program** and get a free sandbox of Tableau Cloud. For more information about the developer program, visit `https://www.tableau.com/developer`.

How to do it...

There are two ways we can authenticate in our Tableau Cloud or Tableau Server environment using the TSC:

- Using your username and password
- Using a personal access token

A **Personal Access Token** (**PAT**) allows users to sign in to the Tableau REST API without exposing their username and password. Because of this, PATs are considered extremely secure and the recommended authentication method for automated scripts and to interact with the REST API.

1. To create a PAT for your Tableau user, you first need to log in to your Tableau Cloud or Tableau Server environment. Then go to **My Account Settings** by clicking on your profile picture in the top-right corner of the Tableau UI, as shown in *Figure 9.1*.

Figure 9.1 – Accessing your user account settings in Tableau Cloud or Tableau Server

2.   At the top, you'll see different tabs. Select the **Settings** tab, scroll down, and look for the **Personal Access Tokens** section.

3.   Type a token name – for example, `python` – and then click on the **Create Token** button. A new window will appear with the secret of the PAT. Copy the secret string and save it somewhere safe as we will need it during our authentication with the TSC.

4.   Click **Done** once you have copied the secret to close the window.

5.   With our PAT ready, it's time to start coding in Python. Open your programming tool or **integrated development environment** (IDE) of choice (Visual Studio Code, Notepad++, Sublime, Pycharm, etc.) and save the file with a `.py` extension – for example, `tableau_authentication.py`.

6.   Start by importing the TSC library we installed in the *Getting ready* section of this recipe to allow our file to use the TSC. To do so, type the following code at the beginning of your file to import the library with an alias of TSC to refer to it while coding:

```
import tableauserverclient as TSC
```

7.   The first step to sign in to our Tableau Cloud or Tableau Server account is to specify our account. The `Server` class of TSC contains the attributes that represent Tableau Cloud or Server. It's also recommended to always use the latest REST API version supported by your Tableau Server or Tableau Cloud instance, so we will use the `user_server_version = True` argument to do so. With these two things in mind, let's create our instance of `TSC.Server`. In my case, because I'm using Tableau Cloud, I'll need to include the first part of my Tableau Cloud site URL, like this:

```
server =TSC.Server(
    'https://10ax.online.tableau.com',
    use_server_version = True
)
```

8. With the `Server` class defined to be able to point to our Tableau instance, now we need to specify our authentication credentials using the PAT created in *Step 3* and the `PersonalAccessTokenAuth` class. This class defines the information required in the sign-in request, including three attributes, following this structure: `PersonalAccessTokenAuth(token_name, personal_access_token, site_id=''):`

- `Token_name`: The name we gave to our PAT in *Step 3*

- `Token_secret`: The secret created and copied in *Step 3*

- `Site_id`: The name of our Tableau site

    To use the class, we need to create a new instance with those three attributes. For example, if in *Step 3* I created a PAT named *python*, my PAT secret is *vNbpPlaeRRK4m3OT0RZiywt*, and the name of my Tableau site is *mydevsite*, then I can create a new class, `PersonalAccessTokenAuth`, named `tableau_auth` like this:

    ```
    tableau_auth = TSC.PersonalAccessTokenAuth(
        'python', 'vNbpPlaeRRK4m3OT0RZiywt',
        site_id = 'mydevsite'
    )
    ```

9. Finally, we need to pass the request object to the `auth.sign_in` method of TSC to sign in to our Tableau environment, and that will also manage the authentication token. We will call this method from the server object created in *Step 7*. This means we can authenticate as shown here:

    ```
    server.auth.sign_in(tableau_auth)
    ```

    When authenticating, the REST API returns three values: the token, the site ID, and our user ID. This means we can try to print the authentication token to check if everything worked as expected:

    ```
    print(server.auth_token)
    ```

    Run the code and check that everything works fine. If so, the last line of code should print a long string of text: our authentication token that will be used in subsequent calls.

10. The authentication token created will keep us signed in for 240 minutes (4 hours) or until the `auth.sign_out` method is called. Let's try it to sign out:

    ```
    server.auth.sign_out()
    ```

    Now, if we try to print the authentication token again, like in *Step 9*, we will get an error that says *Missing authentication token. You must sign in first.* This confirms we are no longer authenticated in our Tableau Cloud site.

You have just learned how to use the TSC to authenticate in your Tableau Server or Tableau Cloud environment. Now it's time to keep learning and start working with our Tableau Site programmatically.

See also

- If you need help installing Python, there's an easy-to-follow guide at this link: `https://www.howtogeek.com/197947/how-to-install-python-on-windows/`. There are also plenty of tutorials online to do so.

- For more details about the prerequisites of TSC, refer to the official documentation: `https://tableau.github.io/server-client-python/docs/#confirm-prerequisites`.

Updating a user's role using the REST API

In the previous recipe, we learned how we can authenticate in Tableau Cloud using the REST API and Python with the TSC. Let's use what we just learned to do something with our Tableau Cloud environment, such as updating a user's role and license.

Getting ready

Imagine you have a user or users that, after receiving some Tableau training sessions, you want to promote from Viewer users to Explorer users. Maybe you have lots of them and you don't want to do this manually, or maybe this is a process that might happen quite often, and you want to do it programmatically. The TSC and the REST API is a great way to perform this type of action.

In my case, I have just a couple of users on my Tableau Cloud site as it's a developer site (*Figure 9.3*). What I might want to do is promote the Tableau user from Viewer to Explorer.

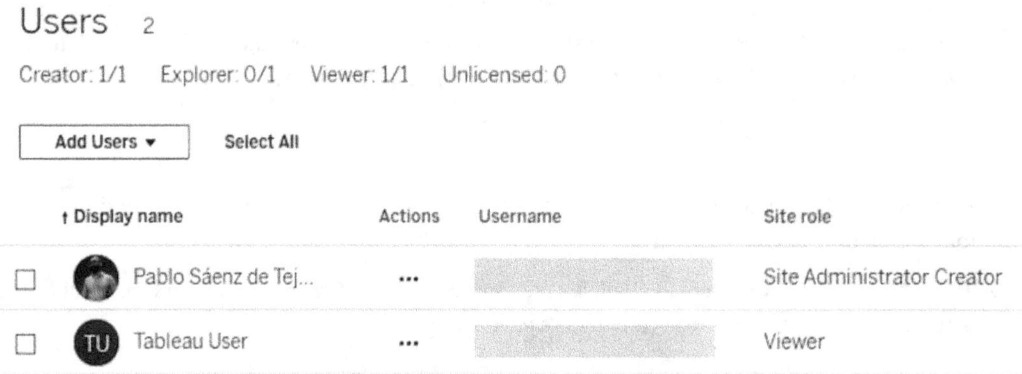

Figure 9.2 – Users on a Tableau Cloud site

To update a user's information using the TSC, we will need to follow two different steps:

1. First, we need to know the ID of the user we want to update. For this task, we will use the `users.get` method, which returns a `UserItem` object with a list of users and a `PaginationItem` object to iterate through the results. This method will allow us to get the ID of the user we want to update.

2. Then, we will use the `users.update` method to update the role using the user ID from the previous method as a parameter.

For authenticating, we will also simplify things a little by using the `with` block, which allows us to run additional code inside the block, calling the `sign_out` method automatically after the block execution completes.

Let's see how we can do this using the TSC and REST API.

How to do it...

1. We will start setting up the authentication as we did in the last recipe. Open a new file in your programming tool or IDE of choice, save it with a `.py` extension, and type the following:

```python
import tableauserverclient as TSC
tableau_auth = TSC.PersonalAccessTokenAuth(
    'tokenName',
    'tokenSecret',
    site_id='siteName'
)
server = TSC.Server(
    'https://10ax.online.tableau.com',
    use_server_version=True
)
```

2. Replace `tokenName` and `tokenSecret` with your own token name and secret, as we learned in the previous recipe. Also, update `siteName` with the name of your Tableau Cloud site and replace `https://10ax.online.tableau.com` if your Tableau Cloud site URL is different.

3. Now let's start by using the `with` block with the `users.get` method to get a list of the users on our site. Add the following lines of code to your `.py` file:

```python
with server.auth.sign_in(tableau_auth):
    all_users, users_pagination=server.users.get()
    print([user.id for user in all_users])
    print([user.name for user in all_users])
    print([user.site_role for user in all_users])
```

The Python script should print three different lists with the user IDs, the user names, and the site role of each user.

4. Now, let's store the ID of the user we want to update in a variable. In my case, the user's full name is `Tableau User`. We could run a `for` loop to find and store the full name of the user we are interested in, adding a few additional lines of code inside the `with` block, which should look like this in the end:

```python
with server.auth.sign_in(tableau_auth):
    all_users, users_pagination=server.users.get()
    print([user.id for user in all_users])
    print([user.name for user in all_users])
    print([user.site_role for user in all_users])
    user_id = ''
    for user in all_users:
        if user.fullname == 'Tableau User':
            user_id=user.id
        else:
            None
    print('The user ID: '+ user_id)
```

The output should be something like in *Figure 9.3*. Of course, your user ID, name, and roles will be different than the ones shown in the screenshot.

```
['e408a3d3-835f-406f-9a83-7905289a9d5f', 'cc4bf83d-4fe0-4950-b6fc-d572fb809772']
['pablo@                      ', 'info@                      ']
['SiteAdministratorCreator', 'Viewer']
The user ID: cc4bf83d-4fe0-4950-b6fc-d572fb809772
```

Figure 9.3 – Output printing user ID, username, and site role

5. Now we have the ID of the user we want to update stored in our `user_id` variable. With it, we can use the `users.get_by_id` method to get the `UserItem` class of that user and update the `site_role` attribute using the `users.update` method. We just need to add three simple lines of code to our file to achieve our goal. Just add the following at the end of your file and inside the `with` block:

```python
target_user = server.users.get_by_id(user_id)
target_user.site_role = 'Explorer'
server.users.update(target_user)
```

Congratulations! If you query the same user again or access the user's sections in Tableau Cloud, you should see the new role already applied to your user.

How it works...

The process is quite simple. The code we just wrote authenticates to our Tableau Cloud environment using the REST API and then gets all the details about all the users in our environment.

Then, we store the user ID of the user we want to update using the user's full name, and we pass the user ID into another call to get the concrete user details. We then first update the site role of the `UserItem` class we asked for in Python and then send our request to update the user with the new site role specified.

There's more...

You can do much more with the TSC and your Tableau users. There are also methods to add users to or remove users from Tableau, return a list of favorite content, or even the groups the users belong to.

The methods you'll need to use for those tasks are `users.add`, `users.remove`, `users.populate_favorites`, and `users.populate_groups`.

Some use cases for which these methods might be useful are as follows:

- Automating the addition or removal of users based on your company rules (for example, removing users who haven't logged in for a certain amount of time)

- Automatically upgrading the site role of users who have received internal Tableau training

- Getting the favorite workbooks of a user to show a detailed list in a company's internal web portal outside of Tableau

See also

- For additional information about the user resources for the TSC, check the official documentation here: `https://tableau.github.io/server-client-python/docs/api-ref#users`

- You can also check the full details about the user methods of Tableau's REST API: `https://help.tableau.com/current/api/rest_api/en-us/REST/rest_api_ref_users_and_groups.htm`

Updating a workbook's owner using the REST API

The TSC allows us to not only interact with users, like in the previous recipe, but also with other elements of our Tableau environment such as connections, data sources, groups, projects, subscriptions, tasks, or **workbooks**.

In this recipe, we will learn how we can interact with our Tableau workbooks to update a workbook's owner.

This might be a very good approach if we have internal requirements of only specific users owning production-ready dashboards or to programmatically update a significant number of workbooks if several users leave our company and we want to transfer their ownership to other users.

Getting ready

If, as in the previous recipe, we authenticate into Tableau Cloud with the TSC, then we query all the users and update one of them, in this case, we will add a bit more complexity using the **Workbook methods** and the **WorkbookItem class**, which allows us to get information about workbook attributes such as ID, description, size, or tags, among many others.

Here are the steps we will follow:

- Authenticate into Tableau Cloud

- Get information about the published workbooks in Tableau Cloud

- Get information about the user we want to be the new workbook owner

- Update a concrete workbook's owner

Let's start.

How to do it...

As in the previous recipe, we will start by authenticating in Tableau Cloud as we learned in the first recipe of this chapter, but we will also import the pandas library to make it easier to look at all the workbook details:

1. Open a new file in your programming tool or IDE of choice, save it with a `.py` extension, and type the following:

```python
import tableauserverclient as TSC
import pandas as pd
tableau_auth = TSC.PersonalAccessTokenAuth(
    'tokenName','tokenSecret', site_id='siteName'
)
server = TSC.Server(
    'https://10ax.online.tableau.com',
    use_server_version=True
)
```

2. Replace `tokenName` and `tokenSecret` with your own token name and secret, as we learned in the previous recipe. Also, update `siteName` with the name of your Tableau Cloud site and replace `https://10ax.online.tableau.com` if your Tableau Cloud site URL is different.

3. Now we will use the `with` block with the `workbooks.get` method to get a list of the workbooks on our site and print each of them on a separate line by adding the following lines of code to your `.py` file:

```python
with server.auth.sign_in(tableau_auth):
    all_workbooks_items, workbooks_pagination = (
        server.workbooks.get()
    )
    for workbook in all_workbooks_items:
        print(workbook)
```

4. Another approach is to create a DataFrame with the fields we are interested in and print the DataFrame. For example, if we wanted to show the name, ID, and owner of each workbook, we could add the following code to our Python file:

```python
workbooks_df = pd.DataFrame({
    'Workbook Name': [
        workbook.name for workbook in all_workbooks_items],
    'Workbook Id': [
        workbook.id for workbook in all_workbooks_items],
    'Owner': [
        workbook.owner_id for workbook in all_workbooks_items]
})
print(workbooks_df)
```

This will print a DataFrame of three columns and one row per workbook, as in *Figure 9.4*.

```
                          Workbook Name  ...                                 Owner
0                Personal Expense Dashboard  ...  e408a3d3-835f-406f-9a83-7905289a9d5f
1                           Habit Tracker  ...  e408a3d3-835f-406f-9a83-7905289a9d5f
2                          Sleeping trends  ...  e408a3d3-835f-406f-9a83-7905289a9d5f
3                Daily Running Comparison  ...  e408a3d3-835f-406f-9a83-7905289a9d5f
4           Expenses by Vendor Comparison  ...  e408a3d3-835f-406f-9a83-7905289a9d5f
5                   Admin Insights Starter  ...  dd0a5ffc-44a6-4aec-8391-44fe54bbcc25
6                Superstore Basic Dashboard  ...  e408a3d3-835f-406f-9a83-7905289a9d5f
7               Country Global Sales Report  ...  e408a3d3-835f-406f-9a83-7905289a9d5f
8                 Average Pay by Department  ...  e408a3d3-835f-406f-9a83-7905289a9d5f
9                  Water Reservoirs in Spain  ...  e408a3d3-835f-406f-9a83-7905289a9d5f
10           Water Reservoirs in Spain Packt  ...  e408a3d3-835f-406f-9a83-7905289a9d5f
11   Quality of life in 85 European cities  ...  e408a3d3-835f-406f-9a83-7905289a9d5f
12                                 Chapter 7  ...  e408a3d3-835f-406f-9a83-7905289a9d5f
13               Basic Book Reading Analysis  ...  e408a3d3-835f-406f-9a83-7905289a9d5f

[14 rows x 5 columns]
```

Figure 9.4 – Output of workbooks using a DataFrame

5. If I want to update the owner of the workbook called **Water Reservoirs in Spain Packt**, which is in the 10th position of my DataFrame, I could first select that concrete workbook:

```
Workbook_to_update = all_workbooks_items[10]
```

6. Now, as in the previous recipe, get a list of the users in the Tableau Cloud account, and get the ID of the user that you want to be the new owner – here, called `Tableau User`:

```
all_users, users_pagination=server.users.get()
user_id = ''
for user in all_users:
    if user.fullname == 'Tableau User':
        user_id=user.id
    else:
        None
```

7. Lastly, I can update the workbook item using the user ID stored in the `user_id` variable and update the workbook in Tableau Cloud:

```
workbook_to_update.owner_id = user_id
server.workbooks.update(workbook_to_update)
```

Done! The workbook owner has been updated. You could check it through the Tableau Cloud website or again query all the workbook information using the TSC.

See also

For more information about the `Workbook` methods and `WorkbookItem` class of the TSC, visit `https://tableau.github.io/server-client-python/docs/api-ref#workbooks`.

Using your data sources beyond visualizations with VizQL Data Service (VDS)

In today's business world, doing more with your data is more important than ever.

Data teams spend a significant amount of time preparing their data sources and data models in Tableau to make analysis fast, easy, and reliable for their organizations. And many people have been desiring to do more with their Tableau-published data sources for a long time, such as deeper automations and integrations with other applications.

The VDS API is a new API developed by Tableau to allow you to access data from your published data sources through programmatic queries via APIs rather than traditional visualizations, helping you use your data in many more ways than just Tableau dashboards.

Getting ready

For this recipe, we will use **Postman**. Postman is an API platform that simplifies the API lifecycle, allowing developers to build and collaborate on APIs efficiently.

There are different ways you can use Postman, from the web, the Postman CLI, a Visual Studio Code extension, or a desktop application compatible with Windows, macOS, and Linux, which is probably the most common one.

For this recipe, we will use the desktop application, which you can download at this link: `https://www.postman.com/downloads/`

To get started, download the Postman version compatible with your operating system, install it and create a Postman account at `https://www.postman.com/` if you don't have one.

How to do it...

Once Postman is installed on your computer and your account created, it's time to learn how we can query data from a published data source:

1. First, go to the Salesforce Developers Postman Collection repository at this link: `https://www.postman.com/salesforce-developers/salesforce-developers/collection/x06mp2m/tableau-apis?ctx=documentation`.

2. Look for the Tableau APIs folder on the left panel, click on the three dots next to the folder and click on **Create a fork**. Creating a fork allows you to contribute and use the elements in the collection.

3. In the new window that will appear, change the fork label if needed, select a workspace to add the collection to, and in the **Environments to fork** make sure you select the **Tableau REST API Environment** from the dropdown menu. Then, click on **Fork Collection**.

4. Postman should then navigate directly to the new collection you just forked. On the left panel, click on **Environments**, and then in the environments list, double click on the environment you just forked. Here is where all the variables for the environment are stored. Update the **Current value** column of the following variables:

    *   `Server`: This should be the base url of your Tableau Cloud environment. For example: 10ax.online.tableau.com

    *   `Content-url`: This should be the name of your Tableau site as it appears in Tableau Cloud's url. For example: mytableausite

    *   `Admin-PAT-name`: The name of your Personal Access Token. If you don't know how to create a Personal Access Token check the recipe **Authenticating in Tableau's REST API** in this same chapter.

    *   `Admin-PAT-secret`: The secret of your Personal Access Token.

Make sure to save the changes clicking **Save** at the top of the screen.

5. On the left panel, click on **Collections** and look for the collection name you forked in *Step 2*. Double click on it and expand the **Sample Workflows** folder and then expand the **VizQL Data Service Queries** folder.

6. Double click the **Sign in (JWT)** request inside the folder to open it. This request uses JSON Web Tokens to authenticate into Tableau Cloud, but we will edit the request to use Personal Access Tokens instead. Once you have double clicked the request, look for the **Body** tab in the middle section of the screen and replace the text for the following:

```
<tsRequest>
    <credentials personalAccessTokenName="{{admin-PAT-name}}"
    personalAccessTokenSecret="{{admin-PAT-secret}}">
        <site contentUrl="{{content-url}}" />
    </credentials>
</tsRequest>
```

This should allow us to get the Personal Access Token details we saved in our environment variables as well as our Tableau Cloud Site details. Make sure you save the changes by clicking **Save** at the top of the screen.

7. Now click **Send**, Postman should send an authentication request using our PAT to Tableau cloud and we should get a response at the bottom of the screen with a credentials Token and our site Id. These two strings will be saved automatically to our environment variables.

8. Now we need to get the ID of a datasource we want to query using the VizQL Data Service. To do so, we need to go back to Tableau Cloud. Sign into Tableau Cloud and look for a data source you want to query. In my case, I have uploaded the `ch1_visits.csv` file from *Chapter 1* as a data source. My data source is called **Visits**. To get the **ID** of the datasource, navigate to the datasource in Tableau Cloud and click on the "I" icon to get the datasource details as shown in *Figure 9.5*. The Id is under the field **LUID**.

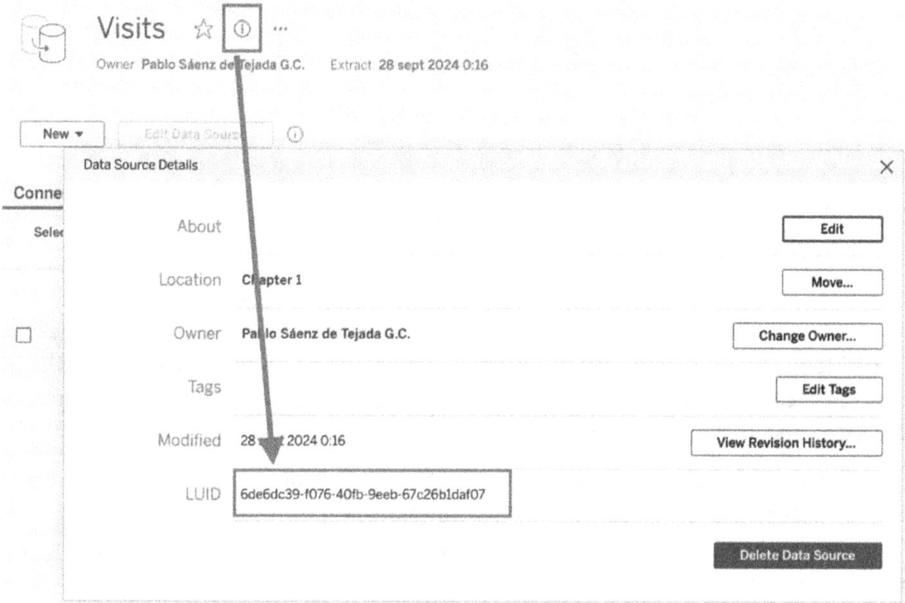

Figure 9.5 – Getting the Id or Luid of a datasource in Tableau Cloud

9. Copy the Id of the datasource, go back to Postman and navigate again to Environments on the left panel. Open again the environment name as in *step 4*, and update the **Current value** of the variable **datasource-id** pasting the text of the datasource Id or Luid. Make sure you **Save** the changes as before.

10. With all our environment variables ready, now it's time to query the data source with VDS. Click on the **Collections** tab on the left menu bar.

11. Navigate again to the **VizQL Data Service Queries** folder and open the **Query Datasource** request.

12. On the main section of the Postman Window, click on the **Body** tab and select **raw** in the radio button options.

13. The coding section should show the body of the request we will send to the VDS API. By default, it should look like this:

```
{
    "datasource": {
        "datasourceLuid": "{{datasource-id}}"
    },
    "options": {
        "returnFormat": "OBJECTS"
    },
    "query": {
        "fields": [
```

```
    {
        "fieldCaption": "Category"
    },{
        "fieldCaption": "Sales",
        "function": "SUM"
    }
    ]
  }
}
```

This request will get the Tableau environment, look for our datasource specified in the datasource id variable. Then, it will query some columns: `Category`, and `Sales`, aggregating the latest. However, because this is just a template, and we don't have those variables in our data source, we need to update the `columns` section of the request.

If you remember from *Chapter 1*, our `vh1_visits.csv` table has columns such as `Doctor ID` and `Duration in Minutes`. If I want to query the average duration of the visits of each doctor ID in descending order to three decimal places, I could replace the `query` section to have a body request such as the following:

```
{
  "datasource": {
    "datasourceLuid": "{{datasource-id}}"
  },
  "options": {
    "returnFormat": "OBJECTS"
  },
  "query": {
    "fields": [
        {
            "fieldCaption": "Doctor ID"
        },
        {
            "fieldCaption": "Duration in Minutes",
            "fieldAlias": "Avg Visit Duration",
            "function": "AVG",
            "sortPriority": 1,
            "sortDirection": "DESC",
            "maxDecimalPlaces": 3
        }
    ]
  }
}
```

As you can see, we can customize the output, giving aliases to the columns, defining aggregations, sorting directions and sorting priorities, and even the number of decimals to quantitative numbers.

> **Use the remote column names**
>
> It's important to remember that the fieldCaption must be the fieldCaption returned from the **Request data source metadata** method. This method provides information about the data fields, such as field names, data types, and descriptions. You have also this request available in the Postman collection in the VizQL Data Service Queries example, named **Read Metadata**.

14. With the body request ready, click the **Send** button at the top right of the Postman window. At the bottom of the screen, you should see the body of the API response in a JSON format, with every single doctor ID, and the average visit duration to three decimal places.

Congratulations! You have just used the VDS API to query your Tableau-published data source and get an answer in JSON format.

There's more…

One of the amazing things about the VDS API is that it not only allows you to query the fields already available in your data sources but also allows you to perform calculations based on those fields and create new values like you do when you create a calculated field in Tableau.

For example, if I wanted to calculate the average duration in a different way, by summing the visit duration in minutes and dividing it by the distinct number of patients each doctor sees, I could add an additional column in the body of my request, like this:

```
{"fieldCaption": "Duration_Per_Patient",
"calculation": "SUM(Duration in Minutes)/
COUNTD(Patient_ID)"}
```

In this case, `fieldCaption` is not a field in my data source, but the unique name of the calculation I want to return. In the `calculation` section, I define the formula I want to calculate, like we normally do with calculated fields.

See also

For more information about the VDS, check the official documentation: `https://help.tableau.com/current/api/vizql-data-service/en-us/docs/vds_whats_new.html`

Geocoding addresses with TabPy, Tableau Prep, and openrouteservice

One of Tableau's strengths is its power with maps and geographical data. But if we want to map addresses, we need the latitude and longitude of each one. How can we convert addresses into coordinates to map our data?

The answer lies in using the following:

- **TabPy**: A Tableau extension that allows us to execute Python scripts, thereby expanding Tableau's capabilities.

- **Tableau Prep**: To create a flow that allows us to load our starting addresses, execute the Python script, check the results, and save them where we want: a local file, a database, in Tableau Cloud, Tableau Server, or Salesforce Data Cloud.

- **openrouteservice API**: An API that allows, among other services, the conversion of addresses into latitudes and longitudes, thereby letting us search for each address and automatically transform it into latitude and longitude. In other words, we can use this API to geolocate postal addresses.

Getting ready

Before we start, we will need to make sure TabPy is installed on our computer and create an account and token in OpenRouteService to use their API.

TabPy can be installed both locally and on a server for global use. To keep things simple, we'll install TabPy locally on our computer.

First, we'll need to install Python if you don't have it already. I'll assume you have Python installed on your computer, but if not, I recommend following the instructions on the official website at https://www.python.org/downloads/, depending on your operating system.

Once we have Python installed, it's time to install TabPy, but it's advisable to first install and update pip. To do this, in your computer's command line, run the following:

```
python -m pip install --upgrade pip
```

After installing and updating pip, we can install the TabPy package by executing the following code in the command line:

```
pip install tabpy
```

Great! We now have TabPy installed, although we won't use it just yet. There are a few more modules we'll need in our Python script, so it's important to make sure we have them installed. In the terminal or command line, execute the two following code lines:

```
pip install pandas
pip install requests
```

The next thing we need is a service that transforms a postal address into its latitude and longitude. Today, there are many such services: Amazon Geocoding, Mapbox Geocoding, Google Geocoding API, and openrouteservice, among many others.

The reason I'm using the last one in this case is because it has a free usage of 1,000 addresses per day.

To start, we need to go to the openrouteservice website at `https://openrouteservice.org/` and click on the **Log In** button in the top-right corner. Click on the **Go Sign up Now** at the top on the next page to sign up and be able to use openrouteservice.

With those things ready, we can start learning how to geocode addresses with Tableau Prep, TabPy, and openrouteservice.

How to do it...

We will start by making sure we can use the openrouteservice API before moving to Tableau Prep:

1. Go to the openrouteservice login screen at `https://openrouteservice.org/` and sign in using the **Log In** option in the navigation menu at the top using the credentials created before.

2. Once logged in, you should see at the top of the screen an API Key tab and a Basic Key field with your **API Key** or **Token**.

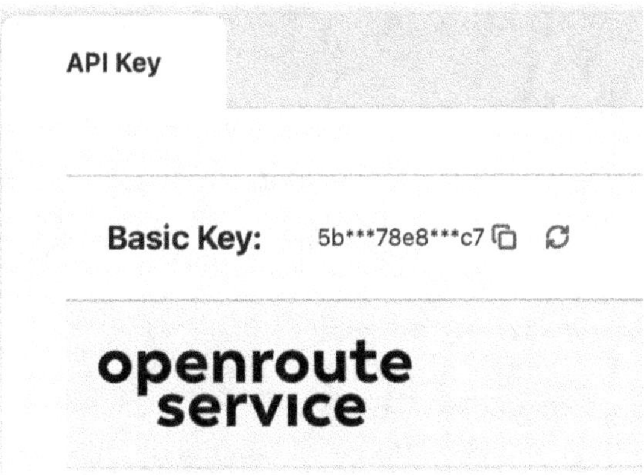

Figure 9.6 – Creating a new token in openrouteservice

3. Copy the token key as we will need it later in our Python script.

4. Perfect. With our openrouteservice API key ready, we can move on to the Python script that will transform addresses to latitude and longitude. TabPy has some requirements we need to meet:

- The script must use a function that specifies the pandas DataFrame as an argument to get our data from Tableau Prep.

- The function must return the results in a pandas DataFrame using the supported data types by TabPy and Tableau Prep: `string`, `decimal`, `integer`, `boolean`, `date`, or `datetime`.

- We will need to use a `get_output_schema` function to define the output schema that we need after our script calls the Google Geocoding API.

5. Create a new `.py` file in your favorite coding tool or IDE (Visual Studio Code, Sublime, Notepad++, PyCharm, etc.) and type the following script or use the one shared at the beginning of the recipe. The script will look for an address, country, postcode, region, and locality fields in the file, and return the address provided with its latitude, longitude, and a confidence number between 0 and 1 of the geocoding result for each address:

```python
import requests
import pandas as pd
import time


def geocode_address(df):
    lat = []
    lon = []
    confidence = []

    # OpenRouteService API key
    mykey = 'paste-here-ors-api-key'
    headers = {'Accept': 'application/json'}

    for i in df.index:
        try:
            # Build URL with structured parameters
            base_url = 'https://api.openrouteservice.org/
                        geocode/search/structured'
            params = {
                'api_key': mykey,
                'address': df['address'][i].strip(),
                'country': df['country'][i].strip(),
                'postalcode': df['postcode'][i].strip(),
                'region': df['region'][i].strip(),
                'locality': df['locality'][i].strip(),
                'size': 1
            }
```

```python
        # Make the API request
        geocode_result = requests.get(
            base_url, params=params,
            headers=headers)
        data = geocode_result.json()

        # Extract coordinates
        if 'features' in data and data['features']:
            coordinates = data['features'][0][
                'geometry']['coordinates']
            lt = coordinates[1]   # Latitude
            lg = coordinates[0]   # Longitude
            conf = data['features'][0][
                'properties'].get('confidence', 0)
        else:
            lt = 0
            lg = 0
            conf = 0

        confidence.append(conf)
        lat.append(lt)
        lon.append(lg)

        # Rate limiting - be nice to the API
        time.sleep(1)

    except Exception as e:
        print(f"Error processing address {df['address'][i]}:
            {str(e)}")
        confidence.append(0)
        lat.append(0)
        lon.append(0)

# Create result dataframe
result_df = pd.DataFrame({
    'address': df['address'],
    'confidence': confidence,
    'latitude': lat,
    'longitude': lon
})

return result_df
```

```python
def get_output_schema():
    return pd.DataFrame({
        'address': prep_string(),
        'confidence': prep_decimal(),
        'latitude': prep_decimal(),
        'longitude': prep_decimal()
    })
```

6. Replace `paste-here-ors-api-key` with the API key from openrouteservice we created in *Step 4* of the recipe.

7. Let's do a quick recap: we have set up the openrouteservice API key and we have a Python script that should meet the TabPy requirements to get a list of addresses and geocode them, returning each address with latitude and longitude fields. Now it's time to start using TabPy and Tableau Prep to finish completing the process. Open a command-line window or terminal and start TabPy by typing the following:

    tabpy

    TabPy should be now ready to use.

8. Now let's open Tableau Prep Builder and configure the TabPy extension. We can do this through **Help | Settings and Performance | Manage Analytics Extension Connection**, as shown in *Figure 9.7*.

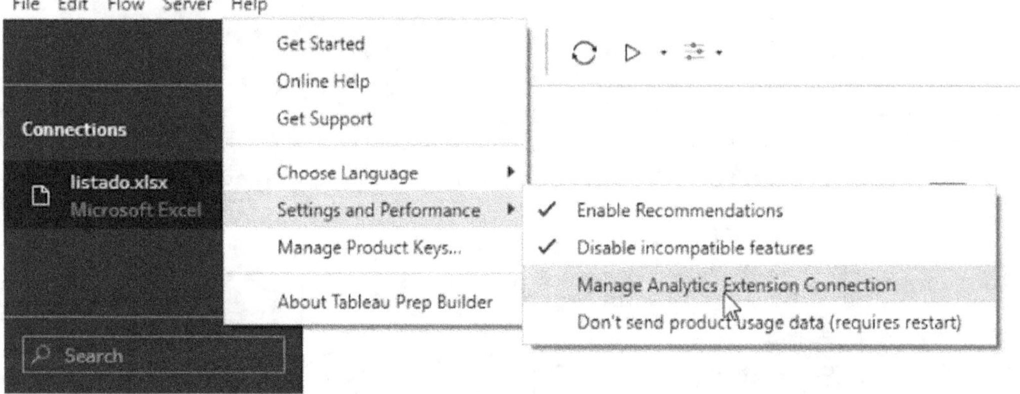

Figure 9.7 — Accessing the Manage Analytics Extension Connection in Tableau Prep

9. Select TabPy in the drop-down menu and type `localhost` for **Server** and `9004` for **Port**. Then, click on **Sign In** to configure the extension and allow Tableau Prep Builder to use TabPy.

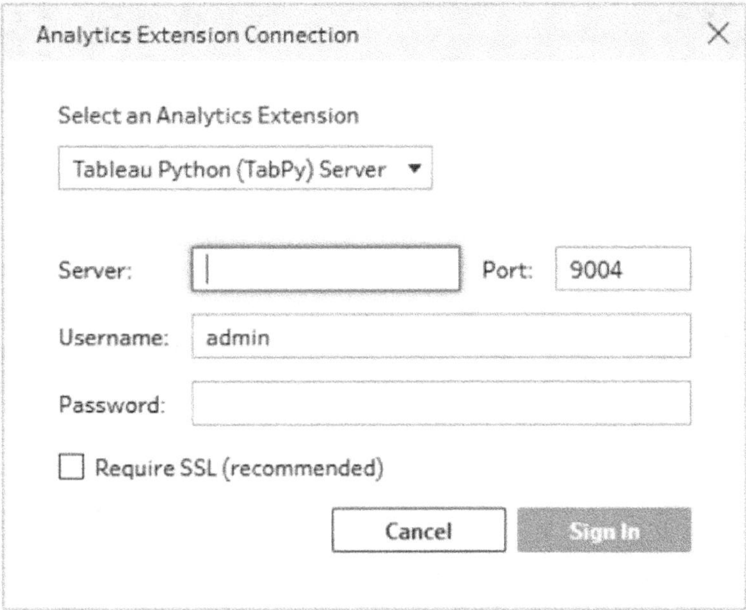

Figure 9.8 – Manage Analytics Extension Connection settings

10. Now we need to create a flow with Tableau Prep Builder and use the script we created and TabPy. Open Tableau Prep Builder and load the `addresses.csv` file shared in the GitHub repository shared at the beginning of the chapter. Make sure all the fields are string fields, you might need to modify the data type of the postcode field from integer to string.

11. Once the data is loaded, add a script step or node to the flow. To configure it, make sure you select **Tableau Python (TabPy) Server** as the connection type, select the `.py` file you created in *Step 5* or downloaded from the GitHub repository, and type `geocode_address`, the name of the Python function in the script we will use, as shown in *Figure 9.9*.

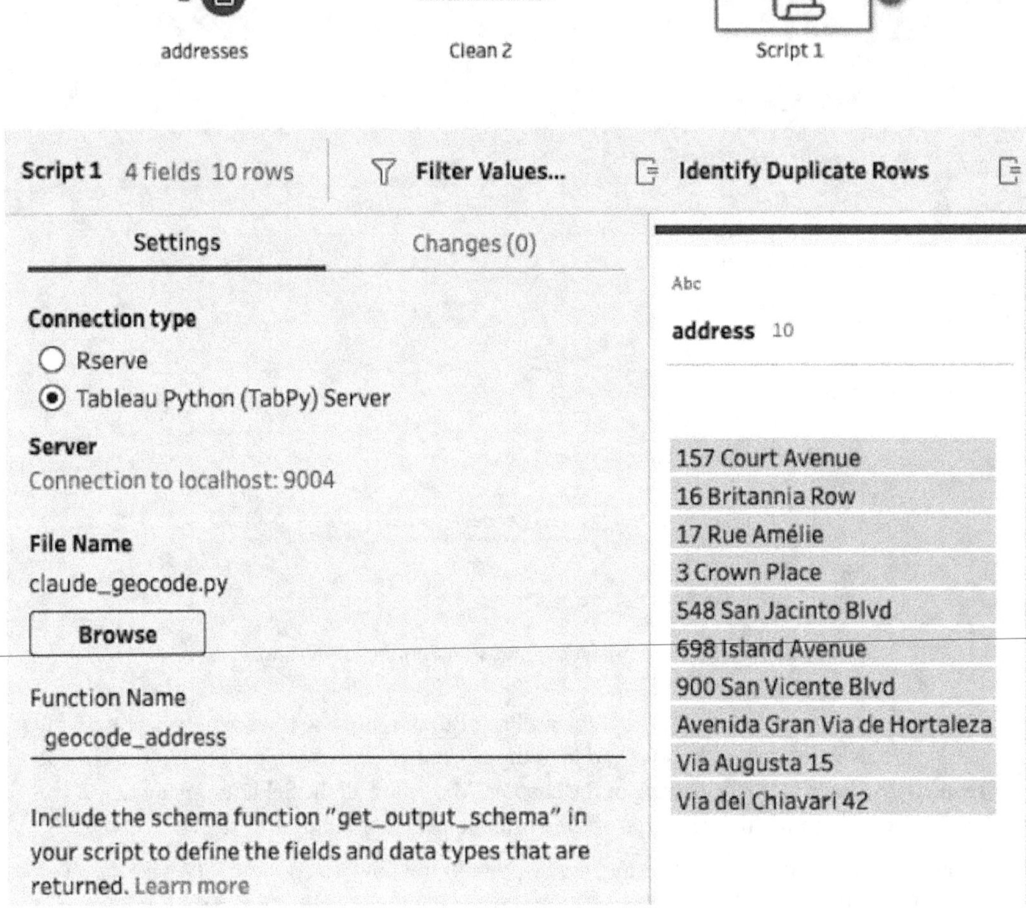

Figure 9.9 – Script node configuration in Tableau Prep

12. Now, add a new clean step or node to the flow. If everything went well, you should see the latitude and longitude of your addresses already geocoded as in *Figure 9.10*.

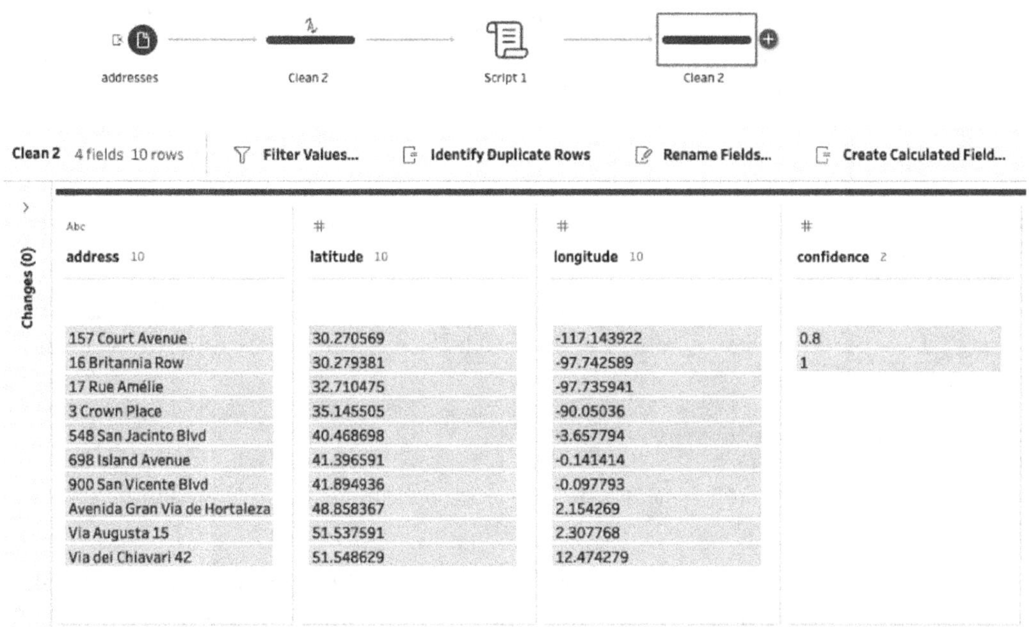

Figure 9.10 – Output of the geocode TabPy script

Well done! You have combined the openrouteservice API with TabPy to geocode addresses. Now you can save the output data and analyze it.

> **Alternative geocoding services**
>
> openrouteservice is a free service that allows you to geocode around 1,000 addresses every 24 hours. There are other geocoding services with fewer restrictions but with costs associated, such as the Google Maps Geocoding API. For real production use cases, it might be interesting to update the code to use alternative paid services with fewer API request restrictions.

Finding all workbooks connected to a specific database with the Metadata API and GraphQL

You might be asking yourself, what is the **Metadata API**? The Tableau Metadata API indexes all the content on your Tableau Cloud site or Tableau Server. This includes workbooks, data sources, flows, and metrics, and then, through the indexing, it also identifies databases, files, tables, and columns used.

The interesting thing about the Metadata API is that, through indexing, it also gathers information about the lineage of all that content. This allows Tableau administrators and data stewards to discover data, track lineage or perform impact analysis in a fast and efficient way.

Getting ready

Before we start using the Metadata API with GraphQL, we need to make sure we have the Metadata API set up and ready to use it.

The good thing is this is already enabled and ready for you if you are using Tableau Cloud. If you are using Tableau Server, a server admin must first enable the metadata service using the following command on Tableau Server:

```
tsm maintenance metadata-service enable
```

For this recipe, we can use our Tableau Cloud Developer environment to avoid requiring setting up anything.

Then we have to log in to our Tableau Server or Tableau Cloud environment and access it through our browser. If you are using Tableau Cloud, the URL in your browser once you access Tableau Cloud should look something like this:

```
https://10ax.online.tableau.com/#/site/mysitename/home
```

The first part of the URL might be different, and instead of **10ax**, it could be **us-west-2b** or any similar text depending on the region where your Tableau Cloud environment is hosted.

To access the Metadata API and GraphQL, just delete the text after `.com` in your URL and type `/metadata/graphiql/` afterward.

Your URL should be something like this:

```
https://10ax.online.tableau.com/metadata/graphiql/
```

Then, press *Enter*, and you should have access to GraphQL to use the Metadata API.

Now we can start querying the Metadata API and get all workbooks connected to a specific database.

How to do it...

The GraphQL language allows you to write a query specifying the objects, and even objects inside those objects, you are interested in and get the results you need.

Generally, GraphQL queries have a shape similar to this:

```
query query_name {
  <object_to_query> (<arguments>) {
    <attribute>
    <attribute> {
      <attribute>
    }
  }
}
```

Then specify the type of object we want to query, such as databases, tables, workbooks, views, or even columns, fields, and calculated fields, as well as the information we want from that object.

Let's build our first GraphQL query to get all the databases in Tableau Cloud:

1. On the left side of the screen, type the following query:

    ```
    query my_databases {
      databases {
        name
        id
        connectionType
      }
    }
    ```

2. Then click the **Play** button on the top menu and see the results on the right side. You should get a list of all the databases available in Tableau Cloud with the name, ID, and connection type of each of them, as in *Figure 9.11*.


```
{
  "errors": [
    {
      "message": "Obfuscation is disabled with your site settings so your results have been automatically filtered to contain only the
results you have permissions to see",
      "extensions": {
        "severity": "WARNING",
        "code": "PERMISSIONS_MODE_SWITCHED",
        "properties": {
          "databases": [
            "permissionMode"
          ]
        }
      }
    }
  ],
  "data": {
    "databases": [
      {
        "name": "SFC_SAMPLES_EUFRANKFURT_SAMPLE_DATA",
        "id": "07c010ed-6aee-1db6-24d9-29df85c8d55c",
        "connectionType": "snowflake"
      },
      {
        "name": "PERSONAL",
```


Figure 9.11 — Sample results of the Metadata API and GraphQL

3. We could add more fields to the query, such as all the workbooks connected to each database:

```
query my_databases {
  databases {
    name
    id
    connectionType
    downstreamWorkbooks {
      id
      name
      projectName
    }
  }
}
```

Now we will get not only the details of each database but also every single workbook connected to each database and their details, as in *Figure 9.12*.

```
{
  "name": "PERSONAL",
  "id": "4c763694-5402-4fe8-1abc-646bf9f696e1",
  "connectionType": "snowflake",
  "downstreamWorkbooks": [
    {
      "id": "691293b9-5e0b-0e0e-1eea-dfe39adbd533"
      "name": "Personal Expense Dashboard",
      "projectName": "Finance"
    },
    {
      "id": "848aa347-c224-06f3-15fd-1239768ed359"
      "name": "Daily Running Comparison ",
      "projectName": "Finance"
    },
    {
      "id": "b9eebbef-5599-6baa-0491-31d3f7dc1fab"
      "name": "Basic Book Reading Analysis",
      "projectName": "Personal Life & Habits"
    }
  ]
},
{
  "name": "d4b3286e-ea09-4ec4-8687-9481ccb9978d",
  "id": "5871be4c-d097-b82a-5bc8-039f5c9c1795",
  "connectionType": "hyper",
  "downstreamWorkbooks": []
},
{
  "name": "666309e6-d9ba-422e-960f-26ba5daa0636",
  "id": "622d8f95-6415-3a4d-1be2-7538b8900cc6",
  "connectionType": "hyper",
  "downstreamWorkbooks": [
    {
      "id": "38292aa9-9673-7bbc-8f0b-ee9409cd19b2"
      "name": "Admin Insights Starter",
      "projectName": "Admin Insights"
    }
  ]
},
```

Figure 9.12 – Databases queried using the Metadata API, GraphQL, and downstream workbooks

4. Let's reduce the scope of our query a bit and learn how we can filter the databases we are querying. To filter our results, we can add a `filter` argument just after specifying the object we want to query (databases, in our example), like this:

```
query my_databases {
  databases (
    filter: {id:"4c763694-5402-4fe8-1abc-646bf9f696e1"}
  ) {
    name
    id
    connectionType
    downstreamWorkbooks {
      id
      name
      projectName
    }
  }
}
```

You can replace the string between the double quotes for one of your databases. The result will be a query that returns all workbooks connected to that specific database and the ID and name of the workbook and the project where the workbook is located.

There's more...

The great thing about the Metadata API and GraphQL is that it not only allows you to query objects downstream, such as workbooks connected to a database, but also upstream.

Imagine we want to query a database with the workbooks connected to it exactly as we just did, but also include the tables of the database each workbook is connected to.

We could achieve this by querying `upstreamTables` inside the workbooks:

```
query my_databases {
  databases (filter: {id: "4c763694-5402-4fe8-1abc-646bf9f696e1"}) {
    name
    id
    connectionType
    downstreamWorkbooks {
      id
      name
      projectName
      upstreamTables {
        name
      }
    }
  }
}
```

There are plenty of possibilities to better understand the content in your Tableau Cloud environment and its dependencies with the Metadata API.

See also

- For more details and information about Tableau's Metadata API, check the official documentation: `https://help.tableau.com/current/api/metadata_api/en-us/docs/meta_api_examples.html`

- You can find additional examples of Metadata API queries in Tableau's GitHub repository: `https://github.com/tableau/metadata-api-samples/tree/master/samples`

Using the Metadata API and GraphQL to document calculated fields created by your users

In the previous recipe, we learned how to use the Metadata API GraphQL to query all the workbooks connected to a specific database.

One of the most interesting features of the Metadata API is that it not only allows you to query content such as databases, workbooks, flows, and views in Tableau Cloud or Server but also to go deeper and even analyze the calculated fields used inside workbooks.

This can be very useful to perform a very detailed analysis of how your users are using Tableau and, for example, discover whether there are common calculations that might be worth including in the tables and views of the database, instead of leaving it in the hands of the analysts.

This might also be useful to reduce possible errors and to speed up the analyst's workflow because if there are common calculations being made in a lot of different dashboards, that probably means there's a common need that the Data Engineering team might need to solve.

Let's see how we can use the Metadata API to check calculations being used in our workbooks.

Getting ready

To start using the Metadata API, we will follow the same steps as in the last recipe. You can check the full details there but, basically, go to your Tableau Cloud or Tableau Server page using a browser, replace anything after `.com` in the URL with `/metadata/graphiql/`, and press *Enter*. Your URL should be something like this: `https://10ax.online.tableau.com/metadata/graphiql/`.

How to do it...

1. First, let's start by querying all the calculated fields in Tableau Cloud. We can achieve this using a very simple query with GraphQL and the Metadata API, such as the following:

```
query my_calculations {
  calculatedFields {
    id
    name
    formula
  }
}
```

The query should return a full list of our calculations with the internal ID Tableau uses for the field, the calculated field name, and the formula, as in *Figure 9.13*.

```
"data": {
  "calculatedFields": [
    {
      "id": "00f517b6-0280-a0e0-e9ee-51ce0916022a",
      "name": "Created At (local)",
      "formula": "DATEADD('hour', [Timezone], [Created At])"
    },
    {
      "id": "01f93d0f-40e1-3cc7-1e34-9b1a87ebd341",
      "name": "Agua_Actual",
      "formula": "FLOAT(REPLACE([Agua Actual],\",\",\".\"))"
    },
    {
      "id": "06272be7-7a5b-4d9e-3276-6504446e4801",
      "name": "avg(0)",
      "formula": "avg(0)"
    },
    {
      "id": "0823925d-6437-bea6-12bd-1ff65f148ac1",
```

Figure 9.13 – Calculated fields returned by the Metadata API

2. This is not a bad start, but probably not very useful because we don't know the data sources, tables, or databases each calculation is being used with. Let's approach the problem the other way around. Let's query all the calculations from every single field of a specific table on my Tableau Cloud site, like this:

```
query all_fields_and_calcs_from_a_table {
  tables (filter: {id:"6acfe17c-6407-89df-e0c0-e9376f625c79"}) {
    name
    id
```

```
        columns {
           name
           referencedByFields {
              name
              referencedByCalculations {
                 name
                 formula
                 downstreamSheets {
                    id
                    name
                    workbook {
                       name
                    }
                 }
              }
           }
        }
     }
  }
}
```

How it works...

The query might look complex, but it is easier than it seems. We are completing the following tasks:

- Filtering a specific table and querying the table name and ID

- Querying all the columns from the table

- Querying all the fields that refer to those columns

- Querying all the calculations that refer to those fields

- Querying the sheets and workbooks where those calculations are used

The query returned some interesting insights. For example, *Figure 9.14* shows that there's a field called **FECHA** in the table (*Fecha* means *Date* in Spanish).

The field is being referred to by a calculation called **Semana** (*Week* in Spanish), basically truncating the date to a weekly format. That calculation is then used in five different sheets of a concrete workbook.

```
{
  "name": "FECHA",
  "referencedByFields": [
    {
      "name": "Fecha",
      "referencedByCalculations": [
        {
          "name": "Semana",
          "formula": "DATE(DATETRUNC(\"week\",[Fecha]))",
          "downstreamSheets": [
            {
              "id": "0b66b1e8-b8e1-b74a-c7e2-a9ebc9bae5d2",
              "name": "Evolución anual",
              "workbook": {
                "name": "Water Reservoirs in Spain"
              }
            },
            {
              "id": "6ce73348-399a-8d5b-a7db-f794d4d121b6",
              "name": "% Agua Embalsada",
              "workbook": {
                "name": "Water Reservoirs in Spain"
              }
            },
            {
              "id": "75452e04-9215-3659-df37-54bbc4124240",
              "name": "KPI Agua Embalsada vs año anterior (2)",
              "workbook": {
                "name": "Water Reservoirs in Spain"
              }
            },
            {
              "id": "bfbf50e7-b2dc-0b60-5a67-e6110985aded",
              "name": "Agua embalsada por cuenca",
              "workbook": {
                "name": "Water Reservoirs in Spain"
              }
            },
            {
              "id": "e0b1746e-71ac-a2ea-c686-7d325f3ba189",
              "name": "Fecha",
              "workbook": {
                "name": "Water Reservoirs in Spain"
              }
            }
          ]
        },
```

Figure 9.14 – Getting all the sheets connected to a concrete calculation of a table field

This is a perfect example of how we can use the Metadata API to identify a calculation that might be a good idea to process in the database. A date calculation being used in several views probably means there's a frequent need for our analyst to query the data on a weekly basis and not just on a daily basis.

Computing the calculation in the database instead of it being done individually by each analyst can achieve the following:

- Improve dashboard performance

- Reduce mistakes

- Increase our analysts' productivity

- Allow for better governance as the calculation is done in a single place instead of in different workbooks and dashboards

There are plenty of possible use cases for the Metadata API. Give it a try and get the most out of it!

Get This Book's PDF Version and Exclusive Extras

Scan the QR code (or go to `packtpub.com/unlock`). Search for this book by name, confirm the edition, and then follow the steps on the page.

Note: Keep your invoice handy. Purchases made directly from Packt don't require an invoice.

10

Core Techniques for Impactful Data Design

The ability to create insightful and engaging dashboards is not just a skill – it's a game changer. Effective dashboards can make the difference between strategic insights and missed opportunities. This chapter will help you navigate the complexities of dashboard design, ensuring that your work stands out and delivers real value in any context.

The goal of this chapter is to help you gain a deep understanding of the technical principles and best practices for creating high-impact dashboards. You'll explore how to precisely tailor your design to meet the needs of your audience, strategically apply color to enhance data interpretation, and select the most effective chart types to convey your message clearly. Furthermore, you'll learn how to develop a comprehensive style guide to maintain visual consistency and utilize advanced tables to enrich your dashboards with sophisticated data insights.

In this chapter, we'll be covering the following recipes:

- Design for your audience
- Use color with purpose
- Choose correct chart types
- Develop a style guide
- Enhance your tables

Design for your audience

Designing dashboards with your audience in mind is key to creating data visualizations that are both effective and impactful. By prioritizing the needs and preferences of your end users, you ensure that the dashboard not only delivers relevant insights but also enhances usability and engagement. Understanding your audience's goals and data literacy helps tailor the design to meet their requirements. When a dashboard is aligned with users' expectations, it becomes a powerful tool that effectively communicates data and drives actionable outcomes. This recipe will highlight the key considerations you must address as a developer or a creator of data products.

How to do it...

- **Understand your target audience**: Identifying and understanding your target audience is crucial for designing a dashboard that effectively meets your users' needs and preferences. Gaining insights into what information your users seek and what questions they are trying to answer will put you in a better position for effective communication, so you can tailor the design and content to provide relevant and actionable insights.

  Begin by engaging with key stakeholders to understand their strategic goals and specific data requirements. Next, gather detailed specifications on users' roles, data literacy, and design preferences. Ensure to analyze their current data usage patterns and pain points; this will help to identify what features and metrics are most valuable. You can also develop user personas to represent different segments of your audience, which can help tailor the dashboard's functionality and interface. By incorporating these basic principles in your dashboard development process, you can ensure that the dashboard design is optimized for usability, relevance, and effectiveness, leading to the creation of a user-centric data visualization tool.

- **Select appropriate visualizations**: The effectiveness of data communication hinges on how well the visual elements represent and clarify the information. Selecting the right chart type for your data ensures that information is presented in a way that aligns with the users' objectives and enhances their ability to make informed decisions. For instance, line charts are ideal for showing trends over time and pie charts are useful for illustrating proportions. Choosing visualizations that align with the type of data and the specific insight helps avoid misinterpretation and enhances clarity. Please refer to the *Choose correct chart types* recipe for more information and resources on this topic.

- **Provide context**: Data without context can be misleading or difficult to grasp, leading to incorrect conclusions or misinformed decisions. Contextual elements such as explanatory text, tooltips, or annotations offer clarity by guiding users through the meaning of data points, trends, or metrics. This added information ensures that even users unfamiliar with the data can comprehend its relevance and make informed choices based on the insights presented.

Consider including clear descriptions or titles that explain the purpose of each visualization. Use tooltips or hidden objects to provide additional details when users hover over or select specific data points; these elements can offer explanations without cluttering the dashboard. Ensure to add annotations or callouts to highlight key trends, outliers, or important changes in the data. These elements should be concise but informative, giving users the right amount of information to interpret the data effectively.

- **Maximize your data-ink ratio**: Edward Tufte introduced the concept of the **data-ink ratio** in *The Visual Display of Quantitative Information*, defining it as the proportion of ink or pixels dedicated to displaying meaningful data versus extraneous decorative elements. A high data-ink ratio ensures that visualizations remain clear, concise, and free from unnecessary clutter, allowing the audience to focus on the insights rather than distractions.

  To effectively implement this principle in your visualizations, begin by eliminating non-essential design elements that do not contribute to data interpretation. Reduce excessive gridlines, redundant labels, and extraneous decorative elements. Simplify charts by using minimal colors and remove background shading. Finally, ensure that you emphasize key insights by structuring data in a logical, narrative-driven manner that guides the audience's focus and enhances understanding. By prioritizing essential information and removing distractions, you can enhance readability, improve comprehension, and create more polished, professional-looking visuals.

  Please note that while the data-ink ratio is a powerful guideline for creating efficient visualizations, it should not be treated as a rigid rule! The goal is to enhance understanding, not strip away all design elements. In some cases, adding subtle visual cues, such as a light gridline or a minimal accent color, can improve clarity without introducing clutter. The key is to balance simplicity with effectiveness, ensuring that your visualization remains both functional and engaging.

- **Design for all skill levels**: Being mindful of diverse user skill levels is extremely important when creating dashboards that will be used by a broad audience with varying degrees of technical proficiency. Some users may be data experts who can easily navigate complex visualizations, while others may need a more straightforward interface to make sense of the information. Balancing the needs of both groups ensures that the dashboard provides value to all users, preventing frustration for those who are less tech-savvy while still offering advanced features for more experienced individuals.

  Make sure you take concrete steps to identify your audience's technical capabilities through user research or feedback. Provide clear, concise explanations and tooltips for less experienced users, while ensuring that interactive elements such as filters or drilldowns are intuitive. Use a clean, simple layout with minimal distractions for clarity, but incorporate advanced features such as customizable views or detailed analytics for tech-savvy users. By offering both simplicity and depth, you can create a dashboard that serves a diverse audience effectively, making data accessible and actionable for all.

- **Build for multi-device use**: Optimizing your dashboards for multi-device viewing is crucial as users increasingly access dashboards on a range of devices, including desktops, tablets, and smartphones. Designing with multiple screen sizes in mind ensures that dashboards remain functional across all platforms. Begin by understanding the different display constraints for each device. For instance, on smaller screens such as mobile devices, available space is limited, and charts or text that appear clear on a desktop may become cluttered or unreadable. To counter this, you should use responsive design techniques to create layouts that automatically adjust based on the device being used.

  In Tableau, this can be achieved by leveraging device-specific layouts, where you can create tailored views for desktop, tablet, and phone formats. These layouts allow for adjusting font sizes, resizing charts, and modifying navigation elements to suit each screen type. A key consideration is maintaining a clean, minimalistic interface and prioritizing the most essential data points. By doing so, you prevent overwhelming the user on smaller screens. Testing the dashboard on actual devices rather than relying solely on desktop previews is another best practice to catch issues such as responsiveness, screen lag, or element misalignment.

- **Design for performance**: Dashboard performance has a direct impact on user experience, operational efficiency, and adoption rate. Slow-loading dashboards or those with laggy interactions can frustrate users, leading to decreased productivity and potentially causing users to abandon the tool altogether.

  Addressing performance early on helps prevent issues that can hinder user experience in the long run. Make sure to establish performance benchmarks based on user needs and expectations, to determine acceptable load times, interaction responsiveness, and data refresh rates. Setting these goals upfront helps guide design decisions and performance optimization efforts. Please refer to *Chapter 4* for more information and resources on this topic.

There's more...

The **Monitor-Analyze-Detail (MAD)** framework provides a tiered information delivery system that caters to varying levels of user expertise and needs. Building on the principles of effective dashboard design, the MAD framework, developed by USEReady, offers a novel approach to organizing and presenting data.

The MAD framework is structured as a pyramid with three distinct layers; see *Figure 10.1*.

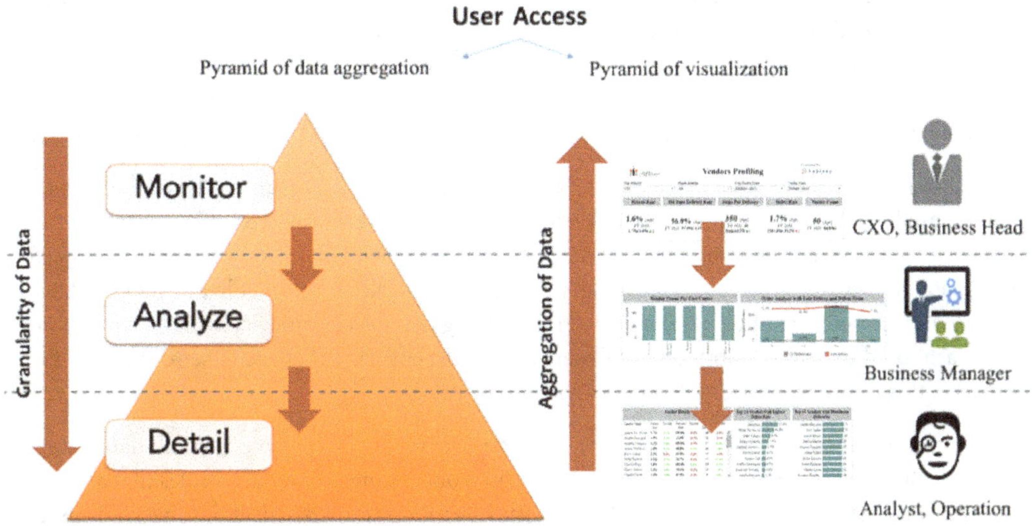

Figure 10.1 – Three distinct layers of the MAD framework developed by USEReady

Each layer serves a specific function:

- **Monitor:** The top layer offers a high-level overview of KPIs and trends. It uses graphical summaries such as charts and scorecards to present critical metrics at a glance. This layer is designed for executives and senior managers who need to quickly assess the overall business performance and identify major trends without delving into detailed data. For example, an executive might use this layer to review company-wide sales figures and key metrics.

- **Analyze:** The middle layer enables users to dive deeper into the data, exploring KPIs from multiple perspectives. This layer supports the use of filters, time frames, and other analytical tools to uncover trends and patterns. For instance, a sales manager might use this layer to investigate sales performance by region or product category, adjusting filters to examine various dimensions and gain more detailed insights.

- **Detail:** The bottom layer provides granular, atomic-level data for thorough analysis and troubleshooting. It often includes transaction-level details and enables users to perform deep dives into specific data points. A data analyst might access this layer to drill down into individual sales transactions to identify the root causes of sales anomalies or deviations.

The MAD framework enhances dashboard usability by offering a clear, hierarchical structure for data presentation. It allows users to start with a high-level overview and drill down into more detailed information as needed, without being overwhelmed by data complexity. This layered approach supports both casual users, who need quick insights, and analysts, who require in-depth data exploration. By minimizing the number of clicks required to access information and providing a logical flow, the MAD framework improves the efficiency of data interaction and decision-making.

Consider a company that needs to design a sales dashboard for both executives and sales representatives. Executives might require a high-level view of overall sales figures, trends, and key metrics, which can be efficiently provided through the *Monitor* layer. Sales representatives, on the other hand, might need detailed data on individual sales transactions, performance by client, or specific product insights, which can be accessed through the *Detail* layer. By applying the MAD framework, the company can create a dashboard that serves both types of users effectively, ensuring that each user can access the information they need with minimal effort and maximum clarity.

To effectively implement the MAD framework, begin by identifying the key metrics and data points relevant to your audience. Design the *Monitor* layer with concise, high-level summaries that address the primary business questions. Ensure that the *Analyze* layer offers interactive features that allow users to explore data from various angles. Finally, include the *Detail* layer for users who need to conduct thorough investigations or perform detailed analyses.

See also

To learn more about the MAD framework, you can read the following blog post: *MAD Framework for Actionable Dashboards: A Comprehensive Guide by USEReady* (`https://www.useready.com/blog/mad-framework-for-actionable-dashboards`).

Use color with purpose

Color serves an essential purpose in dashboard design. When used correctly, color can drive focus, emphasize critical data points, and create an intuitive visual flow. The right color choices can highlight important trends, differentiate categories, and create a visual hierarchy that simplifies complex information and enhances comprehension. This recipe will provide practical guidance on choosing color schemes, avoiding common pitfalls, and ensuring your dashboards are both visually engaging and data-driven.

How to do it...

- **Apply color theory**: Learning the basics of color theory is important because it provides a foundation for understanding how colors interact and influence perception. Color theory explains the relationships between colors and how color combinations can evoke specific emotions or guide attention. In dashboard design, color theory helps in selecting colors that not only enhance visual appeal but also improve readability, highlight key insights, and convey data effectively.

Begin by selecting color schemes based on the relationships in the color wheel. Use complementary colors for contrast or analogous colors for a more harmonious feel, depending on the data's purpose. Tools such as Adobe Color or Tableau's built-in color pickers can help you experiment with different palettes. Additionally, consider the context of your data and use color to guide attention to key metrics, ensure readability, and maintain consistency. Incorporating color theory into your design process will result in dashboards that are visually effective and aligned with the message you want to convey.

- **Leverage color hierarchy**: Color hierarchies can help users visually prioritize and navigate the information presented. By using different shades or intensities of a color, you can create a clear distinction between primary and secondary data, ensuring that key insights stand out while less critical information remains visible but not overwhelming. For instance, darker shades can be applied to highlight primary data points or focus areas, while lighter shades can represent supporting or background data. This approach reduces the cognitive load, guiding users' attention naturally through the dashboard and making the content easier to digest.

  Start off by identifying the key information that needs to stand out and assign it more prominent, darker colors. Then, use progressively lighter shades for secondary or contextual data. It's important to ensure the shades still maintain enough contrast for clarity, even when differentiating between layers of information. You can use tools such as Tableau's color gradient options to create smooth transitions between intensities, making the hierarchy intuitive. Additionally, avoid using too many layers or shades, as this can become confusing; keep the hierarchy simple and consistent throughout the dashboard to maintain a clean and user-friendly design

- **Use fewer colors**: While color can be a powerful tool in dashboard design, overusing it can lead to confusion and visual clutter. Too many colors can overwhelm users, making it harder for them to focus on key insights or understand relationships within the data. This often results in a dashboard that feels chaotic rather than informative. When every data point is highlighted and none stand out, the viewer struggles to prioritize what's important. Limiting the number of colors in a dashboard helps to simplify the visual experience and ensure clear communication of insights.

  To effectively reduce colors in a dashboard, start by limiting your color palette to five or fewer hues; if more categories require differentiation, opt for a two-color scheme, highlighting the most important category with a distinct color and using a muted tone, such as gray, for less critical data. You can also adjust color intensity to further enhance readability. Opting for softer, more subdued hues rather than highly saturated colors reduces visual strain and prevents distractions. This careful adjustment of color intensity ensures that the most critical data points stand out without overwhelming the viewer. Softer colors also make it easier for users to focus on key data points without being sidetracked by overly bright or competing elements.

- **Customize color palettes**: Custom color palettes offer several key benefits. First, they can be used to ensure that your visualizations align with your organization's branding, reinforcing a consistent and professional look. Custom palettes also allow for greater control over how data is represented, enabling you to highlight key elements more effectively. Additionally, custom palettes provide flexibility in accommodating accessibility needs, such as colorblind-friendly designs, ensuring that your dashboard remains inclusive and functional for a wide range of users.

To create a custom color palette, start by using a color palette generator such as Adobe Color, Coolors, or Paletton. These tools allow you to experiment with various color combinations and generate palettes based on your preferences. You can input specific hexadecimal codes, adjust color sliders, or explore predefined themes to find a harmonious set of colors that suit your project. Once you've crafted a palette you like, you can usually export it in various formats for use in design applications. Many of these tools also provide options to save and share palettes, making it easy to integrate custom colors into your dashboards and maintain consistency across different visualizations.

You can easily import your newly created custom color palettes into Tableau by editing the `Preferences.tps` file, which is an XML file where custom color schemes can be defined. The `Preferences.tps` file is found in the `My Tableau Repository` folder on your local computer. You can open this file in a text editor and manually input your desired colors using hexadecimal codes to create a new palette, as in *Figure 10.2*.

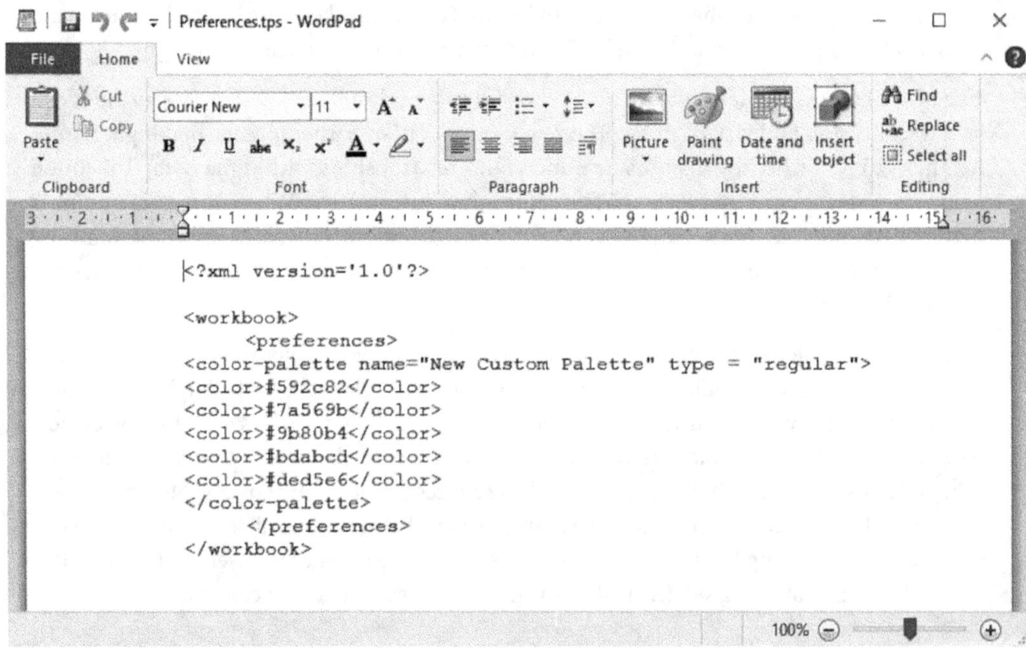

Figure 10.2 – Creating a custom color palette by modifying the Preferences file

You can also define multiple palettes, whether sequential, categorical, or diverging, depending on the needs of your dashboard. Once the colors are set, save the file and restart Tableau to apply the custom palettes.

Alternatively, within Tableau's interface, you can assign specific colors directly to data elements by selecting marks and choosing colors through the drag-and-drop feature. This allows for more flexibility in matching your visualizations to specific branding or design requirements, making your dashboards more visually consistent.

- **Prioritize readability and accessibility**: Addressing accessibility limitations in dashboard design is crucial for creating an inclusive user experience. When colors lack sufficient contrast, important information can become difficult to read, leading to misinterpretation. This issue is even more pronounced for users with visual impairments or color vision deficiencies such as colorblindness, who may struggle to distinguish between certain hues. Accessible design builds trust with users by ensuring that everyone, regardless of their visual abilities, can navigate and interpret the dashboard effectively, leading to a more seamless interaction.

  Begin by selecting colors with high contrast between text and background elements. You can use tools such as WebAIM's color contrast checker, which allows you to test and confirm whether your color combinations meet the required standards, such as the **Web Content Accessibility Guidelines (WCAG)**. These standards recommend a contrast ratio of at least 4.5:1 for normal text and 3:1 for larger text. Additionally, be mindful of colorblind users by using colorblind-friendly palettes or testing your dashboard through external simulators such as Coblis or Colour Simulations. Colour Simulations provides a convenient real-time solution for testing your dashboard's color theme. It also gives you the flexibility to preview how your dashboard will appear to users with various color vision deficiencies; see *Figure 10.3*. You can easily adjust colors directly within the simulator to optimize your dashboard's readability and inclusivity with minimal effort, all from your desktop.

  Additionally, try to avoid relying on color alone to convey information, and ensure to incorporate text labels, patterns, or icons to reinforce meaning. Finally, regularly test your design with a diverse user base to ensure that it remains accessible across different devices and environments.

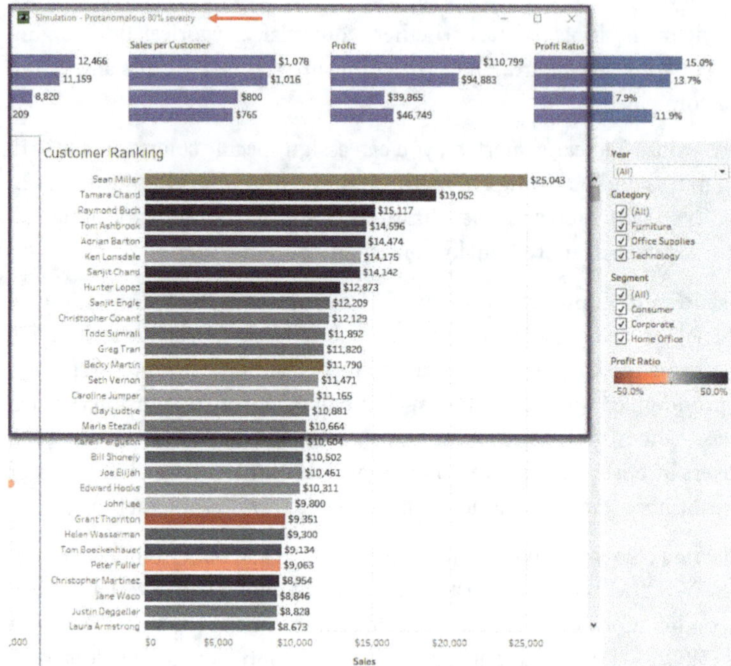

Figure 10.3 – Testing the color palette using Colour Simulations application

See also

- Explore the Adobe Color Wheel and generate custom palettes: `https://color.adobe.com/create/color-wheel`

- Learn to import custom color palettes in Tableau: `https://help.tableau.com/current/pro/desktop/en-us/formatting_create_custom_colors.htm`

- Download Colour Simulations: `http://www.coloursimulations.com/`

- Explore thousands of trending color palettes from Coolors: `https://coolors.co/palettes/trending`

- For a step-by-step process on how to create a color palette, read *Building a Color Palette for Tableau* by Luke Stanke at phData: `https://www.phdata.io/blog/building-a-color-palette-for-tableau/`

Choose correct chart types

The power of a well-chosen visualization lies in its ability to transform complex data into clear, actionable insights. However, the wrong chart can lead to confusion, misinterpretation, and poor decision-making, ultimately diminishing the value of your data analysis. Misleading visuals can obscure important trends or exaggerate insignificant details, causing users to make misguided choices. In this recipe, you'll uncover fundamental approaches to chart selection, designed to help your visualizations clearly communicate their message and prevent the confusion that can result from improper chart choices.

How to do it...

- **Tailor charts to data and purpose**: Understanding your data and objectives is the cornerstone of effective data visualization. Before you can choose the right chart, it's crucial to thoroughly analyze the type of data you're working with – whether it's categorical, numerical, temporal, or geographical. Each data type requires a different approach to visual representation. Equally important is defining the objective of your visualization. Are you trying to compare different categories, show a distribution, illustrate relationships, or break down a composition? Knowing your objective will guide you to the most appropriate chart type. Lastly, consider your audience; a visualization tailored to their level of understanding and needs will be far more impactful. For instance, technical audiences might benefit from more complex charts, while general users may need simpler, more intuitive visuals. By connecting these elements – data type, objective, and audience – you ensure that your visualizations are not only accurate but also effective in conveying the intended insights. Once you've selected a chart, create initial drafts and seek feedback from your audience. Use this feedback to refine your visualizations, ensuring they are clear and effective.

- **Steer clear of common chart pitfalls**: Earlier in this chapter, we discussed the importance of selecting the right chart for your data, emphasizing that certain chart types are well-suited for specific purposes while others may not be as effective. For instance, while pie charts are useful for comparing a few categories, they aren't ideal for spotting trends or showing changes over time. If the wrong chart format is chosen, it can confuse or mislead the viewer.

Figure 10.4 shows a pie chart with 12 categories that can be difficult to interpret, especially when paired with white text on bright backgrounds.

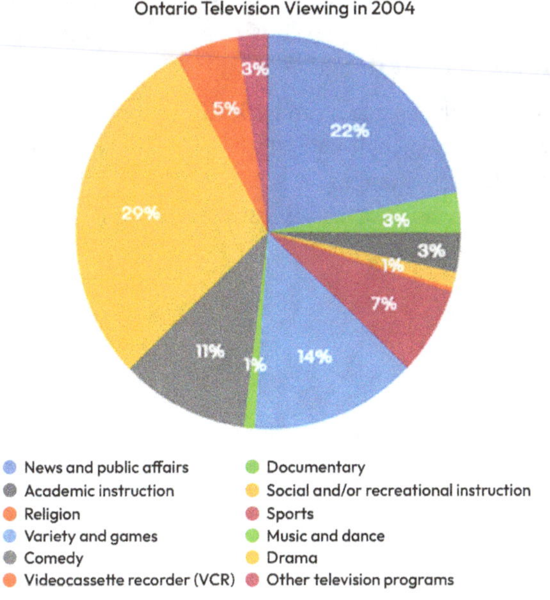

Figure 10.4 – An example showing the wrong chart choice for the data

Another major pitfall is **axis truncation**, where the axis doesn't start at zero. This can exaggerate differences between data points, making small variations seem more significant than they are. For instance, a truncated y axis might show a slight revenue increase as a sharp rise, leading decision-makers to believe growth is stronger than reality (*Figure 10.5*).

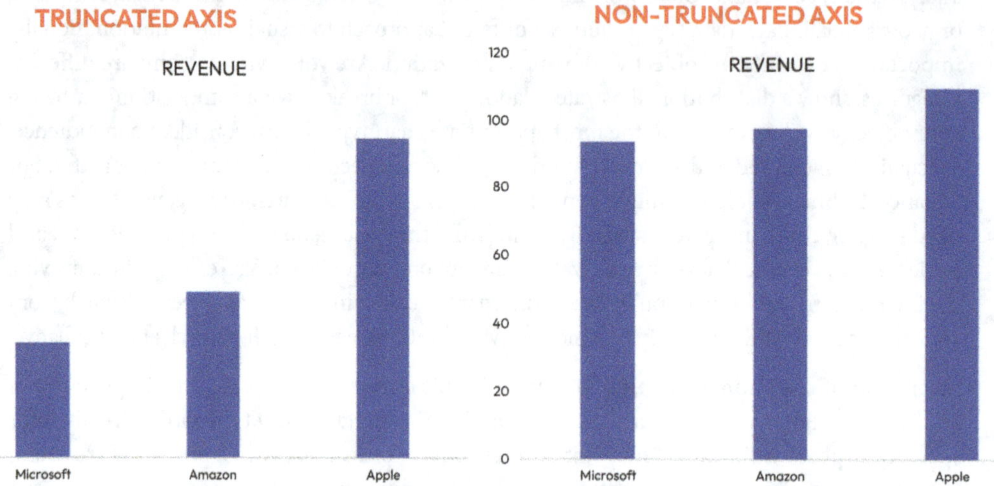

Figure 10.5 – An example showing exaggerated differences in revenue due to axis truncation

Another issue is **reversing the axis**, which flips the expected flow of information. In *Figure 10.6*, the y axis showing gun-related deaths was flipped so that higher numbers are displayed at the bottom and lower numbers are at the top. This creates a false impression that gun deaths are decreasing when, in fact, they are rising.

Reversing the axis distorts the data and can trick viewers into drawing incorrect conclusions. It's a deceptive practice because people naturally expect the y axis to follow the standard format, with higher values at the top. Changing this convention can obscure the reality of the data, leading to a skewed interpretation of critical issues such as gun violence.

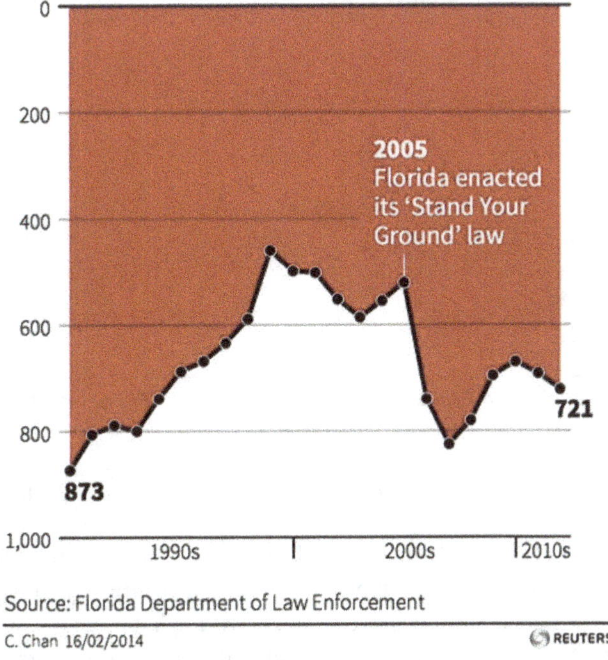

Figure 10.6 – A misleading chart with a reversed y axis

Omitting data points can create a skewed picture by hiding important fluctuations or trends. Leaving out critical data points might make a business appear more stable or successful than it is – for example, focusing on a rising sales trend during the first few months of a year while ignoring the subsequent decline in sales. In *Figure 10.7*, we see a downward trend in gasoline prices in Canada from May 2019 to February 2020, but this short time frame was chosen to give the impression that prices were consistently falling.

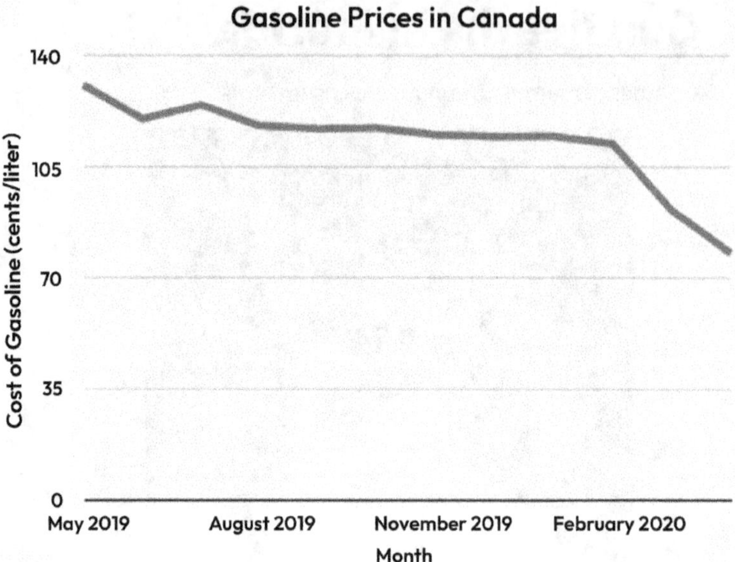

Figure 10.7 – An example showing a purposefully chosen short timeframe

In reality, if we extend the timeframe beyond February 2020 to November 2021, as shown in *Figure 10.8*, we will likely see a more complete and accurate picture of gasoline prices in Canada. Over a longer period, fluctuations such as price increases might become evident, challenging the initial impression of a consistent downward trend. This is a classic example of cherry-picking data - selecting a short period that supports a particular narrative while ignoring the broader context that may reveal a different trend.

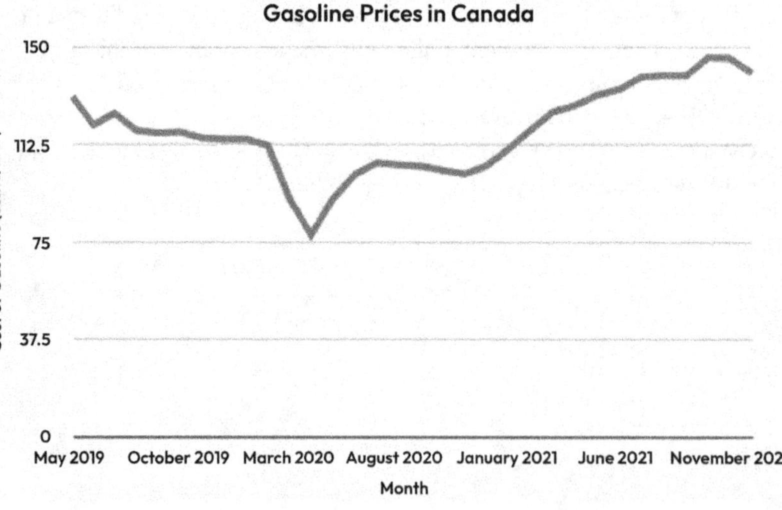

Figure 10.8 – An extended timeframe of the same data in Figure 10.7

Lastly, if you've ever studied statistics, you've likely encountered this phrase: "*Correlation does not imply causation.*" It emphasizes that just because two trends move together, it doesn't mean one is causing the other or that they are meaningfully connected. Take a look at *Figure 10.9*, which displays a line graph of the decline in Canadian automotive apprenticeship registrations alongside nectarine production. These two factors have nothing in common; they are unrelated variables that just happen to decrease at a similar rate over the same period of time.

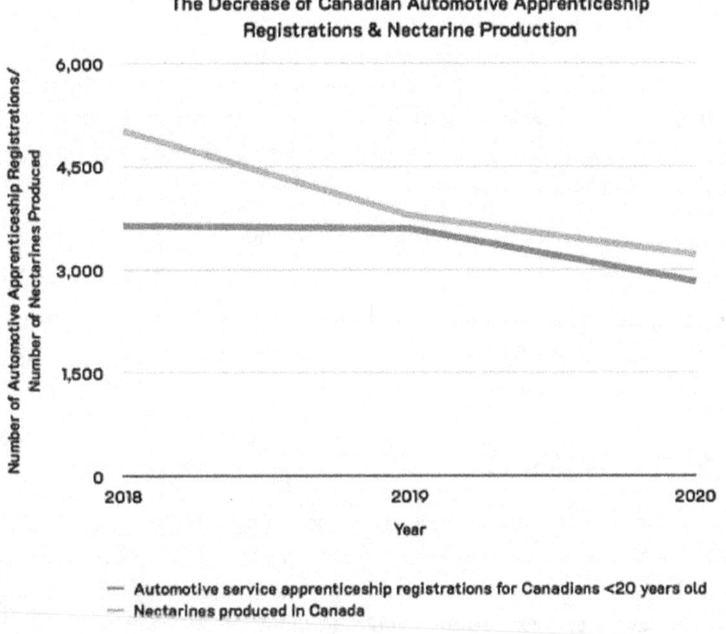

Figure 10.9 – An example showing two unrelated trends moving together in the same direction

In all cases, ensuring accurate, transparent, and complete visualizations is essential for driving reliable business insights.

- **The art and science of chart selection**: The process of selecting the most appropriate chart type is a nuanced balance between aesthetics and functionality. On the functional side, understanding the technical attributes of various chart types is crucial. For example, line charts are superior for depicting trends over time due to their continuous data representation, while scatter plots reveal relationships between variables by plotting data points on an x and y axes making them ideal for identifying correlations and clusters.

From an aesthetic perspective, the visual design of charts impacts how easily and effectively the information is conveyed. Elements such as color schemes, label placement, and chart scaling play significant roles in enhancing readability and ensuring that the chart aligns with the user's data interpretation needs. For instance, a well-chosen color palette can differentiate data series and make complex charts easier to understand.

Continuous learning is essential to master chart selection. This involves staying updated with the latest developments in data visualization techniques, tools, and best practices. Regularly reviewing case studies, participating in webinars, and engaging with professional communities help in adapting to evolving standards and integrating new insights into your visualizations. Tools such as Tableau are continuously updated with new features and functionalities, so keeping abreast of these changes ensures that your visualizations remain effective and cutting-edge.

See also

- To explore different chart types and guided tutorials on how to create them, see the *Tableau Chart Catalog* by Kevin Flerlage on Tableau Public: `https://public.tableau.com/app/profile/kevin.flerlage/viz/TheTableauChartCatalog/TableauChartExamples`

- Use the following Chart Chooser from Highcharts to find the correct chart type based on your data and objectives: `https://www.highcharts.com/chartchooser/`

- You can also use the Visual Vocabulary published by Andy Kriebel to assist in selecting the correct chart: `https://public.tableau.com/app/profile/andy.kriebel/viz/VisualVocabulary/VisualVocabulary`

Develop a style guide

Creating a style guide for your organization ensures consistency and clarity in visualizations across teams and projects. It standardizes color schemes, fonts, chart types, and formatting rules, making dashboards easier to interpret. By following a well-defined style guide, everyone can quickly align on design expectations, reduce time spent on revisions, and maintain a professional, polished look that reinforces the organization's branding. Ultimately, your style guide should outline everything needed to help a Tableau developer achieve a consistent design across various data products while keeping time and effort to a minimum.

How to do it...

- **Format**: When choosing the format for your style guide, a great option is to create it directly in Tableau. This allows you to publish it on the Tableau server, making it easily accessible to developers and creators. Hosting the guide on your server also serves as a reminder to update it as your organization's branding evolves. Providing a link to the style guide in onboarding materials can help new Tableau users quickly familiarize themselves with the standards. Additionally, you can also create a digital document, such as a PDF or a shared cloud-based file, which is both accessible and easy to update to ensure that all team members can access the latest version at any time.

- **Typography and fonts**: To implement a standardized approach to fonts in your style guide, begin by selecting fonts that align with your organization's branding. Document the font family, size, and color for different text elements –titles, subtitles, labels, and tooltips. For example, you might specify that all titles use Arial Bold, 15 pt, and all body text uses Arial, 10 pt. Create a section in your style guide where these details are clearly outlined, along with visual examples of each. Additionally, you can include best practices for text alignment, spacing, and contrast to maintain readability across dashboards. Finally, make sure the guide includes instructions on how to apply these fonts consistently in Tableau by adjusting formatting options in the dashboard and worksheet settings.

- **Color palettes**: To define organization-approved color schemes, start by selecting a few core colors and then use them consistently across all dashboards. Please refer to the *Use color with purpose* recipe at the beginning of this chapter to review the basic principles behind color choices. Once a set of colors is chosen, document each with its hex and RGB codes. For instance, a primary blue might be listed as #005B96 (RGB: 0, 91, 150), and a highlight orange as #F2A900. Next, compile these into your style guide and document each color's purpose – primary, secondary, or highlight. Include visual examples of how these colors should be applied in different chart types, such as bar charts or heatmaps.

  To make this more actionable in Tableau, update the `Preferences.tps` file to predefine these custom palettes, to allow users to quickly apply them across dashboards. Document usage guidelines to ensure consistency, such as using specific colors for KPIs or categories. Finally, keep this document up to date as organizational needs evolve and make it easily accessible for your team.

- **Number and date formats**: Consistent number and date formatting is crucial for ensuring clarity and professionalism in dashboards. When users see uniform formats, it reduces confusion and allows them to quickly interpret the data without distractions. Standardizing formats such as currency, percentages, and dates ensures that metrics are presented in a clear, familiar way, improving the overall user experience. It also helps to maintain consistency across different reports, making it easier for teams to collaborate and for stakeholders to trust the data presented.

  To implement consistent number and date formatting in your Tableau style guide, start by defining how numbers and dates should appear across all dashboards. For numbers, decide on the use of decimal places, thousand separators, and currency symbols. For example, you might specify that large numbers use a comma separator (for example, 1,000) and percentages always display one decimal (for example, 45.7%). For dates, standardize formats such as MM/DD/YY or MM/YY depending on your audience, such as the example in *Figure 10.10*. Document these rules in your guide with clear examples, such as "*For sales data, use $#,##0.00*" or "*Display dates as MMM-YYYY in all trend charts.*" Include instructions on how to apply these formats in Tableau by customizing the number format and date properties in the default field settings for consistency across all reports.

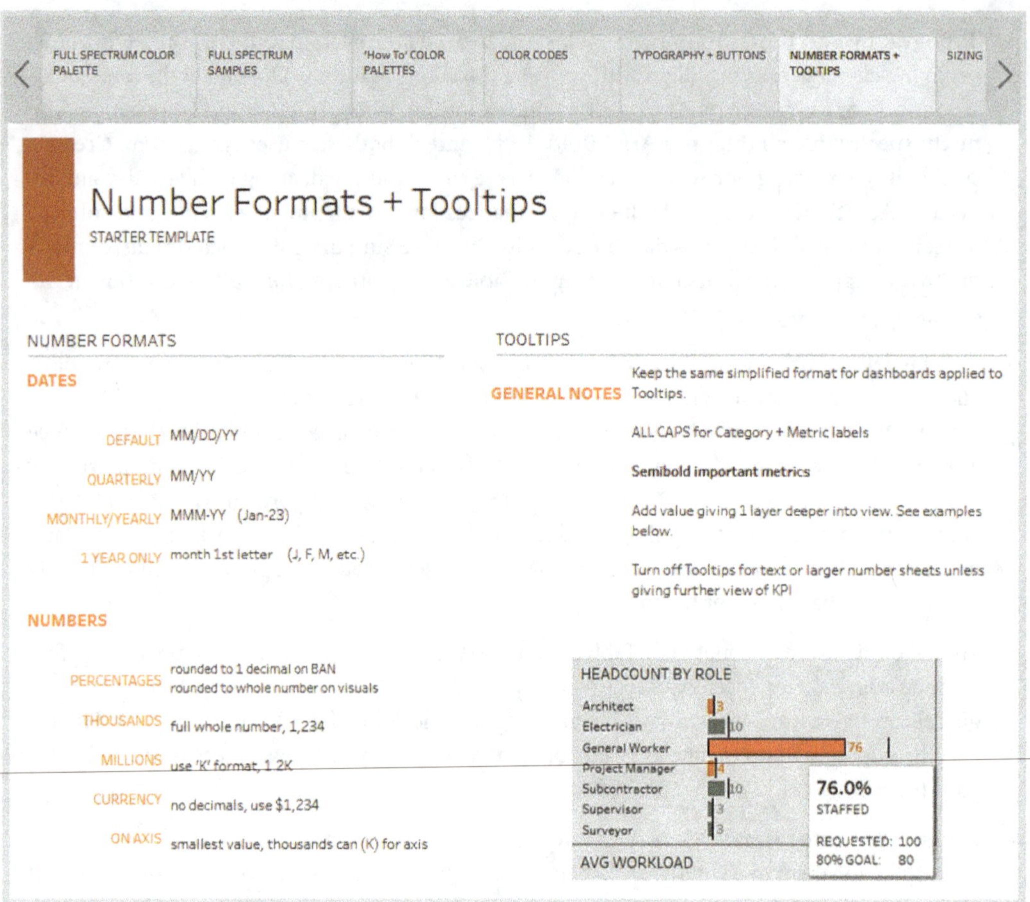

Figure 10.10 – Documenting number and date formats in a style guide

- **Layout and spacing**: Consistent layout and spacing are vital for improving clarity. Proper use of padding and white space prevents overcrowding, making it simpler for users to focus on key information without feeling overwhelmed. It also enhances readability and ensures a professional appearance, fostering a more intuitive and effective user experience. Consistent alignment and grouping help users quickly locate and interpret data, improving overall legibility.

Ensure to establish clear guidelines for both inner and outer padding, as well as the use of white space. Define standard inner padding, such as a 10-pixel margin between charts, filters, and text boxes, to ensure elements are not too close. For outer padding, specify a 20-pixel margin from the edges of the dashboard to provide breathing room and prevent clutter. Document these rules in your style guide with visual examples showing optimal padding and the effective use of white space to enhance readability. Emphasize the importance of consistent alignment and spacing, using Tableau's grid and alignment tools to maintain a clean, organized layout.

- **Branding and logos**: Incorporating branding and logos effectively is important for reinforcing your company's identity while ensuring the data remains the focal point. Proper use of brand assets helps to establish a professional and cohesive look that aligns with your organization's image, making dashboards instantly recognizable. However, it's crucial to balance branding with data presentation to avoid distracting from the information being conveyed. By providing clear guidelines on size, placement, and usage, you can maintain a strong brand presence without compromising the clarity and effectiveness of your data visualizations.

  Start by specifying precise dimensions for logos, such as 150 x 50 pixels, and determine their fixed placement, such as in the top-right corner, to ensure consistency across all dashboards. Include examples in your style guide showing the appropriate use of logos and brand elements, such as subtle placement in headers or footers, and avoid excessive use that could distract from the data. Provide instructions on integrating these elements in Tableau by customizing dashboard headers and backgrounds, ensuring they reinforce your brand's identity while maintaining a focus on data clarity.

  Include technical steps for integrating these elements in Tableau, such as uploading logos through the dashboard's image object and adjusting their size and positioning within the layout. Clear documentation ensures that branding is applied uniformly, preserving a professional appearance without detracting from the data's primary focus.

- **Annotation and labels**: Proper use of annotations and labels is important for providing additional context and insights without taking focus away from the key visual elements. Clear guidelines ensure that annotations are concise and strategically placed, which helps users quickly understand important points without visual clutter. Well-designed tooltips and labels also enhance the interpretability of the data, allowing users to access detailed information on demand without crowding the visual space.

  Begin by defining standard practices for annotations, such as using short, concise text with a font size of 8 pt to avoid overpowering the data. Specify where and how to position tooltips, ensuring they appear only when hovering over key data points and contain relevant, focused information. Document these rules in your style guide with examples of annotated charts and tooltips, including screenshot annotations showing optimal placement and formatting. Include instructions for configuring these features in Tableau, such as setting up tooltips through the Tooltip shelf and using the Annotations feature for adding context to specific data points. This structured approach ensures that annotations and labels provide valuable insights without cluttering the visualization.

- **Interactive elements**: Standardizing interactive elements such as filters, actions, and parameters is crucial for ensuring intuitive navigation and a seamless user experience, as it helps users quickly understand and utilize these elements without confusion.

You can begin by defining uniform styles for filters and parameters, including font size, color, and placement. Make sure to document specific guidelines for filter types, such as dropdowns or sliders, and their default settings. Provide examples in your style guide showing how filters should be aligned and grouped, and how actions should be configured to trigger specific responses. Include technical steps for setting up these elements in Tableau, such as configuring filter actions in the **Dashboard Actions** menu and setting parameter controls in the **Parameters** pane.

- **Dashboard templates**: Using dashboard templates offers several key benefits. First, templates provide a standardized framework, which ensures that dashboards adhere to design and functional guidelines, reducing the time needed for development and promoting a cohesive visual style. Second, templates significantly speed up the development process by providing pre-designed layouts and components, reducing the need to recreate elements from scratch. This efficiency not only saves time but also reduces the likelihood of errors and inconsistencies. Additionally, templates help maintain best practices by incorporating standard elements such as filters, labels, and interactive features, ensuring that all dashboards follow the same functional principles. By using templates, teams can collaborate more effectively, as everyone works from the same foundational design.

You can begin by creating a set of dashboard templates that include predefined layouts, color schemes, and other visual elements, as shown in *Figure 10.11*. Include these templates in your style guide, with detailed descriptions of each template's layout and purpose. For instance, provide a template for a sales dashboard with designated areas for KPIs, charts, and filters, and another for a performance report with specific sections for trend analysis and metrics. Include technical instructions on how to utilize these templates in Tableau and ensure that your documentation includes steps for modifying the templates. By standardizing the use of templates within your organization, you can guarantee a uniform, professional appearance across all reports.

Figure 10.11 – An example showing a dashboard template

- **Dashboard size**: Choosing the right dashboard size for different devices ensures that visualizations are displayed correctly across various screens. Standardizing dashboard sizes helps maintain usability, whether users are accessing reports on desktops, tablets, or mobile devices.

  Begin by defining standard dimensions for each device category, such as desktops, tablets, and mobile phones. Document these dimensions in your style guide, including examples of how dashboards should be adjusted to fit these sizes. Provide guidelines on how to configure these settings in Tableau. Ensure your guide addresses how to test dashboards on different devices to verify that they render correctly and maintain usability.

- **Accessibility considerations**: Incorporate guidelines to ensure visualizations are accessible to all users, including considerations for color blindness and readability. It's important to keep WCAG in mind to help make dashboards more comprehensible and usable for everyone.

  To implement this, start by defining guidelines for color usage, such as selecting colorblind-friendly palettes that utilize colors easily distinguishable by individuals with common forms of color blindness. Document these guidelines in your style guide, including examples of color combinations and their application in various chart types. Provide technical steps for checking color accessibility in Tableau, such as using colorblind simulation tools or third-party accessibility checkers. Additionally, include recommendations for font size and contrast, ensuring text is readable against background colors. Ensure you document how to use Tableau's formatting options to adjust text and background contrast to meet accessibility standards.

- **Version control and updates**: Maintaining an up-to-date style guide is important to ensure it remains relevant and effective as your organization evolves. Effective version control and regular updates help keep the style guide aligned with current best practices and technological advancements.

  Start by establishing a version control system, such as using a shared document repository with version tracking features, such as Git or a similar platform. Document each update with clear version numbers and detailed change logs to track modifications and improvements. Include examples of how to update sections of the style guide, such as adding new guidelines for emerging dashboard features or revising color palettes based on feedback. Ensure that updates are reviewed and approved by relevant stakeholders to maintain accuracy and consistency. Provide instructions on how to communicate changes to all users and incorporate feedback into future revisions. By following these steps, you ensure that your style guide remains a dynamic resource that adapts to ongoing changes and continues to support effective dashboard design and development.

See also

Explore this in-depth style guide on Tableau Public, crafted by Karinna Spitalnick from InterWorks: `https://public.tableau.com/app/profile/karinna.riddett/viz/SampleStyleGuide_16823485802430/SampleStyleGuide`.

Enhance your tables

Humans process visual information more quickly and effectively than plain text. This principle is grounded in the science of data visualization, which highlights how visual representations can accelerate understanding and perception. Advanced tables in Tableau leverage this insight by transforming traditional, static text tables into interactive and dynamic data tools.

Unlike plain text tables, which can be limited and cumbersome, advanced Tableau tables offer a range of features designed to enhance data interpretation and analysis. Moreover, they incorporate advanced formatting techniques, which visually emphasize critical data points and trends, making it easier for users to quickly spot anomalies or significant changes. In this recipe, you'll take on the exciting challenge of building an advanced Tableau table from scratch. This will give you the opportunity to explore how to push the boundaries of what a Tableau table can achieve. Let's get started!

Getting ready

This recipe uses the `Sample-Superstore` dataset provided by Tableau, which can be accessed directly from the **Data Connection** pane on the **Home** page under the **Saved Data Sources** section.

How to do it...

To design our custom table, shown in *Figure 10.12*, we'll approach the task through four key steps. First, we'll develop the necessary calculations to establish the table structure and define the level of detail for the view. Second, we'll customize the mark types using the **Marks** card. Third, we'll refine the table by formatting the marks and ensuring a clean, professional presentation. Finally, we'll incorporate a date axis into the view, enabling the inclusion of simple sparklines for added insight.

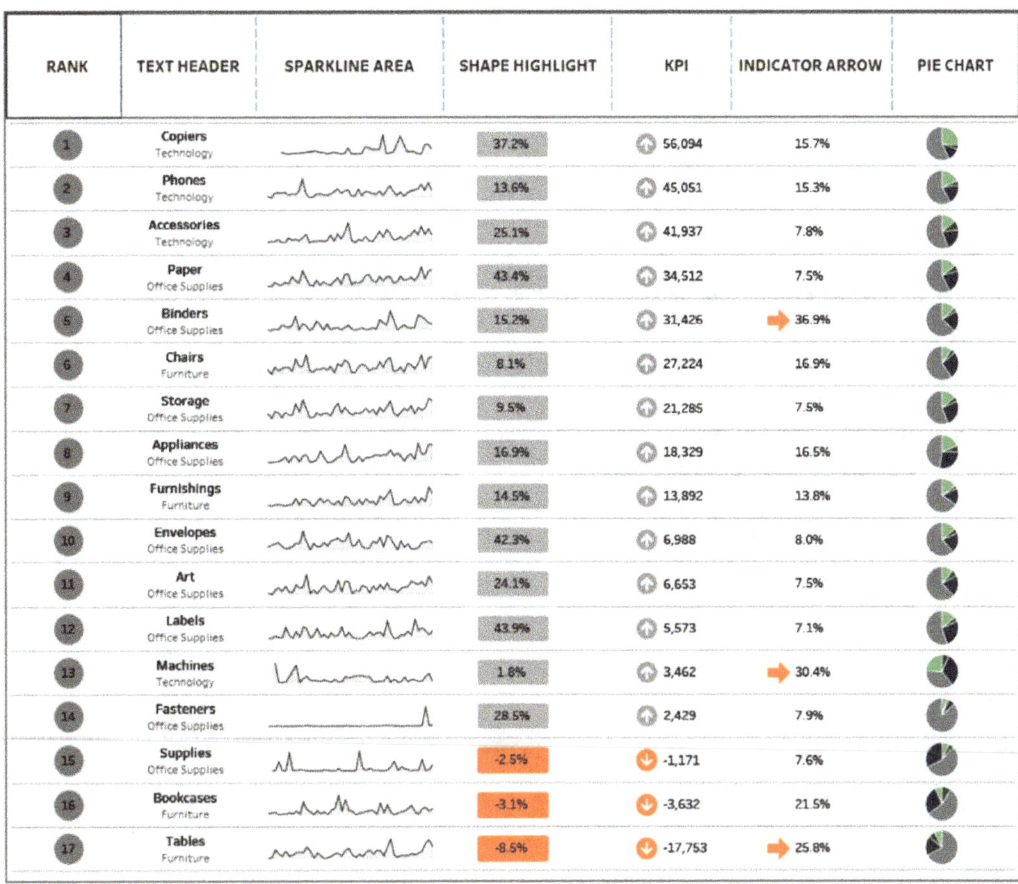

Figure 10.12 – An illustration of the advanced table you'll build in this recipe

Follow these steps:

1. Let's start by creating six custom calculations, each of which will generate a unique axis to represent the columns in the table. For each calculated field, enter the following syntax in the calculation editor: `MIN(0.0)`. To maintain consistency, name each calculated field from the header above. While you can technically use any number for this trick, it's common to use zeros with decimal places. This approach ensures the axis is treated as a float data type, allowing for finer incremental adjustments, as illustrated in *Figure 10.13*. You can adjust the positioning of the data points by modifying the calculation – for instance, using `MIN(-1.0)` to move points closer together or `MIN(0.1)` to space them farther apart.

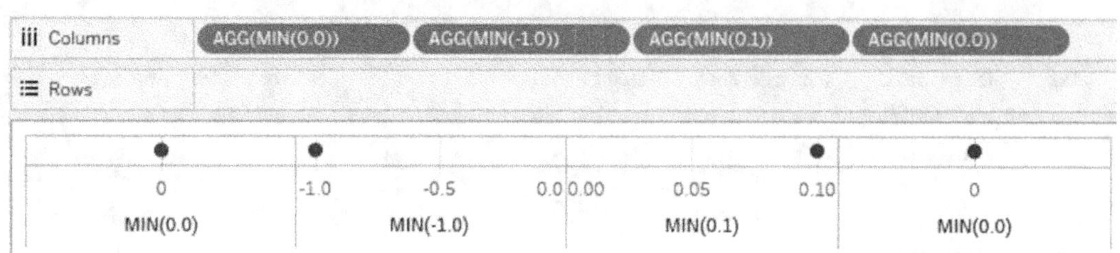

Figure 10.13 – Adjusting the spacing of the data points with custom calculations

2. Next, place your newly created calculated fields on the **Columns** shelf and set the level of detail to **Sub-Category** by dragging the **Sub-Category** dimension onto the **Rows** shelf (*Figure 10.14*). This setup will now allow you to independently manage each measure in the view by customizing the **Marks** card for each of your measures.

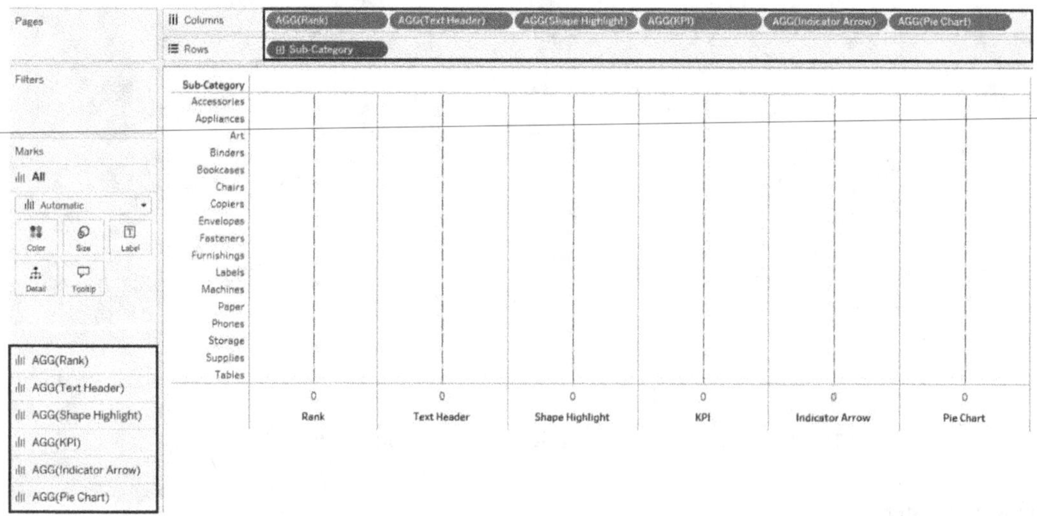

Figure 10.14 – Managing measures independently through the Marks card

3. With the core structure in place, the next step is to customize each field in the **Marks** card. Let's begin with the rank. We want to rank each sub-category based on profit. To do this, use the following calculation to compute the rank by profit: RANK(SUM([Profit])). In the **Marks** card, set the mark type to **Circle** and add the **Rank by Profit** calculation to the label. Be sure to verify the scope, ensuring the rank is computed for each sub-category (*Figure 10.15*).

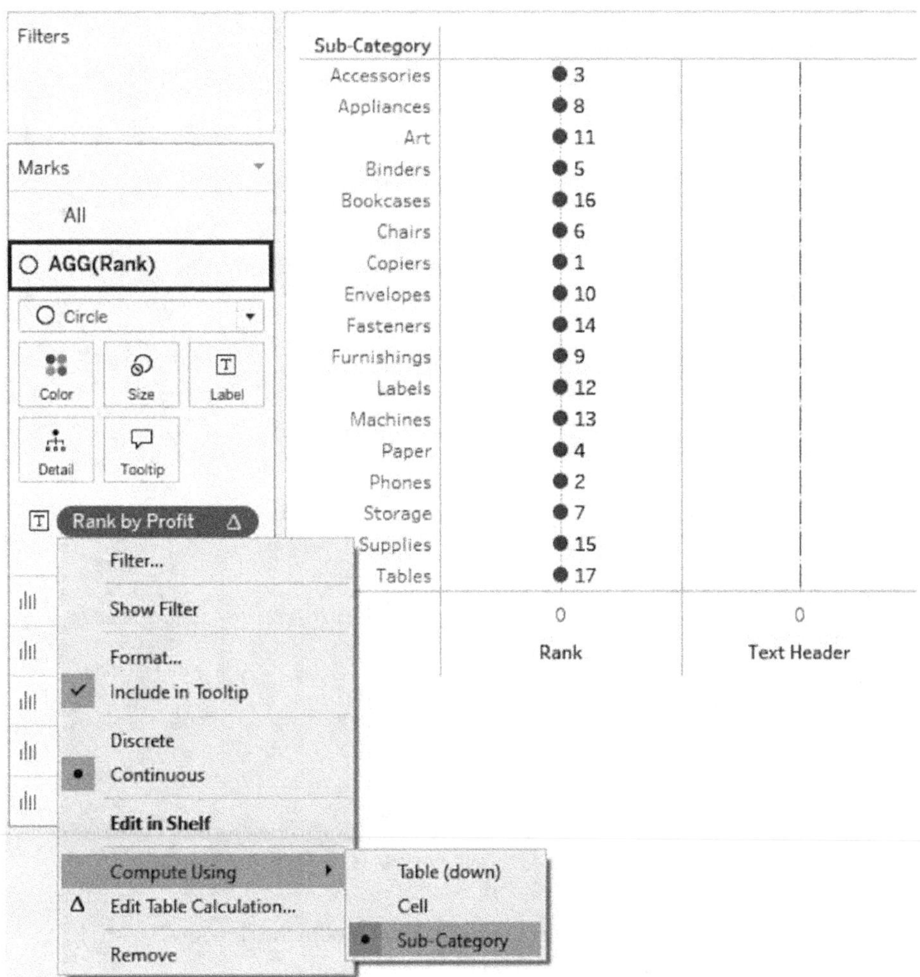

Figure 10.15 – Applying a table calculation to rank each item within a defined scope

4. For the text headers, we want to display both the sub-category name and its corresponding category. To do this, set the mark type to **Text** and add both fields to the **Text** shelf, ensuring that **Sub-Category** appears first (*Figure 10.16*). To maximize the view, select **Entire View** from the dropdown in the toolbar menu.

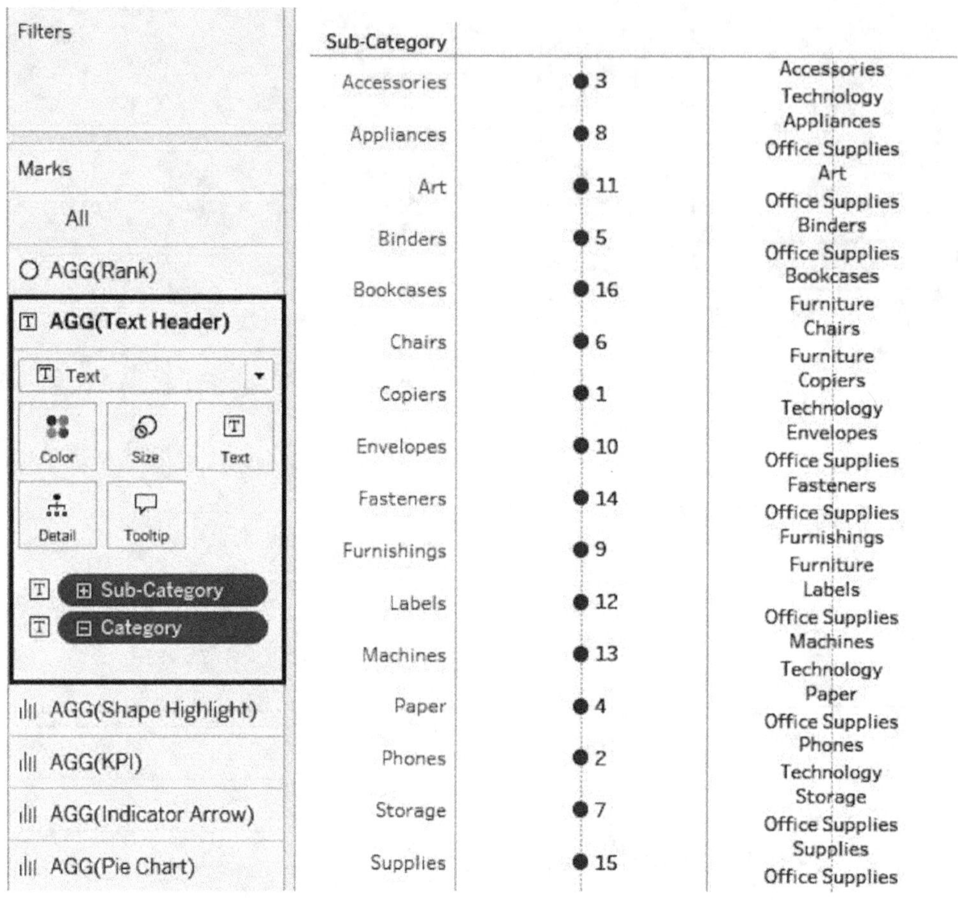

Figure 10.16 – Creating a text header to display both the category
name and its corresponding sub-category

5.   To create our shape highlight, change the mark type to **Shape** and add the **Profit Ratio** field to the **Label** shelf (*Figure 10.17*). In this example, I'm using a custom vector from `flaticon.com`, but you can use any rectangular image of your choice. For instructions on how to import a custom shape into Tableau, please refer to the *See also* section at the end of this recipe.

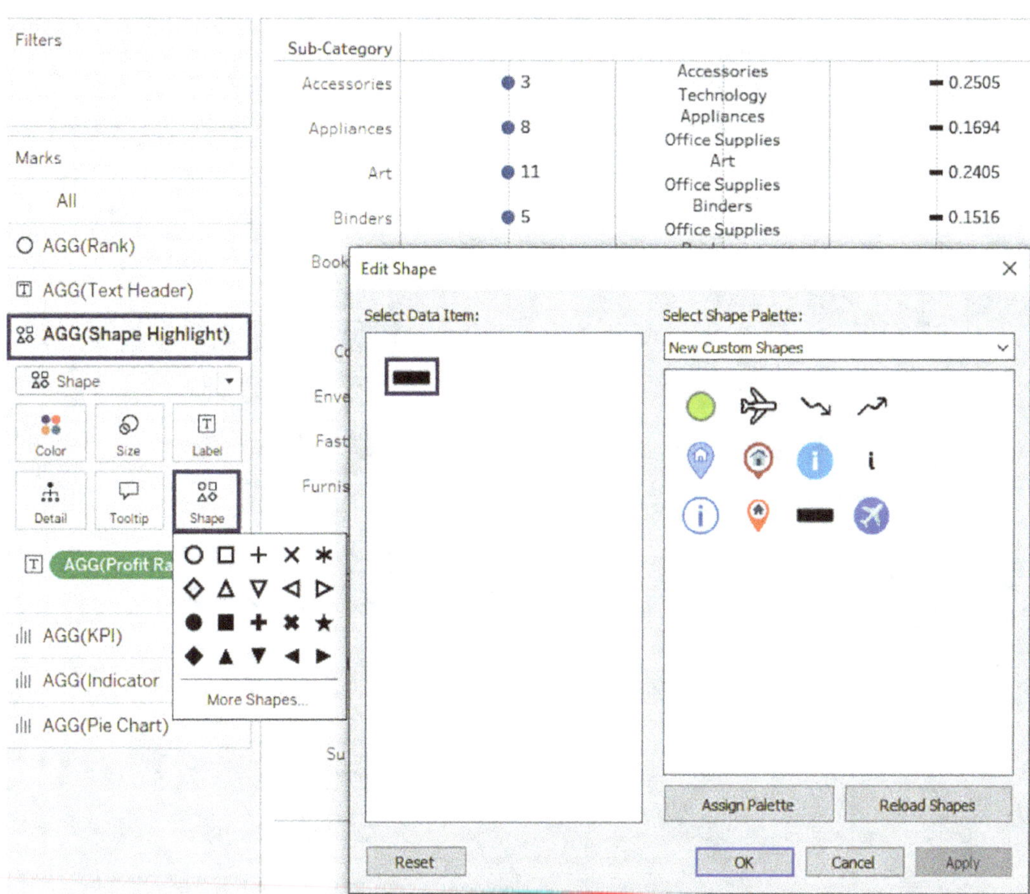

Figure 10.17 – Using a custom shape to highlight measures that meet predefined conditions

6. The KPI indicator will show the total sum of profit by sub-category and use an up or down arrow to represent positive and negative profit values, respectively. In the **Marks** card, add **Profit** to the label, and set the mark type to **Shape**. Next, create the following calculation: `IF SUM([Profit]) >= 0 THEN 1 ELSE -1 END`, name it `Profit (+/-)`, and add it to the **Shape** shelf. Assign two shapes from the **Arrows** shape palette: an upward arrow for the value of `1` and a downward arrow for `-1` (*Figure 10.18*).

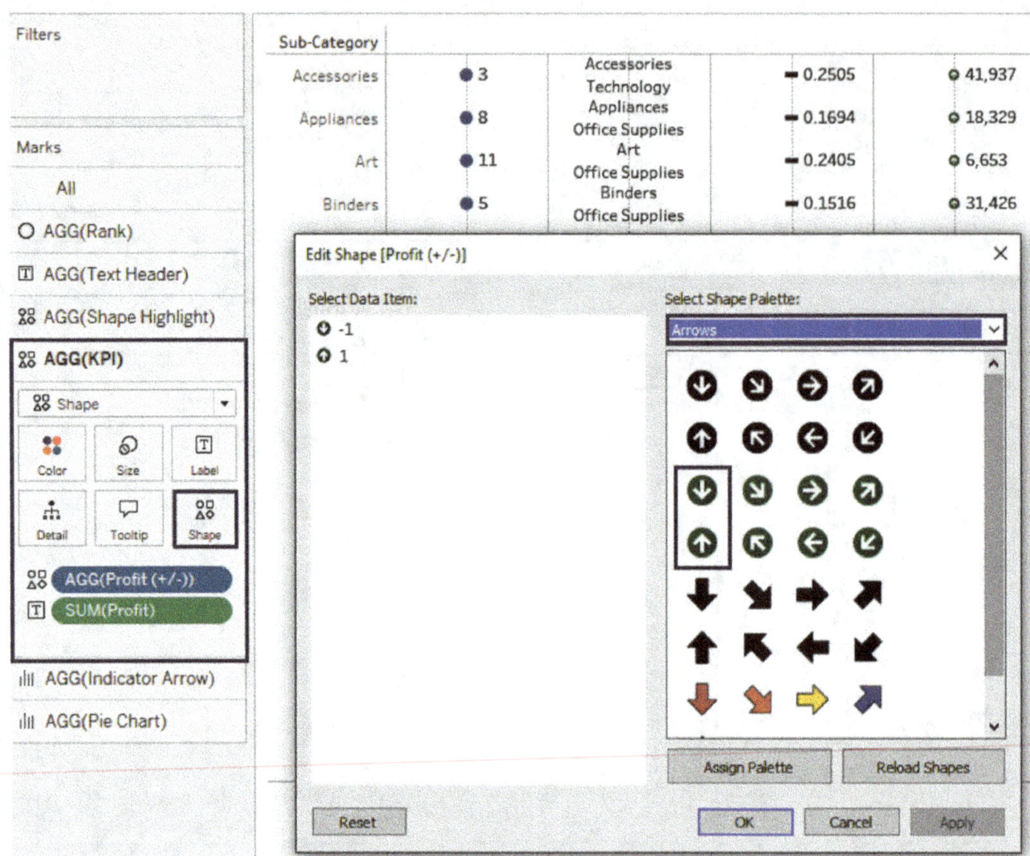

Figure 10.18 – Displaying KPI value trends using arrows to show gains and losses

7. The indicator arrow will point to the average discount by sub-category and highlight items with a discount greater than 25%. Start by placing the **Discount** measure on the **Label** shelf and changing the aggregation from **Sum** to **Average**. Set the mark type to **Shape** and create a new calculated field: `AVG([Discount]) > 0.25`. Add this calculation to the **Color** shelf, assigning orange to represent values evaluated as `true` and white for values evaluated as `false`. Next, choose your shape from the **Arrows** shape palette and format the values as percentages with one decimal place (*Figure 10.19*).

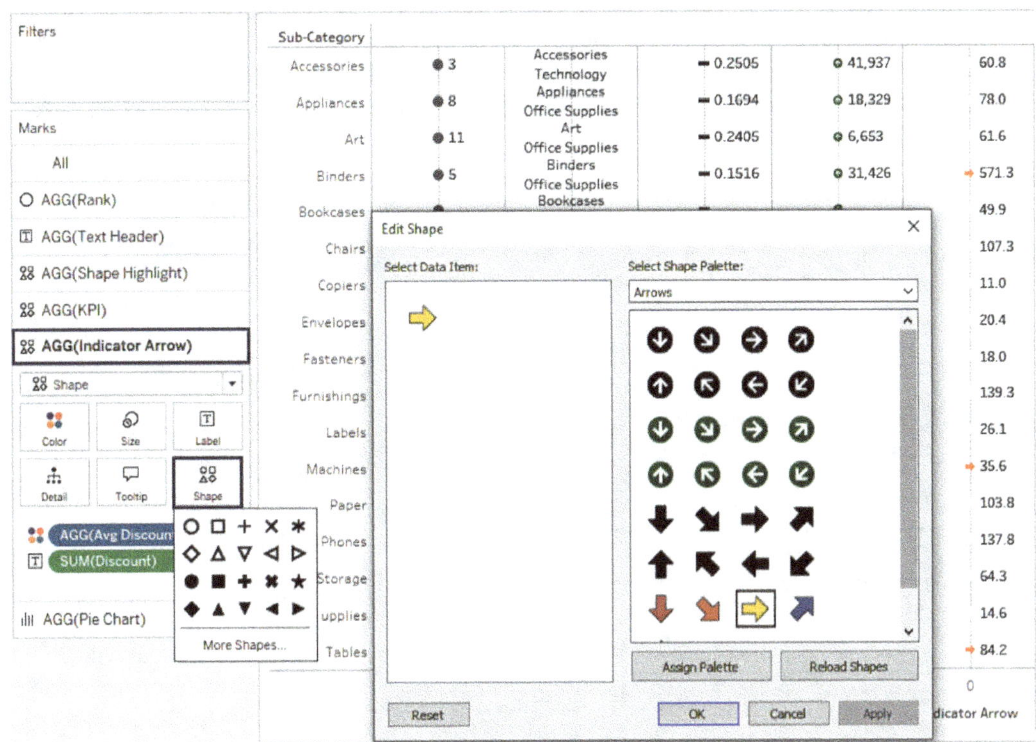

Figure 10.19 – Emphasizing table values with indicator arrows when they match predefined conditions

8. Finally, let's create our mini pie chart! This chart will visualize the total profit by ship mode. Start by changing the mark type to **Pie** and then place **Ship Mode** on the **Color** shelf to differentiate each slice. Next, add **Profit** to the **Angle** shelf to control the size of each slice based on the profit value (*Figure 10.20*). This will give us a clear, proportional representation of how profit is distributed across different ship modes.

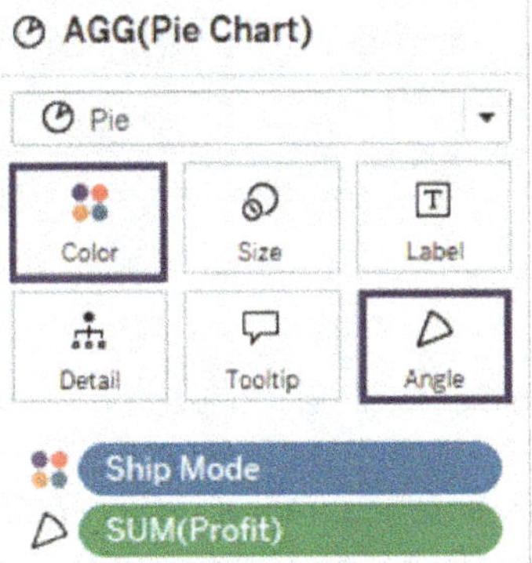

Figure 10.20 – Using the Angle and Color shelves to configure the pie chart

9. Next, we need to revisit each metric and customize our table using the **Marks** card. Let's start with **Rank** and work our way down. To enlarge the circle, adjust the slider on the **Size** shelf by moving it to the right. Then, go to **Label | Alignment** and select **Center** to position the rank inside the circle (*Figure 10.21*).

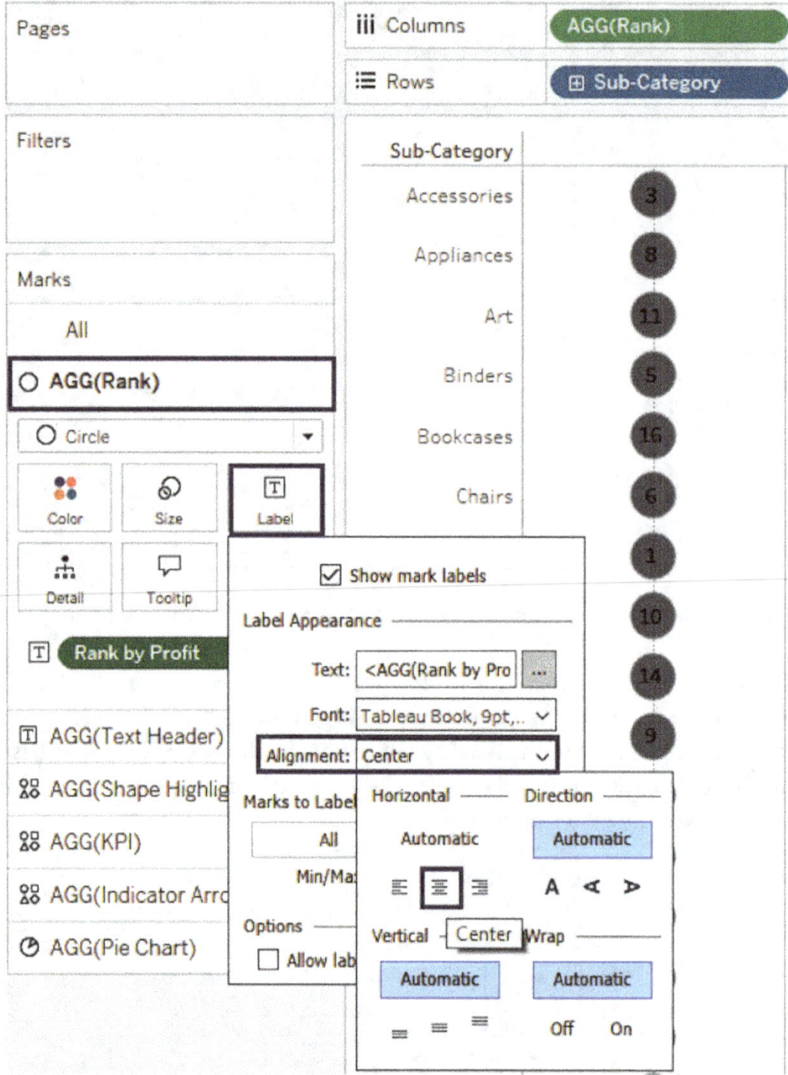

Figure 10.21 – Aligning the rank label to appear centered within the circle

10. Modify the text header by increasing the **Sub-Category** font size to **10** and making it bold. For **Category**, use a dark gray color to ensure the focus remains on the **Sub-Category** name.

11. Adjust the shape highlight size by selecting **Size** and moving the slider to the right until you achieve the desired size and center-align the **Profit Ratio** values. Create a new calculated field to check whether the profit ratio is greater than 0: `[Profit Ratio] > 0`. Add it to the **Color** shelf. Assign orange to values less than or equal to `0` and gray to values greater than `0`. Ensure the **Allow labels to overlap** option is unchecked in the **Label** settings to display text values. Finally, set the number format to a percentage with one decimal place.

12. Apply similar color logic to the KPI shape by placing the previously created `Profit (+/-)` field on the **Color** shelf. Use a two-step diverging color palette, assigning orange to represent negative values and gray for positive values (*Figure 10.22*).

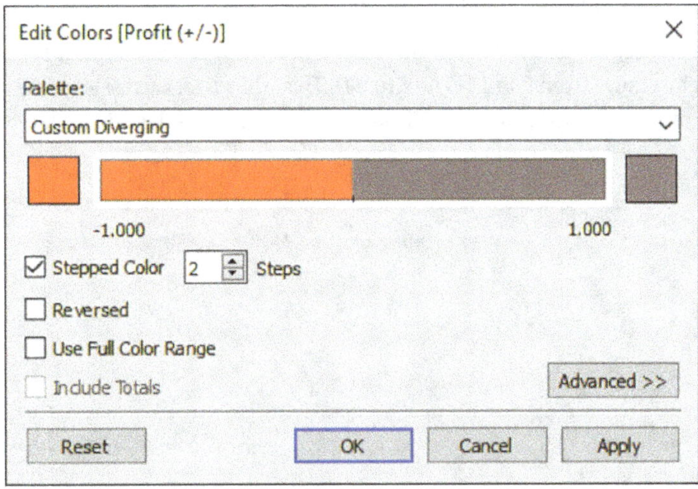

Figure 10.22 – Setting up a two-step diverging color palette to highlight positive and negative values

13. Resize the indicator arrow and pie chart using the **Size** shelf and customize the pie segment colors with the following color codes: **#8dbfa8**, **#26897e**, **#4f6980**, and **#b3b7b8**.

14. At this stage, the table will need some cleanup, including removing unnecessary zero lines and axis headers and resizing cells. Right-click on the table, select **Format | Lines**, and set **Grid Lines** and **Zero Lines** to **None**. To resize cells, you can either do it manually (*Figure 10.23*) or go to **Format | Cell Size**.

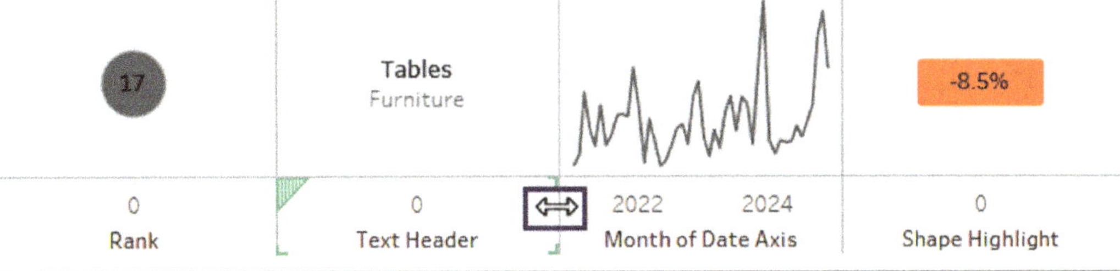

Figure 10.23 – Adjusting table cell width manually

15. If you plan to add additional chart types requiring a continuous date axis, I recommend saving all formatting until the end. This step can distort the current view and often necessitates extra formatting adjustments. An easier way to simplify this process is by creating a separate view for the sparkline and then combining it with the current view on a dashboard. This method avoids many of the time-consuming formatting steps. That said, I'd still like to guide you through the process of adding the sparkline directly to our existing table. To include a continuous date axis, we need to create three additional calculations. For the first calculation, reference **Order Date** inside the calculation editor and save it as `Date Axis`.

16. Drag **Date Axis** to the **Columns** shelf and select **Month** as the continuous date value. Ensure the mark type is set to **Line** in the **Marks** card.

17. Let's create our second calculation to normalize the sales values within a specified window, scaling them to a range from 0 to 1 (*Figure 10.24*). This will adjust each sales value proportionally, based on its relative position to the minimum and maximum sales within the window.

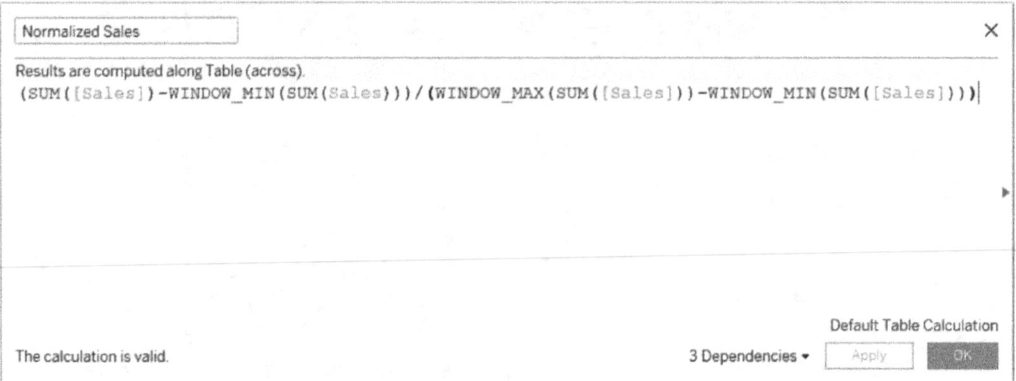

Figure 10.24 – Normalizing the sales values within a defined window

18. Let's reference **Normalized Sales** in the next field, called `Y-Axis` (*Figure 10.25*). This method ensures that individual data points are treated separately while enabling relative comparisons across multiple marks in the window. Drag the **Y-Axis** field to **Rows** and set the scope to compute using `Table (across)`.

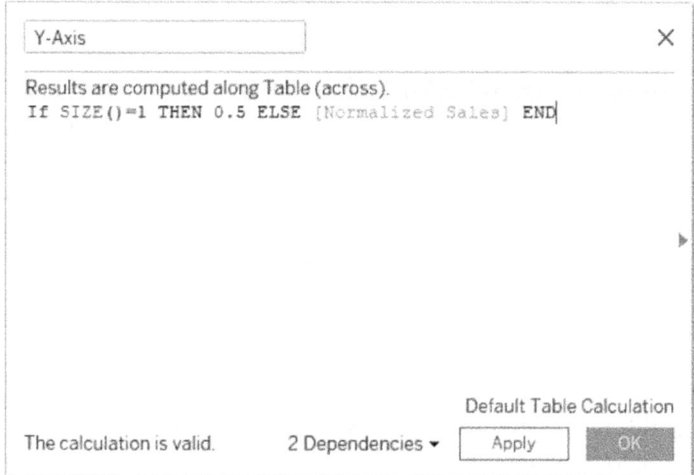

Figure 10.25 – Leveraging the size function to partition the table

19. If the chart becomes distorted after adding **Y-Axis**, you'll need to adjust the formatting of each measure. This is why I strongly recommend saving this step for last. To create the sparkline area chart, duplicate the **Date Axis** field and place both copies side by side on the **Columns** shelf. Change the mark type of the duplicated **Date Axis** to **Area** and create a dual axis. You can also adjust the color and reduce the opacity of the area chart to achieve the desired appearance.

20. For the final step, you can sort your sub-categories in the table from most profitable to least profitable by right-clicking the **Sub-Category** dimension on **Rows** and configuring the sort, as shown in *Figure 10.26*.

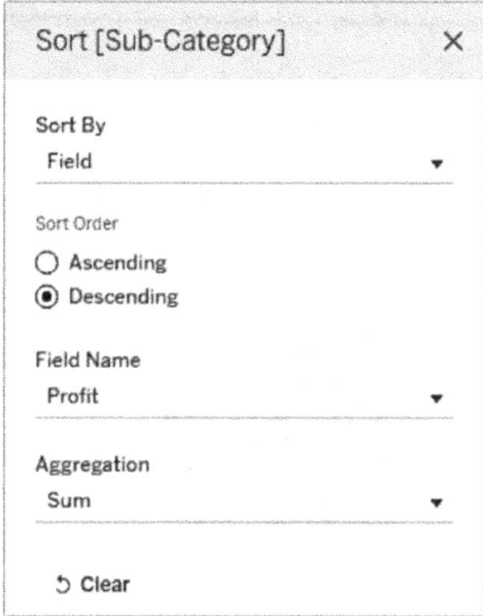

Figure 10.26 – Sorting the sub-categories in descending order of profitability

There's more...

If you're looking for more detailed guidance on creating advanced tables, there's a fantastic YouTube tutorial created by Samuel Parsons (refer to the *See also* section). It demonstrates how to create 14 different chart styles, providing detailed step-by-step walk-throughs and a downloadable Tableau workbook. This resource is a great way to further enhance your skills and explore various techniques. I highly recommend experimenting with these advanced techniques to explore their capabilities and see how they can enhance your data visualizations. Engaging with these methods can be both a valuable learning experience and an enjoyable way to deepen your understanding.

See also

- Take a look at this blog for guidance on creating advanced Tableau tables: `https://policyviz.com/2023/02/23/super-advanced-tableau-tables/`

- Access the advanced Tableau tables dashboard for download on Tableau Public: `https://public.tableau.com/app/profile/sparsonsdataviz/viz/SuperAdvancedTableauTables/ExampleCharts?publish=yes`

- For a comprehensive tutorial on creating advanced tables, check out the following YouTube video by Samuel Parsons: `https://www.youtube.com/watch?v=62tiC50xinE`

- Check out this blog by Luke Stanke, *26 Ways to Enhance Your Tables in Tableau*: `https://www.phdata.io/blog/enhancing-tables-in-tableau/`

- For detailed steps on how to import custom shapes, see the following: `https://interworks.com/blog/ccapitula/2015/01/16/tableau-essentials-formatting-tips-custom-shapes`

Join our community on Discord

Join our community's Discord space for discussions with the authors and other readers:

`https://packt.link/ds`

Index

www.packtpub.com

Subscribe to our online digital library for full access to over 7,000 books and videos, as well as industry leading tools to help you plan your personal development and advance your career. For more information, please visit our website.

Why subscribe?

- Spend less time learning and more time coding with practical eBooks and Videos from over 4,000 industry professionals

- Improve your learning with Skill Plans built especially for you

- Get a free eBook or video every month

- Fully searchable for easy access to vital information

- Copy and paste, print, and bookmark content

Did you know that Packt offers eBook versions of every book published, with PDF and ePub files available? You can upgrade to the eBook version at packtpub.com and as a print book customer, you are entitled to a discount on the eBook copy. Get in touch with us at customercare@packtpub.com for more details.

At www.packtpub.com, you can also read a collection of free technical articles, sign up for a range of free newsletters, and receive exclusive discounts and offers on Packt books and eBooks.

Other Books You May Enjoy

If you enjoyed this book, you may be interested in these other books by Packt:

Tableau Certified Data Analyst Certification Guide

Harry Cooney, Daisy Jones

ISBN: 978-1-80324-346-7

- Connect to various data sources, essential for data analysis journey
- Master data transformation with Tableau Desktop and Tableau Prep Builder
- Explore the full range of calculation types, from basic to advanced
- Structure and filter data, including sets, bins, and hierarchies
- Add analytical functionality to visualize data insights
- Merge charts to create interactive dashboards and compelling data stories
- Customize visuals at workbook, chart, and dashboard levels
- Publish and manage content on Tableau Cloud, sharing insights with ease

Mastering Tableau 2023, Fourth Edition

Marleen Meier

ISBN: 978-1-80323-376-5

- Learn about various Tableau components, such as calculated fields, table calculations, and LOD expressions
- Master ETL (Extract, Transform, Load) techniques using Tableau Prep Builder
- Explore and implement data storytelling with Python and R
- Understand Tableau Exchange by using accelerators, extensions, and connectors
- Interact with Tableau Server to understand its functionalities
- Study advanced visualizations and dashboard creation techniques
- Brush up on powerful self-service analytics, time series analytics, and geo-spatial analytics
- Find out why data governance matters and how to implement it

Packt is searching for authors like you

If you're interested in becoming an author for Packt, please visit `authors.packtpub.com` and apply today. We have worked with thousands of developers and tech professionals, just like you, to help them share their insight with the global tech community. You can make a general application, apply for a specific hot topic that we are recruiting an author for, or submit your own idea.

Share your thoughts

Now you've finished *Tableau Cookbook for Experienced Professionals*, we'd love to hear your thoughts! Scan the QR code below to go straight to the Amazon review page for this book and share your feedback or leave a review on the site that you purchased it from.

`https://packt.link/r/1835469744`

Your review is important to us and the tech community and will help us make sure we're delivering excellent quality content.